KEY ISSUES IN THE NEW KNOWLEDGE MANAGEMENT

D0061314

KM KNOWLEDGE
Ci MANAGEMENT
CONSORTIUM
INTERNATIONAL

About KMCI Press

Powerful Knowledge for Knowledge Professionals

KMCI Press is an exciting publishing partnership that unites the Knowledge Management Consortium International (KMCI), the leading organization for knowledge management professionals, and the Business group and Digital Press imprints of Butterworth–Heinemann, one of the premier publishers of knowledge management books.

KMCI Press publishes authoritative and innovative books that educate all knowledge management communities, from students and beginning professionals to chief knowledge officers. KMCI Press books present definitive and leading-edge ideas of the KMCI itself, and bring clarity and authoritative information to a dynamic and emerging profession.

KMCI Press books explore the opportunities, demands, and benefits knowledge management brings to organizations and define important and emerging knowledge management disciplines and topics, including:

- Professional roles and functions
- Vertical industry best practices and applications
- Technologies, including knowledge portals and data and document management
- Strategies, methodologies, and decision-making frameworks

The Knowledge Management Consortium International (KMCI) is the only major not-for-profit member organization specifically for knowledge management professionals, with thousands of worldwide members including individuals in the professional and academic fields as well as leading companies, institutions, and other organizations concerned with knowledge management, organizational change, and intellectual capital.

For information about submitting book proposals, please see our Web site at http://www.kmci.org.

Titles from KMCI Press

The Springboard: How Storytelling Ignites Action in Knowledge-Era Organizations   Stephen Denning

Knowledge Management Foundations   Steve Fuller

World Congress on Intellectual Capital Readings   Nick Bontis

Enterprise Information Portals and Knowledge Management   Joseph Firestone

The New Knowledge Management—Complexity, Learning, and Sustainable Innovation   Mark McElroy

KEY ISSUES IN THE NEW KNOWLEDGE MANAGEMENT

JOSEPH M. FIRESTONE, PH.D.
MARK W. McELROY

KM Ci PRESS

KNOWLEDGE
MANAGEMENT
CONSORTIUM
INTERNATIONAL

BUTTERWORTH
HEINEMANN

An imprint of Elsevier Science
Amsterdam Boston Heidelberg London New York Oxford Paris
San Diego San Francisco Singapore Sydney Tokyo

Butterworth–Heinemann is an imprint of Elsevier Science.

∞ Recognizing the importance of preserving what has been written, Elsevier Science prints its books on acid-free paper whenever possible.

Library of Congress Cataloging-in-Publication Data
Firestone, Joseph M.
    Key issues in the new knowledge management / Joseph M. Firestone, Mark W. McElroy.
        p.   cm.
Includes bibliographical references and index.
    ISBN 0-7506-7655-8 (pbk. : alk. paper)
    1. Knowledge management.   2. Organizational learning.   I. Title: New knowledge management.   II. McElroy, Mark W.   III. Title.

    HD30.2.F57 2003
    658.4′038—dc21

                                                                    2003045315

British Library Cataloguing-in-Publication Data
A catalogue record for this book is available from the British Library.

The publisher offers special discounts on bulk orders of this book.
For information, please contact:

Manager of Special Sales
Elsevier Science
200 Wheeler Road
Burlington, MA 01803
Tel: 781-313-4700
Fax: 781-313-4882

For information on all Butterworth–Heinemann publications available, contact our World Wide Web home page at: http://www.bh.com

10 9 8 7 6 5 4 3 2 1

Printed in the United States of America

Cover art created by Svend-Eric Filby of Svend Design in Lebanon, NH (www.svend.com)

CONTENTS

Preface, xiii

Acknowledgments, xvii

Introduction: What Is the New Knowledge Management (TNKM), and What Are Its Key Issues?, xix

What Is the New Knowledge Management? xix
What Are Its Issues? xxi
Who this Book Is For, xxvi
How to Use This Book, xxvi
References, xxvi

Chapter 1
THE KNOWLEDGE CONUNDRUM   1

Introduction, 1
On Definition, 2
Definitions of Knowledge, 3
World 2 Definitions, 11
World 3 Definitions, 13
Data, Information, Knowledge, and Wisdom, 17
   World 3 Data, Information, Knowledge, and
      Wisdom, 17
   World 2 Data, Information, and Knowledge, 19
Tacit Knowledge and Explicit Knowledge, 20
Polanyi, Implicit Knowledge, and Popper, 21
Individual Level World 2 Knowledge and Motivational
      Hierarchies, 23
Different Types of Knowledge, 26

Conclusion, 26
References, 29

Chapter 2

ORIGIN OF THE KNOWLEDGE LIFE CYCLE   32

Introduction, 32
The Organizational Learning Cycle (OLC)/Decision
    Execution Cycle (DEC), 33
New Problems, Double-Loop Learning, and Popper's
    Tetradic Schema, 37
Learning and Knowledge Production: Combining
    Argyris/Schön and Popper, 39
A Transactional Systems Model of Agent Interaction, 41
    The Motivational Hierarchy, 41
    Aspects of Motivational Behavior in the Transactional
    System, 43
    Sense Making in the Transactional System, 47
The Knowledge Life Cycle (KLC): The Expression of a
    Change in Instrumental Motivation, 48
Conclusion, 57
References, 58

Chapter 3

INFORMATION MANAGEMENT AND
KNOWLEDGE MANAGEMENT   60

Introduction: Approach to KM, 60
Complex Adaptive Systems, 61
The Natural Knowledge Processing System (NKPS), 61
Hierarchical versus Organic KM, 62
Some Definitions of Knowledge Management, 63
Information Management and Knowledge Management, 69
    Knowledge Processes and Information Processes, 70
Definition and Specification of Knowledge Management, 70

Levels of Knowledge Management, 71
Breadth of KM Processes, 76
Targets of Knowledge Management, 80
Social and Technological, Policy and Program
    Interventions, 81
The Classification of KM Activities, 83
More on How Information Management Differs from
    Knowledge Management, 84
Conclusion, 85
References, 86

Chapter 4
GENERATIONS OF KNOWLEDGE MANAGEMENT 88

Three Views of Change in Knowledge Management, 88
The Three Stages of Knowledge Management, 90
Difficulties with the Three-Stages View, 91
The Two Ages of Knowledge Management (with a Third
    Yet to Come), 94
Difficulties with the Two-Ages View, 95
The Two Generations of Knowledge Management, 97
Snowden's Forecast? A Third Age of KM, 104
    KM and Scientific Management, 105
    KM, Content Management, and Context, 105
    Knowledge: Process or Outcome? 110
    Sense Making, Complex Adaptive Systems, and the Third
        Age, 113
    The Cynefin Model and Its Problems, 115
    Cynefin Conclusions, 132
Conclusion: The Three Stages, the Three Ages, the Two
    Generations, and Comparative Frameworks, 134
References, 136

Chapter 5

Knowledge Claim Evaluation:
The Forgotten Factor in
Knowledge Production   142

Introduction, 142
Where Knowledge Claim Evaluation Fits into Knowledge
    Production, 143
The Kind of Knowledge Produced by Knowledge Claim
    Evaluation, 144
A Framework for Describing Knowledge Claim
    Evaluation, 146
  Knowledge Claim Evaluation: Specific, 147
An Approach to Evaluating Knowledge Claim Evaluation and
    Knowledge Claims, 156
  Success Criteria for Knowledge Claim Evaluation, 157
  Realizing Knowledge Claim Evaluation Effectiveness:
      The Theory of Fair Comparison, 158
Knowledge Claim Evaluation Software, 167
  Key Use Cases in KCE Software, 168
  Structural Features of KCE Software, 169
Conclusion: Significance and Questions, 171
References, 173

Appendix to Chapter 5

Two Formal Approaches to
Measuring "Truthlikeness"   177

Introduction, 177
An AHP-Based Ratio Scaling Approach, 178
A Fuzzy Measurement Approach to "Truthlikeness," 187
Other Approaches to Combining Criterion Attributes of
    "Truthlikeness" and KM Knowledge Production, 191
References, 191

Chapter 6
Applications of The Knowledge Life Cycle (KLC) Framework

193

Introduction, 193
The Knowledge Life Cycle (KLC), 196
Knowledge Management Strategy Formulation, 200
Knowledge Management and Knowledge Audits, 204
Modeling, Predicting, Forecasting, Simulating, Impact Analysis,
    and Evaluation, 206
Metrics Segmentation, 210
Sustainable Innovation, 213
Methodology, 218
Information Technology Requirements, 220
Intellectual Capital, 222
Education and Training, 225
The Open Enterprise, 227
New Value Propositions for Knowledge Management, 230
Conclusion, 234
References, 235

Chapter 7
Knowledge Management as Best Practices Systems—Where's the Context?

238

Best Practice: The Lack-of-Context Problem, 238
Knowledge Claims, 239
Metaclaims as Context, 241
A Better Way, 242
Metaclaims in Action, 245
Conclusion, 247
References, 248

Chapter 8

WHAT COMES FIRST: KNOWLEDGE MANAGEMENT OR STRATEGY?   249

Introduction, 249
Biased Methodologies, 250
The Strategy Exception Error, 251
Strategy and the New Knowledge Management, 254
Where Knowledge Management Belongs, 256
Conclusion, 257
References, 259

Chapter 9

KNOWLEDGE MANAGEMENT AND CULTURE   261

Introduction, 261
Alternative Definitions of Culture, 261
Culture or Something Else?, 264
What Is Culture, and How Does It Fit with Other Factors
     Influencing Behavior?, 264
  Do Global Properties Exist?, 270
Culture and Knowledge, 271
Conclusion: Culture and Knowledge Management, 272
References, 273

Chapter 10

A NOTE ON INTELLECTUAL CAPITAL   275

Introduction, 275
Social Innovation Capital, 278
False Linearity, 279
A False Orientation, 283
Two Systems, Not One, 284
Conclusion, 287
References, 289

Chapter 11

CONCLUSION   290

Vision of the New Knowledge Management, 290
The New Knowledge Management Landscape, 294
  More on Defining Knowledge, 296
  The Origin of the KLC, 298
  Knowledge *Process* Management and Information
    Management, 299
  Supply- and Demand-Side Knowledge Processing, 302
  Meta-Claims and Best Practices, 304
  Knowledge Claim Evaluation, 305
  The Centrality of the Knowledge Life Cycle, 309
  KM and Strategy, 312
  KM and Culture, 315
  The Open Enterprise, 317
  Intellectual Capital, 319
  Information Technology and the New KM, 321
The Future of the New KM, 323
  SECI Model, 323
  The EKP, 325
  Framework for Analysis of KM Software, 325
  Role of Credit Assignment Systems in KM Software, 326
  TNKM Metrics, 326
  TNKM and Terrorism, 326
  The Open Enterprise, Again, 328
  Communities of Inquiry (CoI), 329
  Knowledge Management Methodology, 329
  Value Theory in Knowledge Management, 330
  The New Knowledge Management and Knowledge
    Management Standards, 332
  References, 335

Glossary of Acronyms, 337
Index, 339
About the Authors, 351

PREFACE

In early 1998, the Knowledge Management Consortium (KMC), later to become the KMCI ("I" for International), was just getting started and one of us (Firestone) became a founding member, soon to be followed by the other (McElroy) in October 1998. We first met at a KMCI mini-conference session at the KM Expo Conference in October 1998 in Chicago. At the time, Joe was working on knowledge management metrics and thereafter on basic knowledge management theory, and on Artificial Knowledge Management Systems (AKMSs), a concept very closely related to his previous Distributed Knowledge Management System (DKMS) idea. He was also working on epistemology for Knowledge Management and on complex adaptive systems, as well. Mark was working in the areas of sustainability, systems modeling, and complex adaptive systems.

Joe's work on the AKMS/DKMS paradigm developed through the fall of 1998, and he produced a paper on enterprise knowledge management modeling and the DKMS for the KM Expo-hosted conference already mentioned and also two working papers for a rather premature, but very exciting, KMCI standards conference held in Silver Spring, Maryland, in January 1999. One of these papers was on a Knowledge Base Management System (KBMS) standard, and the other was on an Artificial Knowledge Management System (AKMS) standard. Both papers, and a number of others written since that time, as well as a recent book, helped to develop work in the Enterprise Knowledge Portal (EKP) area as reflected in a number of chapters in this book.

Before meeting Joe in the fall of 1998, Mark had become deeply involved in the study of management applications of complexity theory via the New England Complex Systems Institute (NECSI). In April 1998, he presented a paper at NECSI's first conference on complexity in management in Toronto entitled, "Complexity, IT, and the Interprise." In his paper, Mark introduced the idea of "unmanaging" knowledge, an early reference to what would later become the *Policy Synchronization Method* (discussed variously throughout this book), according to which enhancements in innovation can be achieved not so much by managing knowledge, but by managing the conditions in organizations in which knowledge is produced and integrated. Mark's interest in the development of a complexity-inspired approach to KM became the basis of his introduction to Joe later that year and of their affiliation ever since.

At about the same time that Joe published the first article on the EKP (in March 1999), both of us continued to be involved in significant work at the KMCI on the foundations of knowledge management. That work, done primarily in collaboration with each other, led to the initial formulation of the Knowledge Life Cycle (KLC) framework for knowledge processing and to the first sharp distinctions among business processing, knowledge processing, and knowledge management. The KLC also became the basis for Mark's definition of the second-generation knowledge management concept in 1999, and its subsequent adoption as the KMCI orientation to KM.

We have continued to collaborate in developing the KLC concept since its origination in the spring of 1999 and in developing a knowledge management framework based on it. Many of our publications on the foundations of KM are available at www.dkms.com, at www.macroinnovation.com, and at www.kmci.org. Mark has also published *The New Knowledge Management* (2003), while Joe has published *Enterprise Information Portals and Knowledge Management* (2003), both in the same KMCI Press series in which this book appears. Both are milestone publications in the development of The New Knowledge Management (TNKM).

All of our recent work has been done against the backdrop of, and with an eye toward, the broader work in TNKM. That work now encompasses not only the foundations of knowledge management and conceptual frameworks of the KLC and KM, but additional work on sustainable innovation, social innovation capital, KM strategy, the open enterprise, knowledge management metrics, knowledge management framework methodology, and the relationship of enterprise information portals and the full range of IT products to knowledge management.

The context for this work is all of the above. The more specific context, however, lies in the KMCI Certified Knowledge and

Innovation Manager (CKIM) KM certification program. It is in that program that our key issues approach to KM has been developed. From it, we have confirmed the idea that the most important value proposition for Knowledge Management (KM) is to enhance *organizational intelligence*, the ability of an organization to adapt to its environment. Adaptation ultimately is based on new, relevant, and effective knowledge. So to adapt over time, an organization must be able to *innovate sustainably*. It must be able to recognize problems, to respond to them with tentative solutions (new ideas), to eliminate those solutions that have errors, and thus to create or produce high-quality knowledge that can support more effective decisions. The idea of error elimination is particularly important here, since its systematic employment is one of the prime distinguishing elements in TNKM from other approaches in second-generation knowledge management.

In the course of enhancing organizational intelligence, moreover, it turns out that openness in Knowledge Processing is a requirement that is paramount in realizing this goal. Such openness, in turn, is a protection against malfeasance and corruption. So, it turns out that TNKM, in seeking organizational intelligence, is at the same time providing an antidote to the poison of corporation corruption and its corrosive effects on commerce, the capital markets, and the international economic system, more generally. *Knowledge Management is primarily about management activities performed with the intention of enhancing Knowledge Processing.* And this book is about beginning to lay out the key issues besetting systematic study of how this might be done from the perspective of TNKM, a new KM paradigm. These issues include the nature of knowledge, the origins of knowledge processing in business processing, the nature of KM, change in KM, applications of the KLC, KM best practices and their context, the position and status of KM strategy in the enterprise, the role of culture in KM, the nature of a normative model for KM called the open enterprise, the role of IT in KM, the state of the field of intellectual capital, and much more that we don't have the space to cover in this book.

What we do hope to accomplish is to raise consciousness about TNKM, to demonstrate its attractiveness as an approach to KM, some of the specific accomplishments it already has to its credit, and to indicate the full range of problems it points to that are crying out for solutions. You shall know the quality of a new paradigm by the fruitfulness of the problems it identifies and by the solutions to these problems it suggests. We want you to get to know the *new* knowledge management paradigm, its problems, and some of its solutions through this book. If we are successful, you will join us in the great work of "practicing" TNKM with the objective of making our organizations, both public and private, more open, agile, resilient, adaptive, and innovative in the face of change, and more honest and ethical in the face of temptation.

Joseph M. Firestone, Ph.D.
Alexandria, Va.

Mark W. McElroy
Hartland Four Corners, Vt.

October 15, 2002

ACKNOWLEDGMENTS

There are many we would like to thank for contributing to this book. Some were other authors that greatly influenced our views. Others are friends or colleagues who read our work at one time or another, or heard one of our presentations and were kind enough to provide us feedback that was important in developing our ideas further. Others helped with production of the book.

Among the authors who have been most influential in shaping our views were Karl Popper for his theory of knowledge and its generation; Charles Sanders Peirce for his fallibilism and open-minded pragmatism; Carl Hempel and Willard Van Orman Quine for their writings on theoretical networks; Everett W. Hall for his work on value theory; John Atkinson and David Birch for their research on motivation and action; Thomas L. Saaty for his pioneering work on the Analytic Hierarchy Process (AHP) and on the theory of ratio scale measurement; Henry Mintzberg for his research into the behavior of executives; John Holland for his work on complex adaptive systems and emergence; Paul Thagard for his work on scientific change and revolution; Ralph Stacey for his application of complexity theory to learning in human social systems; Mark A. Notturno for his work on Karl Popper, especially his very fine book *Science and the Open Society*; and Verna Allee for her recent work on value networks.

Among friends, some of whom are also authors, we'd like to thank Steven A. Cavaleri, former President of KMCI and our collaborator in this work; Arthur J. Murray for his help in improving the KMCI Certified Knowledge and Innovation Manager program; Professor Richard W. Chadwick, who some years ago collaborated with Joe in developing the *flow of behavior framework* used in the book; and Dr. Kenneth W. Terhune, who collaborated with Joe in developing the *motivational framework* used here. We thank all of you for the attention you've paid to our work and for the help you've given us.

Those who were important in producing this book include Professor Francisco Javier Carrillo, who reviewed our book proposal and encouraged us to proceed with this project. We have worked most closely on this book with Karen Maloney of Butterworth–Heinemann, who as chairperson of the KMCI Press Board approved the adjustments and changes that occur in any substantial book project; and Katie Hennessy and Kyle Sarofeen, who managed the editorial work for B–H. We thank you all for your help in producing this book. Finally, Joe would like to thank Bonnie, who is unfailing in her good humor and support for his various writing projects and who frequently seems even more enthusiastic than he is in bringing them to a successful conclusion; and Mark would like to thank Amy, whose encouragement and belief in his work during the past five years has meant everything to him.

Joseph M. Firestone
Alexandria, VA

Mark W. McElroy
Hartland Four Corners, VT

October 15, 2002

Introduction:
What Is The New
Knowledge
Management
(TNKM), and What
Are Its Key Issues?

What is the New Knowledge
Management (TNKM)?

At its core, "The New Knowledge Management" (TNKM) is the name for the body of issues, models, and practices representing the broadening of scope of knowledge management from a concern with knowledge sharing, broadcasting, retrieval, and teaching, collectively *knowledge integration*, to a concern with these things, as well as *knowledge making, or knowledge production*. The idea of TNKM arises from McElroy's (1999) analysis of two fundamental types of KM concerns.

McElroy (1999) has characterized the concern with Knowledge Integration as "supply-side" knowledge management, because it assumes that knowledge already exists in the enterprise and that the problem of KM is to facilitate the *supply* of the right preexisting knowledge to the right person at the right time. He has further characterized (1999) the concern with knowledge making as "demand-side" KM, because it assumes that knowledge must be produced in response to the demand for it, and that people self-organize around the demand for knowledge production to create structures that will succeed in fulfilling the demand. While the theory and practice of knowledge management first concerned themselves mainly with supply-side considerations (first-generation KM), KM has broadened in recent years and is now concerned with both supply- and demand-side issues (second-generation KM).

First-generation knowledge management is the set of frameworks, models, practices, techniques, etc., that reflect supply-side-only concerns. Second-generation knowledge management is the set of frameworks, models, practices, techniques, etc., that involve treatment of *both* supply- and demand-side side concerns. The New Knowledge Management (TNKM) is a variant of second-generation thinking that includes specific developments underway at the Knowledge Management Consortium International (KMCI), including the open enterprise, the enterprise knowledge portal, the KM metrics framework, positions on KM standards, intellectual capital, the role of complex adaptive systems (CAS), sustainable innovation, KM methodology, and other new developments. One way to look at TNKM is to consider it a new "paradigm," but in using that term we do not want to carry over Kuhn's (1970) connotation of a relatively closed political ideology impervious to fundamental criticism. Rather, we agree more with Karl Popper's view of paradigms (1970) as frameworks that can always be transcended by developing still broader frameworks containing the older ones. If we accept that TNKM is a paradigm that is open to change and further development, then clearly that paradigm needs detailed articulation of its various components and aspects, so that it may be developed further through critical examination, error elimination, and learning. That articulation is a process the authors have been undertaking through many previous and projected articles, presentations, classes and workshops, and books on TNKM.

KMCI Press has already published two books that reflect the TNKM perspective: *The New Knowledge Management*, by Mark W. McElroy (2003), and *Enterprise Information Portals and Knowledge Management*, by Joseph M. Firestone, Ph.D. (2003). The purposes of this book are to go more deeply into many of the subjects raised in the earlier works; to set TNKM in the context of the social sciences; and to encourage the evolution of KM as a discipline. Most important, however, it is intended to look at TNKM from the point of view of the issue, so that its most important subject areas may be distinguished, the core of TNKM revealed, and the significance of its key problem areas brought home to the KM Community.

Key Issues in The New Knowledge Management is a pivotal book in the development of the TNKM paradigm, because it is this book that moves from the general statement of TNKM principles and outlook to a statement of a set of issues, problems, and "puzzles" that are identified as critical to the paradigm and that are illuminated by it. This book covers many of the primary problem areas in TNKM, but for reasons of space we leave many such areas for a future work.

Having identified TNKM in broad and general terms, let us now turn to the various issues we will address in this book.

What Are Its Issues?

There are many key issues in knowledge management, but there are few books that look at KM from an issues point of view. So we think the field is ready for an issues book and that this one will fill that need. Here are the issues we have selected, the reasons why we selected them, and the features that will emerge from our treatment and that we hope will make this book a significant contribution for readers interested in KM.

The Knowledge Conundrum (Knowledge Wars)

The nature of knowledge is a perpetual issue in Knowledge Management. As Verna Allee (2002) says: "How you define knowledge determines how you manage it." It is a mark of the lack of integration of this field that so many definitions of knowledge, many diametrically opposed to one another, still circulate and are given some measure of credence. Progress will not be made in KM until there is a macro-level attempt to address a few key concepts of knowledge. TNKM has a point of view on this issue, and Chapter 1 on the knowledge conundrum will provide a comprehensive analysis of the warring concepts of knowledge and then will present the TNKM point of view as one that integrates most of them. For readers, this chapter will provide a guide to the perplexed and an alternative that they can use in coming to their own decisions about the monistic, dualistic, or pluralistic character of knowledge.

The Nature of Knowledge Processing (Origin and Character of the Knowledge Life Cycle)

Knowledge processes produce knowledge. They are the primary focus of KM. In TNKM, McElroy (2003) described the Knowledge Life Cycle (KLC) framework and demonstrated its organizing power for those who practice Knowledge Management. But he could not, for reasons of space, provide an in-depth examination of the foundations of the KLC in individual and group motivation. Chapter 2 will provide a theory about how the KLC arises and what its relationship is to the Organizational Learning Cycle (OLC), or as we like to call it, the Decision Execution Cycle, or DEC. This chapter will also provide an analysis of double-loop learning (Argyris 1993), Popper's problem-solving model (Popper 1972), a transaction-based social psychological framework of sociocultural interaction, and "sense making" (Weick 1995)—a very hot topic in KM currently—in DEC and KLC processes.

Information Management or Knowledge Management?

Here is a truly central issue defining the boundaries of Knowledge Management. The very existence of the field depends on this distinction. If it cannot be made coherently, then everything reduces to information management, and there is no basis for the practice and discipline of KM. TNKM has its own perspective on this distinction. It is a clear perspective and in developing it in Chapter 3, we will provide a clear, bright line distinguishing KM from IM. We will also provide a framework of KM activities to guide KM practice.

Generations of Knowledge Management: Three Views

One of the bases of TNKM is in Mark McElroy's distinction between first- and second-generation knowledge management. Now there are two other views of change in KM: a "three-stage" theory offered in a recent issue of *KM World* by Mark Koenig (2002), and an "age" theory offered by David Snowden (2002). Chapter 4 will examine all three views of change, compare them, and will show that the TNKM view is the only viable alternative among the three. In the process, it will critique Snowden's increasingly popular Cynefin Model and demonstrate that TNKM offers all of its advantages in addressing change, dynamism, complexity in organizations, and variety, without having to embrace the oversimplicity, paradox, contradiction, and inaccuracy in historical reconstruction that beset Cynefin.

The Role of Knowledge Claim Evaluation in Knowledge Production

Many current approaches to KM ignore the essential role of knowledge claim evaluation, or validation, a key subprocess in the KLC, in producing knowledge. Chapter 5 addresses this issue and presents a framework for knowledge claim evaluation in producing organizational knowledge. It will also discuss the relevance of the framework for software applications. This framework will be the first of its kind in KM. It will provide a basis for firms to customize their own methodologies for knowledge claim evaluation, knowledge production, and, by extension, innovation, and will also provide a basis for software applications such as enterprise knowledge portals.

Applications of the Knowledge Life Cycle Framework: Theory and Practice in TNKM

Increasingly, theorists in knowledge management are offering conceptual frameworks or models of knowledge processing. The proof of a conceptual framework is in the assistance it provides in enhancing KM practice by supplying a set of categories and relationships that may be used for description, analysis, and planning. Chapter 6 will examine the issue of what the KLC is good for. Specifically, it will provide an account of the support provided by the KLC framework in various areas of practice including: strategy formulation, KM and knowledge audits, modeling, predicting, forecasting, simulating, metrics segmentation, policy and program formulation, methodology, IT requirements, Intellectual Capital, and education and training.

KM as Best Practices Systems—Where's the Context?

A mainstay of first-generation KM has been the *best practice system*, a database solution that catalogs information and stories about business process approaches that were apparently associated with successful outcomes in the past. The guiding idea is that the best practices described in these cases may be reused successfully when similar situations arise. Chapter 7 questions this idea by discussing the problem of "context" in best practices, and by providing an answer to this problem. This answer shows that present best practices systems are anything but that.

What Comes First: KM or Strategy?

Few issues in knowledge management provoke more fiery debate than the question of how KM relates to strategy and who it should report to. Is KM the servant of strategy? Or does KM somehow transcend it? Should KM initiatives be independent of strategy and not subordinate or answerable to their makers? Should strategy be seen as just another kind of knowledge claim, a product of knowledge processing? If so, and if KM is all about enhancing knowledge processing, then isn't business strategy arguably downstream from KM, and not the reverse?

Further, if strategy is indeed nothing more than just another (set of) knowledge claim(s), then instead of viewing KM as a tactical tool for the fulfillment of strategy, shouldn't we, instead, be thinking of strategy as *an outcome of knowledge processing*, the quality of which is the chief concern of KM, and not the fulfillment of strategy? Or is KM an implementation tool for strategy? And if so, should the complexion and mission of KM change whenever business strategies change? In Chapter 8 we will examine these issues, as well as the closely related question of where KM should reside in the management hierarchy.

Is Culture a Barrier in KM?

It's become almost cliché to attribute failures in KM programs to the effects of culture. In Chapter 9 we confront this issue head-on, analyze various reasoning patterns using the idea of culture, and place culture in the context of many other factors that impact the success or failure of KM. We also analyze the relationship of culture to knowledge, a topic that has not generally been addressed clearly in the KM literature. The reader will come away from this chapter with (a) an understanding that culture is composed in large part of knowledge predispositions, and (b) an extension of the conceptual framework of TNKM, enabling clear thinking about the role of culture in KM.

Foundations of Intellectual Capital Frameworks and the Need to Broaden Them

Intellectual Capital (IC) models usually take the form of taxonomies. Market Value is at the top of a hierarchy; types of capital contributing to market value are at the lower levels. IC models are used to segment indicators or metrics, which may then be used to evaluate the market value of companies. Chapter 10 examines the pattern of models of Intellectual Capital and then critiques the thinking that lies behind it. Out of this comes the idea of innovation-related social capital as a new, legitimate form of intangible capital missing from contemporary models and also the view that what conventional accounting desperately needs in order to resolve its quandary over IC is a strong dose of new thinking from complexity science, organizational learning, and TNKM.

Conclusion: The Knowledge Management Landscape, the Vision of Knowledge Management, and the Future of TNKM

We end in Chapter 11 by presenting the vision and program of TNKM. In particular, we will draw from the previous analysis an account of the major problems and issues that we must continue to address to advance TNKM's program of development.

WHO THIS BOOK IS FOR

Communities that would be interested in the book include:

- The KM community
- The organizational learning community
- The innovation management community
- The IT and portal communities
- The R&D community
- The HR and OD communities
- The intellectual capital management community
- The "complexity theory as applied to business" community
- The systems thinking community
- The "system dynamics as applied to business" community

The following management communities will also be interested:

- CIOs (interested in tracking developments in KM)
- HR directors (interested in business methods that lead to improvements in the value of "human capital" and learning strategies)
- OD practitioners (interested in anything that relates to strategies for improving organizational performance)
- CFOs (rapidly rising interest in growing and "valuing" intellectual capital and reporting on same via the finance function)
- CEO/Executive (interested in any approach that results in increased rates and relevance/quality of innovation as a source of competitive advantage)

HOW TO USE THIS BOOK

Read the first three chapters first. Chapters 4 to 9 may be read in any order. Chapters 10 and 11 are best read last.

REFERENCES

Allee, V. (2002), "12 Principles of Knowledge Management" *American Society for Training and Development*, Alexandria, VA.

Argyris, C. (1993), *Knowledge for Action*, San Francisco, CA: Jossey-Bass.

Firestone, J.M. (2003), *Enterprise Information Portals and Knowledge Management*, Boston, MA: KMCI Press/Butterworth–Heinemann.

Koenig, Michael E.D. (2002), "The Third Stage of KM Emerges," *KMWorld* 11, No. 3 (March, 2002), 20–21, 28.

Kuhn, T. (1970), *The Structure of Scientific Revolutions*, Chicago, IL: University of Chicago Press (1970 edition).

McElroy, M.W. (1999), "The Second Generation of KM," *Knowledge Management* (October 1999) pp. 86–88.

———— (2003), *The New Knowledge Management: Complexity, Learning, and Sustainable Innovation*, Boston, MA: KMCI Press/Butterworth–Heinemann.

Nonaka, I. and Takeuchik, H. (1995), *The Knowledge Creating Company*, New York, NY: Oxford University Press.

Popper, K.R. (1970), in I. Lakatos and A. Musgrave (eds.), "Normal Science and Its Dangers," *Criticism and the Growth of Knowledge*, Cambridge, UK: Cambridge University Press.

Popper, K.R. (1972), *Objective Knowledge*, London, England: Oxford University Press.

Snowden, D. (2002), "Complex Acts of Knowing; Paradox and Descriptive Self-Awareness", *Journal of Knowledge Management*, forthcoming.

Weick, K. (1995), *Sense Making In Organisations*, Beverly Hills, CA: Sage Publications.

Chapter 1

THE KNOWLEDGE CONUNDRUM

INTRODUCTION

Since knowledge management became a popular phrase in the mid-1990s, practitioners have labored under the burden of varying and sometimes vague definitions of the field. It is a frequent occurrence at meetings of practitioners discussing KM Metrics, KM Methodology, or KM approaches that someone suddenly asks, "What do we mean by knowledge management?" It's a still more frequent occurrence that multiple answers are forthcoming in such meetings. Part of the reason for this lack of consensus on a basic definition distinguishing the fundamental process characterizing KM from other business processes is lack of consensus about how to define "knowledge" itself. Most writers about knowledge management apparently believe that they should keep discussion of the nature of knowledge to a minimum and either use the term implicitly, or alternatively, offer the definition they prefer with little or no explanation about why they prefer that specific definition.

This chapter critically surveys alternative definitions of knowledge used in the KM literature, and on the basis of this critique proceeds to offer our own construction of this key term and relates our views to other important questions related to knowledge. The topics we will cover include:

1

- On definition
- Definitions of knowledge
- World 2 definitions
- World 3 definitions
- World 2 data, information, and knowledge
- Tacit knowledge and explicit knowledge
- Polanyi, implicit knowledge, and Popper
- Individual level World 2 knowledge and motivational hierarchies
- Different types of knowledge

ON DEFINITION

Many in Knowledge Management (KM) prefer to avoid defining it. Their view is that definition is a sterile, time-wasting pastime contributing little or nothing to the real work of KM. Our view is different. It is that definition is an important early step on the road to specifying one's cognitive map of knowledge processing and KM and to ultimately developing quality models useful for developing KM solutions. We also think that arguments over definition are not fruitless arguments, but important exchanges about what is a good starting point for developing a cognitive map of KM.

The purpose of a definition is not to provide necessary and sufficient conditions for its use. Instead, its purpose is to answer a question like: "What do you mean by knowledge management?" with a short, *incomplete* answer that:

- allows the questioner to infer something more of the cognitive map (or conceptual map, or semantic network) of the target of the question; and
- facilitates the beginning of further communication and perhaps learning relative to that cognitive map.

A definition, in other words, is the "elevator speech" (the 30-second expression of the idea; see Moore 1991, 159–162) representing, however imperfectly, the cognitive map of the person offering it. That is, when communicating with others about any term, you can:

- Refuse to explain it;
- Define it;

■ Specify it;
■ Construct a cognitive map of it.

Which would you rather do in response to a basic question from someone either at the beginning of a conversation or at a briefing? Do nothing? Give the "elevator speech?" Give the five-minute overview? Or give the whole briefing?

And if there's disagreement over a specific definition there are a number of good reasons why that might be the case, other than mere love of philosophical disputation. First, the definition may not provide enough of the definer's cognitive map to evaluate his or her statements using the concept. Second, the definition may not distinguish the concept from other concepts. Third, the definition may redefine the term beyond common usage in a manner that promotes confusion in communication. (This is a frequent occurrence due to the desire of communicators to acquire the "halo effect" of certain terms for their frequently different concepts.) And fourth, those disagreeing may forecast that a bad model will result (in wasted time and effort) from the starting place for model construction provided by a particular definition.

So, once again, why bother to define? Answer: to save time in responding to a questioner, to create a basis for further communication with others, and last, to specify a cost-effective starting place for further specification, measurement, and modeling.

DEFINITIONS OF KNOWLEDGE

There is no consensus on the nature of knowledge. Nor has there ever been in the history of human thought (Jones 1952). Here's a brief and far from comprehensive survey of definitions offered by writers and researchers in knowledge management.

Knowledge is:

■ "Justified true belief": This is the venerable definition of many philosophers, especially of empiricists who believe knowledge claims can be justified by facts (Goldman 1991). It also is the definition adopted by Nonaka and Takeuchi (1995, 58).
■ "Information in context": This is a definition that may have its roots in Cartesian rationalist epistemology. In that conceptual

framework, its import is that a knowledge claim is valid if it fits without contradiction and adds to the systematic coherence of a larger framework of knowledge (Aune 1970). That is, the rationalist view that knowledge is information in context and that context is what makes it knowledge derives *from the more complete idea* that information is justified as knowledge when it is coherent with a larger deductive system within which it fits. In this formulation, the validity criterion and the theory of truth are the same. They form a coherence theory of truth and validation, where coherence means that a knowledge claim is consistent with its broader context. In other words, according to the Cartesian rationalist version of the information in context view, information is knowledge when and if (because) it is validated by consistency with its context.

The rationalist view of knowledge as information in context is only one variant of that view. A second is the pragmatist idea that information that is useful in a situational context of decision and action is knowledge. This view does not focus on logical consistency with other knowledge claims in a system. Instead, it focuses on how instrumental a piece of information is as a tool for action. A further variant of the pragmatist view results from those who do not believe that mere information, our linguistic expressions recorded in documents, information systems, or other cultural products can ever be knowledge. This variant views knowledge as belief and suggests that the utility of information in context is determined by the belief knowledge that exposure to the information produces.

■ "Knowledge is understanding based on experience": This is an idea that is central to modern pragmatism and its associated epistemology (James 1907). It's also a standard definition found in English language dictionaries. Since it refers to "understanding," it is clearly a definition of knowledge focused on belief.

■ "Knowledge is experience or information that can be communicated or shared" (Allee 1997, 27). Even though Allee refers to experience here, her emphasis is clearly on sharable information and community, not beliefs (27).

■ "Knowledge, while made up of data and information, can be thought of as much greater understanding of a situation, relationships, causal phenomena, and the theories and rules (both explicit and implicit) that underlie a given domain or problem." (Bennet and Bennet 2000, 19). Here Bennet and Bennet refer to knowledge as "understanding" of situations, relationships, and causal phenomena but associate data, information, theories, and rules, and also "understanding" of them with knowledge.

■ "Knowledge can be thought of as the body of understandings, generalizations, and abstractions that we carry with us on a permanent or semi-permanent basis and apply to interpret and manage the world around us . . . we will consider knowledge to be the collection of mental units of all kinds that provides us with understanding and insights." (Wiig 1998). Wiig clearly defines knowledge as a form of belief.

■ "The most essential definition of knowledge is that it is composed of and grounded solely in *potential acts* and in those signs that refer to them" (Cavaleri and Reed 2000, 114). This is another definition originating in pragmatism and specifically in the work of Charles S. Peirce. A definition offered in the same spirit is "knowledge is social acts," provided by Ralph Stacey (1996).

■ "Knowledge is the capacity for effective action." This definition is the one favored by the organizational learning community (Argyris 1993, 2–3).

■ "Knowledge is a fluid mix of framed experience, values, contextual information, and expert insight that provides a framework for evaluating and incorporating new experiences and information. It originates and is applied in the minds of knowers. In organizations it often becomes embedded not only in documents or repositories but also in organizational routines, processes, practices, and norms" (Davenport and Prusak, 1997, 5).

We will discuss these views shortly, but first we want to introduce the framework we prefer for looking at knowledge.

We distinguish three types of knowledge:

■ World 1 knowledge—encoded structures in physical systems (such as genetic encoding in DNA) that allow those objects to adapt to an environment;

- World 2 knowledge—beliefs and belief predispositions (in minds) about the world, the beautiful, and the right that we believe have survived our tests, evaluations, and experience;
- World 3 knowledge—sharable linguistic formulations, knowledge claims about the world, the beautiful, and the right, that have survived testing and evaluation by the agent (individual, group, community, team, organization, society, etc.) acquiring, formulating, and testing and evaluating the knowledge claims.

All three types of knowledge are about encoded structures in one kind of system or another that arguably help those systems to adapt. The World 1, World 2, and World 3 distinctions were introduced by Karl Popper (1972, 1994, Popper and Eccles 1977). Popper also defined the distinction between World 2 and World 3 knowledge (1972, 106–122, 1994, Chap. 1) (Popper and Eccles, 1977, 36–50). But he did not define either type of knowledge in precisely the terms we have used.

It is comparatively easy to accept Popper's distinction between the World 1 material and World 2 mental objects that underlies the distinction between World 1 and World 2 knowledge. It is much harder however, to accept the reality of World 3 objects and therefore World 3 knowledge. Following Popper, we propose that there are things that affect our behavior which (1) are not part of World 1 or World 2, (2) are *made* by intelligent beings, (3) are sharable among us in that they provide sharable content for those exposed to them, and (4) are partly autonomous once created by us. World 3 objects include theories, arguments, problems, works of art, symphonies, constitutions, public policy statements, and all the cultural objects that express content.

While Popper called these objects "World 3," he was quick to recognize that such objects come in many varieties and indicated that he thought that World 3 had many different regions. He had no strong feelings about whether these regions should all be called World 3 products or whether we should break things out into a number of distinct worlds based on the differences among art, science, music, law, truth, beauty, justice, and other cultural products. We agree with his views and also think that it makes little difference how we label the different World 3 regions as long as we recognize that all are cultural products, that humans create them, and that their function is to help us adapt.

Among World 3 products, we have already named problems and knowledge claims as key objects. Thus, knowledge claims exist within any organization or social system and are among its World 3 products. Among World 2 objects we have distinguished beliefs and belief predispositions of various kinds. Later on we will present a much richer view of the psychology of psychocultural interaction.

So in World 2 we have beliefs and belief predispositions, and in World 3 linguistic expressions in the form of knowledge claims. Where, then, is knowledge? As we indicated earlier, knowledge is found in both World 2 and World 3 in those beliefs, beliefs predispositions, and knowledge claims that have best survived our attempts to test and evaluate them against competitors. Thus, in our view, knowledge is a term applied to the best performing beliefs, belief predispositions, and knowledge claims of an agent—that is, the individual or group that holds the belief or belief predisposition, or expresses the knowledge claims in question—in the course of the agent assessing the performance of those claims.

Our definitions of Worlds 2 and 3 knowledge do not require that knowledge be true. In fact, our position is that knowledge claims are fallible and that while a particular knowledge claim may be true, and that its function is to state what is true, even those that we call "knowledge" may prove false in the future if they fail to survive our tests. If knowledge need not be true, then clearly it cannot be called objective on grounds that it is true.

Further, World 2 belief knowledge, even though it has survived individual tests and evaluations, since it is fallible, also has the problem that it is not sharable among agents. Thus, such knowledge is personal and psychological, and the beliefs that constitute it do not exist outside the knowing subject that holds them. In exactly this sense, World 2 belief knowledge is subjective.

On the other hand, World 3 knowledge claims, once created, do exist outside the knowing subjects that created them, do not die with these subjects, and, in addition, are sharable among these knowing subjects and others that may not encounter them until years after their creation. Further, the track record of testing and evaluating knowledge claims also exists outside the knowing subjects involved in creating it and is sharable among knowing subjects interested in the knowledge claims. So this sharability of knowledge claims and their track records makes them "objective" in a way that beliefs and belief predispositions are not.

If knowledge claims are "objective," what may be said about the objectivity of World 3 knowledge itself? We have already defined World 3 knowledge as composed of the best surviving knowledge claims of an agent. But this notion implies that knowledge is the product of a classification decision by the agent producing that knowledge. So what, exactly, is "objective" about this classification decision that may well be dependent on ideological or political criteria that are biased and therefore essentially subjective in nature? The answer is that in the general case there is nothing necessarily "objective" about such decisions, nor need there be to ensure that the knowledge produced by the decision is "objective."

The reason for this is that the classification decision need not be correct for the resulting "knowledge" to be objective. Nor need it follow a decision procedure that conforms to any recognizable notion of rationality (though the knowledge that emerges from it would certainly be higher quality if it did, and therefore an "objective" decision procedure is certainly preferable to one that is not objective).

Rather, the objectivity of the knowledge produced lies in the sharable nature of the knowledge claims that have been classified as knowledge and the metaclaims constituting the track record of testing and evaluation. The sharable nature of these claims always makes the decision to classify a knowledge claim as knowledge subject to review. Thus, it has no effect on the objectivity of knowledge that the classification decision is made by one particular agent rather than another, because the designation "knowledge" for a particular knowledge claim carries no greater connotation of "objectivity" than the objectivity that inheres in the unclassified knowledge claims themselves.

The distinction between World 2 and World 3 knowledge, and particularly the use of the term "knowledge" for World 3, is frequently hard to accept. A particularly direct objection to our characterization is the following.

World 3 expressions of knowledge are not the same as knowledge in the World 2 sense because they are *expressions of knowledge*, not knowledge. They are vestiges of knowledge. To call them knowledge is a little bit like calling a person's shadow a form of "person" because it expresses the shape of a person whose very essence can be deciphered from a study of the shadow. Therefore, shadows are "objective" people.

This argument, though trenchant and attractive, has many problems. First, we do not say that World 3 knowledge claims are the same as World 2 knowledge. World 2 knowledge is belief knowledge; most of it is not even reducible to language; most of it is predispositional in character and is not even conscious. And all of it is subjective in the sense that it cannot be shared with other agents. Second, World 3 knowledge claims are not expressions of belief knowledge as claimed just above.

It is a fallacy to think that we can faithfully express or copy our belief knowledge except in the most superficial sense. Rather than being expressions of belief knowledge, knowledge claims are simply products that we create in an effort to help us solve problems. They are one type of linguistic expression. What do they express? *What the claims say*, not what the authors believe. We do not know the correspondence between what the authors say and what they believe. Nor does the truth of the expressions—the knowledge claims—have anything to do with the truth of a person's beliefs. Truth as a coherent philosophical construct is a relationship between linguistic entities and facts. *It is not a relationship between beliefs and facts*. It is not even clear what the analogous relationship between beliefs and facts is, but it is not truth.

Third, World 3 knowledge claims are not "vestiges of knowledge." They are not because they are a resultant of belief knowledge, situational forces, cultural and social structural influence, and individual creativity expressed in the creation of World 3 objects. So, much more goes into creating them than just belief knowledge.

They are also not vestiges because as linguistic objects, they have an entirely different character than beliefs and are in no sense a "leftover" or "vestige" of them. They are also not vestiges because while beliefs cannot be shared with others, these knowledge claims can be shared, and this sharability characteristic makes them more testable, more open to evaluation, more open to gradual refinement over time, and more useful in both solving problems and in generating new problems that can lead to further progress than beliefs can.

Finally, in the passage: "To call them knowledge is a little bit like calling a person's shadow a form of 'person' because it expresses the shape of a person whose very essence can be deciphered from a study of the shadow. Therefore, shadows are 'objective' people," such ideas express an entirely false analogy. In the analogy, the person is the reality and the shadow is the representation of it we use to try to divine its essence. But in the World 2/World 3 contrast, reality is the system and environment within which we have to act, and our problem is to understand that reality so that we can achieve our goals in that context. At any given time, our belief knowledge is the "shadow" of reality present in our minds, and our problem is to refine this shadow, this understanding, so that we can use it to act more successfully. How do we do that?

We do it by combining with others to create linguistic expressions, cultural products that are representations of reality themselves, more shadows. But there are differences between these shadows and the belief shadows. First, unlike belief shadows, with these knowledge claim-based shadows, we can at least formulate the idea of truth correspondence coherently. Second, we can test and evaluate these knowledge claims in collaboration with other people, so that we can create organizational knowledge. Third, we can share these shadows with others in order to refine them and to test them against alternative shadows, so that eventually we can arrive at a shadow that has performed better in the face of our tests. Fourth, when our construction of our knowledge claim shadows is, for the time being, complete, we can use these shadows to reshape our belief shadows, so that these "belief shadows" that we must rely upon to make decisions, provide us with better results.

This last point is of paramount importance. Following Popper's account (Popper and Eccles 1977, 120–147), evolution begins within World 1. When biological creatures evolve, they first achieve their goals through limited adaptive and learning capabilities. They have brains but do not have minds. Minds evolve as control mechanisms for the brain. And as we have seen, minds allow agents to develop belief "shadows" for tracking reality and enhancing adaptation. However, the shadows created by mind alone cannot incorporate an objective shared perspective on reality. Therefore their fit with external conditions is less than ideal.

So evolution proceeds further. It creates creatures that not only have brain, mind, and consciousness, but also creatures that have language and culture. These creatures can use language and culture to create "shadows" that do incorporate a sharable perspective on reality, and this perspective, in turn, with continued inquiry, can produce "shadows" that benefit from this shared perspective and that can even correspond closely with reality. In other words, the creation of language and culture creates more objective "shadows" (knowledge claims) that place constraints on the personal, subjective "shadows" (beliefs) of the mind. These subjective shadows, in turn, help it to better understand reality, which it must do if it is to fulfill its role as the controller of behavior.

This brings us to the end of our attempt to *introduce* our own knowledge framework. Later we will expand it to cover knowledge outcomes in detail, and still later knowledge processing and knowledge management. In conclusion, we note that in many organizations, there is little concern with World 1 knowledge, and with the beautiful, and only slightly greater concern with the right, so we are left with Worlds 2 and 3 knowledge of reality as the outcomes of knowledge processes that are of primary concern to knowledge management. Let us now consider some of the definitions of knowledge surveyed earlier in light of their internal difficulties and the World 2/World 3 distinction.

WORLD 2 DEFINITIONS

■ The definition of knowledge as "justified true belief" has the difficulty that we cannot know for certain that any knowledge belief, no matter how well validated, is true. Yet some knowledge claims, the well validated ones, are what we mean by knowledge. It also has the additional difficulty that "justification" of knowledge claims cannot be accomplished through the testing and evaluation processes that comprise validation, because no finite amount of evidence can provide a warrant for inferring that a knowledge claim is true. And nether can a finite amount of evidence force one to accept the conclusion that a knowledge claim is false. In short, the problem with justified true belief as a definition of knowledge is that we can neither "justify" knowledge claims nor ever know for certain whether they are true. So, if knowledge is justified true belief, we are led to the conclusion that there is no knowledge, a conclusion that is unacceptable as a foundation for knowledge management.

■ The definition of World 2 knowledge we provided earlier implies that knowledge is not the same thing as "understanding" whether qualified by experience, or greater understanding, or insight. Understanding, for one thing, is conscious. When we understand something, we are aware of our understanding in consciousness. Knowledge in World 2, on the other hand, can refer to unconscious predispositions of various kinds that we cannot make conscious. Further, we may hold beliefs that we have not tested and evaluated, understand those beliefs completely, but not believe that those beliefs are knowledge because they have not been tested and evaluated. For at least these two reasons, "understanding" is not a sufficient condition of knowledge, and therefore the pragmatist (James), Bennet and Bennet, and Wiig definitions are called into question.

■ Nor is World 2 knowledge the same thing as experience we can share. Some tacit knowledge, as characterized by Polanyi (1958, 1966), is inexpressible. We know it but cannot tell it. This kind of World 2 knowledge is impossible to share. So if we accept Polanyi's idea of personal, tacit knowledge, on those grounds alone we must also accept that knowledge is not always experience we can share. Even beyond such tacit knowledge, however, there is an even more important reason why World 2 knowledge is not the same thing as experience we can share, and that is that World 2 knowledge whether tacit or not is internal to our minds and ultimately private. Since no one has direct access to the mind of another, there is no way to directly share the experience of another.

■ Other than through ostensive demonstration, which does not share personal experience, the way we attempt to share experiences with others is primarily by using language-based communication, visuals, and art, in other words, World 3 knowledge claims, to describe our experiences to others. But clearly neither our descriptions of our experiences, nor our demonstrations, are the same as our subjective experiences. There is an irreducible *epistemic gap* between these external things and our inner experience. What we are sharing with others is not our World 2 beliefs, but our World 3 expressions of knowledge claims resulting from these beliefs, or our expressions of these World 2 beliefs, or our demonstrations comprised of actions reflecting our beliefs.

So the above definitions of World 2 knowledge have serious difficulties as accounts of it. In our view, World 2 knowledge is belief that the agent holding it has "justified" by subjecting it to the agent's testing and evaluation process. But it need not be true, and it cannot be "justified" by logical rules of whatever kind. World 2 knowledge is an immediate precursor of our decisions, and we use it to make them. Such knowledge is "subjective" in the sense that it is agent-specific and cannot be directly shared with others.

World 2 knowledge exists at levels above the individual, as well as at the individual level of analysis. That is, an "agent" "holding" World 2 knowledge can be a group, a team, an organization, even a nation, as well as an individual. Much research on culture (Triandis et al. 1972, Bateson 1972, Kluckhohn and Strodtbeck 1961, Morris 1956, McClelland 1961, Firestone and Oliva 1971, Glenn 1966, DeCharms and Moeller 1962), national character (Terhune 1970, Duijker and Frijda 1960), civil strife (Firestone 1972), and political integration (Deutsch 1963, Merritt 1966, Namenwirth 1969, Feierabend and Feierabend 1966), suggests that group cognitive predispositions (including belief and knowledge predispositions) are a useful concept in accounting for group behavior. If we do not recognize the existence of such predispositions, we restrict World 2 knowledge to the level of the individual. Such individual World 2 knowledge is "personal," in the sense that other individuals do not have direct access to one's own knowledge in full detail, and therefore cannot "know" it as their own belief. We will return to the idea of group cognitive predispositions in Chapter 9.

WORLD 3 DEFINITIONS

Five of the knowledge definitions we surveyed earlier may be viewed as World 3 definitions. These are knowledge as "information in context," knowledge as "a potential act," knowledge as "social acts," knowledge is the "capacity for effective action," and knowledge is "a fluid mix of framed experience, values.... All five definitions have severe problems. Here they are:

First, the idea that knowledge is information in context suggests that knowledge is linguistic in character because the term "information" is almost never used to characterize belief and World 2 objects. But this definition doesn't distinguish knowledge from information, because information can have every bit as much context as knowledge.

What distinguishes knowledge from information from the viewpoint of the agents distinguishing one from the other is *the content of the **validation contexts** of knowledge, and the extent to which it tests and evaluates competing knowledge claims.* The history of an organization's tests of knowledge claims and their competitive performance determines the validity of such claims. So the validation context is the aspect of context that is all-important in distinguishing knowledge from information, and if we wish to use the *information in context* idea to define knowledge, it would be much closer to the mark to define knowledge as information in its validation context, rather than simply as information in context.

Second, World 3 knowledge is also not the same thing as a "potential act" and "those signs that refer to them," or as "social acts." To see this, first note that potential acts are not beliefs, but abstractions, forecasts that are World 3 objects themselves. And we express such potential acts, as Peirce indicated, with the signs that refer to them.

However, *not every potential or social act is a knowledge claim, much less a tested or evaluated knowledge claim.* Though every potential act may either be or imply a knowledge claim relating the act to its anticipated consequences, unless we already have validated the knowledge claim implied by the potential act, it is just information, no different than any alternative potential knowledge claim act. So the definition of knowledge as a potential act raises the question of how potential acts that are knowledge claims are tested and evaluated.

Third, the definition of knowledge as "social acts" raises the same concerns as we just expressed for knowledge construed as potential acts. Social acts are also not beliefs but are either material (World 1) in character, or insofar as they are potential social acts, they are, as we have said, World 3 objects. And as World 3 objects we must address the question of whether they are knowledge claims, and if they are, whether they have been tested and evaluated and whether they have survived better than competitive alternatives.

Fourth, "knowledge is the capacity for effective action" is a World 3 definition insofar as the capacity referred to is the possession of sharable knowledge resources such as problems, theories, models arguments, information systems, policies, programs, etc. This definition of knowledge has the political scientist's problem. That is, knowledge may be a *necessary* condition for effective action. But it is not sufficient. Effective action also requires (a) the *intention* to use one's knowledge, and (b) the *capability or power* to take those effective actions.

Our fifth World 3 definition is Davenport and Prusak's:

> Knowledge is a fluid mix of framed experience, values, contextual information, and expert insight that provides a framework for evaluating and incorporating new experiences and information. It originates and is applied in the minds of knowers. In organizations it often becomes embedded not only in documents or repositories but also in organizational routines, processes, practices, and norms (Davenport and Prusak 1997, 5).

This definition, with its reference to "framed experience," "contextual information," "framework," and "embedding in documents," etc., is squarely in the World 3 rather than the belief camp. But as with the other definitions reviewed it ignores the role of testing and evaluating knowledge claims in distinguishing knowledge from information.

Instead of any of the above definitions, we think that World 3 knowledge consists of models, theories, arguments, descriptions, problem statements, etc., that have survived our tests and evaluations. It consists of linguistic formulations or expressions (World 3 information also exists). It is not psychological in nature or even sociological, though it is made by intelligent agents. We talk about the truth, or nearness to the truth of such World 3 objects, and of knowledge defined as descriptions, models, theories, or arguments that are closer to the truth than their competitors (Popper 1972).

This kind of knowledge is not an *immediate* precursor to decisions. It impacts decisions only through the impact it has on (World 2) beliefs. These beliefs, in turn, immediately impact decisions. This kind of knowledge (World 3 objects), further, is "objective."

It is objective in the sense that it is not agent specific and is shared among agents as an object whether or not they believe in it. It is also not "personal," because (a) all agents in the organization have access to it, and (b) it emerges from the interaction of a number of agents. Finally, it is objective because, since it is sharable, we can sensibly talk about its organizational validation. To understand the essence of World 3 knowledge we can do no better than to quote Karl Popper (1972, 116) who first formulated this idea of "objective knowledge," on the objective knowledge content in books:

> A man who reads a book with understanding is a rare creature. But even if he were more common, there would always be plenty of misunderstandings and misinterpretations; and it is not the actual and somewhat accidental avoidance of misunderstandings which turns black spots on white paper into a book or an instance of knowledge in the objective sense. Rather, it is something more abstract. It is its possibility or potentiality of being understood, its dispositional character of being understood or interpreted, or misunderstood or misinterpreted, which makes a thing a book. And this potentiality or disposition may exist without ever being actualized or realized.
>
> To see this more clearly we may imagine that after the human race has perished, some books or libraries may be found by some civilized successors of ours (no matter whether these are terrestrial animals that have become civilized, or some visitors from outer space). These books may be deciphered. They may be those logarithm tables never read before, for argument's sake. This makes it quite clear that neither its composition by thinking animals nor the fact that it has not been actually read or understood is essential for making a thing a book, and that it is sufficient that it might be deciphered.
>
> Thus, I do admit that in order to belong to the third world of objective knowledge, a book should—in principle or virtually—be capable of being grasped (or deciphered or understood, or "known") by somebody. But I do not admit more.

The distinction between World 2 and World 3 knowledge raises the issue of which type of knowledge should be the object of KM.

- Can World 2 knowledge be managed by organizations?
- To what extent is World 2 knowledge about an organization determined by organizational interaction, rather than individual predispositions and interactions not manageable by the organization?
- Where does the distinction between Worlds 2 and 3 knowledge leave the much better known distinction between tacit and explicit knowledge?

■ Or the less well known distinction between "implied knowledge" and codified knowledge? These questions will be considered in due course.

DATA, INFORMATION, KNOWLEDGE, AND WISDOM

Many writers have addressed the distinctions among data, information, and knowledge. (See, for example, Allee 1997, Bellinger 1998, Beller 2001, Murray 2000, Barquin 2001.) Our own version will provide a necessary background to taking up future issues on the distinctions between data management and knowledge management, and information management and knowledge management. What are the differences among data, information, and knowledge in human organizations? That depends on whether we're talking about World 3 or World 2 phenomena. Let us consider World 3 first.

World 3 Data, Information, Knowledge, and Wisdom

What are the differences among World 3 data, information, and knowledge in human organizations? Data, information, and knowledge all emerge from the social process. They are global properties of an organization, or its constituent agents, depending on the organizational level that is the focus of analysis. They are inter-subjective constructs, not personal data, information, or knowledge. Organizational data, information, and knowledge are World 3 objects.

A datum is the value of an observable, measurable, or calculable attribute. Data are more than one such attribute value.

Is a datum (or are data) information? Information is always provided by a datum, or by data, because data are always specified in some conceptual context. And, it is important to note, the conceptual context is one that expresses data in a structured format. Without that structured format we would not call it "data." *So data are a type of information.* They are a type of information whose conceptual context provides the data with structure and whose purpose is to represent observation.

Information, in more general terms, is data plus conceptual commitments and interpretations, or such commitments and interpretations alone. Information is frequently data extracted, filtered or formatted in some way.

Organizational knowledge is a subset of organizational information, not a superset. But it is a subset that has been extracted, filtered, formatted—that is, processed, in a very special way. It is information that has been subjected to and that has passed tests and evaluations aimed at eliminating errors and seeking the truth. It is information that has been enhanced by the record and experience provided by the validation process. Ideally, this enhanced information is that which is most truthlike (see Chapter 5).

This brings us to the Case of the Misconceived Pyramid. In treating the distinctions among data, information, and knowledge, it is often assumed that these are arranged in a pyramid with data, the most plentiful type, at the bottom; information produced from data above it; knowledge produced from information through the hard work of refining, or "mining," above it, and wisdom produced from knowledge, the rarest of all, at the top. This makes a nice picture (Figure 1.1). But if data and knowledge are also information, what happens to the pyramid?

Figure 1.2 presents a new picture. In it, information is not made from data. Data and knowledge are made from preexisting information. That is, "just information," data, knowledge, and problems are used in the *knowledge life cycle* to produce more information, including new knowledge. In effect this figure is saying, "Get

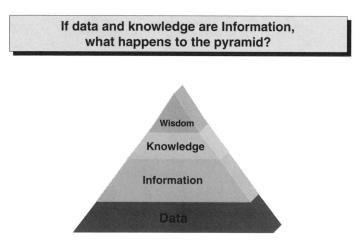

Figure 1.1
The Case of the Misconceived Pyramid

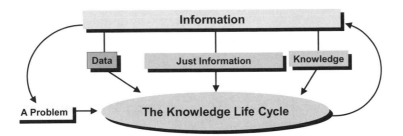

Figure 1.2
Get Rid of the Pyramid, Get On to the Cycle

rid of the pyramid; get on to the cycle." We will go into much greater detail about the nature of the Knowledge Life Cycle (KLC) in later chapters.

What has happened to wisdom in this new image? Wisdom is knowledge of what is true or right coupled with "just" (in the sense of justice) judgment about action to achieve what is right. Another definition is the application of knowledge expressed in principles to arrive at prudent, sagacious decisions about conflict situations. Both these definitions are consistent with the parable of Solomon, but they suggest that wisdom is ambiguous. It is either (a) a form of knowledge (i.e., also information) about doing what is right or (b) a kind of decision (in which case it's not information, but a type of action in a business process). That is, depending on how it is defined, wisdom may not be the same kind of thing as data, information, or knowledge.

World 2 Data, Information, and Knowledge

Earlier, we defined World 2 knowledge as beliefs (in minds) about the world, the beautiful, and the right that have survived our tests and evaluations. What if the beliefs do not survive or we cannot decide if they have or not? Then we have information. Are surviving beliefs "information," as well as knowledge? They are nonrandom structures, and as such fit Shannon's (1948) definition of information. So, there is no reason to deny knowledge the appellation information, as well.

Where do data come into this picture? "World 2 data" must refer to beliefs about observational experiences. These beliefs are like other beliefs in that we view them as validated, unvalidated, or invalidated by our experience, and also they fit into and relate to the general structure of the rest of our beliefs. So they, like World 2 knowledge and information, are also information.

What about the pyramid? Does the pyramid image (see Figure 1.1) make sense for World 2 data, information, and knowledge? Again, our experience argues against it. Data are not the foundation from which we produce information, from which we produce knowledge, from which we produce wisdom. Instead, we are born with *genetically encoded knowledge* (World 1 knowledge) that enables us to interact with the external world and to learn (Popper 1972, 71–73). This knowledge is more plentiful in quantity than all of the knowledge we will acquire through learning for the rest of our lives. We use it to approach the world with predispositions and beliefs. With these we create and structure experience, and from the process of doing this we produce new data, information, and knowledge continuously and in no particular order.

How do we do this? Once again it is through the Knowledge Life Cycle (KLC). The KLC, visualized in Figure 1.2 (and in a more detailed fashion in later chapters), produces both World 3 and World 2 data, information, and knowledge. And within its processes, World 2 and World 3 phenomena alternate in influencing the production of each other as the KLC operates through time.

TACIT KNOWLEDGE AND EXPLICIT KNOWLEDGE

A widely recognized distinction in knowledge management circles is Polanyi's distinction (1958 and 1966) between tacit, personal knowledge and explicit, codified knowledge. By tacit knowledge, Polanyi meant "committed belief" that is contextual in character and difficult to express. In fact, he characterized some tacit knowledge as inexpressible, or "ineffable," and stated that "we can know more than we can tell." He also saw knowledge as inhering in mental models that provide the knower with a gestalt. Moreover, the context of the gestalt provides one way in which we can understand the tacit component of knowledge. In a gestalt, we can distinguish the portions we focus attention on from the background context that helps to establish the pattern of the gestalt, or that is used as a tool to integrate the focal portions into a more comprehensive whole. The "focal" knowledge in the pattern receives our attention and notice. The "tacit" or background knowledge, on the other hand, while much more extensive and absolutely necessary to the pattern, is not noticed and remains unarticulated.

The importance of the tacit/explicit distinction for KM is emphasized in Nonaka and Takeuchi's (1995) account of *The Knowledge Creating Company*. They assume that knowledge is created through the interaction between tacit and explicit knowledge, and they postulate four different modes of knowledge conversion:

- from tacit to tacit (called socialization);
- from tacit to explicit (externalization);
- from explicit to explicit (combination); and
- from explicit to tacit (internalization).

Since the appearance of Nonaka and Takeuchi's very popular book, the distinction between tacit and explicit knowledge and the idea that knowledge management is about encouraging these four modes of conversion in a kind of spiral model of upward progress has informed the knowledge management programs of many companies.

POLANYI, IMPLICIT KNOWLEDGE, AND POPPER

In considering Polanyi's distinctions, let us begin by noticing that the tacit/explicit distinction is a dichotomy that oversimplifies his more detailed account of knowledge and the gestalt concept. That is, Polanyi indicates that much tacit knowledge can be made explicit, and that there is some that remains ineffable and can never be expressed. Further, he even distinguishes "implicit beliefs," (1958, 286–294), suggesting a third category of knowledge: implicit beliefs, defined as those "held in the form of our conceptual framework, as expressed in our language" (ibid., 286–287).

In short, Polanyi identifies tacit knowledge that can't be expressed, tacit knowledge that can be made explicit, and implicit knowledge as defined above. So, we believe that the Nonaka and Takeuchi interpretation of Polanyi's work is too simple. If we agree that tacit knowledge is sometimes composed of beliefs we cannot express, and that explicit knowledge is made of expressed beliefs, then that leaves a third category: those cognitions or beliefs that, while not focal or explicit, are expressible, given the environmental conditions effective in eliciting them. We will call this category implicit knowledge, while recognizing that it contains not only those nonfocal or assumed portions of our conceptual frameworks, but any nonfocal beliefs that can be brought into focus and made explicit. So now we have a three-way distinction relevant to the study of knowledge conversion: explicit, implicit, and tacit. It is also useful to view this three-way classification from the point of view of Popper's distinction between World 2 and World 3. That is, Popper's objective knowledge (World 3) is obviously all explicit and codified, and involves the expression of Polanyi's "focal knowledge." To the extent that we can think of "implicit knowledge" in the World 3 sense, its character is very different from World 2 implicit knowledge. The latter is based on a psychological association with focal knowledge that is part of a gestalt. World 3 implicit knowledge, in contrast, is knowledge that is logically implicit in explicit knowledge (in linguistic formulations), in the sense that it can be derived from such knowledge.

On the other hand, some of Popper's World 2 mental phenomena are obviously personal and "tacit" in the sense that (by definition) they may represent mental objects that cannot be focused in expressible psychological orientations. Other World 2 mental phenomena represent objects that can be focused in such orientations and are therefore *implicit*. Finally, there are still other World 2 phenomena that represent explicit, focal beliefs, situational orientations that express explicit linguistic knowledge in the mind. Such tacit, implicit, and explicit phenomena in the mind are all unobservable abstractions or "hidden variables." They are hypothetical constructs (MacCorquodale and Meehl 1948) whose characteristics must be inferred using measurement instruments, models, surveys, observation, etc.

Note, also, that all explicit statements are not about World 3 objects and all personal, tacit knowledge is not about World 2. Thus, if we say that we know that the "many-worlds" interpretation of quantum theory is true, this explicit statement is about our *belief* that the many-worlds interpretation is true. It is an explicit statement about a World 2 object. It converts our implicit knowledge (our validated belief) into an explicit knowledge claim about our belief. It is not a direct statement about the (World 3) many-worlds model. It also does not convert our implicit knowledge orientation into explicit linguistic knowledge in the sense that we have fully and faithfully transformed our implicit psychological orientation into an explicit, codified form. That cannot be done because our implicit belief is not a linguistic formulation, and the epistemic gap between internal, non-linguistic psychological connections and internal or external linguistic formulations is irreducible.

On the other hand, if we say that the many worlds interpretation of quantum theory is true, this explicit statement is about quantum theory, the linguistic formulation, itself. It is about a World 3 object, not our World 2 belief. It is a description of the relationship that we claim exists between quantum theory and reality and is in no way a claim about what we believe.

On the other hand, we can also hold subjective knowledge (beliefs) about either subjective states or about World 1 or World 3 objects. Our procedural knowledge about how to make lamb stew is about World 1, for example, because it is made up of World 2 belief predispositions about how to act (World 1) to manipulate the (World 1) components to make the stew. So subjective knowledge is in no way restricted to knowledge about World 2 objects.

Individual Level World 2 Knowledge and Motivational Hierarchies

It is a general characteristic of the various current discussions about the nature of (World 2) knowledge and the foundations of knowledge management that the relation of such knowledge to psychological motivation is not explicitly considered. One can see this clearly by noting that tacit/implicit and explicit knowledge are all viewed as situationally oriented beliefs by contemporary writers on KM. (See, for example, Nonaka and Takeuchi 1995, 57–61). But what are beliefs? They are cognitions, or perhaps at most cognitions combined with evaluations, and both of these represent situationally fixed psychological orientations, rather than general psychological predispositions. The knowledge management literature simply does not recognize World 2 *knowledge predispositions* of individuals even though it is these predispositions that are the product of an agent's knowledge processing experience and the motivator of its knowledge processing decisions.

Figure 1.3 presents the agent, the individual, group, team, or organization as a decision-maker executing the transactions that are the atomic components of business processes. World 2 knowledge is contained in the goal-directed agent and is composed of the memories, values, attitudes, and situational orientations of agents. World 3 knowledge is contained in the cultural conditions that make up part of social ecology. Thus, Figure 1.3 illustrates the role of World 2 knowledge as an immediate precursor of decisions and transactional behavior in the organizational system, as well as the role of World 3 knowledge as a cultural factor shaping psychological orientations in general and World 2 knowledge in particular.

Figure 1.4 illustrates the incentive system of an agent (see Birch and Veroff 1966, Atkinson 1964, Atkinson and Birch 1978), the complex of motivational predispositions that intervenes between the situational stimuli and the behavior of any agent. Figure 1.4 shows

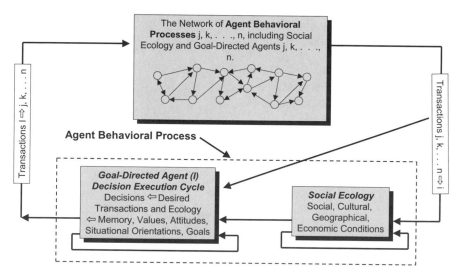

Figure 1.3
The Flow of Behavior Among Agents

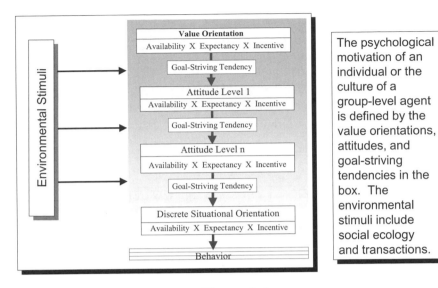

Figure 1.4
The Incentive System of an Agent

the goal-directed agent depicted in Figure 1.3 in more detail. It views agent behavior as the product of an interaction of the agent's situation with a hierarchy of motivational predispositions, including value orientations (Kluckhohn and Strodtbeck 1961, Morris 1956), and various levels of increasingly focused attitudinal predispositions. These predispositions, combined with the external situation, finally produce a situational orientation which is the immediate precursor of goal-striving, instrumental behavior, such as business process behavior, and which includes both the tacit and explicit knowledge responsible for decision making and behavior.

The availability and expectancy factors in Figure 1.4 refer to an agent's predispositions to perceive certain classes of behavior alternatives and resources as available for acting (availability), and certain expected consequences as likely to result from implementing the various alternatives (expectancy). The incentive factor refers to the negative or positive attraction, the intensity of affect or emotion, which the perceived consequences of particular alternatives have for the agent. The motive factor is the strength of the goal-striving predispositions resulting from the interaction of the other three factors. The availability and expectancy factors in this framework are cognitive in character, and the incentive factor is emotional or affective. *Interactions of these factors are knowledge or belief predispositions of agents, and they are an essential part of the World 2 knowledge system of an agent.* They play a vital role, not only in decision making, but in learning. And they provide a large part of the continuity of individual behavior and knowledge seeking that we observe in the knowledge life cycle and other business process behavior.

DIFFERENT TYPES OF KNOWLEDGE

Our discussion so far has highlighted a number of different definitions and conceptions of knowledge. Some of these we have rejected as confused, ambiguous, vague, or contradictory, and others we have distinguished as identifying different types of knowledge. Table 1.1 summarizes the discussion so far and adds some more information. Its categorization is based on the following distinctions:

- Worlds 1 (material), 2 (mental) and 3 (artifact-based) knowledge
- Situational knowledge and knowledge predispositions
- Tacit, implicit, and explicit knowledge
- Psychologically implicit knowledge and logically implicit knowledge

Table 1.1 provides a framework that is our proposal for solving the knowledge conundrum. The types defined there are World 1 knowledge; World 2 situational, tacit, implicit, or explicit knowledge; World 2 predispositional knowledge; World 3 types of explicit knowledge (24 types); and by implication World 3 implicit knowledge (also 24 types depending on the type of knowledge it may be derived from).

CONCLUSION

We believe that if the classification framework in Table 1.1 does not solve the knowledge conundrum, it at least provides a much better foundation for knowledge management than has existed previously.

Table 1.1
A Knowledge Typology

Domains/Attributes	World 1 Knowledge	World 2 Situational Knowledge	World 2 Knowledge Predispositions	World 3 Knowledge
Encoded	✓	✓	✓	✓
Validated	✓	✓	✓	✓
Tacit	NA	✓	NA	NA
Implicit	NA	Knowledge that is associated with other knowledge, not explicit, but can be made so	NA	Knowledge that may be derived from explicit knowledge using logic
Explicit	NA	✓	NA	1. Structured database knowledge claims 2. Descriptive factual statements 3. Conceptual models 4. Data models object models 5. Computer simulation models 6. Planning models 7. Analytical models 8. Measurement models 9. Predictive models

(Continued)

Table 1.1
(Continued)

Domains/ Attributes	World 1 Knowledge	World 2 Situational Knowledge	World 2 Knowledge Predispositions	World 3 Knowledge
				10. Impact models
				11. Assessment models
				12. Application software
				13. Validation criteria, perspectives and frameworks
				14. Methods
				15. Methodologies
				16. Formal language utilities
				17. Semiformal language utilities
				18. Meta-knowledge claims
				19. Planning knowledge claims
				20. Descriptive knowledge claims
				21. Factual knowledge claims measurements of abstractions
				22. Knowledge claims about impact, cause, and effect
				23. Predictive knowledge claims
				24. Assessment knowledge claims

It resolves the conflict between those who believe in mental knowledge and those who believe in knowledge embedded in artifacts by pointing out that these are different types of knowledge, and that they in turn differ from knowledge embedded in biological organisms or other agents in the material world. It introduces the important distinction in the area of mental knowledge between predispositional knowledge and situational knowledge, a distinction that has been largely ignored in KM in all of the hubbub surrounding the discussion of belief knowledge. It recognizes the distinctions among tacit, explicit, and implicit knowledge. And finally, it recognizes that implicit beliefs and knowledge claims implied by preexisting explicit knowledge are two different things. We will return to this framework and its distinctions frequently in chapters to follow. And we will find that all its types of knowledge are accounted for by, and have their place in, knowledge processing and specifically in the knowledge life cycle, to whose origins we now turn.

REFERENCES

Allee, V. (1997), *The Knowledge Evolution: Expanding Organizational Intelligence*, Boston, MA: Butterworth–Heinemann.

Allee, V. (2000), "Reconfiguring the Value Network," available at: http://www.vernaallee.com/reconfiguring_val_net.html.

Argyris, C. (1993), *Knowledge for Action*, San Francisco, CA: Jossey-Bass.

Atkinson, J. (1964), *An Introduction to Motivation*, New York, NY: Van Nostrand.

Atkinson, J.W. and Birch, D. (1978), *Introduction to Motivation (2ⁿᵈ edition)*, New York, NY: Van Nostrand.

Aune, B. (1970), *Rationalism, Empiricism, and Pragmatism*, New York, NY: Random House, 1970.

Axelrod, R. (1976), *The Structure of Decision*, Princeton, NJ: Princeton University Press.

Barquin, R. (2000), "From Bits and Bytes to Knowledge Management," January–February, 2000, www.e-gov.com also available at: www.barquin.com.

Bateson, G. (1972), "The Logical Categories of Learning and Communication," in G. Bateson, *Steps to an Ecology of Mind*, New York, NY: Chandler Publishing, Company.

Beller, S. (2001), "The DIKUW Model." *National Health Data Systems*, April, 2001, available at www.nhds.com/toc.htm.

Bellinger, G. (1998), "Data, Information, Knowledge and Wisdom" at http://www.radix.net/~crbnblu/musings/kmgmt/kmgmt.htm.

Bennet, A. and Bennet, D. (2000), "Characterizing the Next Generation Knowledge Organization" *Knowledge and Innovation: Journal of the KMCI, 1, no. 1*, 8–42.

Birch, D. and Veroff, J. (1966), *Motivation: A Study of Action*, Belmont, CA: Brooks/Cole.

Cavaleri, S. and Reed, F. (2000), "Designing Knowledge Generating Processes", *Knowledge and Innovation: Journal of the KMCI, 1, no. 1*, 109–131.

Cavaleri, S. and Reed, F. (2001), "Organizational Inquiry: The Search for Effective Knowledge," *Knowledge and Innovation: Journal of the KMCI, 1, no. 3*, 27–54.

Cox, E. (1994), *The Fuzzy Systems Handbook*, Cambridge, MA: Academic Press.

Cox, E. (1995), *Fuzzy Logic for Business and Industry*, Rockland, MA: Charles River Media.

Davenport, T. and Prusak, L. (1997), *Working Knowledge: How Organizations Manage What They Know*, Boston, MA: Harvard Business School Press.

DeCharms, R. and Moeller, C. (1962), "Values Expressed in American Children's Readers: 1800–1950," *Journal of Abnormal and Social Psychology, 64*, 136–142.

Deutsch, K. (1963), *The Nerves of Government*, New York, NY: The Free Press.

Duijker, H. and Frijda, N. (1960), *National Character and National Stereotypes*, Amsterdam, NV: North-Holland.

Feierabend, I. and Feierabend, R. (1966), "Aggressive Behavior within Polities: A Cross-National Study," *Journal of Conflict Resolution, 10*, 249–271.

Firestone, J. (1972), "The Development of Social Indicators from Content Analysis of Social Documents," *Policy Sciences, 3*, 249–263.

Firestone, J. and Oliva, G. (1971), "National Motives and National Attributes: A Cross-Time Analysis," *General Systems, 16*, 93–124.

Glenn, E. (1966), "A Cognitive Approach to the Analysis of Culture and Cultural Evolution", *General Systems, 11*.

Goldman, A. (1991), *Empirical Knowledge*, Berkeley, CA: University of California, 1991.

James, W. (1907), *Pragmatism*, New York, NY: Longmans.

Jones, W.T. (1952), *A History of Western Philosophy*, New York, NY: Harcourt, Brace and World.

Kluckhohn, F. and Strodtbeck, F. (1961), *Variations in Value Orientations*, New York, NY: Harper & Row.

Kosko, B. (1992), *Neural Networks and Fuzzy Systems*, Englewood Cliffs, NJ: Prentice-Hall.

MacCorquodale, K. and Meehl, P. (1948), "On a Distinction between Hypothetical Constructs and Intervening Variables," *Psychological Review*, *55*, 95–107.

McClelland, D.C. (1961), *The Achieving Society*, Princeton, NJ: Van Nostrand.

Merritt, R. (1966), *Symbols of American Community: 1735–1775*, New Haven, CT: Yale University Press.

Moore, G. (1991), *Crossing the Chasm*, New York, NY: HarperBusiness.

Morris, C. (1956),*Varieties of Human Value*, Chicago, IL: University of Illinois Press.

Murray, A. (2000), "Knowledge Systems Research," *Knowledge and Innovation: Journal of the KMCI, 1, no. 1*, 68–84.

Namenwirth, J. (1969), "Some Long and Short-Term Trends in One American Political Value: A Computer Analysis of Concern with Wealth in 62 Party Platforms," in Gerbner, G. et al., (eds.) *Analysis of Communications Content*, New York, NY: John Wiley & Sons.

Nonaka, I. and Takeuchi, H. (1995), *The Knowledge Creating Company*, New York, NY: Oxford University Press.

Polanyi, M. (1958), *Personal Knowledge* (Chicago, IL: University of Chicago Press, 1958).

Polanyi, M. (1966), *The Tacit Dimension*, London, UK: Routledge and Kegan Paul.

Popper, K.R. (1972), *Objective Knowledge*, London, England: Oxford University Press.

Popper, K.R. (1994), *Knowledge and the Body-Mind Problem*, (edited by Mark A. Notturno), London, UK: Routledge.

Popper, K.R and Eccles, J.C. (1977), *The Self and Its Brain*, Berlin, Germany: Springer.

Shannon, C.E. (1948), "A Mathematical Theory of Communication," *Bell System Technical Journal*, *27*, 379–423, 623–656.

Stacey, R.D. (1996), *Complexity and Creativity in Organizations*, San Francisco, CA: Berrett-Koehler Publishers.

Terhune, K. (1970), "From National Character to National Behavior: A Reformulation for Prediction", *Journal of Conflict Resolution*, *14*, 203–263.

Triandis, H.C. et al. (1972), *The Analysis of Subjective Culture*, New York, NY: Wiley.

Wiig, K. (1998), in Yogesh Malhotra's compilation at www.brint.com.

Chapter 2

ORIGIN OF THE KNOWLEDGE LIFE CYCLE

INTRODUCTION

The journey to knowledge management may begin, as we have in Chapter 1, with the formulation of a basic conceptual framework for defining and specifying knowledge, but it must continue with a consideration of the processes that produce knowledge and with a conceptual framework that provides a cognitive map of these processes. Such a framework is sometimes called a Knowledge Life Cycle (KLC) framework.

KLC frameworks (McElroy 1999, 2000, 2000a, 2003; Firestone 1999, 2000, 2000a, 2000b, 2003) are getting increasing attention as people begin to accept that knowledge management is about managing the KLC. Alongside the KLC concept, though, many others have been concerned with the Organizational Learning Cycle (OLC) concept and its role in knowledge processing and KM. Some even believe that there is no separate KLC and that only the OLC exists. This chapter shows that the KLC is a separate framework from the OLC, and that, in fact, KLC processes originate in the OLC and then feed back into it. The alternation between KLCs and OLCs is both basic to knowledge processing and grounded in human psychology, both at the individual level and group level. This alternation is the foundation of knowledge management as a distinct process and discipline.

THE ORGANIZATIONAL LEARNING CYCLE (OLC)/DECISION EXECUTION CYCLE (DEC)

The organizational learning literature provides a number of examples of frameworks that depict a cyclic-agent behavioral process of decision, action, experiential feedback, and then adjustment followed by new action. Such frameworks are not new. For example, Ackoff (1970, 100) specifies a decision cycle of four steps: (1) decision making, (2) implementation, (3) evaluation, and (4) recommendation, with information being fed into each of the four steps. More recently, David Kolb and Roger Fry (1975) and Kolb (1984) identify an "experiential learning cycle" composed of (a) active experimentation, (b) concrete experience, (c) reflective observation, and (d) abstract conceptualization. Firestone (1997, 1997a, 1998, 2000a) identifies a decision execution cycle including (1) acting, (2) monitoring, (3) evaluating, and (4) planning, and specifies "use cases" for each of these steps. Haeckel (1999, 75–92) distinguishes (a) Act, (b) Sense, (c) Interpret, and (d) Decide, and characterizes the sense and interpret steps as "sensing," or creating meaning out of noise. He also associates the act and decide steps in the cycle as adaptively "responding" to the environment, and further, characterizes organizations as "sense" and "respond" systems on the basis of this "adaptive loop."

Haeckel also points out (81) that "adaptive loops may or may not be *learning* loops." By this he means that many adaptive loops are "learned processes" that involve responses to environmental changes based on predetermined rules. Real learning, he believes, only occurs in response to changes in environmental context that stimulate organizations to create new adaptive responses. We will return to this point a bit later.

Another slightly different formulation of the OLC idea was presented by Ralph Stacey (1996). Stacey distinguishes three steps: (1) act, (2) discover, and (3) choose. "Discover" incorporates activities similar to the sense and interpret, and monitoring and evaluating activities identified by others.

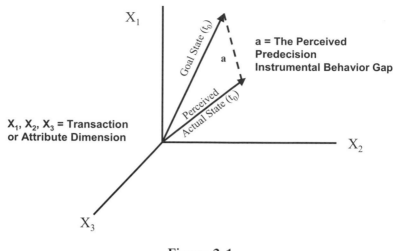

Figure 2.1
The Gap Motivating Action

Our own formulation of the OLC or decision cycle idea is based on Firestone's previous formulations (1997, 1997a, 2000a). In this view, the Decision Execution Cycle (DEC) is motivated by a perceived gap between an agent's goal state and the actual state of the world the agent is trying to manage. Figure 2.1 expresses the gap idea.

The DEC is instrumental behavior whose purpose is to close the perceived instrumental behavior gap. Figure 2.2 illustrates the DEC.

The generic task patterns or *phases* of any decision/execution cycle are: planning, acting (including deciding), monitoring, and evaluating. **Planning** is a knowledge production and knowledge integration activity. It means setting goals, objectives, and priorities, making forecasts as part of prospective analysis, performing cost/benefit assessments as part of prospective analysis, and revising or reengineering a business process. It involves capturing and using data, information, and knowledge to produce a plan, an instance of World 3 planning knowledge.

Acting means performing the specific domain business process (to be defined later) or any of its components. Acting involves *using planning knowledge, along with other World 3 and World 2 knowledge*, to make and implement decisions, but acting does not by itself produce new knowledge.

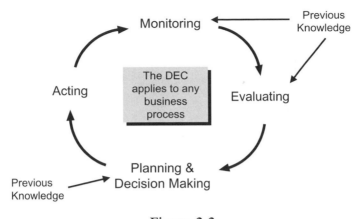

Figure 2.2
The Decision Execution Cycle

Monitoring means retrospectively tracking and describing activities and their outcomes. Monitoring involves gathering data and information, modeling processes, and using previous knowledge to produce new descriptive, impact-related, and predictive knowledge about the results of acting. Monitoring is another activity involving (this time World 2 and World 3) knowledge production and knowledge integration.

Evaluating means retrospectively assessing the previously monitored activities and outcomes as a *value network* (Allee 2000). Evaluating means using the results of monitoring along with previous knowledge to assess the results of acting and to produce knowledge about the descriptive gaps between business outcomes and tactical objectives and about the normative (benefits and costs) impact of business outcomes. Evaluating is yet another form of activity that produces and integrates both World 2 and World 3 knowledge.

Note that the DEC applies to any business process in a manner to be discussed shortly and that monitoring, evaluating, planning, and acting (including decision making), *use* previous knowledge. Where does the previous knowledge used in the DEC come from? It comes most immediately from what we call the Distributed Organizational Knowledge Base (DOKB). The DOKB is the combination of previous (World 2) knowledge beliefs and belief predispositions of enterprise agents and artifact-based validated (and explicit) knowledge claims, and meta-information (or metaclaims) stored in both

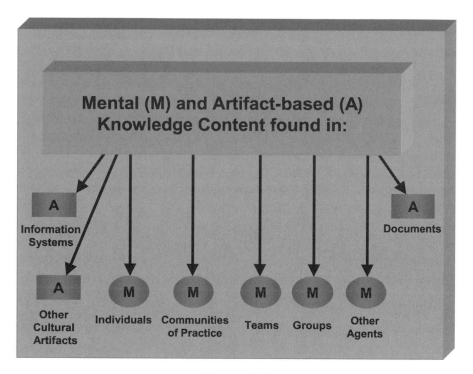

Figure 2.3
Previous Knowledge: The Distributed Organization
Knowledge Base

electronic and nonelectronic enterprise repositories (World 3). Figure 2.3 illustrates the DOKB.

The role of the DOKB may be expressed clearly using Argyris and Schön's notion of single-loop learning (1974). Figure 2.4 illustrates the idea that the DOKB provides the *governing knowledge* that agents use to adjust their behavior in the face of new knowledge about events and conditions based on monitoring following action. The governing knowledge combines with knowledge gained from perceptions of events and conditions to produce what Argyris and Schön call single-loop learning.

The DOKB is an aspect of all structures incorporating organizational knowledge such as normative business processes, plans, organizational cultural expressions, organizational strategy, policies, procedures, and information systems. Coupled with information

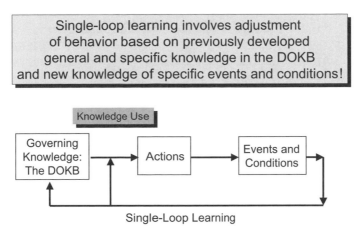

Figure 2.4
Single-Loop Learning Based on Argyris and Schön

from external sources, the knowledge in these structures impacts behavioral business processes through the acting phase of the Decision Execution Cycle. The DEC, in turn, through its monitoring, evaluating, and planning phases generates new adaptive problems as well as new knowledge about specific conditions for later increments of the DEC.

NEW PROBLEMS, DOUBLE-LOOP LEARNING, AND POPPER'S TETRADIC SCHEMA

Single-loop learning involves only the use of previously generated knowledge, to produce new knowledge about specific events and conditions and to make adjustments to actions. The process presents no problems (i.e., epistemic gaps) to be solved. But when single-loop learning doesn't work in adapting to changes in the environment, agents must solve problems by creating new governing knowledge. This process of arriving at solutions to problems and thus creating new governing knowledge is what Argyris and Schön called "double-loop learning" (DLL) (1974). The relevance of the double-loop metaphor is illustrated in Figure 2.5.

Argyris and Schön's DLL concept doesn't tell us very much about how problems are solved and new knowledge created. For that we

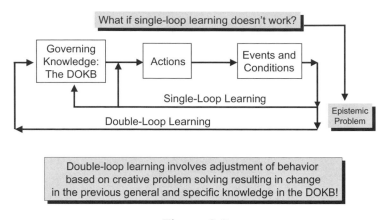

Figure 2.5
Double-Loop Learning (Loosely) Based on Argyris and Schön

turn to Karl Popper's problem-solving framework (1972, 1994; Popper and Eccles 1977). Popper saw the growth of knowledge as basic to human experience, to our nature as adaptive creatures, and as an emergent consequence of our trial-and-error efforts to solve adaptive problems while relying both on our previous knowledge and our experience. His view of knowledge production, illustrated in Figure 2.6, is simple but focused on essentials.

One begins with a problem (P_1), then through conjecture (we call it knowledge claim formulation) one arrives at a tentative solution (typically at multiple tentative solutions) (TS). Next, one tests and evaluates the tentative solution (refutation) in order to eliminate errors (EE), as Popper suggests *before they eliminate us*. We call this knowledge claim validation, or evaluation.

The result is that some solution or solutions will have survived our testing and evaluation better than others. These and the results of our efforts at error elimination are new knowledge. But invariably new knowledge suggests new problems (P_2), which, in turn, trigger successive episodes of Popper's schema. The measure of our progress is that the new problem resulting from our efforts is a better one to have than the old problem. So, over time, we observe the growth of knowledge and the emergence of more and more sophisticated problems.

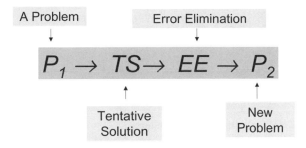

- 'Problems' in this context are epistemic problems
- Tentative Solutions are produced by 'Knowledge Claim Formulation'
- Error Elimination will later be called 'Knowledge Claim Evaluation'

Figure 2.6
Popper's Tetradic Schema: A Framework for Adaptation

An interesting implication of the distinction between single- and double-loop learning and the focus on problem solving as a process that is different from merely applying already existing governing knowledge is the change in the immediate focus of motivation, as we move from single-loop adjustments followed by immediate action to double-loop problem solving followed by new governing knowledge. In brief, instrumental behavior focused on action producing new governing knowledge *represents a shift in motivation* from instrumental behavior focused on action intended to close the original gap driving the DEC to a focus on action intended to produce new governing knowledge. Or to put this another way, the shift to problem solving represents a shift to a second DEC, one focused on problem solving or knowledge production alone. We will return to this idea shortly.

LEARNING AND KNOWLEDGE PRODUCTION: COMBINING ARGYRIS/SCHÖN AND POPPER

Though this has somehow escaped notice before, it is plain that Popper's tetradic schema fits nicely into Argyris and Schön's DLL idea, providing more flesh to its bare bones. Figure 2.7 combines the

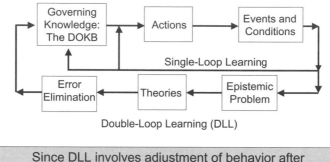

Double-Loop Learning (DLL)

Since DLL involves adjustment of behavior after creative problem solving, we identify it with Popper's theory.

Figure 2.7
Double-Loop Learning—Combining Argyris/Schön and Popper

main ideas of Argyris/Schön and Popper and expresses the key idea that problems can arise out of the DEC that cannot be solved by mere single-loop adjustment—and that these problems are solved through the double-loop problem life cycle and the tetradic schema laid out by Popper, rather than through the initial DEC focused on a direct business goal.

Figure 2.7 also has important implications for an account of knowledge production. Knowledge is produced both in DECs through single-loop learning and in Problem Life Cycles (PLCs) through double-loop learning. The kind of knowledge produced by DECs, once again, is knowledge about specific events and conditions including what they are (monitoring based on sensory perceptions and available technology), our assessment of them (evaluating based on available valuational perspectives) and how we deal with them (planning according to the routine application of preexisting knowledge). The DEC, then, is the process we follow in order to close *operational gaps* in our lives.

The kind of knowledge produced by PLCs, on the other hand, is knowledge about specific conditions based on new perspectives and generalized knowledge relating to new theories and models, new ontologies, epistemologies, and methodologies. It is knowledge produced and integrated in response to adaptive problems that goes beyond knowledge about mere adjustments to behavior based on preexisting knowledge available from the DOKB. Thus, the PLC is the process we follow in order to close *epistemic gaps* in our lives, not *operational* ones.

A Transactional Systems Model of Agent Interaction

We have presented the origin of the problem life cycle as the response to a failure in single-loop learning to adjust behavior in the DEC to meet the challenges of the environment. But what is the context and motivational basis for problem solving adaptive responses arising out of the DEC? First, it is the transactional social system environment of agent behavioral responses illustrated in Figure 1.3. In the figure, all agents are viewed as part of the social network that is this social system. Within this network, all agents respond to transactions and social ecology constrained by their motivational hierarchies or incentive systems.

The Motivational Hierarchy

Take a closer look at the agent behavioral process from the viewpoint of the specific agent highlighted at the bottom of Figure 1.3. Figure 2.8 illustrates the incentive system of an agent (See Birch and Veroff 1966, Atkinson 1964, Atkinson and Birch 1978) by identifying two levels of motivational predispositions that intervene between the situational orientation, environmental stimuli, and behavior of any agent. Figure 2.8 views agent behavior as the product of an interaction of the agent's situation with a hierarchy of motivational predispositions, including value orientations (Kluckhohn and Strodtbeck 1961, Morris 1956), and one level of more focused attitudinal predispositions. These predispositions, combined with the external situation, produce a situational orientation which is the immediate precursor of goal-striving, instrumental behavior, such as business process behavior, and which includes both the tacit and explicit knowledge responsible for decision making and behavior.

Alert readers will recognize the above as a simplified version of the process illustrated in Figure 1.4 and described in Chapter 1. Here we want to make clear the evolution of the simple three-level framework to the more complex concept described in Chapter 1. The bridge to

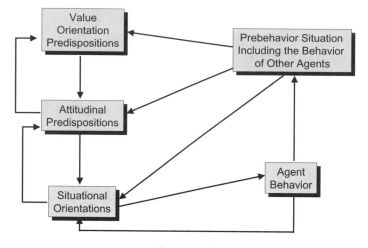

Figure 2.8
*The Immediate Prebehavior Context: A Three-Level
Motivational Hierarchy*

that more generalized concept is in Figure 2.9, which shows the interaction of the external situation with a motivational or attitudinal
level defined at some arbitrary level of specificity "k." Figure 2.9
shows that for any arbitrary attitudinal level "k," there will always
be an arbitrary level of greater situational generality above it and an
arbitrary level of greater situational specificity below it. Thus, the
number of attitudinal levels between value predispositions and
situational orientations is potentially infinite, because that number is
a matter of the modeler's choice.

Figure 1.4 illustrates the motivational hierarchy in its most complete form and highlights the availability, expectancy, incentive, and
motive aspects of motivation. The availability and expectancy factors
refer to an agent's predispositions to perceive: certain classes of behavior alternatives and resources as available for acting (availability), and
certain expected consequences as likely to result from implementing
the various alternatives (expectancy). The incentive factor refers to
the negative or positive attraction, the intensity of affect or emotion,
which the perceived consequences of particular alternatives have for
the agent. The motive is the strength of the goal-striving predispositions resulting from the interaction of the other three factors. The
availability and expectancy factors in this framework are cognitive in

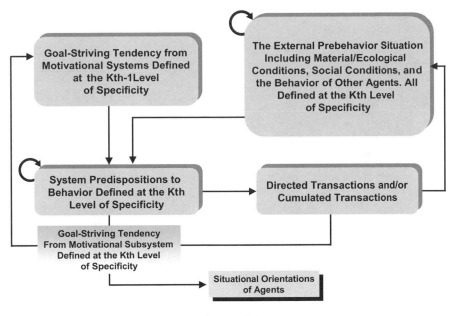

Figure 2.9
Generalization: A Motivational Subsystem

character, and the incentive factor is emotional or affective. *Interactions of these factors are knowledge or belief predispositions of agents, and they are an essential part of the World 2 knowledge system of an agent.* They play a vital role, not only in decision making, but in learning. And they provide a large part of the continuity of individual behavior and knowledge seeking that we observe in the knowledge life cycle and other business process behavior.

Aspects of Motivational Behavior in the Transactional System

What are the relationships among motivation, learning, knowledge, and behavior? To understand these we need to consider how agents interpret the environmental stimuli they perceive.

- ■ An agent interprets environmental stimuli in terms of whether they constitute resources and opportunities (social ecology) or cooperation (transactions). This is environmental encouragement.

■ An agent interprets environmental stimuli in terms of whether they constitute constraints (social ecology) or conflict (transactions). This is environmental resistance or inertia.

■ Any situation involving instrumental behavior has an environmental encouragement/resistance mix.

■ To social encouragement, the agent responds with goal-striving tendencies and transactions perceived as contributing to reaching the goal-state. This we call *steering* behavior.

■ To social resistance, the agent responds in a variety of ways depending on its expectancy concerning the ease or difficulty involved in closing the instrumental behavior gap in the face of social resistance. If resistance is seen as "moderate," the agent will respond with *coping behavior*.

■ There are two classes of coping behavior:

   ■ A habitual pattern of regulatory behavior applying previous knowledge more or less according to a procedure, routine, or rule, and *producing new knowledge* about specific events and conditions based on such procedures, routines, or rules. This is single-loop learning.

   ■ A novel development and selection among tentative solutions and decision alternatives involving *learning* new ways of coping with the environmental resistance. This, of course, is double-loop learning and Popperian problem solving.

Habitual/regulatory coping behavior continues instrumental behavior toward its original goal. But problem solving represents a temporary *interruption* of instrumental behavior in whose first step a new problem is defined: a problem viewed in terms of a gap between what we know and what we need to know to cope with environmental resistance. So a problem-solving situation encountered in the context of coping behavior, with its gap between what we know and what we need to know, *arouses its own incentive system*, the incentive to learn. And this motivation, reinforced by the initial motivation toward goal attainment, drives what we might call a problem, or adaptive, life cycle.

The Problem Life Cycle (PLC) is appropriately called that because it is about the birth and death of problems. Their birth occurs in the context of coping behavior when regulatory behavior fails and trial-and-error search behavior begins. Their death occurs when the problem is solved and the agent returns to the DEC with new governing knowledge. Problem Life Cycles are basic to the motivation of all intelligent agents.

Figure 2.10 illustrates the DEC again, this time with the idea that the monitoring, evaluating, and planning phases in the DEC may involve the selection of *either* regulatory or problem-solving coping behavior on the part of an agent. If regulatory behavior is selected, then single-loop learning applies along with use of the DOKB. If problem-solving behavior is selected, that "kicks-off" double-loop learning and the Problem Life Cycle (also including use of the DOKB).

The relationship of the PLC to the DEC is illustrated in Figure 2.11. *The Problem Life Cycle is a process composed of many Decision Execution Cycles all motivated by the learning incentive system!* This view is suggested by Popper's tetradic schema. The development of tentative solutions (Knowledge Claim Formulation), followed by error elimination (Knowledge Claim Evaluation), will clearly involve

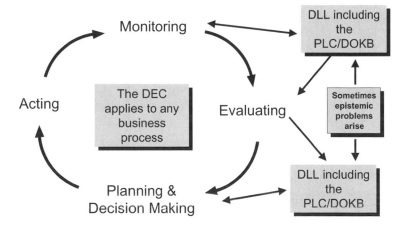

Figure 2.10
The Decision Execution Cycle "Kicks Off" the Problem Life Cycle (PLC)

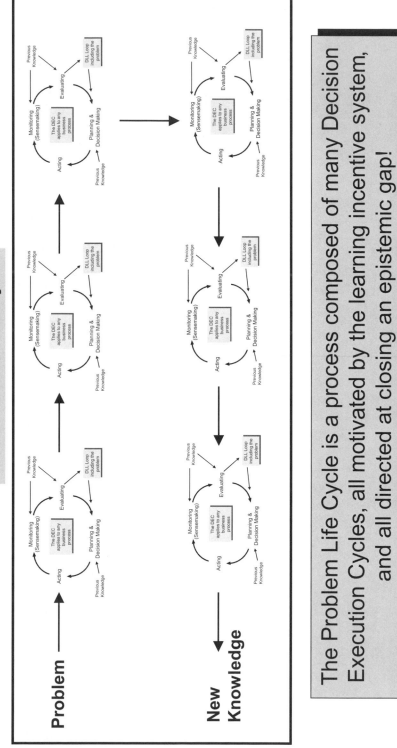

Figure 2.11

Problem Life Cycles and Decision Execution Cycles

many different activities that must be generated by multiple DECs. These are related to one another in that all are motivated by the motivational response aroused by the gap between what the agent knows and what it needs to know.

Since the PLC is made up of DECs, and since all DECs may spawn PLCs, it is relevant to ask whether DECs comprising a PLC may initiate higher-level PLCs. The answer is yes. DECs comprising knowledge claim formulation or knowledge claim validation may themselves initiate new PLCs, which contribute to the primary PLC initiated by the original DEC motivated by the original instrumental behavior gap.

Sense Making in the Transactional System

Recently, writers in knowledge management such as Ralph Stacey (2001) and David Snowden (2002) have begun to rely on ideas about "sense making" developed by Karl Weick (1995) over the past 30 years. These ideas are based on the outlook of those who believe that "reality is socially constructed" (Berger and Luckmann 1967). While the perspective presented here is different in many ways from Weick's, it has many similarities to that perspective. In particular, the importance of the following characteristics is common to sense making and the transaction framework:

- Identity construction (the idea that agents and systems create their own identities in the process of adapting to their environments);
- Monitoring (sense making) after action (the idea that monitoring is a response to action and that it involves filtering and interpretation of external stimuli and is not a process that "mirrors" reality in any recognizable way);
- Sense making partly shapes (enacts) sense making environments; social interaction shapes social ecology (the idea that sense making considered broadly as monitoring and evaluating determines action, which in turn impacts social ecology over time);
- Sense making occurs in social settings (monitoring occurs in the social interaction framework); and
- Sense making (and DEC activity) is ongoing.

In general, the transactional systems framework differs with the sense making outlook on two points. First, we don't accept that reality is socially constructed. Our knowledge of reality is certainly mediated by our social networks, along with our psychological predispositions and biological heritage, but it is also influenced by reality itself, which exists, we believe, apart from our social construction of it. And second, we also believe, in contrast to many who espouse the sense making orientation, that knowledge claims should not be validated by social consensus, but by continuing testing and evaluation aimed at error elimination. Apart from these two very important departures, the outlooks of sense making and the transactional systems approach are similar.

The Knowledge Life Cycle (KLC): The Expression of a Change in Instrumental Motivation

The Knowledge Life Cycle (KLC), in an organizational context, is a description of instrumental behavior and motivation which, rather than being aimed at achieving an operational or business outcome goal-state, is focused instead on reaching a certain epistemic or knowledge outcome goal-state. Having provided a framework explaining in general terms how this shift occurs and how the PLC originates from the DEC, we will now explain how the DEC and the PLC relate to business processes, knowledge processes, and knowledge management.

Figure 2.12 illustrates the idea that any behavioral business process (including knowledge and knowledge management processes) may be viewed as a network of linked activities driven by World 2 knowledge, aimed at producing outcomes of value to those performing the activities. A linked sequence of activities performed by one or more agents sharing at least one objective is a *task*. A linked, but not necessarily sequential, set of tasks producing results of measurable value to the agent or agents performing the tasks is a *task pattern*. A cluster of task patterns, not necessarily performed sequentially, often performed iteratively, incrementally, and adaptively, is a *task cluster*. Finally, a hierarchical network of interrelated, purposive activities of intelligent agents that transforms inputs into valued outcomes, a cluster of task clusters, is a *business process*.

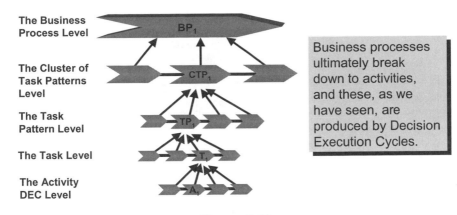

Figure 2.12
The Activity to Business Process Hierarchy

Business processes ultimately break down to activities, and these, as we have seen, are produced by decision execution cycles. Business processes are performed and managed by agents. Agents, if they're groups, have an internal culture. At the same time the cultural component of social ecology also impacts the agent decision execution cycles that ultimately comprise business processes.

Business processes and business management together constitute the business processing environment that produces business outcomes such as sales, profits, and ROI in an enterprise. Figure 2.13 illustrates this simple relationship.

Since business processing environments are comprised of decision execution cycles, they will, from time to time and as illustrated in Figure 2.14, spawn problems. These problems can be solved only through problem life cycles or double-loop learning cycles. In the context of organizations we call these knowledge processes (added in Figure 2.15) or knowledge life cycles (added along with the DOKB in Figure 2.16).

Figure 2.16 shows that the knowledge life cycle is comprised of (1) problems generated by business processes, (2) knowledge processes, and (3) the DOKB containing the outcomes of knowledge processes, as well as knowledge about special events and conditions produced in the DEC. The DOKB is also used in the business processing environment, and this environment, in turn, creates new problems and new instances of the KLC. We have seen that

Figure 2.13
The Business Processing Environment and Business Outcomes

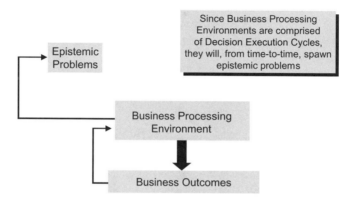

Figure 2.14
The Business Processing Environment and Epistemic Problems

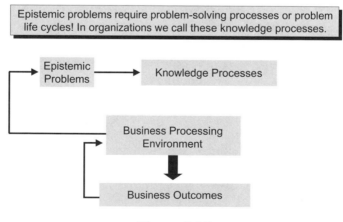

Figure 2.15
Knowledge Processes

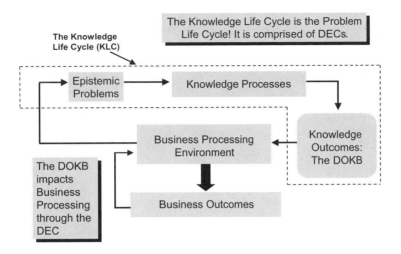

Figure 2.16
Knowledge Outcomes: The Distributed
Organizational Knowledge Base

business processes are comprised of DECs and that these processes spawn problems if these DECs cannot adapt to environmental stimuli through regulatory behavior and therefore must turn to Problem Life Cycles (PLCs). **In the organizational context these PLCs are called KLCs,** and they too are comprised of DECs, that, in turn, can spawn their own problems and new higher-level instances of the KLC.

A more granular view of the KLC is presented in Figure 2.17.

Knowledge production is initiated in response to problems produced by decision cycles in business processes. It produces new Organizational Knowledge (OK), including Surviving Knowledge Claims (SKCs), Undecided Knowledge Claims (UKCs), and Falsified Knowledge Claims (FKCs), and information about the status of these. All of the above are codified, explicit, World 3 objects. OK is composed of all of the foregoing results of knowledge production. It is part of what is integrated into the enterprise by the Knowledge integration process.

The knowledge production process, in combination with previous agent predispositions, also produces *beliefs related to the World 3 knowledge claims.* These are World 2 objects, predisposing various organizational agents to action. In some instances, they are

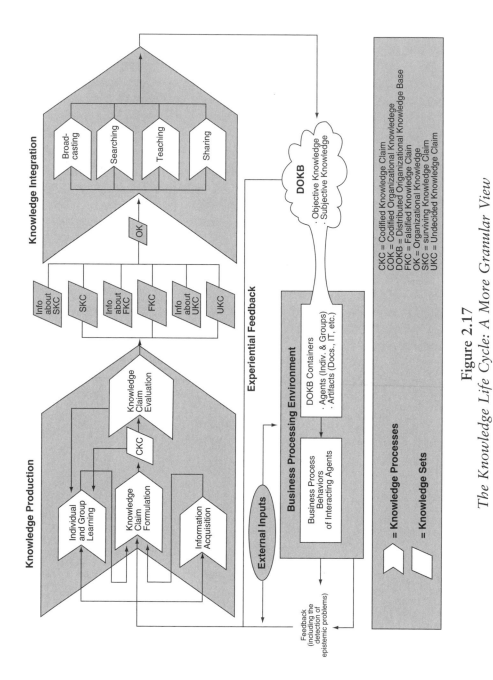

Figure 2.17

The Knowledge Life Cycle: A More Granular View

52

predispositions that correspond to organizational knowledge; in other instances they are predispositions that reflect awareness of validated or surviving knowledge claims but contradict them, or supplement them, or bear some other conceptual relationship to them. At the individual level these beliefs are in part tacit, since all of them are not expressible linguistically by the individuals holding them, or implicit since some that are neither tacit nor explicit may not have been verbally expressed but can be. Where these beliefs have been validated by the individuals, or other intelligent agents holding them, they constitute World 2 knowledge held by those agents. But they are not organizational knowledge. Rather, they are outputs of the organizational knowledge processing system experienced at the level of individual agents.

The knowledge integration process takes organizational knowledge and, by integrating it within the organization, produces that portion of the DOKB constituting new knowledge produced by the KLC, in contrast to the portion of it produced by the DEC through single-loop learning (e.g., implicit knowledge of balance while riding a bicycle). Integrating means communicating organizational knowledge content to the organization's agents with the purpose of making them fully aware of existing organizational knowledge. This also requires making the knowledge available in knowledge stores that agents can use to search for and retrieve knowledge. The result of knowledge integration is that the content of new codified organizational knowledge is available in both accessible and distributed knowledge stores and, in addition, is reflected in the predispositions of agents all across the enterprise. As we indicated earlier, the DOKB is the combination of distributed World 3 and World 2 knowledge content.

The DOKB, in its turn, has a major impact on structures incorporating organizational knowledge such as normative business processes, plans, organizational culture, organizational strategy, policies, procedures, and information systems. Coupled with external sources, these structures then feed back to impact behavioral business processes through the acting phase of the DEC. The DEC, in turn, generates new problems in the planning, monitoring, and evaluating phases to be solved in the next round of knowledge processing, i.e., in new KLCs.

"Drilling down" into knowledge production, the KLC view is that information acquisition, and individual and group learning in the service of problem solving, impact on knowledge claim formulation, which, in turn, produces Codified Knowledge Claims (CKCs). These, in their turn, are tested in the knowledge claim evaluation task cluster, which entails a critical examination of knowledge claims including, but not limited to, empirical testing, which then produces new Organizational Knowledge (OK).

The Individual and Group (I&G) Learning task cluster or subprocess is *recursive* in the sense that I&G learning is itself a KLC at the level of system interaction just below the global level, while I&G learning at the second level is itself a KLC at the level below, and so on until individual learning and knowledge production is reached. KLCs, therefore, occur at the group and individual levels of analysis as well as at the organizational level of analysis. They produce knowledge claims that have been validated from the perspective of the individual or the group as the case may be, but from the perspective of the organization they are unvalidated information, or unvalidated claims. Figure 2.18 illustrates the recursive nesting of KLCs and the DECs that comprise them in an organization.

The key task cluster that distinguishes Knowledge Production from information production is Knowledge Claim Evaluation (or validation). It is the subprocess of criticism of competing knowledge claims, and of comparative testing and assessment of them, that transforms knowledge claims from mere information into

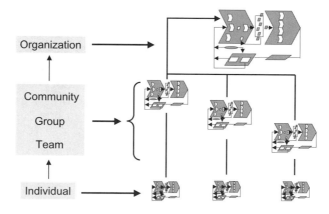

Figure 2.18
Nesting of Knowledge Life Cycles in an Orgnization

tested information, some of which passes organizational tests and therefore becomes, from the organizational point of view, new knowledge (i.e., truthlike information).

In other words, as we stated in Chapter 1, the difference between information and knowledge is validation. But what is validation? Is it testing and evaluation of knowledge claims (World 3), or testing and evaluation of beliefs (World 2)? Testing and evaluation of knowledge claims is public and sharable in the sense that the claims themselves are sharable, and the tests and their results are sharable. That is why World 3 knowledge is objective. Testing and evaluation of beliefs is private and personal. It is this difference that makes World 2 knowledge subjective. In the context of the enterprise, then, knowledge claim evaluation involves the testing of World 3 objective knowledge, not World 2 subjective knowledge.

Validation is not the same thing as justification. Justification is the process of proving that a knowledge claim is true. Validation, or knowledge claim evaluation, never proves anything with certainty. It simply provides (a) a record of how well competing knowledge claims stand up to our tests or (b) personal experience of how well competing beliefs stand up to our tests. Justification of knowledge claims and beliefs is impossible, but validation or evaluation of them is not.

Since validation is just our process of testing and evaluating knowledge claims or beliefs, the practice of it will vary across individuals, groups, communities, teams, and organizations. A particular entity may use validation practices based on explicit rules or specified criteria to compare knowledge claims, but it need not. Agents are free to change their tests or criteria at any time, to invent new ones, or to apply ad hoc tests and criticisms in validation. That is, validation is a free-for-all; it is just the process by which knowledge claims and beliefs run the gauntlet of our skepticism and our criticism.

Looking at knowledge production from the viewpoint of agents at different levels of organizational interaction, and keeping the role of knowledge claim evaluation in mind, it follows that individual and group learning may involve knowledge production from the perspective of the individual or group. But from the perspective of the enterprise, what the individuals and groups learn is information, not knowledge. Similarly, information acquired may be knowledge from the perspective of the external parties it is acquired from, but not knowledge to the enterprise acquiring it, until it has been validated as such.

Figure 2.17 also illustrates that knowledge validation has a feedback effect on individual and group learning. This occurs because individuals and groups participating in knowledge claim evaluation are affected by their participation in this process. They both produce World 3 organizational knowledge in the form of codified and validated knowledge claims, and also experience change in their own "justified" beliefs (i.e., they generate World 2 knowledge) as an outcome of that participation.

Drilling down into knowledge integration, organizational knowledge is integrated across the enterprise by the broadcasting, searching/retrieving, teaching, and sharing task clusters. These generally work in parallel rather than sequentially. And not all are necessary to a specific instance of the KLC. All may be based in personal non-electronic or electronic interactions.

Knowledge production and knowledge integration, their subprocesses, task clusters, etc., like other value networks, are, like the PLCs discussed earlier, composed of decision cycles through which agents execute their roles in these value networks. This means that planning, acting, monitoring, and evaluating also apply to knowledge processes and to activity in the KLC, though here the instrumental motivation is focused on learning rather than on primary business outcomes.

That is, KLC processes are executed by agents performing KLC DECs, and therefore engaging in planning, acting, monitoring, and evaluating oriented toward knowledge production and knowledge integration goals. But there is also an even higher level of knowledge processing. The higher level knowledge producing and knowledge integrating activities initiated by problems occurring in KLC DECs are KM-level knowledge producing and knowledge integrating task clusters, because they address problems in knowledge processing about how to plan, how to monitor, how to evaluate, or how to implement activities in order to attain knowledge processing goals. These problems are solved by producing and integrating KM-level knowledge. Figure 2.19 illustrates the origin of KM knowledge processes in problems originating in KLCs and in other knowledge management processes that are goal-directed toward managing knowledge processing.

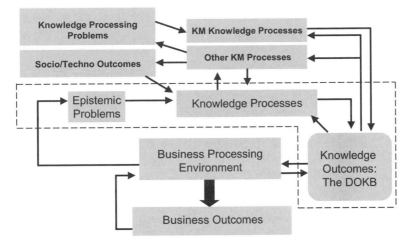

Figure 2.19
Knowledge Management

CONCLUSION

In this chapter we have explained the origins of the KLC. We have shown that the KLC is a separate framework from the DEC/OLC. KLC processes both originate in the DEC/OLC, are comprised of DECs themselves, and then feed back into DECs at the business process level. Yet KLCs are not the same as DECs. Rather, they are higher-level processes or value networks, patterns of DECs integrated by motivation toward knowledge production and integration goals, rather than primary business goals commonly found in sales, marketing, manufacturing, and other business processes.

We have seen that the alternation between KLCs and OLCs is both basic to knowledge processing and grounded in human psychology, both at the individual level and group level. It is an alternation between different types of motivation, and this alternation is the foundation of a distinction between business processing and knowledge processing, and between the latter and knowledge management. This last distinction is the basis of knowledge management as a distinct process and discipline. Without it there can be no knowledge management—a point we will examine in much greater detail in Chapter 3.

REFERENCES

Ackoff, R. (1970), *A Concept of Corporate Planning*, New York, NY: Wiley-Interscience.

Allee, V. (2000), "Reconfiguring the Value Network," available at: http://www.vernaallee.com/reconfiguring_val_net.html.

Argyris, C. (1993), *Knowledge for Action*, San Francisco, CA: Jossey-Bass.

Argyris, C. (1991), "Teaching Smart People How to Learn," *Harvard Business Review* (May–June, 1991). 99–109.

Argyris, C. and Schön, D. (1974), *Theory in Practice: Increasing Professional Effectiveness*, San Francisco: Jossey-Bass.

Atkinson, J.W. (1964), *An Introduction to Motivation*, New York, NY: Van Nostrand.

Atkinson, J.W. and Birch, D. (1978), *Introduction to Motivation*, (2nd *edition*), New York, NY: Van Nostrand.

Berger, P. and Luckmann, T. (1967), *The Social Construction of Reality*, Garden City, NY: Doubleday Anchor.

Birch, D. and Veroff, J. (1966), *Motivation: A Study of Action*, Belmont, CA: Brooks/Cole.

Firestone, J.M. (1997), "Object-Oriented Data Warehousing", *White Paper No. 5*, *Executive Information Systems, Inc.*, Wilmington, DE, August, 1997, Available at: http://www.dkms.com/White_Papers.htm.

Firestone, J.M. (1997a), "Distributed Knowledge Management Systems (DKMS): The Next Wave in DSS", *White Paper No. 6*, *Executive Information Systems, Inc.*, Wilmington, DE, August 23, 1997, Available at: http://www.dkms.com/White_Papers.htm.

Firestone, J.M. (1998), "Basic Concepts of Knowledge Management", *White Paper No. 9*, *Executive Information Systems, Inc.*, Wilmington, DE, June 24, 1998, Available at: http://www.dkms.com/White_Papers.htm.

Firestone, J.M. (1999), "The Metaprise, the AKMS, and the Enterprise Knowledge Portal," *Working Paper No. 3*, *Executive Information Systems, Inc.*, Wilmington, DE, May 5, 1999, Available at : http://www.dkms.com/White_Papers.htm.

Firestone, J.M. (2000), "Accelerated Innovation and KM Impact," *Financial Knowledge Management* (Q1, 2000), 54–60.

Firestone, J.M. (2000a), "Knowledge Management: A Framework for Analysis and Measurement," *White Paper No. 17*, *Executive Information Systems, Inc.*, Wilmington, DE, October 1, 2000, Available at: http://www.dkms.com/White_Papers.htm.

Firestone, J.M. (2000b), "Enterprise Knowledge Portals: What They Are and What They Do," *Knowledge and Innovation: Journal of the*

KMCI, *1*, *no. 1*, 85–108. Available at :
http://www.dkms.com/White_Papers.htm.

Firestone, J.M. (2003), *Enterprise Information Portals and Knowledge Management*, Boston, MA: KMCI Press/Butterworth–Heinemann.

Haeckel, S.H. (1999), *Adaptive Enterprise*, Boston, MA: Harvard Business School Press.

Kluckhohn, F. and Strodtbeck, F. (1961), *Variations in Value Orientations*, New York, NY: Harper & Row.

Kolb, D. (1984), *Experiential Learning*, Englewood, Cliffs, NJ: Prentice-Hall.

Kolb, D. and Fry, R. (1975), "Toward an Applied Theory of Experiential Learning", C. Cooper (ed.), *Theories of Group Process*, London: John Wiley & Sons.

McElroy, M.W. (1999), "The Second Generation of KM," *Knowledge Management* (October 1999) pp. 86–88.

McElroy, M.W. (2000), "Integrating Complexity Theory, Knowledge Management, and Organizational Learning," *Journal of Knowledge Management* Vol. 4 No. 3 (2000), pp. 195–203.

McElroy, M.W. (2000a), "The New Knowledge Management," *Knowledge and Innovation: Journal of the KMCI* 1 (October 15, 2000, Vol. 1, No. 1), pp. 43–67.

McElroy, M.W. (2003), *The New Knowledge Management: Complexity, Learning, and Sustainable Innovation*, Boston, MA: KMCI Press/ Butterworth–Heinemann.

Morris, C. (1956), *Varieties of Human Value*, Chicago, IL: University of Illinois Press.

Popper, K.R. (1972), *Objective Knowledge*, London, England: Oxford University Press.

Popper, K.R. (1994), *Knowledge and the Body-Mind Problem* (edited by Mark A. Notturno), London, UK: Routledge.

Popper, K.R. and Eccles, J.C. (1977), *The Self and Its Brain*, Berlin, Germany: Springer.

Snowden, D. (2002), "Complex Acts of Knowing; Paradox and Descriptive Self-awareness," *Journal of Knowledge Management*, 6, no. 2 (May) 1–14.

Stacey, R.D. (1996), *Complexity and Creativity in Organizations*, San Francisco, CA: Berrett-Koehler.

Stacey, R.D. (2001), *Complex Responsive Processes in Organizations: Learning and Knowledge Creation*, New York, NY: Routledge.

Weick, K. (1995), *Sense Making In Organizations*, Beverly Hills, CA: Sage Publications.

Chapter 3

INFORMATION
MANAGEMENT AND
KNOWLEDGE
MANAGEMENT

INTRODUCTION: APPROACH TO KM

Some approaches to knowledge management seem to view any manipulation of knowledge as knowledge management. In this view, knowledge sharing, knowledge production, and knowledge transfer are knowledge management. In this view, knowledge use is knowledge management. In this view, knowledge management is part of every business process. But is knowledge management really everything and anything having to do with knowledge and knowledge processing?

The obvious answer is no. We sharply distinguish knowledge use and knowledge processing from knowledge management. Knowledge use occurs whenever any agent makes a decision. It is part of every business process (See Figure 2.17). Knowledge processing is knowledge production and knowledge integration (McElroy 1999, Firestone 1999), two distinct knowledge processes constituting the Knowledge Life Cycle (KLC) (see Figure 2.17).

Knowledge management is *knowledge process management*; that is, the management of knowledge production, knowledge integration, the KLC, and their immediate outcomes (Firestone 2000, 2000a, McElroy 1999). A key aspect of knowledge process management is innovation in knowledge processes to enhance performance of the KLC.

COMPLEX ADAPTIVE SYSTEMS

A Complex Adaptive System (CAS) is a goal-directed open system attempting to fit itself to its environment. It is ". . . composed of interacting" adaptive "agents described in terms of rules" (Holland 1995, 10) that are applicable with respect to some specified class of environmental inputs. "These agents adapt by changing their rules as experience accumulates" (ibid.). The interaction of these purposive agents, though directed toward their own goals and purposes, results in emergent, self-organizing behavior at the global system level. This emergent behavior in a sustainable CAS is, itself, adaptive.

Emergent behavior is behavior that cannot be modeled based on knowledge of the system's components. It is the ability of CASs to adapt, along with their emergent behavior that distinguishes them from simple adaptive systems and from Newtonian systems that lack adaptive capacity.

THE NATURAL KNOWLEDGE PROCESSING SYSTEM (NKPS)

The NKPS is a CAS. It is a system marked by ongoing, conceptually distinct, persistent, adaptive interaction among intelligent agents (a) whose interaction properties are not determined by design, but instead emerge from the dynamics of the interaction process itself; and (b) whose agent interactions produce, maintain, and enhance the distributed knowledge base produced by the interaction. An enterprise NKPS includes mechanical and electrical organizational components, such as computers and computer networks, as well as human and organizational agents. An intelligent agent is a purposive, adaptive, self-directed object. The notion of a Distributed Organizational Knowledge Base (DOKB) was defined in Chapter 2.

Hierarchical versus Organic KM

A central issue in KM is whether it should be hierarchical in nature, focusing on designing and implementing a set of well articulated rule-governed business processes implementing knowledge production or knowledge integration, handed down by knowledge managers, and implemented in a manner reminiscent of business process re-engineering; or whether KM should be organic in the sense that it focuses upon implementing policies that support "natural" tendencies of existing knowledge processing patterns occurring in communities of practice and generally outside the formal lines of organizational authority. The hierarchical approach is frequently called "Newtonian," while the organic approach is often called the "knowledge ecology" approach.

The organic approach gets a boost from scientific research on Complex Adaptive Systems (CAS) (Holland 1995, 1998, Kauffman 1995). CAS theory supports the idea that there is an NKPS in any organization that is comprised of independent, autonomous individuals, teams, and groups, whose self-organized interaction produces emergent knowledge. This knowledge, in turn, is the chief means organizations use to adapt to their environments and maintain their identity.

Put simply, the objective of KM is to leverage and enhance the natural tendencies toward knowledge production of the NKPS with appropriate policies and above all to do nothing to interfere with these natural tendencies. The motto of organic KM is: "Above all, do no harm!"

CAS theory is very different in character from the essentially Newtonian classical theory of economics based on supply and demand. But it shares with it the idea that the system in question, in this case the NKPS, will naturally, and without interference from management, perform well in producing and integrating knowledge. There is a disposition, then, among those who believe in CAS theory to be conservative about interfering with existing KM and knowledge processing patterns under the assumption that they are natural. The issue, however, is: Are they "natural," or are they simply the result of previous management interventions that distort the natural tendencies of the organizational system to produce and integrate knowledge? If the situation is the latter, then the implication is that KM should not take a hands-off attitude, but instead should attempt to intervene to restore the natural, productive tendencies of the NKPS.

Thus, concrete situations in real enterprises may require different postures toward KM interventions. But we lack clear criteria for evaluating when we have an NKPS that requires laissez-faire KM, and when we have one that requires a more active approach. Without such criteria for making evaluations, the policy posture that follows from a belief in organic KM is hard to apply and should be approached with caution. The same applies to the reengineering approach. It can easily exacerbate problems in knowledge processing caused by previous ill-advised interventions.

SOME DEFINITIONS OF KNOWLEDGE MANAGEMENT

Rather than doing a full survey of the field (not consistent with our desire to focus on a number of issues in a relatively small space), our purpose here is to raise and address key issues arising from typical attempts to define KM. To fulfill this purpose it is convenient to rely on a range of definitions provided at Yogesh Malhotra's (1998) well known web site and a variety of views beginning with Malhotra's own definition.

Malhotra (1998)

> Knowledge Management caters to the critical issues of organizational adaptation, survival, and competence in the face of increasingly discontinuous environmental change. . . . Essentially, it embodies organizational processes that seek synergistic combination of data and information processing capacity of information technologies, and the creative and innovative capacity of human beings.

Malhotra looks at KM as a synthesis of IT and human innovation!

> While information generated by computer systems is not a very rich carrier of human interpretation for potential action, knowledge resides in the user's subjective context of action based on that information. Hence, it may not be incorrect to suggest that knowledge resides in the

user and not in the collection of information, a point made two decades ago by West Churchman, the leading information systems philosopher.

In this definition, it is not clear what management is. Or what knowledge is. It is not clear what information is. If knowledge is personal, does that mean that Malhotra rules out organizational knowledge? And why is information, as well as knowledge, not personal? Does Malhotra think there is something about personal information that automatically makes it valid and therefore "knowledge"? Is everything we believe "knowledge" just by virtue of our believing it? If so, this is a highly subjectivist view of knowledge and derivatively of KM.

Sveiby (1998)

. . . Both among KM-vendors (researchers and consultants) and KM-users (read short descriptions of what companies and other practitioners are doing) there seem to be two tracks of activities—and two levels. Track KM = Management of Information. Researchers and practitioners in this field tend to have their education in computer and/or information science. They are involved in construction of information management systems, AI, reengineering, groupware, etc. To them, knowledge = objects that can be identified and handled in information systems. This track is new and is growing very fast at the moment, assisted by new developments in IT.

This definition begs the question of defining KM. It doesn't define "management" or "knowledge." And it doesn't distinguish knowledge from information, or knowledge management from information management.

Track KM = Management of People. Researchers and practitioners in this field tend to have their education in philosophy, psychology, sociology or business/management. They are primarily involved in assessing, changing and improving human individual skills and/or behaviour. To them Knowledge = Processes, a complex set of dynamic skills, know-how, etc., that is constantly changing. They are traditionally involved in learning and in managing these competencies individually—like psychologists—

or on an organisational level—like philosophers, sociologists or organisational theorists. This track is very old, and is not growing so fast.

"Knowledge" is clearly not a process. "Learning," "KM," and "knowing" are processes, but knowledge itself, the outcome of processes such as learning and knowing, is not a process.

Sveiby's two alternative "definitions" of KM are presented by him as originating with others, identifying two schools of thought. Our remarks just above are not intended to state that either view is subscribed to by him as the correct definition of KM. Rather, our remarks should be interpreted as directed at the views stated without the implication that Sveiby subscribes to them. We note, however, that his statement of them declines to offer a critique of either, and that he prefers to remain above the fray.

Ellen Knapp (PWC) (1998)

We define knowledge management as "the art of transforming information and intellectual assets into enduring value for an organization's clients and its people."

Knapp thinks it is more important to tell us that KM is an "art" than it is to tell us what management is and what exactly it is we are managing. "Intellectual assets" is far too vague a construct to define the scope of KM. "Transforming" is not managing, and things other than knowledge can have "enduring value." In other words, this definition confuses acting upon information with managing knowledge; and knowledge processing with knowledge management. It is a characteristic error, committed again and again in knowledge management circles.

University of Kentucky (1998)

Knowledge is a vital organization resource. It is the raw material, work-in-process, and finished good of decision making. Distinct types of knowledge used by decision makers include information, procedures, and heuristics, among others. . . . A variety of computer-based techniques for managing knowledge (i.e., representing and processing it) have been and will continue to be devised to supplement innate human knowledge management skills. As a field of study, knowledge management is concerned with the invention, improvement, integration, usage, administration, evaluation, and impacts of such techniques.

Rather than being the "finished good of decision making" (a nice turn of phrase), knowledge is the finished good *for* decision making. In any event, it is hard to see the distinction between information and procedures and heuristics, since these appear to be information also. Moreover, this definition limits KM to "computer-based techniques," a limitation neither acceptable to the KM community in general, nor justified by the common concept of management, which encompasses far more than computer techniques.

Karl Wiig (1998)

Knowledge management in organizations must be considered from three perspectives with different horizons and purposes:

Business Perspective—focusing on why, where, and to what extent the organization must invest in or exploit knowledge. Strategies, products and services, alliances, acquisitions, or divestments should be considered from knowledge-related points of view.

Management Perspective—focusing on determining, organizing, directing, facilitating, and monitoring knowledge-related practices and activities required to achieve the desired business strategies and objectives.

Hands-On Operational Perspective—focusing on applying the expertise to conduct explicit knowledge-related work and tasks.

Karl Wiig, one of the more systematic thinkers in the field of knowledge management today, is the closest so far on the management side. The business perspective focuses attention on resource allocation, certainly a managerial activity. The management perspective identifies a number of management activities. The "hands-on" perspective recognizes that knowledge managers must also do knowledge processing. But as we've seen in Chapter 1, Wiig's definition of knowledge as "understandings" and "mental units" is highly debatable and clearly falls entirely on the World 2 side of things. So his definition of KM doesn't orient us toward managing, producing, and/or integrating World 3 knowledge, or toward managing how either World 2 or World 3 information is validated and hence becomes "knowledge."

R. Gregory Wenig (1998)

> Knowledge Management (for the organization): consists of activities focused on the organization gaining knowledge from its own experience and from the experience of others, and on the judicious application of that knowledge to fulfill the mission of the organization. . . .
>
> Knowledge: Currently, there is no consensus on what knowledge is. . . . The definition that I have found most useful when building systems is as follows: knowledge is understanding the cognitive system possesses. It is a construct that is not directly observable. It is specific to and not residing outside the cognitive system that created it. Information, NOT knowledge, is communicated among cognitive systems. A cognitive system can be a human, a group, an organization, a computer, or some combination.

Wenig's definition is strong on many of aspects of World 2 knowledge, especially on the distinction between individual knowledge and collective knowledge, and on the idea that it is a kind of information (World 3 knowledge) and not World 2 knowledge that is communicated among cognitive systems. But Wenig's definition is weak on the activities comprising KM and how they are distinguished from knowledge processing activities.

Philip C. Murray (1998)

> Our perspective at Knowledge Transfer International is that knowledge is information transformed into capabilities for effective action. In effect, knowledge is action. . . .
>
> For KTI, knowledge management is a strategy that turns an organization's intellectual assets—both recorded information and the talents of its members—into greater productivity, new value, and increased

competitiveness. It teaches corporations, from managers to employees, how to produce and optimize skills as a collective entity.

If knowledge were action, we wouldn't need two words. In fact, there is a great gap between knowledge and action and even between knowledge and the capability for action. As we have seen in Chapter 1, knowledge is a necessary condition for effective action, but it is not sufficient by itself. Not only knowledge, but also power and other resources are required for effective action to occur, as is the will to take such action. Also, let us not forget that information combined with capability and intention is also sufficient for action, but not for success. Finally, KM is a process and not a strategy as specified in Murray's view.

Tom Davenport (1998)

Knowledge is: "information with value, from the human mind" (adapted from *Information Ecology*, by Tom Davenport).

KM is: "Processes of capturing, distributing, and effectively using knowledge" (Davenport 1994).

"Information with value" is getting close to knowledge. But what kind of value? Information can have value for producing knowledge and yet not be knowledge itself. Thus, in producing knowledge, one may select from among a number of competing models. All may be of value in providing the context for an assessment which validates only one of them as knowledge, but that doesn't change the fact that all but one are just information.

This specific definition of KM, further, does not cover the interpersonal and decision-making aspects of KM. Moreover, why are "capturing," "distributing," and "using" knowledge, distinctively knowledge management, as opposed to knowledge processing, which consists of activities that all knowledge workers as well as knowledge managers engage in? Here, then, is another case of someone confusing knowledge processing with knowledge management.

Most definitions of KM suffer from the lack of careful treatment of both "management" and "knowledge." It's almost as if KM experts think that "knowledge management" is not a form of "management" and therefore does not have to be defined or characterized in a manner consistent with well established meanings of that term.

The above definitions are striking in that they tell us so little. Why do KM definitions tell us so little about (a) the activities that are part of KM and (b) the target of those activities?

The situation with respect to "KM" is very similar to what we have already found with regard to "knowledge." There is no consensus on definition and attempts to define KM are relatively superficial. It is a case of another key concept in KM being defined so vaguely and ambiguously that research and writing on KM is weighed down with conceptual baggage and difficulties in communication, inhibiting both the search for KM knowledge and effective KM decision making. Our own attempt to solve the problem of definition begins with consideration of the differences between information management and knowledge management.

INFORMATION MANAGEMENT AND KNOWLEDGE MANAGEMENT

What is the difference between Information Management (IM) and Knowledge Management (KM)? Both concepts refer to managing (handling, directing, governing, controlling, coordinating, planning, organizing) processes and the products of those processes. In addition, since knowledge is a form of information (see Chapter 2), it follows that KM is a form of IM. More specifically, KM is a more robust form of IM that provides management of activities not necessary in specifying the concept of information management.

One difference between basic IM and KM is that basic IM focuses on managing how information is produced and integrated into the enterprise, while KM does the same with respect to knowledge. A second difference between basic IM and KM is that basic IM focuses on managing a more narrow set of activities than KM. The two information processes managed by an organization are information production and information integration. The two basic knowledge processes are knowledge production and knowledge integration.

Since knowledge processes are more inclusive in the sense that there are classes of activities in knowledge processes not found in basic information processes, let us first examine a framework for looking at knowledge processes. Then we will be able to arrive at how basic information processes are different from augmented information/knowledge processes, by cutting out some of the knowledge activities in knowledge processes. After completing that examination, we will begin to address knowledge management and basic information management in more detail.

Knowledge Processes and Information Processes

Knowledge production includes (a) knowledge claim formulation, (b) individual and group learning, and (c) information acquisition. It also includes (d) knowledge claim evaluation activity. Knowledge integration includes (a) knowledge broadcasting, (b) searching/ retrieving), (c) teaching, and (d) knowledge sharing. The two knowledge processes, once again, may be viewed as part of the KLC, a knowledge "value network" (Allee 2000). The KLC and the interaction of the two knowledge processes are illustrated in Figure 2.17. The major task clusters within knowledge production and knowledge integration are also illustrated in Figure 2.17.

Basic information processes are different from knowledge production and integration processes in that they lack knowledge claim evaluation and therefore fail to distinguish between knowledge claims that are surviving, falsified, or otherwise. Information Production includes information acquisition, individual and group learning, even knowledge claim formulation, but excludes knowledge claim evaluation. So the information "life cycle" or value network is incomplete in comparison with the knowledge life cycle. Similarly, information integration includes broadcasting, searching/retrieving, teaching, and sharing, but what is being broadcasted, searched for, retrieved, taught, and shared is information rather than knowledge. Let us now turn to a more detailed discussion of the nature of KM interventions before returning to the question of differences between KM and IM.

Definition and Specification of Knowledge Management

KM is a management discipline that seeks to enhance organizational knowledge processing. KM is also human activity that is part of the interaction constituting the Knowledge Management Process (KMP) of an agent or collective.

This last definition reduces KM to the definition of the KMP. *The KMP is an ongoing, persistent, purposeful interaction among human-based agents through which the participating agents manage (handle, direct, govern, control, coordinate, plan, organize, facilitate, enable, and empower) other agents, components, and activities participating in basic knowledge processing (knowledge production and knowledge integration), with the purpose of contributing to the creation and maintenance of an organic, unified whole system, producing, maintaining, enhancing, acquiring, and transmitting the enterprise's knowledge base.*

This definition in effect defines the KMP as a process aimed at the management of knowledge processes and their outcomes. But this is only the beginning in specifying the character of KM. We need now to specify KM by providing a classification based on a multidimensional view of KM activities.

We can distinguish among organizations along five important KM dimensions, thereby providing the basis of a useful classification. These are:

- the number of levels of knowledge management interaction an organization has implemented;
- the breadth of knowledge management activities it has implemented at each level;
- the target(s) of knowledge management activity;
- whether a knowledge management intervention is a social process intervention or a technology intervention; and
- whether the intervention is a policy or program intervention.

Levels of Knowledge Management

By levels of knowledge management interaction, we mean to distinguish multiple levels of KM process activity arranged in a hierarchy. In principle, and, at least with respect to knowledge production, the hierarchy has an infinite number of levels. The hierarchy is generated by considerations similar to those specified by Bertrand Russell (Russell 1919, Whitehead and Russell 1913) in his theory of types, and Gregory Bateson (1972) in his theory of learning and communication.

Knowledge processes occur at the *same* level of agent interaction as other business processes, even though they are about those processes. Let us call this business process level of interaction *Level Zero* of enterprise Complex Adaptive System (CAS) interaction (Waldrop 1992).

At this level, preexisting knowledge is used by business processes and by knowledge processes to implement activity. And in addition, knowledge processes produce and integrate knowledge about business processes using (a) previously produced knowledge about how to implement these knowledge processes, (b) infrastructure, (c) staff, and (d) technology, whose purpose is to provide the foundation for knowledge production and knowledge integration at *Level Zero*. But from where does this infrastructure, staff, knowledge, and technology come? Who manages them, and how are they changed?

They do not come from, by, and through the *Level Zero* knowledge processes—these only produce and integrate knowledge about business processes such as sales, marketing, or manufacturing processes. Rather, this is where *Level One* of CAS interaction, the lowest level of knowledge management, comes in.

This *Level One* KM process interaction is responsible for producing and integrating knowledge about *Level Zero* knowledge production and integration processes to knowledge workers at *Level Zero*. It is this knowledge that is used at both *Level Zero* and *Level One* to implement knowledge processes and KM knowledge and information processing. Let us call this *Level One* knowledge the Enterprise Knowledge Management (EKM) model.

The KM process and EKM model at *Level One* are also responsible for providing the knowledge infrastructure, staff, and technology necessary for implementing knowledge processes at *Level Zero*. In turn, knowledge processes at *Level Zero* use this infrastructure, staff, and technology to produce and integrate the knowledge used by the business processes. The relationships between *Level One* KM and *Level Zero* knowledge and business processes are illustrated in Figure 3.1.

Knowledge about *Level Zero* knowledge processes, as well as infrastructure, staff, and technology, change when *Level One* KM process interactions introduce changes. That is, changes occur: when the *Level One* KM process produces and integrates new knowledge about how to implement *Level Zero* knowledge processes; and when it adds or subtracts from the existing infrastructure, staff, and tech-

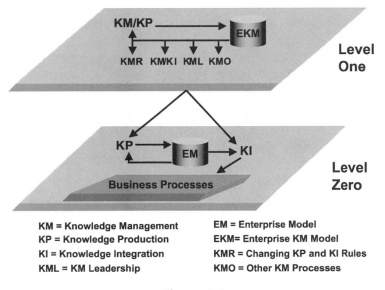

KM = Knowledge Management   EM = Enterprise Model
KP = Knowledge Production   EKM= Enterprise KM Model
KI = Knowledge Integration   KMR = Changing KP and KI Rules
KML = KM Leadership   KMO = Other KM Processes

Figure 3.1

Relationships Between Level One *Knowledge Management and*
Level Zero *Knowledge and Business Processes*

nology based on new knowledge it produces. There are two possible sources of these changes.

First, knowledge production at *Level One* can change the EKM model, which, in turn, impacts on (a) knowledge about how to produce or integrate knowledge about (*Level Zero*) business processes, (b) knowledge about how to acquire information or integrate knowledge about *Level One* information acquisition or integration processes (c) staffing, (d) infrastructure, and (e) technology. This type of change, then, originates in the KM *Level One* process interaction itself.

Second, knowledge expressed in the EKM model about how to produce *Level One* knowledge may change. This knowledge, however, is only used in arriving at the *Level One* EKM model. It is not explained or accounted for by it. It is determined, instead, by a KM *Level Two* process and is accounted for in a *Level Two* EKM model produced by this interaction. Figure 3.2 adds the KM *Level Two* process to the process relationships previously shown in Figure 3.1.

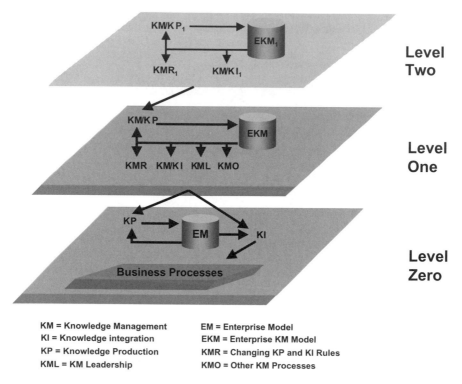

KM = Knowledge Management   EM = Enterprise Model
KI = Knowledge integration   EKM = Enterprise KM Model
KP = Knowledge Production   KMR = Changing KP and KI Rules
KML = KM Leadership   KMO = Other KM Processes

Figure 3.2
Adding Knowledge Management Level Two *to the Relationshop*

Instead of labeling the three levels of processes discussed so far as
Level Zero, Level One, and *Level Two,* it is more descriptive to think
of them as the *knowledge process level, the KM or metaknowledge
process level,* and the *meta-KM or Metaprise level* (Firestone 1999)
of process interaction, respectively. There is no end, in principle, to
the hierarchy of levels of process interaction and accompanying EKM
models. The number of levels we choose to model and to describe
will be determined by how complete an explanation of knowledge
management activity we need in order to accomplish our purposes.

The *knowledge process level* produces knowledge about business
processes and uses knowledge about how to produce (how to innovate) knowledge about business processes. This level cannot change
knowledge about how to produce knowledge. But it *can* change
knowledge about business processes.

The *KM (metaknowledge) process* level produces *knowledge about how to produce knowledge about business processes* (i.e., knowledge processing knowledge). The KM level also uses knowledge about how to produce KM level knowledge *about how to produce knowledge about business processes* (again, knowledge processing knowledge). This level can change knowledge about how to produce knowledge but cannot change knowledge about how to produce KM-level knowledge.

The meta-KM, or *first Metaprise level* (i.e., *Level Two*), produces: (a) knowledge about how to produce knowledge about KM knowledge processes at *Level One*, and (b) knowledge about how to produce KM level knowledge (again, at *Level One*) about how to produce knowledge about knowledge processes for use at *Level Zero*. It uses knowledge about how to produce meta-KM level knowledge about how to produce knowledge about KM knowledge processes. This level can change knowledge about how to produce KM-level knowledge but cannot change knowledge about how to produce meta-KM level knowledge.

Level Three, the meta-meta-KM process, or *second Metaprise level* of interaction, produces knowledge about how to produce meta-KM level-produced knowledge about how to produce knowledge about KM knowledge processes, and uses meta-meta-KM level-produced knowledge about how to produce knowledge about meta-KM level knowledge processes. This level can change knowledge about how to produce meta-KM level knowledge, but cannot change knowledge about how to produce meta-meta-KM level knowledge.

Level Two (the first Metaprise level), then, seems to be the minimum number of levels needed for a view of KM allowing one to change (accelerate) the rate of change in KM level knowledge. And in some situations, where we need even more leverage over our knowledge about how to arrive at knowledge about KM processes, we may even need to go to levels higher than *Level Two*.

Keeping in mind the above distinctions among enterprises according to the level of knowledge management practiced in them, let us talk about KM, meta-KM, mcta-meta-KM level enterprises, and so on. It should be possible to usefully characterize the successful twenty-first century intelligent enterprise, at least on a business-domain specific basis, as a Level X Metaprise, when we have more empirical evidence on how many KM levels are needed for competitiveness in any business domain.

Thus, the relative effectiveness of enterprises practicing different levels of KM is an empirical question, not something we should assume as given. While it is very likely that effectiveness will increase as enterprises move from the KM level to higher levels, there may be a point at which diminishing returns set in. Or there may even be a point at which movement up the ladder of levels leads to negative returns relative to the investment required to add a KM level, or leads to fewer returns than alternative investments in other areas. ROI considerations must apply to enterprise KM enhancements, as well as to other enterprise business processes.

Breadth of KM Processes

By breadth of knowledge management processes, we mean the extent to which all of the major KM activities are implemented at any specified KM level of the enterprise. So what are these major KM activities? Here is a conceptual framework that begins to specify them.

Consider Figure 2.12, "The Activity to Business Process Hierarchy." This hierarchy, ranging from activities to processes, applies to knowledge and KM processes as well as to operational business processes. Enterprise KM activities may be usefully categorized according to a scheme of task clusters which, with some additions and changes, generally follows Mintzberg (1973). We use Mintzberg's categorization of activities because it was developed from an extensive empirical study of managerial behavior.

There are three types of KM task clusters: interpersonal behavior, information (and knowledge) processing behavior, and decision making. The task clusters are broken down further into nine more specific types of task pattern activities.

Interpersonal KM behavior includes:

- figurehead
- leadership
- external relationship-building activity

Information and knowledge processing behavior includes:

- KM knowledge production
- KM knowledge integration

Decision making includes:

- changing knowledge processing rules
- crisis handling
- allocating KM resources
- negotiating agreement with representatives of other business processes

In the following pages we will specify these nine areas of KM activity.

Interpersonal Behavior

Figurehead or Ceremonial Representation KM Activity

This activity focuses on performing formal KM acts such as signing contracts, attending public functions on behalf of the enterprise's KM process, and representing the KM process to dignitaries visiting the enterprise. Such symbolic representation is an aspect of all managerial activity. Managers have authority. Part of what maintains that authority is the symbolism used and manipulated by them to express the legitimacy of their authority and to claim it.

Figurehead activity in the KM area is similar to that in other areas of executive activity. Methods such as personal networking, meetings, public appearances, Web-enabled representing, and infrastructure such as intranet facilities used for figurehead activity, conference and presentation rooms, fax, telephone facilities, etc., are also similar. What is perhaps different is the focus of figurehead activity on conferences, meetings, and events where knowledge processing and knowledge management are the primary topics of interest.

Leadership

This includes setting policy, hiring, training, motivating, monitoring, and evaluating KM and some knowledge processing staff. It also includes persuading non-KM agents within the enterprise of the validity of KM process activities. That is, KM leadership activity includes building political support for KM programs, projects, and knowledge processes within the enterprise and influencing the climate and norms within which knowledge processing will occur, so that knowledge production will be enabled. Finally, leadership activities cut across all the other nine categories of KM activities. That is, leadership is an aspect of each of the nine classes of KM activities.

That leadership activities are central to KM is axiomatic. Leadership is a key management activity in any business process, and knowledge and KM processes are business processes. Again, what is different here is the focus on leadership of knowledge production and integration activities and on changing knowledge processing rules such as those impacting knowledge claim evaluation. And in the area of resource allocation, the focus on allocating software applications supporting knowledge production, integration, and management is different.

Building Relationships with Individuals and Organizations External to the Enterprise

This is another political activity designed to build status for KM and to cultivate sources of support for KM external to the enterprise. To build new external relationships requires joining professional associations, serving on committees, attending and presenting at conferences, visiting colleagues and allies, forming strategic alliances and partnerships, and networking individual contacts. There is no magic here, just the need to design and implement a systematic program to generate alliances and close relationships with individuals. These personal relationships are essential for information acquisition at the KM level. Some information can only be acquired through personal networks. Building external relationships means performing those activities intended to produce friendships, alliances, and "partnerships" with decision makers external to one's own company. These relationships are essential for providing "role models" for knowledge managers.

Knowledge and Information Processing

Knowledge Production Is a KM as Well as a Knowledge Process

KM knowledge production is different in that it is here that the "rules," frameworks, perspectives, and methodologies for knowledge production used at the level of knowledge processes are specified.

Keep in mind that knowledge production at this level involves planning, descriptive, cause-and-effect, predictive, and assessment knowledge about the two fundamental *Level Zero* knowledge processes, as well as these categories of knowledge about *Level One* interpersonal, knowledge integration, and decision-making KM activities. The only knowledge not produced by *Level One* knowledge production is knowledge about how to accomplish knowledge production at *Level One*. Once again, the rules, perspectives, etc., constituting this last type of knowledge are produced at *Level Two*.

KM Knowledge Integration

KM knowledge integration is affected by KM knowledge production and also affects knowledge production activities by stimulating new ones. KM knowledge integration at any KM level also plays the critical role of diffusing "how-to" knowledge to lower KM and knowledge process levels. But the essential character of knowledge integration at the KM level is unchanged from that at the basic KLC at *Level Zero*.

Decision-Making Activities

Changing Knowledge Processing Rules

The task clusters of information acquisition, individual and group learning, knowledge claim formulation, knowledge claim evaluation, broadcasting, searching/retrieving, teaching, and sharing are all composed of tasks. Knowledge workers execute these tasks, and knowledge managers produce the processing "rules" contributing to the execution of the tasks. Knowledge managers also change the rules once they produce new knowledge about them. Essentially this involves making the decision to change knowledge processing rules and causing both the new rules and the mandate to use them to be transferred to the lower level. The term "rules" here should be interpreted liberally, as signifying perspectives, customs, frameworks, etc., as well as rules. We are not claiming that *Rules* produced by knowledge managers necessarily govern, or should govern, all or even most knowledge production. On the contrary, rules govern most knowledge production in business process DECs. But in KLCs knowledge is frequently produced through the use of novel perspectives and frameworks as well as rules.

Crisis Handling

Crisis handling involves such things as meeting CEO requests for new competitive intelligence in an area of high strategic interest for an enterprise and directing rapid development of a KM support infrastructure in response to requests from high level executives. Crisis handling does not occur in KM as frequently as it does in other management processes. But when it does occur, it is a significant KM activity.

Allocating Resources

Allocating resources for KM support infrastructures, training, professional conferences, salaries for KM staff, funds for new KM programs, etc., is also an important KM activity. KM software implementation falls into this category.

Negotiating Agreements

Negotiating agreements with representatives of business processes over levels of effort for KM, the shape of KM programs, the ROI expected from KM activities, etc., is another important area of KM activity. Once again, this activity is not unique to KM. But its lack of distinctiveness makes it no less essential to the practice of KM.

Targets of Knowledge Management

In Chapter 2 and the development above, we indicated that knowledge management manages knowledge processes and their outcomes. Thus, these, rather than business processes and business outcomes, are the targets of knowledge management. This relationship is expressed in Figures 2.19, 3.1, and 3.2, and again in Figures 3.3 and 3.4.

In Figure 3.5, we list the 10 most generalized targets of KM, the KLC subprocesses and their outcomes. This 10-category taxonomy is highly expandable, since each of the subprocesses may be broken down further into task clusters and patterns.

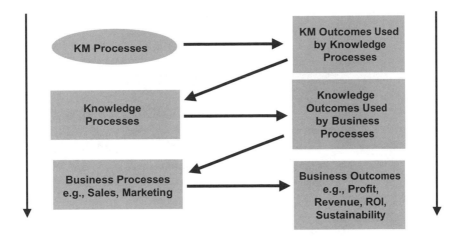

Figure 3.3
From Knowledge Management Processes to Business Outcomes

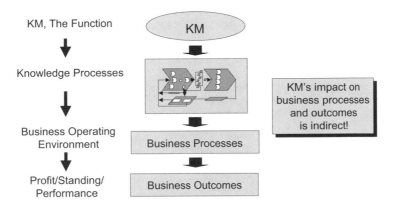

Figure 3.4
A Reference Model for Knowledge Management

Social and Technological, and Policy and Program Interventions

The social dimension of KM interventions deals with people and processes using a variety of tools and methods including recruiting, communities of practice, knowledge cafés, social process redesign, and many others. The technological dimension, of course, deals with

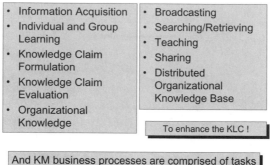

Figure 3.5

Knowledge Management Business Processes Have Different Purposes and Targets

	Demand-Side KM	Supply-Side KM
Social Dimension **(People and Process)**	• Individual Learning • Group Learning • Innovation & IC Mgmt • Communities of Inquiry • KAIZEN Events in Mfg • Think Tanks • Management Planning	• Training Programs • Communities of Practice (CoP) • Knowledge Capture • Storytelling • KM Cultural Initiatives • Operations Mgmt

Technology Dimension **(IT)**	• Knowledge Portals
	• Innovation Mgmt Tools
	• Groupware
	  - Collaboration Apps
	  - Virtual Teaming Tools
	  - E-mail
	• Listserv Discuss'n Grps
		• Information Portals
		• Intranets
		• Information Mgmt
		• Work Product Mgmt
		• Content Mgmt
		• Imaging
		• Groupware

Figure 3.6

Some Examples of Common Knowledge Management Initiatives

technology-based interventions, such as enterprise knowledge portals, community support software, text-mining software, and other KM-related applications. Figure 3.6 provides examples of KM interventions classified by the *social* versus *technology* and demand-side (knowledge production) versus supply-side (knowledge integration) dichotomies. In the classification we are forming here, the demand- and supply-side categories are further broken down into KLC subprocesses and outcomes.

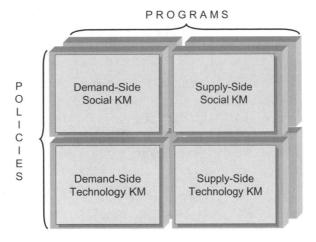

Figure 3.7
Policies versus Programs in Knowledge Management Initiatives

Policy and program KM interventions differ, of course, in their intent and generality. Policies are supposed to be highly general and may require several programs to implement. Programs are more specific in their focus on social and technological targets. Here are two examples:

Policy: Employees shall have meaningful opportunities to engage in self-directed learning.

Program: 3M's Fifteen Percent Rule (Employees may spend up to 15% of their time on self-chosen, self-managed learning, with full management support.)

Thus, we can see that when we add the *policy versus program* dimensions to the *demand- versus supply-side* and *social versus technology* intervention matrix shown in Figure 3.6, we get an even richer framework for categorizing KM strategies and intervention types (see Figure 3.7).

The Classification of KM Activities

This classification of nine KM categories or task clusters is not complete. There are likely other task clusters and patterns we have overlooked. But this classification of activities is specific enough to (along with the level, target, social/technological, and policy/program dimensions) provide the capability to define many types of KM interventions which may then be analyzed for impact and effectiveness. If we assume only two KM levels on the Metaprise dimension, the 9 KM activity categories, the 10 target categories, the two social/technological, and the two policy/program categories, then the KM taxonomy that results specifies a 720-category classification of KM interventions. And this is only the beginning of differentiation, since further category segmentation can easily be developed in both the KM activity and target dimensions and perhaps almost as easily in the social/technological and policy/program dimensions as well.

MORE ON HOW INFORMATION MANAGEMENT DIFFERS FROM KNOWLEDGE MANAGEMENT

IM activities can be defined in analogy to KM activities. There are three categories of IM activities in the information management process: interpersonal behavior; information processing behavior; and decision making.

Interpersonal IM behavior includes:

- figurehead
- leadership
- external relationship-building activity

Information processing behavior includes:

- IM information production (no knowledge claim evaluation)
- IM information integration (only broadcasting, searching/retrieving, teaching, or sharing information, but not knowledge)

Decision making includes:

- changing information processing rules
- crisis handling
- allocating IM resources
- negotiating agreements with representatives of other business processes

The differences between information processes at the IM level and knowledge processes at the KM level therefore arise from the absence of knowledge claim evaluation activity in IM. As a result, broadcasting, searching/retrieving, teaching, and sharing at the IM level are all focused on information and not on knowledge.

CONCLUSION

There have been many attempts to define KM, but remarkably few attempting to specify the activities or processes comprising it. This is one of the mysteries of KM literature. It is as though KM theoreticians have gone from KM abstractions to *stories, case studies, tools, software,* and the rest of the diversity we see in KM without developing further the core concept of the field, and thereby leaving a huge gap (see Figure 3.8) between core definitions and the more concrete objects named above.

If we fill this gap we gain:

■ a better understanding of the scope and meaning of KM, because specification is even more important for understanding than definition;

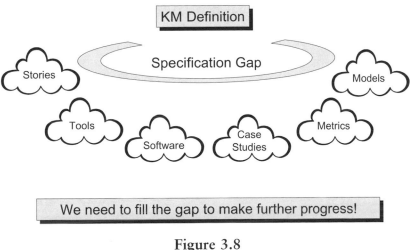

Figure 3.8
A Specification Gap

- necessary language for developing the conceptual framework that can provide the measurement architecture for KM; and
- concepts that become the focus of efforts to develop metrics of KM inputs to the KLC.

On the other hand, if we fail in this specification, we get continued confusion about what KM is and continued inability to evolve a professional discipline that might be based on KM in any sort of meaningful context.

In this chapter, we have developed a KM conceptual framework and contrasted KM and information management. We began with a discussion of differences between KM and IM, then developed a clear definition of KM, and then went on to specify a 720-category classification of KM intervention types based on the Metaprise levels, KM activities, KLC targets, social/technological, and policy/program dimensions. We believe that this framework fulfills the basic need for clarification of the middle ground between definition and various KM objects that has existed in KM for some time. It therefore also provides a new foundation for KM policies, programs, and projects, a foundation that goes way beyond the simple 2 × 2 frameworks that have so far been so popular as a basis for KM programs. Let us hope that the days of oversimplification in KM program design, based on such 2 × 2 frameworks, are over and that the days of realistic consideration of the variety of KM phenomena have arrived. If they have, then this KM framework is a contribution to TNKM that will shortly flourish.

References

Allee, V. (2000), "Reconfiguring the Value Network," available at: http://www.vernaallee.com/reconfiguring_val_net.html.

Bateson, G. (1972), "The Logical Categories of Learning and Communication," In G. Bateson, *Steps to an Ecology of Mind*, New York, NY: Chandler Publishing Company.

Davenport, T. (1994), Quoted in Y. Malhotra, "Compilation of definitions of knowledge management" at www.brint.com.

Davenport, T. (1998), quote in Y. Malhotra, "Compilation of definitions of knowledge management" at www.brint.com.

Firestone, J.M. (1999), "The Metaprise, the AKMS, and the Enterprise Knowledge Portal," *Working Paper No. 3, Executive Information Systems, Inc.*, Wilmington, DE, May 5, 1999, Available at: http://www.dkms.com/White_Papers.htm.

Firestone, J.M. (2000), "Accelerated Innovation and KM Impact," *Financial Knowledge Management*, **1, no. 1**, 54–60, also available at http://www.dkms.com.

Firestone, J.M. (2000a), "Knowledge Management: A Framework for Analysis and Measurement," *White Paper No. 17, Executive Information Systems, Inc.*, Wilmington, DE, October 1, 2000, Available at: http://www.dkms.com/White_Papers.htm.

Holland, J.H. (1995), *Hidden Order*. Reading, MA: Addison-Wesley.

Holland, J.H. (1998), *Emergence*. Reading, MA: Addison-Wesley.

Kauffman, S. (1995), *At Home in the Universe*. New York, NY: Oxford University Press.

Knapp, E. (1998), quote in Y. Malhotra, "Compilation of definitions of knowledge management" at www.brint.com.

Malhotra, Y. (1998) "Compilation of definitions of knowledge management" at www.brint.com.

McElroy, M. (1999), "The Second Generation of KM," *Knowledge Management Magazine* **(October, 1999)**, 86–88.

Mintzberg, H. (1973), "A New Look at the Chief Executive's Job," *Organizational Dynamics*, *AMACOM*, **Winter, 1973**.

Murray, P. (1998), quote in Y. Malhotra, "Compilation of definitions of knowledge management" at www.brint.com.

Russell, B. (1919), *Introduction to Mathematical Philosophy*, London, UK: Allen and Unwin.

Sveiby, K. (1998), quote in Y. Malhotra, "Compilation of definitions of knowledge management" at www.brint.com.

University of Kentucky, quote in Y. Malhotra, (1998) "Compilation of definitions of knowledge management" at www.brint.com.

Waldrop, M. (1992), *Complexity*, New York, NY: Simon and Schuster.

Wenig, R.G. (1998), quote in Y. Malhotra, "Compilation of definitions of knowledge management" at www.brint.com.

Whitehead, A.N. and Russell, B. (1913), *Principia Mathematica*, London: Cambridge University Press.

Wiig, K. (1998) quote in Y. Malhotra, "Compilation of definitions of knowledge management" at www.brint.com.

Chapter 4

GENERATIONS OF KNOWLEDGE MANAGEMENT

THREE VIEWS OF CHANGE IN KNOWLEDGE MANAGEMENT

Knowledge management, new as it is, is changing. There are at least three accounts of how it is changing and about how we should view The New Knowledge Management (TNKM). One account, by Mark Koenig (2002), sees KM as a field that was originally driven by information technology, the Internet, best practices, later lessons learned, and most important, knowledge sharing. This theory sees a second stage of KM as about human factors, organizational learning, and knowledge creation viewed as the conversions among tacit and explicit knowledge. The third stage of KM is the stage of the arrangement and management of content through taxonomy construction and use, and like the first is also heavily biased toward information technology.

The second view of change, by David Snowden (2002), is a bit more subtle than the first. According to this theory, the first age of knowledge management is one in which the word knowledge itself was not at first "problematic," and in which the focus was on

88

distributing information to decision makers for timely use in decisions. The second age replaced the information technology focus with one on tacit/explicit knowledge conversion inspired by Nonaka's SECI model. It is just ending. Snowden contends that the third age *will be* one in which: knowledge is viewed paradoxically as a thing and a flow; context, narrative, and content management will be central to our view of KM; there will be an understanding of organizations as engaged in sense making through utilization of complex adaptive systems phenomena constrained by human acts of free will attempting to order them; and finally, the use of the insights and practices of scientific management will be restricted to appropriate contexts, while "insights and learnings" from theories of chaos and complexity will supplement them in contexts where these new insights are relevant.

The third view of change, first presented by Mark W. McElroy (1999) based on work hosted by the Knowledge Management Consortium International (KMCI) and continuing partly under its auspices since then, views first-generation KM, also called "supply-side KM," as primarily about integrating ("supplying") previously created knowledge through knowledge distribution, sharing, and other integrative activities. It is typically associated with two well-known phrases that serve as the mantras for advocates of the "knowledge sharing" side of KM: (1) *It's all about capturing, codifying, and sharing valuable knowledge*, and (2) *It's all about getting the right information to the right people at the right time*. The third view sees second-generation KM as first appearing in the mid-1990s and as being focused not only on "supply-side" knowledge processing such as knowledge sharing, but also on "demand-side" knowledge processing, or "knowledge-making" in response to problem-induced demands. This combined focus on knowledge integration and knowledge production is the defining characteristic of Second Generation KM (SGKM), or alternatively, The New Knowledge Management (TNKM). But an important aspect of it is also the recognition that organizations are permeated with complex adaptive systems phenomena and that knowledge management in them is about using KM to enable or reinforce self-organization in knowledge processing for the purpose of achieving accelerated sustainable innovation in support of organizational adaptation.

So in light of these contrasting views, questions arise. Which of the three views is correct? Are there two generations, stages, or ages of KM? Is a third age about to begin? Or are there already three? Are the changes best seen as occurring along the information technology dimension? Or along linguistic dimensions, such as taxonomy construction, context, and narrative? Or in terms of whether we view organizations as mechanisms, or CASs, or CASs modified by human "promethean" interventions? Or just in terms of the popularity of different intervention types from one period to another? Or is change in KM best viewed as occurring in terms of the shifting focus of management on the scope of knowledge processing as identified by McElroy? We will answer these questions after we have examined each of the three views in more detail.

THE THREE STAGES OF KNOWLEDGE MANAGEMENT

In Mark Koenig's view (2002, 20), "The initial stage of KM was driven primarily by information technology. That stage has been described . . . as 'by the Internet out of intellectual capital.'"

By this, Koenig means that the development of the Internet and the use of its technology to implement intranets provided the enterprise with an unprecedented tool for knowledge sharing and transfer. Knowledge management was the name introduced to describe the management activity concerned with implementing such solutions, in order to gain competitive advantage and increase productivity and effectiveness.

Further, this activity could be rationalized by its proponents (including large consulting organizations selling their own newly developed expertise in implementing such solutions) in terms of increasing the value of an enterprise's Intellectual Capital (IC). The notion of IC had appeared a few years earlier to account for the increasing disparity between the market value of real world enterprises and their book value as computed using measurable financial indicators and conventional formulae for computing company valuations. In addition to the above, the first stage of KM was also characterized by a focus on "best practices," later revised to a focus on "lessons learned." But it is not clear from Koenig's account what "best practices" and "lessons learned" in KM have to do with the IT focus supposedly dominant in stage one.

So for Koenig, the first stage of KM was about applying technology to accomplish knowledge sharing and coordination across the enterprise. The second stage, on the other hand, was primarily a recognition that KM was not all about applying technology, but rather had also to include a focus on human and cultural factors as essential in implementing KM applications, if failures were to be avoided. Koenig calls attention to the work of Senge (1990) on organizational learning and Nonaka and Takeuchi (1995) on the SECI model and its applications as essential to phase two. Koenig also calls attention to the focus of these works on organizational learning and knowledge creation, but not on systems thinking, which was an important element in Senge's treatment and in the rising popularity of stage two activities. Koenig also mentions the importance of communities of practice in stage two, but neglects to make the connection between the communities of practice emphasis and the thinking of Senge and Nonaka and Takeuchi, or for that matter, between communities of practice and knowledge creation and innovation.

Koenig thinks that the third stage of KM (2002, 21) "is the awareness of the importance of content—and, in particular, an awareness of the importance of the retrievability and therefore of the arrangement, description, and structure of that content." In particular, the third stage is about finding relevant content and about taxonomy development and content management to facilitate this goal.

DIFFICULTIES WITH THE THREE-STAGES VIEW

There are a number of difficulties in Koenig's account of the development of knowledge management. First, the dates in his account of development are unclear. His theory is one of the onset of new KM stages which then exist along with the old. If such a stage theory of KM development is to be applied we need either clear dates to distinguish the beginning of each successive stage, or a clear period of transition in which the previous stage is gradually supplemented by the features of the new stage. Without these criteria it is very hard to characterize a particular period as stage one rather than stage two and to confirm that analysis. Specifically, Koenig claims that stage one precedes stage two and that stage one is about applying IT, while stage two is about the human element in KM. Yet Senge's book, identified as a stage two milestone was written in 1990 much before the trend toward intranets and knowledge sharing applications, supposedly characteristic of stage one, gained momentum. Karl Wiig's work (1989) introducing KM as a field was also written much before the widespread adoption of Internet-based technology in enterprises, and even before Senge's book. And then Wiig wrote three books from 1993 to 1995, looking at KM comprehensively. Even Nonaka and Takeuchi dates from 1995, a date that surely preceded the heyday of so-called stage one KM with its emphasis on intranet-based knowledge sharing and coordination applications.

The same difficulty applies to the supposed transition from stage two to stage three KM. If we are to believe Koenig, it was not until 2001 that content management and taxonomy development became important for KM. However, the 1998 combined KM World/AIIM conference held in Chicago had a major content management element. In fact, attendees were frequently heard by these authors to complain that content management was dominating the conference and that such applications were not KM applications, and that claims to the contrary were merely "vendor speak" hiding the fact that vendors had very few KM applications to offer.

Following that conference, moreover, the conference circuit began to see an explosion of content management and portal conferences. These were frequently closely associated with so-called KM applications. Both types of conferences included sessions on tools for taxonomy development and for increasingly efficient retrieval of information through application of search technology.

While there is no question that the interest in content management and taxonomy development continues to increase, there is no reason to claim that this trend is either later than the second stage or even that such activities are new and go beyond the concerns of the second stage. After all, the concern with taxonomy and content management is about more efficiently retrieving knowledge or information that already exists. Thus, its core motivating concern is not different from Koenig's stage one. That is, taxonomy development and content management are primarily about coordinating and sharing already existing knowledge and only secondarily about aiding knowledge making. So there is a good argument for asserting that Koenig's stage 3 is really just an extension of his stage 1.

Second, another difficulty with Koenig's account is the ad hoc character of its classification of the three stages of KM, apparently based on anecdote and personal observation. There is no underlying conceptual framework organizing the analysis of change. KM supposedly begins as an IT field. Then suddenly, under the influence of Senge and Nonaka, it begins to incorporate the human element, and this element is apparently either discontinuous with what has gone before, or a response to the perceived failure of the IT applications implemented in the first age. It is presented as if it is a mere adaptation to a problem, the problem of getting organizations to accept IT interventions defined as KM projects. Further, a similar ad hoc adaptation is viewed as triggering the move from stage 2 to stage 3. That is, Koenig seems to think that we have a new stage of KM because people realize that they can neither share nor create knowledge without good Web-based navigation to help them "find" it.

The third difficulty with Koenig's view is that its lack of a conceptual framework provides only limited guidance for the further development of KM. He points to the fact that his view suggests that librarians may have an important part to play in taxonomy development as a positive reason for taking it seriously. But what does his analysis imply about knowledge management activities or policies more generally, or about knowledge production, organizational learning, sustainable innovation, intellectual capital, KM metrics, methodologies, and IT requirements for KM applications? That is, once you understand his account, what can you do with it? The answer is very little. Unless one is interested in content management and taxonomy development, there is little of interest in it, or of general significance for the further development of KM. Thus it provides both an inadequate analysis of the past and fails to provide a road map for the future.

In brief, we believe that Koenig's approach to the analysis of stages of KM is much too ad hoc in character, focusing on tools and techniques and not on the broad purposes of KM. As a result, his typology only records shifting fashions, not fundamental shifts in disciplinary concerns. Thus, he cannot recognize that both IT applications in support of KM and taxonomy/content management concerns are not about central issues of knowledge management orientation, but rather are about techniques and tools for supporting such KM orientations. The development of these techniques and tools, however, is driven by the basic orientations and purposes themselves.

So, current content management, taxonomy, and portal application concerns are about supporting knowledge coordination and transfer applications. They are not yet about supporting knowledge making, production, and creation. This is true because first generation KM is still dominant, while Second Generation Knowledge Management (SGKM) (originating as a coherent orientation toward the subject somewhere in the period 1995–1999) is still in the process of taking hold. This point will become clearer as we get into the discussion of the Snowden and McElroy views on change in KM.

The Two Ages of Knowledge Management (with a Third Yet to Come)

According to Snowden (2002, 2) the first age of KM, prior to 1995, was about "the appropriate structuring and flow of information to decision makers and the computerisation of major business applications leading to a technology enabled revolution dominated by the perceived efficiencies of process engineering."

He calls this age "information for decision support." And his characterization of it, as the above quote implies, does not distinguish it from Business Process Reengineering (BPR). In fact, for Snowden, KM in the first age seems to be a species of BPR, which proceeded without recognition of knowledge gained through experience or person-to-person processes of knowledge transfer. Since it ignored these aspects of knowledge, Snowden thinks that the word knowledge itself became problematic in knowledge management by the end of the first age.

Snowden further contends (2002, 2) that the second age of knowledge management began in 1995 with "the popularisation of the SECI Model" after the publication of Nonaka and Takeuchi's *The Knowledge Creating Company* (1995). But he also says that "to all intents and purposes knowledge management started circa 1995" with the publication of this book. That statement, combined with his characterization of the first age as one of information for decision support, raises the question of why there is a first age in his change framework at all, or more properly, why his second age of knowledge management is not his first age.

The second age of KM, in Snowden's view, is characterized by a focus on the SECI model's four processes describing the conversion of knowledge from: explicit to tacit (socialization) tacit to explicit (externalization), explicit to explicit (combination), and tacit to tacit (internalization). He goes on to comment about the misunderstanding of Polanyi's (1958, 1966) views on the nature of the relationship between tacit and explicit knowledge that is prevalent in the second age, specifically that it was "dualistic, rather than dialectical," in contrast with both Polanyi's and Nonaka's understanding of the relationship. But he says little else about the second age, leaving the impression that there was little else to this age of KM.

DIFFICULTIES WITH THE TWO-AGES VIEW

Before moving on to Snowden's characterization of the coming third age of knowledge management, note that his description of the first two ages of KM leaves a lot of open questions. First, was there really no more to the first age of KM than "information for decision support"? If so, then why was the term KM used at all? After all, the field of business intelligence provides information for decision support. So do data warehousing and data mining. So does the still broader category of Decision Support Systems (DSS). So what was the term KM supposed to signify that those other terms do not?

Second, if there was no more than information for decision support to the first age, then what were the attempts to distinguish data, information, knowledge, and wisdom about? What was the development of Xerox's community of practice for the exchange of knowledge among technicians about? What was knowledge sharing at Buckman Laboratories in 1987 and 1992 (Rumizen 1998) about? Where does Hubert St. Onge's (see Stewart, 1999) work on the relationship of customer capital to the learning organization fit? Or Senge's (1990) work on systems thinking? Or Karl Wiig's early introductions to KM (1993, 1994, 1995)?

In brief, Snowden's characterization of the first age of KM as focused on providing information for decision support and implementing BPR schemes suggests much too heavy an emphasis on KM as primarily composed of IT applications to reflect the full reality of the first age. In fact, his failure to take account of the human side of KM during the first age suggests a desire for the same kind of neat distinction we find in Koenig's analysis. In effect, Snowden, like Koenig, seems to want to say that the first age was about technology and the second age was about the role of people in Nonaka's four modes of conversion.

Third, in describing the second age of KM, Snowden's account is, once again, far too spare in its characterization. No doubt the Nonaka and Takeuchi book has had an important and substantial impact on knowledge management, but the period since 1995 has seen important work done in many areas not explicitly concerned with knowledge conversion.

These areas include semantic network analysis, the role of complex adaptive systems theory in knowledge management, systems thinking, intellectual capital, value network analysis, organizational learning, communities of practice, content management, knowledge sharing, intellectual capital, conceptual frameworks for knowledge processing and knowledge management, knowledge management metrics, enterprise information portals, knowledge management methodology, and innovation, to name some, but far from all, areas in which important work has been done. Finally, as indicated by the title of Nonaka and Takeuchi's book, their concern, and a central concern of second generation KM as we shall see shortly, is about "knowledge creation," or knowledge production. It is only secondarily about knowledge conversion.

Nonaka mistakenly identified knowledge creation wholly with knowledge conversion. In our view, however, knowledge conversion only produces belief or psychological knowledge. In the area of producing organizational knowledge as a cultural product, the role of knowledge conversion is focused on only one subprocess in knowledge production: the subprocess of knowledge claim formulation. It doesn't address knowledge claim evaluation or validation, a critical subprocess in the creation of explicit, shared, culturally based knowledge.

Snowden's account of the coming third age of knowledge management is developed much more carefully in his work than his account of the other two ages. But it will be much easier to develop, understand, and critique his forecast of a third age if we provide the third view of change in knowledge management first, and along with it some additional comments on both the Snowden and Koenig interpretations of generations. We now turn to that task.

THE TWO GENERATIONS OF
KNOWLEDGE MANAGEMENT

The third perspective on the evolution of KM distinguishes between two "generations": first and second generation KM (first developed in McElroy 1999). According to this view, a distinction can be made between "supply-side" knowledge management, in which interventions are aimed at knowledge integration, or sharing, and demand-side KM, which is focused, instead, on knowledge production, or making. In the first case, the practice of KM is predicated on the assumption that valuable knowledge already exists; the purpose of KM, then, is to capture, codify, and share it. In the second, no such assumption is made. Before knowledge can be shared, much less captured and codified, it has to first be produced. Thus, supply-side KM focuses on enhancing the "supply" of existing knowledge to workers who need it, whereas demand-side KM seeks to enhance our capacity to satisfy our "demands" for new knowledge.

First generation KM, according to this view, was (and continues to be) supply-side only in its orientation. Second generation practice, however, is *both* supply- and demand-side oriented. Of crucial importance to this view of KM, then, is the contention that knowledge is not only something we share, but is also something we make. Indeed, we can only share knowledge that exists, and knowledge can exist only after it is created—by people.

A cyclical view of knowledge making and sharing—or, more generally, production and integration—therefore comes sharply into focus as a consequence of this third perspective. Rather than assume, as first generation thinkers do, that valuable knowledge already exists and that the sole task of KM is merely to enhance its distribution, second generation thinkers contend, as well, with the problem of knowledge production. It is because of this that second generation KM is more closely aligned with the fields of organizational learning and innovation management than the second age envisioned by Snowden.

Of additional foundational importance to this third view of KM is the distinction it makes between *knowledge processing* and *knowledge management*. This rather fundamental distinction is not made in either the Koenig or Snowden accounts of the evolution of KM. Knowledge processing is precisely the cycle referred to above, through which people in organizations, in response to problems arising in business processes, collectively engage in knowledge production and integration. Knowledge processes, therefore, are social processes through which organizations make and share their knowledge.

Knowledge management, on the other hand, is a management activity that seeks to enhance knowledge processing. Not all organizations support formal knowledge management functions, but all organizations do engage in knowledge processing. The purpose of KM according to this view is to enhance an organization's ability to perform knowledge processing, and ultimately by improving it to enhance the quality of its business process behavior and its ability to adapt to its environment.

Also central to the generational view of KM is the position that knowledge processing in human social systems is a self-organizing affair. That is, people in organizations tend to self-organize in emergent, pattern-like ways around the production and integration of knowledge. We can generally describe the shapes of these patterns using terms like problem detection, intrinsically motivated learning, group and community formation, communities of inquiry or practice, problem solving, knowledge evaluation and adoption, knowledge sharing, and so forth. That these activities are self-organizing and pattern-like in their appearance is explained with the aid of complexity and complex adaptive systems theories in the generational view of KM. Indeed, SGKM is deeply rooted in the application of complex adaptive systems theory to knowledge processing in human social systems, a perspective it applies backwards and forwards in its characterization of how KM has evolved over the years.

While the generational view of KM does point to two distinct bodies of practice that are supply-side on the one hand and demand-side on the other, it does not suggest that the second one started only after the first one ended. Rather, the two streams of practice are concurrent in use and will probably carry on in this way for some time to come.

Consider, for example, the field of Organizational Learning (OL), which is arguably focused on nothing if not demand-side knowledge processing. This is a field that clearly started long before KM (the term) came into fashion in the mid-1990s. The same can be said for the fields of Innovation Management (IM), Organizational Development (OD), and even Human Resources Development (HRD), which has always been concerned with the transfer of knowledge in the form of training and other knowledge sharing programs.

What we have, then, according to the generational view of KM, is two distinct bodies of practice that are separate in content but not necessarily in time. That said, the first generation of KM arguably began quite some time ago, even as early as the late nineteenth/early twentieth centuries with the work of Frederick Taylor (1912), whose scientific management system explicitly called for the capture, codification, and use of what we today would refer to as "best practices." This was supply-side KM in action, since its intent was to enhance knowledge capture and sharing. Later on in the twentieth century, work related to enhancing knowledge production began to appear. This took many forms, including the evolution of R&D and its various methodologies and management schemes, innovation management, organizational learning, and institutionalized science, which has always been concerned with the production of new knowledge. From this perspective, supply- and demand-side KM is more than 100 years old.

Despite this, the term "KM" is considerably younger in age. Its initial appearance in the mid-1990s was clearly tied to supply-side KM, and it wasn't until 1999 that the formal distinction between that sense of the term and the new, or second, sense was introduced using the supply-side/demand-side language. Indeed, it wasn't until McElroy (1999) and his colleagues at KMCI (Firestone 1999, 1999a, 1999b, 1999c) began to think of differences in KM practice as being somehow related to the separate and distinct notion of social knowledge processing that the combined form of supply- *and* demand-side KM was viewed as adding up to a new and unique body of practice (SGKM) deserving of special recognition.

So even though we can say that *both* supply- and demand-side KM were theoretically being practiced in various forms prior to the advent of "KM" as such in the 1990s; they were clearly *not* being practiced, much less compared to one another, in these terms. Nor were they being tied to a formal conceptual distinction between knowledge processing and KM. That dates from the end of the 1990s, following the advent of KM in the mid-1990s in its supply-side form.

Comparing this third view to the other two, we can see important differences. The Koenig view, as we have said, presents an ad hoc classification scheme in which the three "stages" of KM are based more on anecdote and personal observation than on any sort of underlying conceptual framework related to knowledge processing and how it is practiced. The third, generational view, by contrast, relies explicitly on a vision of social knowledge processing, against which all forms of practice in KM can be seen and understood. Indeed, it is SGKM that is associated with a formal articulation of this vision for just this purpose. That articulation is the knowledge life cycle framework, or KLC, as developed and refined by Firestone (Firestone 1999c, Firestone 2000, 2000a, 2000b, 2001, 2002), McElroy (1999, 1999a, 2000a, 2000b, 2002, 2002a, 2002b) and other members of the Knowledge Management Consortium International (KMCI) (Cavaleri and Reed 2000) over the past four years. The KLC framework is illustrated again in Figure 4.1.

Next, because the scope of the KLC is comprehensive in its representation of knowledge processing in human social systems, all forms of KM practice, both current and future ones, can be related to it. Everything we do in KM is designed to have impact on one or more elements of the KLC. A generation of KM, therefore, should not, according to SGKM, be defined in terms of a Koenig-like focus on practice types, tools, or trends. Indeed, such a definition risks losing sight of the central purpose of KM interventions and tools. The appearance and/or departure of different kinds or styles of interventions need not—and should not—have anything to do with our attempts to make sense of them in terms of what their basic purpose is.

What is of more fundamental relevance to analysis of the evolution of KM is what its practitioners are *trying to do*, not what their tools and methods are. Of course, we must be interested in tools and methods, too, but only after we've settled on a purpose, and used it to define the basic thrust of KM. Different flavors of tools come and go, but the purpose of KM is always to enhance knowledge processing.

SGKM's conceptual framework for knowledge processing gives rise to another important distinction between it and the Koenig view of stages. As stated earlier, the Koenig view seems to begin and end with an appreciation of the importance of taxonomy development and content management. Under this logic, the very next issue to pop up on the KM landscape would give rise to a fourth stage, a fifth one after that, and so forth. This is what happens when we define

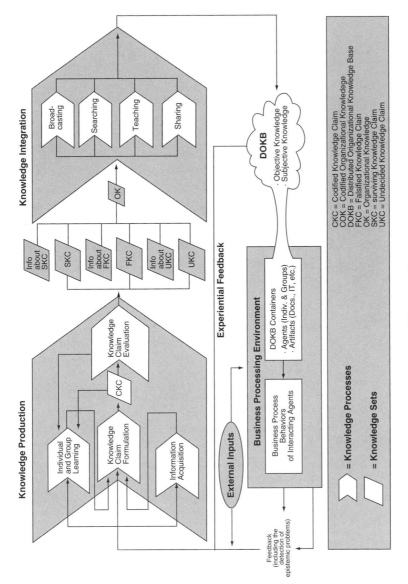

Figure 4.1

The Knowledge Life Cycle (KLC)

101

evolution from the perspective of tools and styles of interventions—each stage becomes too narrow, too tightly bounded, with nowhere else to go, driven by short-term problems and adaptations. Such a specification of stages is ad hoc and lacks depth of insight into what KM is ultimately trying to achieve or have impact on (i.e., to enhance knowledge processing).

By contrast, the third, generational view of KM is relatively free of bias toward intervention types or styles. According to the generational view, new tools and methods are constantly being created and tested, and there's nothing wrong with that. But what shouldn't (or doesn't) change along the way, except very infrequently, is the intended target of their use. Why? Because tools are used in the service of theory, and until such time as theory changes, no fundamental shift in thinking can be said to have occurred. That, and not fluctuations in tool sets or methods, must be the standard of evaluation. Practitioners of KM either seek to have an impact on knowledge production, knowledge integration, or both. Variations in the tools we use don't change such basic objectives.

In comparing the third, generational view of KM to that of Snowden's, the generational perspective can help us add to our earlier critique of his account of the first two ages of KM. First, his account seems to suffer from the same lack of an underlying conceptual framework used to organize his analysis of change.

In the first age, we are encouraged to envision individuals at work whose momentary needs from time-to-time require informational support. Then KM comes to the rescue (or is it IM?), delivers the information, and declares victory. In this view, there is no social system, only individuals. And in this view, there is only the momentary and discrete decision transaction that frames the backdrop for KM, thus failing to distinguish KM, as we pointed out earlier, from data warehousing, business intelligence, or DSS. From the perspective of the third generation view of KM, however, this is an act of knowledge integration (supply-side KM). But this only makes sense in the context of a more comprehensive knowledge processing framework that can help us distinguish knowledge integration from knowledge use. It is a distinction that Snowden does not make, but that is fundamental to first generation, supply-side KM.

In Snowden's second age we are suddenly thrust into the realm of knowledge conversion using Nonaka's SECI model as a reference. This is indeed an improvement over his first age, since his account of the second age characterization at least employs a conceptual framework—some vision of knowledge processing, which arguably goes on between individuals and other individuals, and between groups and individuals and other groups. Nonetheless, we are still left with a fairly narrow frame of reference and a failure to place the Nonaka model into a broader context of knowledge processing or a framework of KM concepts and practice.

This narrow frame of reference, of course, is determined by the scope of the SECI model that Snowden has selected to conceptualize the second age. In the SECI model, knowledge processing is reduced to four kinds of transactions—the "knowledge conversion" transactions reviewed earlier. In using this model as the basis of his second age, Snowden reduces all of KM practice between the years of 1995 and today to a concerted effort on the part of KM professionals to get these four transactions to work better.

Never mind the much broader scope of KM activity observable since 1995 and discussed earlier. Never mind that he takes us from "information delivery" in the first age to "knowledge conversion" in the second, without explaining the difference between information and knowledge in the transition, or why the SECI model is only about knowledge and not information. And never mind, for that matter, that the SECI model, since it, too, does not address this question, could just as easily be seen as a way of converting "misinformation" or "falsified knowledge" from one party to another. Or that it could be seen as a model for generating unvalidated knowledge claims rather than knowledge (Firestone 2000, 2001). Or that it fails to make the distinction among tacit, explicit, and *implicit* knowledge (see Chapter 1, Firestone 2001, 2002; Chapter 7), and not just between tacit and explicit knowledge.

Regarding the term "knowledge," Snowden tells us that it was not problematic at the beginning of the first age, but became so at its end because the first age did not recognize the character of knowledge that was embedded in social interaction and in minds. In the first age, then, we can infer that Snowden thinks that the terms "information" and "knowledge" were used loosely relative to one another, if not interchangeably. Knowledge in the second age, however, took on some special meaning, although he never really tells us what that is. Its special meaning is somehow tied in with the SECI model, the touchstone of the second age. Still, none of this would seem to support the assignment of "age" status to either period in Snowden's account. Why? Because even if we can agree to include the pre-1995 period in which he describes the handling of information and not knowledge at all, these distinctions, from a generational point of view are, like Koenig's ideas, nothing more than "a story" about evolution in tools and methods. They do not point to evolution in the underlying conceptual or analytical frameworks of KM and knowledge processing.

The generational view, on the other hand, has a much easier time of accommodating the phenomena just mentioned without having to resort to the declaration of new ages, stages, or generations. Indeed, they are all mainly about information and/or knowledge transfer or integration. Add them to a long list of other techniques aimed at enhancing knowledge sharing or transfer, and you're still left with one stream of practice: supply-side KM. Thus the generational view comprises a much broader framework than the SECI model, in that it incorporates all of the varied activities of KM practice listed earlier in this paper as occurring since 1995. In fact, SGKM is broad enough to include much, perhaps most, of the aspects that are supposed to distinguish Snowden's third age from SGKM itself. We'll explore this and other problems in the next section on Snowden's forecast.

Snowden's Forecast? A Third Age of KM

Snowden (2002) contends that the third age *will be* one in which:

- knowledge is viewed paradoxically as a thing and a flow;
- context, narrative, and content management will be central to our view of KM;
- there will be an understanding of organizations as engaged in sense making through utilization of complex adaptive systems phenomena constrained by human acts of free will attempting to order them; and
- scientific management with its mechanistic models will be applied to carefully selected targets where it is appropriate, while the outlooks of chaos and complexity theory will be applied to other targets and situations where they are appropriate.

There are a number of ways to look at this forecast. Let us start with its implicit factual claim that the present condition of KM is not characterized by the above attributes.

KM and Scientific Management

Is it true that KM does not now restrict scientific management and its mechanistic models to carefully selected situations where these may be relevant? We think the answer to this question is yes.

We don't know of a single writer on KM who endorses scientific management and its mechanistic models as the dominant approach to KM, and we know of many writers who explicitly reject the relevance of such an approach to most human-based interactions. These writers include: Allee (1997), Amidon (1997), Brown (1995), Brown and Duguid (1991, 2000), Carrillo (1998, 2001) Davenport and Prusak (1997), Denning et al. (1998), Denning (2001), Firestone (1999, 1999a, 2000, 2001), Kuscu, 2001, Leonard-Barton (1995), McElroy (1999, 1999a, 1999b, 2000, 2002), Senge (1990), Wheatley and Kellner-Rogers (1996), among many others. In short, it is simply false that third generation knowledge management, if there is to be one, will be unique in restricting mechanistic management models to only those situations in which they are relevant, since that restriction has already come to pass.

KM, Content Management, and Context

Is it true that KM is not now characterized by context, narrative, and content management, and that therefore this would be a distinctive development in a coming third age or generation of KM? In reviewing Koenig's views we have already pointed out that content management has been a concern in KM for some years now, and also that the 1998 combined KM World/AIIM conference held in Chicago had a major content management element. In fact, many vendors have long confused content management and knowledge management, as if there were nothing more to KM than that.

And since 1998, the ties between knowledge management and content management have grown stronger with the connection that is currently made between enterprise information portals (with substantial content management capabilities) and knowledge processing and KM. In our view, that connection is greatly overdrawn (Firestone 2003, Chaps. 15 and 17). But from Snowden's point of view, content management is at the heart of the third age of KM, even though it certainly has not been far from the attention of KM practitioners since the mid-1990s. Snowden in fact recognizes the close connection between content management and KM prior to the third age. He says (2002, 3):

> Stacey accurately summarises many of the deficiencies of mainstream thinking, and is one of a growing group of authors who base their ideas in the science of complex adaptive systems. That new understanding does not require abandonment of much of which has been valuable, but it does involve a recognition that most knowledge management in the post 1995 period has been to all intents and purposes content management.

So clearly, content management is not a *distinctive* characteristic of any forecasted third age.

Regarding context, Snowden's (2002) use of that term is not transparent. Linked as it is with content management (p. 3) by Snowden, our first interpretation was that he was mainly referring to context analysis in the context of content analysis and management. But his primary concern with context instead comes from the notion that (ibid.):

> . . . human knowledge is deeply contextual, it is triggered by circumstance. In understanding what people know we have to recreate the context of their knowing if we are to ask a meaningful question or enable knowledge use . . .

In other words, the knowledge people have that is directly related to knowledge use is the set of situational beliefs they use to perform acts. And these beliefs are not determined outside of situational contexts, but through the interaction of people with those contexts. Moreover—turning to Stacey (2001)—Snowden suggests that these beliefs (knowledge) are ephemeral, precisely because of their grounding in momentary experiences, or contexts. He seems to be saying that because experiences are fleeting, so, too, must knowledge evoked in the course of experiences be fleeting, as well. In any case, he is clearly suggesting that knowledge beliefs and use are at least partly determined as a function of situational contexts.

Now, as it happens, this last is not a new idea. It is one that has been well known in the social sciences for many decades, and has certainly been well known in social psychology for many, many

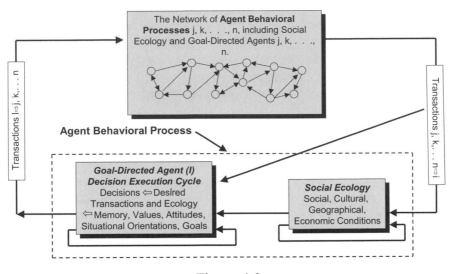

Figure 4.2
The Flow of Behavior Among Agents

years. Figure 4.2 illustrates the idea of an agent making decisions and engaging in transactions with other agents. The beliefs affecting behavior in the diagram are within the agent. The beliefs closest to behavior are the "sense" (Weick 1995, Haeckel 1999) that the agent has made out of the situation. The context is provided by the transactions directed at the agent and also by the social ecology box in the figure, including its physical, social, structural, and cultural components.

The process of interaction going on inside the agent may also be viewed as the decision execution cycle of the agent, illustrated in Figure 4.3. In the figure, sense making is represented by the step called "Monitoring."

Figure 4.4 provides the psychological context of the formation of situational knowledge and beliefs. It shows a hierarchy of psychological predispositions of any agent that are *aroused* by the external situational context, that form an internal psychological context, and that themselves affect the formation of contextual knowledge beliefs. This hierarchy, called an incentive system (Birch and Veroff 1966), produces a situational orientation of the agent. The availability and incentives represent the "sense" the agent has made of the situation.

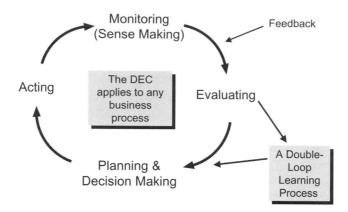

Figure 4.3
The Decision Execution Cycle

The situational incentive refers to the affective orientation produced by the predispositional hierarchy toward the situation. The behavior is the result of the goal-striving produced by the interaction of the availability, incentive, and affective components.

The notion presented in Figure 4.4 is oversimplified in that it ignores the overwhelmingly high probability that behavior in any concrete situational context will simultaneously be motivated by *more than one incentive system.* A contemplated action, in other words, may be associated with a likely outcome having multiple and either conflicting or reinforcing incentive values or value expectations for an agent. So the depiction of a single goal-striving tendency at the bottom of Figure 4.4, just prior to the discrete situational orientation, is incorrect. Instead, visualize a number of conflicting goal-striving tendencies, $G_1 \ldots G_n$, all firing in parallel, and take the resultant of these, along with the environmental stimuli, as affecting the discrete situational orientation.

Nor is this kind of conception of situational knowledge being formed in a context new to knowledge management. Firestone (2001) proposed this framework in an article explicating the notion of "subjective culture" for use in second generation KM. His development of this framework is not connected to any fundamental generational change beyond SGKM, but only to an attempt to strengthen its foundation by clarifying the role of knowledge as belief or belief

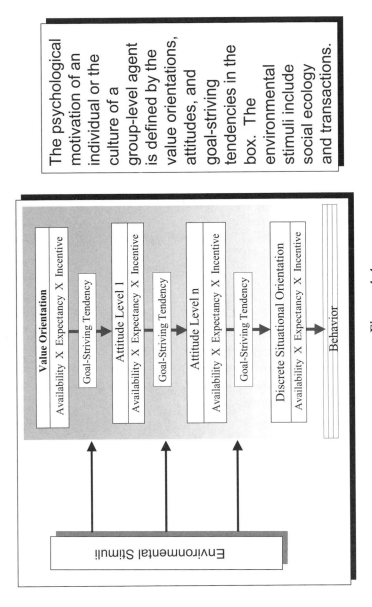

The psychological motivation of an individual or the culture of a group-level agent is defined by the value orientations, attitudes, and goal-striving tendencies in the box. The environmental stimuli include social ecology and transactions.

Figure 4.4
The Incentive System of an Agent

109

predisposition; knowledge as a cultural product; and culture, itself, in business, knowledge, and knowledge management processes.

If the notion of contextual knowledge is not, as Snowden implies, new to KM, is it true that his conceptual development of the idea of context, combining abstraction and culture, is significant enough that it should form the basis of a reorientation of KM and therefore a third age? We believe that the answer to this question is clearly no because:

- descriptions of context in terms of abstraction and culture are much too simple without much more detailed development of the framework;
- context alone neither comprises nor determines knowledge production and integration processes; and
- a revision in the idea of how to categorize context for purposes of description and analysis is not the kind of fundamental change in orientation that signals a new generation, or a new age.

Thus, why wouldn't such a change just fit into the second age? It may not do so, if one defines the second age, as Snowden does, as essentially one in which activity is focused on the SECI model, but if one takes the broader SGKM or TNKM point of view, changes in how we categorize or describe context for the purpose of affecting knowledge production and knowledge integration are just "par for the course" and involve nothing more than further development of the TNKM point of view, rather than a departure *from it* into a new generational outlook.

Knowledge: Process or Outcome?

Is it true that knowledge is not now viewed paradoxically as a thing and a flow and that this view needs to be adopted in order to get past the difficulties associated with viewing knowledge as a thing? Our answer to this challenge is to agree that "knowledge" is not now viewed paradoxically as both a thing and a flow, but also to state in no uncertain terms that to adopt such a view would not solve the problems of knowledge management, but rather would only deepen the degree of confusion and conflicts existing in the discipline.

Let us now examine our reasons for this conclusion by offering responses to some of Snowden's comments on the nature of knowledge as a process and then both a "thing" and a "flow."

Some of the basic concepts underpinning knowledge management are now being challenged: "Knowledge is not a 'thing,' or a system, but an ephemeral, active process of relating." (2002, 3).

Taken from Stacey (2001), this definition suffers from, or at least creates, a process-product confusion. It is fueled by a desire to focus on the dynamics of knowledge creation, rather than only on explicit codified outcomes or mental beliefs. However, we can do this without becoming confused just by distinguishing knowledge processes from knowledge products or outcomes. Knowledge processes are not any less important because we call them "knowledge processes" rather than "knowledge" (the "ephemeral active process of relating").

If we take the view that knowledge is a process, we can no longer talk about knowledge as embedded in cultural products, or even knowledge as beliefs or predispositions in minds. Or knowledge as "true" or "false," since processes are neither true nor false, but only existent or nonexistent.

Also, if we take this view, it doesn't account for the *content* of cultural products or beliefs or predispositions in minds. So we are left with the problem of finding words other than knowledge to describe these very real phenomena. The real question is: What do we gain by calling knowledge "an ephemeral, active process of relating"? What does it do for us? In our view it provides only additional confusion in a field that is already replete with it, because people insist on using words for their halo effect rather than for their descriptive value.

To us it seems clear that knowledge is not a process but an outcome of knowledge production and integration processes. In other words, we believe that knowledge should be viewed as a "thing," not as a process. We also believe that as specified elsewhere (Firestone 2001), knowledge is not a single thing but is divided into three types: physical, mental, and cultural. All are things, and more specifically are encoded structures in systems that help those systems to respond and adapt to changes in their environments.

Next, Snowden says (ibid.):

> ...mainstream theory and practice have adopted a Kantian epistemology in which knowledge is perceived as a thing, something absolute, awaiting discovery through scientific investigation.

To say knowledge is a thing may be Kantian, or sometimes even Platonist for that matter, but to label it in this way is not to criticize the idea on its merits. Furthermore, to say that knowledge is a thing is not to say that it is "absolute," or that it is "awaiting discovery through scientific investigation." That is, knowledge can be (a) a thing; (b) produced by social processes of many kinds, and not just processes of scientific investigation, much less awaiting discovery by the latter; and (c) also can be either false or true. So there is nothing "absolute" about it.

Snowden also says (ibid.):

> In the third generation we grow beyond managing knowledge as a thing to also managing knowledge as a flow. To do this we will need to focus more on context and narrative, than on content.

As far as the third generation (or *age*) being about managing knowledge as a flow is concerned, if by "flow" Snowden means knowledge processing, then we do not agree that this is distinctively third generation but think it is second generation KM and is at least a few years old now, as our discussion of SGKM above indicates. But is this, in fact, what he means by "flow"?

Again, Snowden says (ibid.):

> Properly understood knowledge is paradoxically both a thing and a flow; in the second age we looked for things and in consequence found things, in the third age we look for both in different ways and embrace the consequent paradox.

Here we see a shift in Snowden's view. As we saw above, he begins by characterizing knowledge as a process and creating a process-product confusion, but ends by claiming that it is both a "thing" and a "flow," thereby creating a process-product redundancy (to wit, flows *are* things), which he denies is a redundancy, treats as a seeming contradiction, and terms a "paradox." He then defends paradox, by pointing out that philosophers have learned much from paradox and also that physicists have had to live for many decades with the paradox that electrons are both particles and waves.

This is all very neat, but it is also very problematic: (1) philosophers have learned much from paradox, but this doesn't mean that paradox in the definition of knowledge is good for KM, especially if there is no paradox. (2) It is not true that physicists have concluded that electrons are both particles and waves. Rather, electrons are things that may be described using a particle model under certain conditions and a wave model under others. The reason why there is no contradiction or paradox in this view is that physicists know enough not to claim that electrons are both waves and particles, but that they are a third thing entirely. Indeed, this is the key lesson embodied in the Heisenberg uncertainty principle.

And (3), and most important, Snowden hasn't established the need to call knowledge both a thing and a flow and thereby embrace paradox, contradiction, or redundancy, much less another age of KM founded on paradox. All we need do, instead, as we in fact have done in SGKM, is to say that knowledge is an outcome or product (thing) that is produced by human social processes (process). Thus we have the ability to deal with both dynamics and outcomes in such a conceptualization, an ability that has always existed in systems theory.

So, the effort to establish knowledge first as a process, and then as a "thing" and a "flow," is not persuasive to us. It seems to offer no advantages that the process-product view of SGKM is not already delivering. On the other hand, it offers the disadvantages of logical contradiction, redundancy, or, perhaps, paradox, if one accepts Snowden's assertion, that can only lead a third generation founded on it into unnecessary confusion and perplexity. Our conclusion is that we don't need such a third generation, but that what we do need to do is to continuously tighten the conceptual foundations of SGKM and continue to develop its program of research and practice.

Sense Making, Complex Adaptive Systems, and the Third Age

Is there already an understanding in knowledge management of organizations as engaged in sense making through utilization of complex adaptive systems phenomena constrained by human acts of free will attempting to order them? Or is this a distinctive feature that might provide the foundation for a third generation of KM?

Recognizing the role of complex adaptive systems phenomena in human organizations, "sense making" and knowledge production is very important in understanding the emergence of organizational behavior, organizational knowledge predispositions, organizational learning, and organizational intelligence from interactions among organizational agents. But whether or not recognition of the importance of CAS phenomena and their interaction with purposeful knowledge management interventions creates the need for a new KM generation depends very much on one's view about previous generations.

If you accept Snowden's view that the second age of KM is about knowledge conversion and the Nonaka/Takeuchi program alone, and that it (a) did not focus on knowledge processing, (b) had no emphasis on the situational character of knowledge, (c) is committed to development of mechanistic models of knowledge management, and (d) did not recognize the role of CAS in knowledge processing and knowledge management, then to declare the need for a new generation may make sense. But if you view SGKM, as we do, as a professional discipline developing since 1995 to:

1. emphasize the distinctions among knowledge, sense making, knowledge processing, knowledge management, business outcomes, business processing, and business management;

2. add a focus on knowledge production (rather than just knowledge conversion) and sustainable innovation to a previous focus on knowledge integration;

3. arrive at a conceptual framework that emphasizes the situational character of sense making and belief knowledge; that breaks knowledge production and knowledge integration into subprocesses; that identifies knowledge management activities and their targets in knowledge processing; that makes clear the link between knowledge processing, explicit knowledge production, belief knowledge production, and knowledge use; and that relates all of this to the situational context of sense and decision making and organizational learning cycles;

4. recognize patterns of knowledge processing that emerge from CAS-based interaction tempered by KM initiatives;

5. recognize that KM initiatives must be synchronized with CAS phenomena in order to succeed;

6. deny the relevance of mechanistic management models for knowledge management;

7. emphasize the central role of knowledge claim evaluation (or validation) in KM;

8. emphasize the important role of communities of practice in mobilizing CAS-based interaction and contributing to both knowledge production and knowledge integration;

9. recognize the role of culture in providing a context for knowledge processing and knowledge management;

10. emphasize a coherent theory of knowledge that distinguishes it from data, information, and wisdom;

11. develop a systematic approach to knowledge and KM-related metrics;

12. place the role of information technology in context as an enabler of knowledge processing and KM processing;

13. recognize a model of intellectual capital that sees social innovation processes as an aspect of such capital; and

14. develop and use methodology that incorporates all of the above elements and that is oriented toward problem solving;

then you may feel that everything that is distinctive and useful in Snowden's forecasted third age already exists in the second generation, that is, in TNKM. So from the point of view of TNKM, there is no third age and no need for one.

But even if all of the above is correct, what about Snowden's Cynefin model? Doesn't it suggest that a third age is upon us?

The Cynefin Model and Its Problems

Our treatment of the Cynefin model will be detailed and follows the following pattern: We summarize a bit of the model and then present commentary and criticism. We then repeat this pattern until the analysis is complete. We then offer a summary of the whole discussion and some general perspectives.

The Model: The Cynefin model uses the distinctions between the poles of the context dimensions: high and low abstraction, and teaching and learning cultures to initially create four types. In Snowden's words (2002, 6):

> Cynefin creates four open spaces or domains of knowledge all of which have validity within different contexts. They are domains not quadrants as they create boundaries within a centre of focus, but they do not pretend to fully encompass all possibilities.

The Cynefin model not only specifies four open spaces or domains of knowledge. It also views those spaces (Snowden, 2002, Figure 2) as common sense-making environments.

Commentary: The first problem with the Cynefin model is with the specification of the two context dimensions used to formulate it: culture and abstraction.

Snowden bases his concept of culture on Keesing and Strathern's (1997) work. They distinguish between the sociocultural system (what people do and make) and the ideational system (or what people

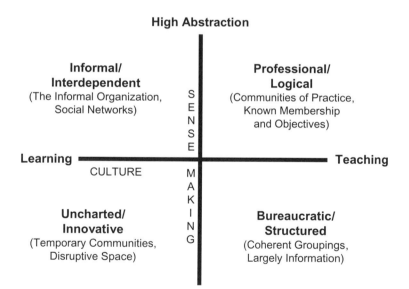

Figure 4.5
The Cynefin Model: Cultural Sense Making (Adapted from David Snowden, 2002)

learn) as two different types of culture. Snowden, however, also notes that the first type of culture is teaching culture and the second type of culture is learning culture. In forming the Cynefin model he then uses the dimension teaching/learning to define an aspect of variation among sense-making environments.

Now, the problem with this is the gross oversimplification of the Keesing/Strathern distinction between the two types of culture. The two types are based on numerous dimensions in Keesing and Strathern, not on the distinction between teaching and learning. To suppose that the teaching/learning distinction is all that is meaningful in the notion of culture for specifying sense-making environments is to make a wildly optimistic and obviously incorrect assumption.

The second context dimension (high/low abstraction) is also specified inadequately by Snowden. Snowden (2002) does not define what he means by abstraction. In Snowden (2000) he comes closer to defining abstraction in the following passage:

> Such communities are working at a high level of abstraction. Abstraction is the process by which we focus on the underlying constructs of data. As Boisot (1998) admirably demonstrates, the process of abstraction is focused on concepts, not percepts. Percepts ". . . achieve their economies by maintaining a certain clarity and distinction between categories, concepts do so by revealing which categories are likely to be relevant to the data-processing task" or information creation. "Abstraction, in effect, is a form of reductionism; it works by letting the few stand for the many."

But this definition of "abstraction" is still unclear. Specifically, we now know that abstraction is a process, but we don't know (from Snowden's account) what we actually do when we abstract and we don't know what "high abstraction" and "low abstraction" mean to Snowden in sense-making environments. We do receive the further information in both Snowden articles that level of abstraction is inversely related to cost of disembodiment or codification. But this idea seems to imply that abstraction is an outcome (actually an attribute of information) rather than a process, as Snowden has designated it in the above quote. In short, we don't know what Snowden means by abstraction. So it's very difficult to evaluate his description of common sense-making environments in terms of high/low abstraction.

The above considerations immediately call into question the Cynefin model. If we have no clear idea of what is meant by "abstraction," and if the distinction between teaching and learning cultures oversimplifies contextual variations due to culture, then how are we to understand the relation of these dimensions to common sense-making environments?

The Model: In Snowden's Figure 2, the domains are labeled "Common Sense Making," so that each of the four constitutes a distinctly different environment for sense making.

Commentary: Snowden's immediate purpose in constructing Cynefin was to specify four distinct sense-making environments that sense makers encounter in their everyday experience in organizations. But is sense making really the primary goal of knowledge processing? And is it the same thing as knowledge production?

Undoubtedly, sense making is an important activity. According to Figures 2, 3, and 4, sense making is a critical step in the decision execution cycle underlying all action and all business process behavior including knowledge process behavior. But sense making, business processing, and knowledge processing are not equivalent. This lack of equivalence raises the question of where sense making stands in relation to knowledge management. Knowledge management is management of knowledge processing and its immediate knowledge outcomes, and business management is management of business processes, generally, and their outcomes. Since sense making is a part of all business process behavior, it falls under the general purview of business management rather than knowledge management, unless the sense making in question is specifically tied to decision execution cycles comprising the various subprocesses of knowledge production and knowledge integration.

This argument raises the question of the specific relevance of a sense-making model such as Cynefin to knowledge processing and knowledge management. Of course, it has *some* relevance to knowledge processing and knowledge management. Both areas are areas of business process behavior, and so both, at the lowest level of decision making and acting involve sense making. But sense making is only one activity in the DEC, and, in addition, patterns of sense making don't speak directly to the dynamics of knowledge subprocesses such as information acquisition, individual and group learning, knowledge claim formulation, and knowledge claim evaluation, and the various knowledge integration subprocesses. So at most even a good model of sense making would not be broad enough in its relevance to define the scope of knowledge management in its third age.

On the other hand, since sense making relates to all decision making through the DEC, a good model of sense making will add to our theoretical and practical understanding of the actions that are the foundation of knowledge processing and knowledge management. So sense making models certainly have a place in providing a better understanding of the decision-making foundation of SGKM processes.

Here is the first of the four environments:

The Model: bureaucratic/structured; teaching, low abstraction

This common sense-making environment emphasizes formal organization, policies, rules, procedures and controls. Snowden emphasizes the explicit, open nature of language, training, and the corporate intranet as important features. He also points out that "its shared context is the lowest common denominator of its target audience's shared context" (2002, 6). In other words, the level of abstraction characterizing the shared context of communications is low.

Commentary: Here, Snowden does not explain why an ideal type of bureaucratic/structured, learning and high abstraction, would not be equally useful as a common sense-making environment—or, for that matter, why the other two ideal type variations based on the teaching/learning and high abstraction/low abstraction dichotomies, bureaucratic/structured, learning and low abstraction, and bureaucratic/structured, teaching and high abstraction, should not also be selected. In other words, he provides no explanation why he settled on the above pattern as the only sense-making environment *within* the bureaucratic structured category. In other words, he doesn't explain the logic behind his specification of the above specific bureaucratic/structured sense-making environment as one of his four primary types of common sense-making environments.

Here is the second of the four environments:

The Model: professional/logical; teaching, high abstraction

This common sense-making environment is characterized by a high level of abstraction in the shared context for communications. It is also characterized by professional individuals, expertise, training, specialized terminology, textbooks, communities of practice, and "efficient knowledge communication," especially among experts.

Commentary: A similar comment can be provided here as we offered for the bureaucratic/structured types. Why specify teaching/high abstraction along with professional/logical? Could not professional/logical sense-making environments involve both learning and low abstraction as well as teaching and high abstraction? Or other combinations of these categories? Of course they can. Do other combinations make sense? We don't know, but we do know that the rationale presented by Snowden for the type he prefers is not clear to us and, we suspect, to other readers as well.

Here is the third of the four environments:

The Model: informal/interdependent; learning, high abstraction

This environment has a high level of abstraction in the shared context of experiences, values, symbol structures, and beliefs. It is focused on the informal organization and its "network of obligations, experiences and mutual commitments." It is also characterized by trust, voluntary collaboration, storytelling, the ability of symbolic languages to efficiently convey large amounts of information through reliance on highly abstract symbol associations, and shared symbol structures. This information can include "simple rules and values that underlie the reality of that organization's culture" (Snowden 1999).

Commentary: Again, the pattern specified by Snowden is not the only pattern that can be specified for informal/interdependent sense-making environments. In particular, we think that low abstraction in the shared context of experiences, values, symbol structures, etc., is also possible in such environments, as is teaching.

Further, the specification that an informal/interdependent environment is characterized by trust and voluntary collaborations is certainly only one possibility. Informal/interdependent sense-making environments may also be characterized by mistrust and socially coerced collaboration, as well. Of course, such a sense-making environment may be less effective at sense making than the one specified by Snowden. But we don't know that yet based on research, while we do know that expectations based on simple ideal types are often frustrated by complex reality.

Here is the fourth of the four environments:

The Model: uncharted/innovative; learning, low abstraction

This environment presents entirely new situations to an organization. It is "the ultimate learning environment," and it is characterized by low abstraction in the shared context of communications among agents in this common sense-making environment.

> Here we act to create context to enable action, through individuals or communities who have either developed specific understanding, or who are comfortable in conditions of extreme uncertainty. Such individuals or communities impose patterns on chaos to make it both comprehensible and manageable (ibid.).

Commentary: Is this really the perfect learning environment? Why would one think that one can learn better without context than with it? This would be true only if one assumes that context is always more constraining than chaos. But certainly this is not always true. In a very real sense, chaos may be the best *un*learning environment, the opposite of what Snowden suggests. Further, why is the environment characterized by low abstraction? If it is truly uncharted, then decision makers can create their own context, with a level of abstraction appropriate to them.

The Model: Snowden tells us that the Cynefin model we have just outlined is based on the distinctions among chaotic, complex, and complicated systems. By complicated systems he means those systems whose cause-and-effect structure is either known or knowable. By complex systems he means those with coherent structures and processes whose cause-and-effect structure cannot be known and whose global behavior is emergent, but which is not explainable in terms of a system's components and their relationships. By chaotic systems he means those systems in which "all connections have broken down and we are in a state of turbulence or eternal boiling."

Commentary: We believe that this typology of systems is incomplete, and that human social systems are not Natural Complex Adaptive Systems (NCASs), such as insect social systems, but Promethean Complex Adaptive Systems (PCASs). That is, we find CAS behavior in them, but such behavior is moderated by the continuous efforts of human agents to create predictable structures that serve their interests. These efforts use normative processes that attempt to simulate cause-and-effect sequences by treating humans as if they are objects that will respond to prescribed stimuli in prescribed ways. However, the behavioral processes corresponding to these normative processes are not processes in complicated systems; rather, they are "complex" processes, always subject to human adaptation and innovation in the face of changing conditions. So PCASs follow neither CAS, nor complicated, nor chaotic patterns, but rather their own patterns that oscillate constantly between different states of relative complexity.

Also, we need to note at this point that the boundary between complicated and complex systems is not hard and fast in the sense that it is obvious when a system belongs to one class or the other. To be a CAS or a PCAS, rather than a complicated system, it is necessary that a system not be "knowable." However, a system that today seems unknown or unknowable may tomorrow be knowable or known. So we can never say for certain that a particular type of system fits into one category or another.

The Model: After introducing these distinctions Snowden asserts that these three system types "map on to the Cynefin model." Chaotic systems map on to the uncharted/innovative common sense-making environment; complex systems map on to the informal interdependent environment; and complicated systems map on to either the professional/logical or bureaucratic/structured environments, depending on whether the targets of decision making are "knowable" complicated systems, or "known" complicated systems.

Commentary: Snowden does not explain the above mappings and it's not at all obvious that they make sense, or even what he means by "mapping." Does he mean to say that the bureaucratic/ structured sense-making environment is a known system? Or that the professional/logical sense-making environment is a "knowable" system? Or that the informal/interdependent sense-making environment is a complex system? Or that the uncharted/innovative sense-making environment is a chaotic system? If that is the meaning of "mapping," it seems invalid on its face, because all organizational sense-making environments are part of a single system, the organizational system. And that system is a type that we have previously called a PCAS. Its nature cannot be changed by interpreting sense-making *environments* as though they were autonomous systems without risking serious misunderstanding of the dynamics of the organizational system.

Indeed, Stacey (1996, 184) himself makes this point in the following passage, in which he discusses the possibility (or not) of human agents being able to separate themselves from the organizational environments of which they are a part in their attempts to manage the creative dynamics of human social systems:

> Do human consciousness and self-awareness somehow enable us to alter the dynamics of the systems that we are a part of and that we constitute with each other when we interact?
>
> At the level of the organization, as at the levels of the individual mind and the group, the answers to these questions must be no. First, it is extremely difficult for members of an organization to sustain enough emotional distance from their roles as participants to also operate as observers. . . . Even when we manage to reflect collectively on the organization we are a part of, we are still not able to alter the fundamental dynamics of that system.

An alternative interpretation and the one we favor because it is most in accord with the interaction philosophy at the base of sense making (see Weick 1995, Smythe 1997), is that Snowden is seeking to correlate his previous construction of sense-making types in the Cynefin model with the types of target systems that each of these environments is most suited for, in terms of the likely success of sense-making activities in these environments in "making sense" of the target systems and successfully dealing with them over time. In other words, this second interpretation is that the sense-making environment Snowden is talking about is comprised of the interaction between a Cynefin sense-making type and one of the four types of target systems he specifies. Such a relationship is illustrated in Figure 4.6. But even though this interpretation initially seems most plausible, further consideration indicates that it, too, would indicate an error by Snowden.

Why should we, for example, use an uncharted, innovative sense-making environment to make sense of a chaotic system? It seems to us that any sense-making environment would work, so long as through it we can recognize that the system that is the target of our sense-making efforts is, in fact, a chaotic system. Similarly, why should an informal, interdependent sense-making environment be necessary to decide that a target system we are interested in is, in fact, a complex system?

So if the second interpretation is correct, Snowden seems to have fallen prey to a subject/object confusion of the organization and the target system that is the object of its sense making. If that's true,

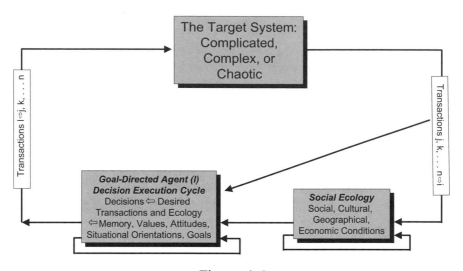

Figure 4.6
An Interactive Sense-Making Environment

then no mapping of the type of the target system to the type of sense-making environment can be taken at face value, and Snowden needs to explain why other mappings of sense-making environments to target systems (e.g., professional/logical to complex systems) are not equally valid.

The Model: Snowden next develops the Cynefin model by associating various characteristics with the four Cynefin sense-making environment/system type combinations. Known space (the domain of bureaucratic structured/teaching/low abstraction/known systems) is associated with best practices, the ability to predict behavior, to prescribe specific policies, and a "feudal" leadership style. Snowden also thinks that people can transform complex or chaotic systems into known systems "through laws and practices that have sufficient universal acceptance to create predictable environments." Once these known systems are created, decision making can proceed by categorizing incoming stimuli and responding "in accordance with predefined procedures" (Snowden 2002, 8).

Commentary: Why should "known space" be associated with a feudal leadership style? Evidently this hypothesis is based on the notion that since the target system in known space is complicated, one needs a bureaucratic/structured sense-making environment governed by feudal leadership, because this is the only type of sense-making environment capable of understanding a complicated known system. Surely this is an instance of the confusion of subject and object in mapping the original Cynefin model onto the systems typology used by Snowden.

Snowden also thinks that known systems can be created from chaotic or complex ones through instituting laws, policies, procedures, etc. All we have to say to that hypothesis is, "Good luck." Known systems cannot be created by fiat. Rather, a known system is a real system that is successfully described by some cause-and-effect theory we have developed. If no such cause and effect structure can be formulated, then normative human social processes cannot substitute for such a structure. Rather, the result of imposing laws and structures on complex systems is a Promethean CAS, not a known system. More likely, it's a dysfunctional PCAS.

As for the idea that chaotic systems may be transformed through leadership into knowable or known systems, this idea is also confused. That is, if a system is really a chaotic system, there are no cause-and-effect relationships that are understandable within it. So how can human agency have any predictable effect on such a system without destroying it? Indeed, is a chaotic system even a system, if its patterns are not understandable even after the fact?

The Model: Knowable space (the domain of professional/logical/teaching/high abstraction/knowable systems) is associated with good practice, expert explanations and predictions of behavior, expertise-enabled management by delegation, codification of expert language, entrainment of thinking, oligarchic leadership based on community "elders," and sensing and responding based on expert understanding. In knowable space, as in known space, humans impose order. But here the order is more "fluid" than in known space. To manage this space, it is necessary to periodically disrupt the body of expert knowledge and shared context, because it can be a barrier to the creation and growth of new knowledge.

Commentary: Why is "knowable space" associated with "entrainment of thinking" to a greater extent than known space? Are professional/logical environments more vulnerable to closed-mindedness than bureaucratic/structural environments? We doubt it. Why is oligarchic leadership necessary to make sense of knowable space? Clearly, it's not. Why should "knowable space" imply that professional/logical sense-making environments using experts, rather than informal/interdependent sense-making environments using knowledge workers, are necessary to make sense of them?

Why are periodic disruptions of the social structures of knowable space necessary to ensure continued effective sense making in this space? The need for periodic disruptions is connected to the assumption that the content of knowledge is determined by an elite that supports a dominant paradigm that in turn controls the growth of knowledge. But what if knowledge production in an organization doesn't work that way? What if knowledge claim evaluation works through continuous testing and evaluation and openness in the evaluation process? What if knowledge is not developed based on consensus, but emerges through a continuous and open evaluation and testing process? This open enterprise model of knowledge production (McElroy 2002, Chap. 1, Firestone and McElroy 2002) would not need periodic disruptions to function well, because it is always open to new ideas. In fact, disruption would not improve knowledge production in such a system. Instead, it would disrupt the functioning of the open knowledge production process and might result in a system of Kuhnian paradigms (Kuhn 1970) supported only by consensus, a system that would require periodic disruption.

The Model: Complex space (the domain of informal/interdependent/learning/high abstraction/complex systems) is associated with self-organization, global pattern emergence, fluidity, stability at the edge of chaos, and emergent leadership based on natural matriarchal or patriarchal authority and respect. Here, according to Snowden, managers should recognize pattern formation early and manage patterns by stabilizing some and disrupting others based on goals, objectives, and values. They may even "seed the space" in hopes of encouraging desirable patterns. But prediction of emergent patterns is not possible in complex space. In this space, agents cannot sense and respond. They must probe first to stimulate and/or understand patterns. Only then can they sense and respond successfully.

Commentary: We agree that leadership in complex space is emergent, but it is also true that in a PCAS emergent leadership must contend with imposed leadership. Also, what is the significance of the comment that emergent leadership in complex space is matriarchal or patriarchal? Is Snowden saying something more here than that such leaders may be either female or male? If so, what?

Also, note the very Promethean tenor of Snowden's comments about complex space. The idea that we can disrupt some patterns and reinforce or stabilize others, and even seed still others suggests scientific management. Since, according to Snowden, we cannot predict emergent patterns in complex space, our ability to predict the outcome of our Promethean interventions is also problematic.

Even if we probe first "to stimulate and understand patterns" and then sense and respond, we don't know whether or not our response will stimulate emergent responses from the system that are unintended. In other words, the possibility of emergent side effects in complex systems suggests care in intervening and a search for as much cause-and-effect, statistical, and expert assessment knowledge about the system as we can muster. We should always keep in mind that something we've categorized as a complex system, may not, in fact, be one. Continued attempts to analyze complex systems as if they are "knowable" are therefore rational, if only to establish the degree to which they are not knowable.

The Model: *Chaos* (the domain of uncharted/innovative/learning/low abstraction/chaotic systems) is associated with lack of structured linkages among components, unpredictable, unfathomable connectivity among these components, and tyrannical or charismatic leadership. According to Snowden, chaotic systems require active crisis management, lead to the disruption of entrained thinking in managers, require regular immersion to "immunize" organizations against chaotic systems, and can be used to advantage if leadership can impose order without loss of control. Snowden also thinks "that what to one organization is chaotic, to another is complex or knowable." Management must proceed in this domain by acting and only then sensing and responding.

Commentary: Why do chaotic systems require active crisis management? Such systems cannot be understood and their behavior cannot be predicted. That is their nature. So why should crisis management of such systems work? Also, how can we immunize ourselves against chaos by immersing ourselves in such systems? Each chaotic system is unique and lacks a cause-and-effect structure. Would repeated exposures to multiple chaotic systems make the next chaotic system any less chaotic or unpredictable? We don't think so. So how can familiarity with them help us to cope?

Snowden also seems to believe in the relativity of chaos to the perspective of the organization beholding it. But this is certainly an unfortunate way of speaking. Surely, systems are either chaotic or not. It is our models of real systems that may vary, so that sometimes we mistake complex or knowable systems for chaotic ones. And what we thought was chaos is therefore either at its edge or even orderly. Finally, does it really help management, as Snowden suggests, to act before sensing and responding to chaotic systems? If they really lack causal structure and are not subject to emergent patterns, then how can our acting first result in a better foundation for sense making and responding? Such systems should be equally unfathomable and uncontrollable regardless of how we proceed through time.

The Model: A central tenet of Snowden's third age proposal is his contention that knowledge will be viewed, paradoxically, as both a thing and a flow. In his first reference to knowledge as flow, Snowden states that "Complex adaptive systems theory is used to create a sense-making model that utilises self-organising capabilities of the informal communities and identifies a natural flow model of knowledge creation, disruption and utilisation." (Snowden 2002, 1). Later on in his discussion of the first age of KM prior to 1995, he says that the focus was on "the appropriate structuring and flow of information to decision makers" (ibid., 2). Next, in what appears to be a reference to flow, he quotes Stacey (2001) as saying, "Knowledge is not a 'thing,' but an ephemeral, active process of relating" (ibid., 3).

Later on, Snowden refers to flow in terms of the movement of knowledge in his discussion of the dimension of Abstraction in his Cynefin model as follows: "The upper and lower levels represent the range of shared context and therefore the range of possible knowledge flow" (ibid., 4). He goes on to say that both forms of culture he depicts in his model are "key to the flow of knowledge within an organization. We need to transfer to new members, in both the society and the organization, knowledge that has been painfully created at cost over previous generations" (ibid., 5).

Finally, in a subsection of his paper entitled "The Natural Flow of Knowledge," Snowden says, "We can now see the sensible pattern of flow of knowledge within an organization," a claim he makes following his presentation of a view of the Cynefin model in which flows are depicted between his four domains. He summarizes his perspective on knowledge flow as follows: "From this perspective we see knowledge as flowing between different states, with different rules, expectations and methods of management" (ibid., 12).

Commentary: Given the importance of the view of knowledge as "flow" to both Snowden's third age and the Cynefin model, it is critical to understand what he means by the term, and why he claims it is paradoxical in relation to the view of knowledge as a "thing." Earlier we noted the confusion caused by this language by pointing out that flows *are* things. Putting that aside, however, we fail to see either the claimed contradiction between the terms in this case, or the paradox between them.

To say that knowledge is something that flows, as most of his statements above would suggest, is not to invoke a contradiction at all or even a paradox. On the other hand, if Snowden were to claim that knowledge is both a thing that does *not* flow, on the one hand, and a thing that *does* on the other, then we would indeed have a contradiction or a paradox. But this does not seem to be what he is saying at all. Rather, what he seems to be saying is that *knowledge flows*—not that knowledge *is* flow, but that it (as a "thing") is subject to movement. With this we agree. But where's the paradox in that?

Another possible interpretation of Snowden's claims about knowledge as flow is that he's really not talking about knowledge at all. Rather, he's talking about a process whose outcomes are knowledge (i.e., learning and innovation). But here we encounter, once again, the product/process confusion we covered before. The flow *of* knowledge (process) should not be regarded *as* knowledge. Both are things but they are not the *same* things. The flow of knowledge occurs between various stages (or states) in the processes of knowledge production and integration, but to say that knowledge flows between the stages of a process is not to say that knowledge *is* a flow.

Turning to other sources for what "flow" could possibly mean to Snowden in this context, we see the term heavily used in two fields closely related to Knowledge Management. One is Complex Adaptive Systems (CAS) theory, a bedrock of Snowden's own hypothesis, and the other is System Dynamics, a closely related field in which the nonlinearity of complex systems is modeled and studied.

To CAS theorists, flows are movements of things between nodes and across connectors in networks (Holland 1995, 23). In Holland's treatment of this subject, he states: "In CAS the flows through these networks vary over time; moreover nodes and connections can appear and disappear as the agents adapt or fail to adapt. Thus neither the flows nor the networks are fixed in time. They are patterns that reflect changing adaptations as time elapses and experience accumulates." (Holland 1995, 23). Now, if this is what Snowden (and Stacey) mean by "ephemeral, active process[es] of relating," (Snowden 2002, 3), again, we fail to see the paradox and see only confusion instead. Holland and other CAS theorists are not claiming that the things that flow across ephemeral networks are the same things as the ephemeral networks themselves. A sharp distinction between the two is made with no paradox involved, nor any need for one. And so we fail to see how the use of the term "flows" in the literature on CASs could be used to support Snowden's claim of a paradox in the view of knowledge or the Cynefin model.

In the System Dynamics arena, "stocks and flows" are central to the lingua franca of the field. Flows in System Dynamics refer to streams of things (which are otherwise held in "stocks") moving at different rates of speed and with different degrees of frequency, with or without delays. But flows *as* things are never confused with the things that they carry. And so here again, we fail to see how the historical use of the term "flows" necessarily leads to any sort of contradiction or paradox.

In sum, while Snowden purports to use the term "flow" as a noun (as in, knowledge *is* flow) in his definition of knowledge, his actual use of the term in his discussion seems confined to its use as a verb (as in, *knowledge flows*). Thus, he never manages to deliver a satisfactory definition for knowledge as flow. On the other hand, to the extent that he implies that flow may be a *process*, the process he refers to is arguably one that produces and/or transfers knowledge, but which is not the same *as* knowledge itself. For all of these reasons, we find Snowden's claim of a paradox in the third age definition of knowledge to be unpersuasive and full of confusions.

The Model: What Snowden's Cynefin model seems to be most fundamentally about is the dynamics of knowledge production and transfer in organizations. As discussed immediately above, this seems to be the thrust of his use of the term flows, although in most cases he seems to be talking more about transfer than production, an understanding which is encouraged by his graphical representation of flows across the boundaries contained in his model (Snowden 2002, Figure 4, p. 9). This seems clearly intended to depict the flow of knowledge (things) from one Cynefin domain to another.

In further support of this view, many references in Snowden's account of the flows within and between his four domains can be found in his description of the model, including the following statement (ibid., 10):

In the third generation, we create ecologies in which the informal communities of the complex domain can self-organize and self-manage their knowledge in such a way as to permit that knowledge to transfer to the formal, knowable domain on a just in time basis.

Elsewhere, he makes similar repeated references to identifying and codifying knowledge, conveying it, transferring it, communicating it, and sharing it. Separately, he refers to knowledge creation, sense making, pattern forming, learning, and innovation—all presumably references to knowledge production, not knowledge sharing or transfer.

Commentary: When viewed from the generational view of KM (McElroy 1999, 2003), Snowden's emphasis on knowledge flows within and across the Cynefin model (sharing and transfer) seems decidedly supply-side in its orientation. Separately, his lesser emphasis on knowledge production would seem to be demand-side in focus. If this is true, what Snowden is attempting to say is that knowledge production and integration are both social processes which occur in different organizational settings, or ecologies, the awareness of which by managers should trigger different styles of interventions and oversight to cope with their effects. But if this is the case, what's the difference between Snowden's account of the coming third age of KM and the second generation of KM that was first identified (McElroy 1999) and articulated four years ago? Further, from a second generation KM point of view, why should we view the Cynefin model as anything other than a personal and parochial depiction (or theory) of knowledge processing that can easily be accommodated within the existing framework of the second generation KLC framework?

Indeed, Snowden's implicit claim that people in organizations tend to self-organize around the production and integration of knowledge is part and parcel of the KLC framework first articulated four years ago—as was the intentional and careful application of CAS theory to KM. Similarly, the view that behavioral patterns in knowledge processing form as a consequence of such self-organizations, and that they tend to oscillate between order, chaos, and complexity was also explicitly embraced in the second generation view of KM developed four years ago. And finally, the notion of choosing management interventions on the basis of awareness of all of this is an idea that first appeared in 1999 (McElroy, ICM speech, April

1999a), and which later led to at least one formally defined method (McElroy and Cavaleri patent, 2000, The Policy Synchronization Method).

So even the idea of crafting management policies with the intention of synchronizing them with the self-organizing patterns of social knowledge processing behaviors in organizations is at least three years old, and is very much a part of second generation thinking. On the basis of all of this, then, we continue to see no compelling reason to accept the claim that a new age in KM is upon us. What is upon us, perhaps, is a new model, formulated in a highly questionable and confusing fashion, that fits within the conceptual framework of second generation thinking, but not a new conceptual framework that would suggest the arrival of a new generation, stage, or age.

Cynefin Conclusions

The Cynefin model is an elaborate construct full of implications and hypotheses, but it is (1) also full of many difficulties and confusions, and (2) as presented by Snowden it does not provide the conceptual framework one needs to compare his coming third age of KM to the first two. We will consider this second conclusion in the next section in a more general context. Here we note the many questions we raised about the Cynefin model in almost every detail. In our view the model should only survive if its foundations are formulated much more rigorously and systematically. The following is a summary of our conclusions about Snowden's Cynefin model:

- ■ The reduction of the concept of cultural variation to the teaching/learning dichotomy should be abandoned even if it costs Snowden his four-category classification of common sense-making environments. Simplicity and ease of exposition to executives desperately trying to understand knowledge management must give way to reality in modeling sense-making environments.
- ■ The concept of abstraction needs to be clarified so its meaning is clear to readers.
- ■ If there are more than four types that can be composed out of the Cynefin fundamental attributes (as is indicated by our questions about alternative sense-making environments that may

have been specified), they should be presented by Snowden. A classification framework must be evaluated as a whole, so that we can better understand the principles behind it. It should not be presented by describing only the categories its author thinks are important, because the unimportant categories may contain important insights that either reinforce or call into question the whole framework. Snowden's mention of, and decision to overlook, his fifth domain in the middle of the Cynefin model is unfortunate in this regard.

- The number of systems used to describe sense-making environments should increase. The existence of PCASs suggests that Snowden's system classification is incomplete. But even if one declined to explore the "mapping" of system types on to sense-making environments, it is very clear that Snowden's four types exhaust only a fraction of the logical possibilities suggested by his underlying concepts, and he provides no reasons for restricting Cynefin to his initial selection of four types.
- The confusion between subject and object in talking about sense-making environments should be clarified, and the one-to-one mapping of system to Cynefin categories should be abandoned.
- The many small questions we have raised above on issues such as how leadership correlates to the different types should be answered.
- The concept of "knowledge as flow" needs to be clarified so its meaning is clear to readers, especially the sense in which its meaning supposedly leads to the paradox claimed by Snowden. Short of that, the "paradox" claim should be abandoned.
- The degree to which the Cynefin model constitutes a material or conceptual departure or evolution from the currently existing (and previously developed) articulation of second generation KM, if at all, should be demonstrated. Short of that, the Cynefin model should be seen as nothing more than a particular, and evidently highly questionable, expression of second generation thinking, the essence of which has already been widely articulated (Albors 2001, Allee 1997, Kelly and Allison 1999, Bennet and Bennet 2000, 2001, Carrillo 1998, 2001, Cavaleri and Reed 2000, 2001, Courtney, Chae, and Hall 2000, Firestone 1998, 1999, 1999a, 1999b, 1999c, 2000, 2000a,

2000b, 2001, 2001a, 2001b, 2002, Kuscu 2001, Loverde 2001, McElroy 1999a, 1999b, 2000a, 2000b, 2001, 2002a, 2002b, 2003, McMaster 1996, Murray 2000).

Even if all of the above points were met and the Cynefin model were made more multidimensional, it could still not serve as the basis for a new generation of knowledge management. The reason for this is that Cynefin is about sense making and decision making; it is not a general conceptual framework that can function as an intellectual umbrella for all activities in the field of KM. Instead, it illuminates one corner of the concerns of KM, the corner that deals with the foundations of (and immediate precursors to) action. It is an important corner, even a fundamental one. But it does not provide a framework for approaching knowledge production and integration, or the role of knowledge claim evaluation in knowledge production, or knowledge management, or KM-related metrics, or sustainable innovation, or a comprehensive information technology system supporting KM, or KM software evaluation, or intellectual capital, or the type of enterprise that will support accelerated sustainable innovation, or many other subjects that are important for the emergent discipline that is KM.

CONCLUSION: THE THREE STAGES, THE THREE AGES, THE TWO GENERATIONS, AND COMPARATIVE FRAMEWORKS

Perhaps the most important differentiator between the three views of change in KM we have analyzed here is the methodology used to analyze change in the three instances. Basically, Koenig and Snowden take a storytelling approach to analyzing changes in the KM evolutionary process, whereas McElroy bases his case for fundamental change on the KLC knowledge processing framework and the distinction between knowledge processing and KM.

Koenig takes an IT approach to KM and basically tells a *story* of changes in IT-related concerns. Thus, he starts by noting that the first stage of KM was about using the Internet for knowledge sharing and transfer. The second stage was a reaction to the failure of the first to live up to its promise by failing to take account of human factors essential to make IT applications successful, and the third stage is about improving the IT side by making it easier for humans to navigate to the information or knowledge they want or need.

This story of changes occurring in response to a desire to make IT-based KM solutions successful does not specify a conceptual framework based on concepts of knowledge, KM, business processing and outcomes. Lacking such a framework, Koenig has no tool to compare the three stages of KM in order to evaluate the comprehensiveness of change in its key elements. That is why his analysis seems ad hoc and questionable from the standpoint of whether the changes he records are really so fundamental as to suggest new stages in the KM evolutionary process.

The situation is little better with Snowden's approach. Boiled down to its essentials, he almost seems to be saying:

- the first age was about applying the BPR notions of Hammer and Champy (1993) on a foundation of Taylor (1912);
- the second age was about applying the vision expressed in Nonaka and Takeuchi (1995);
- the coming third age will be about applying the vision expressed in his own Cynefin model, coupled with Stacey's notions about the paradoxical character of knowledge, and expanded through its synthesis with the Cynefin systems typology.

So, Snowden's story of change is not guided by a conceptual framework providing us categories setting a context for describing change, but rather is a claim that KM proceeds from vision to vision expressed in great books and/or articles. His view provides no guide about what the next fundamental change in KM will bring, because how can we know what the rest of a story might be?

McElroy's (1999) approach to change uses the conceptual framework of the Knowledge Life Cycle (KLC) to analyze the change in KM that he believes suggests there have been two and only two generations so far. The KLC framework clearly distinguishes knowledge production and knowledge integration processes as the two processes comprising knowledge processing behavior. In turn, these fundamental processes are divided into four subprocesses for each process. Figure 4.1 above provides enough detail to allow one to recognize that knowledge processing activities are clustered in either the knowledge production or knowledge integration categories and that KM initiatives have also primarily been concerned with either one or the other. Once that recognition was made it was easy to see that the early period of formal KM, from the early 1990s to at least 1999, has primarily been about knowledge integration, and that SGKM, the *fusion* of concern about knowledge integration with knowledge production, begins only in the late 1990s and is first explicitly formulated against the backdrop of the Knowledge Management Consortium International (KMCI), including the authors' prior works (Firestone 1998, 1999, 1999a, 2000, and McElroy 1999, 1999a, 1999b).

The SGKM "paradigm" of fusion between supply- and demand-side KM now exists alongside the continuing practice of supply-side KM, which is still dominant in the field. But the growing concern with innovation in corporate, government, and intellectual capital circles suggests that further fundamental change in KM is unlikely until there is a much wider embrace of demand-side problems. If, however, fundamental change were to occur, the KLC framework suggests that it will revolve around a reconceptualization of knowledge processing, involving a specification of some new fundamental process in addition to knowledge production and integration, or perhaps a fundamental reconceptualization of knowledge production or knowledge integration processes. The fact that neither the Koenig nor Snowden views of change focus on such an evolution in how we see knowledge processing explains why the changes they focus on do not add up to a new stage, age, or generation of KM.

REFERENCES

Albors, G.J. (2001), "Knowledge Creation in an SME Environment", *Knowledge and Innovation: Journal of the KMCI*, *1*, *no. 2*, 145–160.

Allee, V. (1997), *The Knowledge Evolution: Expanding Organizational Intelligence*, Boston, MA: Butterworth–Heinemann.

Amidon, D. (1997), *Innovative Strategy for the Knowledge Economy: The Ken Awakening*, Boston, MA: Butterworth–Heinemann.

Bennet, A. and Bennet, D. (2000), "Characterizing the Next Generation Knowledge Organization," *Knowledge and Innovation: Journal of the KMCI*, *1*, *no. 1*, 8–42.

Bennet, A. and Bennet, D. (2001), "Exploring Relationships in the Next Generation Knowledge Organization," *Knowledge and Innovation: Journal of the KMCI*, *1*, *no. 2*, 91–109.

Birch, D. and Veroff, J. (1966), *Motivation: A Study of Action*, Belmont, CA: Brooks/Cole.

Boisot, M. (1998), *Knowledge Assets*, Oxford University Press.

Brown, J.S. (1995), "The People Are the Company," *Fast Company*, **1**.

Brown, J.S. and Duguid, P. (1991), "Organisational Learning and Communities of Practice," *Organisation Science*, March, 40–57.

Brown, J.S. and Duguid, P (2000), *The Social Life of Information*, Cambridge, MA: Harvard Business School Press.

Carrillo, F.J. (1998), "Managing Knowledge-Based Value Systems", *Journal of Knowledge Management*, **1, No. 4** (June), 280–286.

Carrillo, F.J. (2001), "Meta-KM: A Program and a Plea", *Knowledge and Innovation: Journal of the KMCI*, **1, no. 2**, 27–54.

Cavaleri, S. and Reed, F. (2000), "Designing Knowledge Generating Processes", *Knowledge and Innovation: Journal of the KMCI*, **1, no. 1**, 109–131.

Cavaleri, S. and Reed, F. (2001), "Organizational Inquiry: The Search for Effective Knowledge," *Knowledge and Innovation: Journal of the KMCI*, **1, no. 3**, 27–54.

Courtney, J., Chae, B. and Hall, D. (2000), "Developing Inquiring Organizations," *Knowledge and Innovation: Journal of the KMCI*, **1, no. 1**, 132–145.

Davenport, T. and Prusak, L. (1997), *Working Knowledge: How Organizations Manage What They Know*, Boston, MA: Harvard Business School Press.

Denning, S. (2001), *The Springboard, How Storytelling Ignites Action in Knowledge-era Organizations*, Boston, MA: KMCI Press/Butterworth Heinemann.

Denning, S. et al. (1998), *What Is Knowledge Management?* Washington, DC: World Bank.

Firestone, J.M. (1998), "Knowledge Management Metrics Development: A Technical Approach," *Executive Information Systems White Paper*, Wilmington, DE, June 25, 1998. Available at http://www.dkms.com/White_Papers.htm.

Firestone, J.M. (1999), "Enterprise Knowledge Management Modeling and Distributed Knowledge Management Systems," *Executive Information Systems White Paper*, Wilmington, DE, January 3, 1999. Available at http://www.dkms.com/White_Papers.htm.

Firestone, J.M. (1999a), "The Artificial Knowledge Manager Standard: A Strawman," *Executive Information Systems KMCI Working Paper No. 1*, Wilmington, DE, Available at http://www.dkms.com/White_Papers.htm.

Firestone, J.M. (1999b), "Enterprise Information Portals and Enterprise Knowledge Portals," *DKMS Brief*, *8*, *Executive Information Systems, Inc.*, Wilmington, DE, March 20, 1999.

Firestone, J.M. (1999c), "The Metaprise, the AKMS, and the Enterprise Knowledge Portal," *Working Paper No. 3*, *Executive Information Systems, Inc.*, Wilmington, DE, May 5, 1999, Available at: http://www.dkms.com/White_Papers.htm.

Firestone, J.M. (2000), "Accelerated Innovation and KM Impact." *Financial Knowledge Management* (Q1, 2000), 54–60.

Firestone, J.M. (2000a), "Knowledge Management: A Framework for Analysis and Measurement," *White Paper No. 17*, *Executive Information Systems, Inc.*, Wilmington, DE, October 1, 2000, Available at: http://www.dkms.com/White_Papers.htm.

Firestone, J.M. (2000b), "Enterprise Knowledge Portals: What They Are and What They Do," *Knowledge and Innovation: Journal of the KMCI*, *1*, *no. 1*, 85–108. Available at: http://www.dkms.com/White_Papers.htm.

Firestone, J.M. (2000c), "Enterprise Knowledge Portals and e-Business Solutions," *White Paper No. 16*, *Executive Information Systems, Inc.*, Wilmington, DE, October 1, 2000, Available at: http://www.dkms.com/White_Papers.htm.

Firestone, J.M. (2001), "Key Issues in Knowledge Management", *Knowledge and Innovation: Journal of the KMCI*, *1*, *no. 3*, 8–38. Available at: http://www.dkms.com/White_Papers.htm.

Firestone, J.M. (2001a), "Knowledge Management Process Methodology", *Knowledge and Innovation: Journal of the KMCI*, *1*, *no. 2*, 85–108. Available at: http://www.dkms.com/White_Papers.htm.

Firestone, J.M. (2001b), "Enterprise Knowledge Portals, Knowledge Processing and Knowledge Management," in Ramon Barquin, Alex Bennet, and Shereen Remez (eds.) *Building Knowledge Management Environments for Electronic Government*, Vienna, VA: Management Concepts.

Firestone, J.M. (2003), *Enterprise Information Portals and Knowledge Management*, Boston, MA: KMCI Press/Butterworth–Heinemann.

Firestone, J.M. and McElroy, M.W. (2002), Certified Knowledge and Innovation Manager (CKIM) Level I Course Notes (Section on the Open Enterprise available from the authors).

Haeckel, S.H. (1999), *Adaptive Enterprise*, Boston, MA: Harvard Business School Press.

Hammer, M. and Champy, J. (1993), *Re-engineering the Corporation*, New York, NY: HarperBusiness.

Holland, J.H. (1995), *Hidden Order*. Reading, MA: Addison-Wesley.

Keesing, R. and Strathern, A. (1997), *Cultural Anthropology: A Contemporary Perspective (3rd edition)*, Belmont, CA: Wadsworth.

Kelly S. and Allison, M.A. *The Complexity Advantage* (New York, NY: Business Week Books/McGraw-Hill, 1999).

Koenig, Michael E.D. (2002), "The third stage of KM emerges," *KMWorld* **11, no. 3** (March, 2002), 20–21, 28.

Kuhn, T. (1970), *The Structure of Scientific Revolutions. 2nd Edition*, Chicago, IL: University of Chicago Press, (1970 edition).

Kuscu, I. (2001), "An Adaptive Approach to Organisational Knowledge Management", *Knowledge and Innovation: Journal of the KMCI*, **1, no. 2**, 110–127.

Leonard-Barton, D. (1995), *Wellsprings of Knowledge*, Boston, Harvard Business School Press.

Loverde, L. (2001), "Intellectual Capital: An M & A Approach," *Knowledge and Innovation: Journal of the KMCI*, **1, no. 3**, 58–88.

McElroy, M.W. (1999), "The Second Generation of KM." *Knowledge Management* (October 1999), pp. 86–88.

McElroy, M.W. (1999a) ICM Speech in Miami, FL, April 1999: "The Knowledge Life Cycle, An Executable Model for the Enterprise." Available at http://www.macroinnovation.com/images/KnlgLifeCycle.pdf.

McElroy, M.W. (1999b) "Double-Loop Knowledge Management," *Systems Thinker* (October 1999, Vol. 10, No. 8), pp. 1–5.

McElroy, M.W. (2000) "Using Knowledge Management to Sustain Innovation," *Knowledge Management Review* (Sept./Oct. 2000, Vol. 3, Issue 4), pp. 34–37.

McElroy, M.W. (2000a), "Integrating Complexity Theory, Knowledge Management, and Organizational Learning," *Journal of Knowledge Management* Vol. 4 No. 3 (2000), pp. 195–203.

McElroy, M.W. (2000b) "The New Knowledge Management," *Knowledge and Innovation: Journal of the KMCI* (October 15, 2000, Vol. 1, No. 1), pp. 43–67.

McElroy, M.W. (2001), "Where Does KM Belong? A Better Solution," *Knowmap: The Knowledge Management, Auditing and Mapping Magazine* (Vol. 1, No. 4, 2001) (www.knowmap.com).

McElroy, M.W. (2002a), "Social Innovation Capital," *Journal of Intellectual Capital* (Vol. 3, No. 1, 2002), pp. 30–39.

McElroy, M.W. (2002b) "A Framework for Knowledge Management," *Cutter IT Journal* (March 2002, Vol. 15, No. 3), pp. 12–17.

McElroy, M.W. (2003), *The New Knowledge Management: Complexity, Learning, and Sustainable Innovation*, Boston, MA: KMCI Press/Butterworth–Heinemann.

McElroy, M.W. and Cavaleri, S.A. (2000), "Policy Synchronization Method", Patent application filed with the U.S. Patent and Trademark Office in September 2000.

McMaster, Michael D. (1996), *The Intelligence Advantage: Organizing for Complexity*, Boston, MA: Butterworth–Heinemann.

Murray, A.J. (2000), "Knowledge Systems Research," *Knowledge and Innovation: Journal of the KMCI*, **1, no. 1**, 68–84.

Nonaka, I. (1991), "The Knowledge-Creating Company," *Harvard Business Review*, November–December.

Nonaka, I. and Takeuchi, H. (1995), *The Knowledge Creating Company.* New York, NY: Oxford University Press.

Polanyi, M. (1958), *Personal Knowledge*, Chicago, IL: University of Chicago Press.

Polanyi, M. (1966), *The Tacit Dimension*, London, UK: Routledge and Kegan Paul.

Rumizen, M. (1998), "How Buckman Laboratories 'shared knowledge' sparked a chain reaction", The Journal for Quality & Participation *1*, 34–38.

Senge, P. *The Fifth Discipline: The Art & Practice of the Learning Organization.* New York, NY: Currency Doubleday, 1990.

Smythe, E. (1997), "Life in Organizations: Sensemaking or Appreciation? A Comparison of the Works of Karl Weick and Geoffrey Vickers," "Unpublished draft", available at:
http://mis.commerce.ubc.ca/smythe/weick.pdf.

Snowden, D. (1999), "Liberating Knowledge" Introductory chapter to *Liberating Knowledge* CBI Business Guide, Caspian Publishing October 1999.

Snowden, D. (2000), "Cynefin: a sense of time and space, the social ecology of knowledge management", in *Knowledge Horizons: The Present and the Promise of Knowledge Management,* ed. C. Despres & D. Chauvel. Butterworth Heinemann October 2000.

Snowden, D. (2002), "Complex Acts of Knowing; Paradox and Descriptive Self-awareness", *Journal of Knowledge Management*, **6, no. 2** (May) 1–14.

Stacey, R.D. (1996), *Complexity and Creativity in Organizations*, San Francisco, CA: Berrett-Koehler.

Stacey, R.D. (2001), *Complex Responsive Processes in Organizations: Learning and Knowledge Creation*, New York, NY: Routledge.

Stewart, Thomas (1999), *Intellectual Capital: The New Wealth of Organizations*, New York, NY: Currency Doubleday.

Taylor, F. (1912), Testimony at Congressional hearing, January 25, 1912.

Weick, K. (1995), *Sense Making In Organisations*, Beverly Hills, CA: Sage Publications.

Wenger, E. (1999), "Communities of Practice: The Key to Knowledge Strategy," *Knowledge Directions: The Journal of the Institute for Knowledge Management*, 48–63.

Wheatley, M. and Kellner-Rogers, M. (1996), *A Simpler Way*, San Francisco, CA: Berrett-Koehler Publishers.

Wiig, K. (1989), *Managing Knowledge: A Survey of Executive Perspectives*, Arlington, TX: Schema Press.

Wiig, K. (1993), *Knowledge Management Foundations—Thinking about Thinking—How People and Organizations Create, Represent, and Use Knowledge*, Arlington, TX: Schema Press.

Wiig, K. (1994), *Knowledge Management: The Central Focus for Intelligent Acting Organization*, Arlington, TX: Schema Press.

Wiig, K. (1995), Knowledge Management Methods: Practical Approaches to Managing Knowledge, Arlington, TX: Schema Press.

Chapter 5

Knowledge Claim Evaluation: The Forgotten Factor in Knowledge Production

Introduction

A lot of attention is paid to acquiring, formulating, distributing, retrieving, and sharing knowledge claims in Knowledge Management, but little attention is devoted to how they are tested and evaluated. Knowledge claim evaluation (KCE), at least in the field of Knowledge Management, is the forgotten factor in knowledge production. In this chapter, we develop a viewpoint on knowledge claim evaluation and discuss how it is and may be carried out. We cover:

- where knowledge claim evaluation fits into knowledge production
- the kind of knowledge produced by knowledge claim evaluation

142

- a framework for describing knowledge claim evaluation
- an approach to evaluating knowledge claim evaluation
- knowledge claim evaluation software

WHERE KNOWLEDGE CLAIM EVALUATION FITS INTO KNOWLEDGE PRODUCTION

KCE is the subprocess of knowledge production that produces both World 3 organizational knowledge and World 2 (belief) feedback to the participants in knowledge production at the organizational level. It is a behavioral subprocess in which agents interact with one another to consider and evaluate previously formulated knowledge claims. The subprocess, like other subprocesses in the KLC, is composed of many Decision Execution Cycles (DECs), which, in their turn, combine into tasks, task patterns, and eventually the subprocess itself.

All the subprocesses in knowledge production are necessary for completing it. But KCE is the only subprocess that distinguishes knowledge production from information production in that it is not necessary for information production, while it is for knowledge production. And as we saw in Chapters 1 through 4, its outcomes are the only ones that distinguish knowledge from information and allow us to lower our risk in decision making, because its outcomes distinguish information that has survived our tests from information that has not and information about which we are undecided. So in a sense, knowledge claim evaluation is the very foundation of, and should be the first priority of, knowledge management, since if it is badly performed, its outcome will be higher risk and erroneous information, rather than higher quality knowledge claims that have survived our attempts at testing and evaluation.

Moreover, since knowledge claim evaluation determines what knowledge is for any agent, including an organization, it also determines what is to be integrated into the organization during knowledge integration, the second primary process in the KLC. In short, knowledge claim evaluation is at the very center of knowledge processing and is also at the core of the distinction between The New Knowledge Management (TNKM) and the earlier first generation of KM. It is knowledge claim evaluation, after all, that provides the basis for distinguishing knowledge from information and for removing the difficulty, characteristic of first generation KM, of distinguishing knowledge management from information management.

Knowledge claim evaluation is also the focal point of the distinction between Second Generation Knowledge Management (SGKM) and TNKM. SGKM views knowledge production as one of the key processes in knowledge production, and also views KCE as the key subprocess in knowledge production. However, SGKM is not necessarily oriented toward error elimination and falsification as the basis of KCE. Other approaches for validating knowledge claims, such as consensus-based or authority-based schemes, are alternatively taken by competing schools of SGKM thought. In contrast, TNKM takes a Popperian approach to KCE and views error elimination and falsification as the heart of the matter.

THE KIND OF KNOWLEDGE PRODUCED BY KNOWLEDGE CLAIM EVALUATION

As we indicated in Figure 4.1, KCE produces World 3 Organizational Knowledge—more specifically, linguistic expressions that have survived testing and evaluation. Figure 5.1 presents a classification of the outcomes of KCE. There are six categories of outcomes illustrated in the figure: Falsified Knowledge Claims (FKC), Undecided Knowledge Claims (UKC), Surviving Knowledge Claims (SKC), and information (actually, meta-information or metaclaims) about knowledge claims in each of the first three categories. These categories, characteristic of TNKM, reflect a falsificationist and error-elimination perspective because they reflect logically possible outcomes from knowledge claim testing and evaluation. Thus, the emphasis is on testing and evaluating knowledge claims and on embracing only those claims that survive our testing. These are World 3 knowledge.

This classificatory representation is only one among many that could be used for knowledge outcomes. Fuzzy set representations comparing knowledge claims are one alternative representation (Firestone 1998), as is a ratio scale (ibid.) of the extent to which knowledge claims have been falsified. We prefer the simple classification here, because knowledge claim evaluation in real organizations is largely qualitative in most situations and, at least in the beginning, consideration of knowledge outcomes as categories is

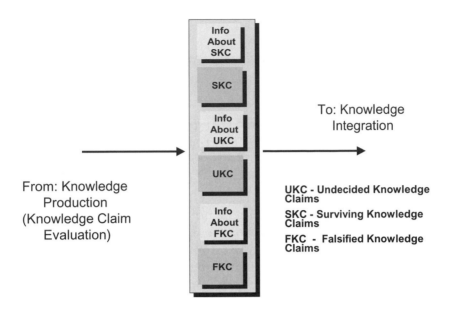

Figure 5.1
New Organizational Knowledge (Artifact-Based)

precise enough for most purposes. We need to be clear, though, that the simple categorization suggested above is not the only comparative framework available, and that especially at the boundaries of the SKC, UKC, and FKC sets, classification will be somewhat arbitrary.

In addition to producing new organizational knowledge, KCE also produces both World 2 and World 3 knowledge for those agents involved directly in it. At the organizational level, this means that any teams, groups, departments, or individuals participating in KCE not only produce organizational knowledge (see Figure 4.1), but also are affected by their experiences and specifically by the transactions they receive and the environment they must deal with in the course of their participation in KCE and in their own DECs that contribute to the KCE. This immersion in the process (see Figures 1.4, 1.5, 2.7, 2.8, and 2.9) produces new World 2 and World 3 knowledge for the agents at the same time it produces contributions to KCE at the organizational level.

To understand this clearly, think about the DECs that comprise the KCE process. Like any other DECs, they are the focus of *single loop learning* and also the initiators of *double loop learning* processes by the agents performing the DECs. Such learning processes produce the new World 2 and World 3 knowledge at the agent level we mentioned just above.

A FRAMEWORK FOR DESCRIBING KNOWLEDGE CLAIM EVALUATION

The key subprocess that distinguishes knowledge production from information production is knowledge claim evaluation. It is the subprocess of criticism of competing knowledge claims, and of comparative testing and assessment of them, that transforms knowledge claims from mere information into tested information, some of which survives our organizational tests and attempts at error elimination and therefore becomes, from the organizational point of view, knowledge.

In other words, the difference between information and knowledge is testing and evaluation of knowledge claims (World 3), or testing and evaluation of beliefs (World 2). Testing and evaluation of knowledge claims is public and sharable in the sense that the claims themselves are sharable and the tests and their results are sharable. That is why we say that World 3 knowledge is objective. Testing and evaluation of beliefs, however, is private and personal. It is this difference that makes World 2 knowledge subjective.

Knowledge claim evaluation is not the same thing as justification. Justification is the process of proving that a knowledge claim is true. KCE never *proves* anything with certainty. It simply provides (a) a record of how well competing knowledge claims stand up to our tests or (b) personal experience of how well competing beliefs stand up to our tests. Justification of knowledge claims and beliefs is impossible, but evaluation of them is not.

Since KCE is just our process of testing and evaluating knowledge claims or beliefs, *the practice of it will vary* across individuals, groups, communities, teams, and organizations. A particular entity may use evaluation practices based on explicit rules or specified criteria to compare knowledge claims, but it need not. Agents are free to change their tests or criteria at any time, to invent new ones, or to apply ad hoc tests and criticisms in evaluation. That is, KCE is a free-for-all; it is just the process by which knowledge claims and beliefs run the gauntlet of our skepticism and our criticism.

Looking at knowledge production from the viewpoint of agents at different levels of organizational interaction, and keeping the role of knowledge claim evaluation in mind, it follows that individual and group learning may involve knowledge production from the perspective of the individual or group, but from the perspective of the enterprise, what the individuals and groups learn is information, not knowledge. Similarly, information gathered through information acquisition may be knowledge from the perspective of the external parties it is acquired from, but not knowledge to the enterprise acquiring it, until it has been evaluated and has survived its tests.

Figure 4.1 also illustrates that knowledge claim evaluation has a feedback effect on individual and group learning. This occurs because individuals and groups participating in knowledge claim evaluation are affected by their participation in this process. They both produce World 3 organizational knowledge in the form of codified and evaluated knowledge claims, and also experience change in their own beliefs (i.e., they generate World 2 knowledge) as an outcome of that participation.

Knowledge Claim Evaluation: Specific

Knowledge claim evaluation is a subprocess of knowledge production in which knowledge claims are subjected to competitive testing and evaluation against alternatives with reference to organizationally held criteria, perspectives, and frameworks to determine the value and veracity of knowledge claims. It is critical in distinguishing knowledge processing from information processing, because it is the only subprocess that is necessary for knowledge processing but not information processing—all other subprocesses in the KLC are common to both.

The evaluation and testing process in real organizations is not a cut-and-dried process in which fixed knowledge claim rivals take prescribed tests and are evaluated against static criteria or fixed rules. Instead, knowledge claim evaluation in organizations is a vortex in which many competing knowledge claims are considered simultaneously against criteria, perspectives, and frameworks that are often being reweighted, reformulated in various ways, and even introduced to or expelled from the decision execution cycles of KCE.

Surviving, falsified, and undecided knowledge claims *emerge* from this vortex of conflict and collaboration in a manner that is not predictable from any simple model. An organization may develop and try to develop and apply a fixed process to be used by agents for knowledge claim comparison and evaluation, so that we can sensibly describe a normative knowledge claim evaluation value network. But the actual KCE subprocess will vary from this normative pattern and will present to the analyst and modeler a CAS pattern of emergence (Holland 1998).

Knowledge Claim Evaluation Contexts

Knowledge claims may be tested and evaluated in the context of interaction with any of the following internal organizational sources:

- Interpersonal peer communications including those found in communities of practice
- Interpersonal expert communications including those found in communities of practice meetings
- E-mail messages
- Web documents
- Web-accessed databases
- Non-Web accessed databases
- Web-enabled communications in communities of practice
- Web-enabled collaborative applications
- Media (CDs, tapes, etc.)
- Printed documents

We offer the above list to emphasize that there are many types of contexts of KCE, but there is little knowledge about the relative effectiveness of each type or combinations of them in supporting KCE interactions. The effectiveness of the context will depend upon the predispositions, situational orientations, and situational contexts that characterize interaction in that context and the nature of the interactions themselves (see Chapters 1, 2, and 4). The predispositions, in particular, must support knowledge claim evaluation and testing. If they constrain it unduly, then the interactions that result partly from them will be ineffective in producing successful KCE. This brings us to process descriptors.

Process Descriptors

Descriptors of KCE are classified into process descriptors, infrastructure descriptors, and knowledge claim descriptors. This section will present the process descriptors of the framework:

- KCE cycle time: every act, sequence of acts, task, etc., in the KLC or any of its subprocesses, such as the KCE, takes time. We refer to the time involved as the cycle time. An increase in efficiency is synonymous with a decrease in cycle time. But increasing efficiency in KCE may conflict with its effectiveness in distinguishing knowledge from information, and specifically may lower it. Everyone is familiar with the trade-off between efficiency and effectiveness. It is expressed in such homilies as "haste makes waste" and "in the long run we're all dead." But in KCE, this trade-off is particularly sensitive, since the desire for efficiency can easily lead to inadequate testing and evaluation and to the survival of a disproportionate number of false knowledge claims. So attempts to decrease cycle time should be sensitive to side effects on effectiveness and other aspects of the KCE subprocess.
- KCE velocity and acceleration (Firestone 2000): the idea of KCE cycle time leads naturally to the notion of KCE velocity, the number of KCE cycles in an organization per unit time (it will be a small number if time is measured in seconds, minutes, hours, days, or even weeks). Velocity, in turn, leads to the idea of acceleration, the change in KCE velocity divided by the change in time. Both of these attributes of KCE are useful in comparing its level of efficiency across organizations, and the direction and magnitude of change in efficiency that they are experiencing.
- Intensity of collaborative activity in KCE: the production of knowledge at the organizational level is a collaborative activity. Collaboration refers to agents working together on a sustained basis to achieve their goals. These goals may or may not be held in common (the collaborative process may be delivering different benefits to each participant and serve different purposes for each). The intensity of their collaborative activity refers to the frequency with which they work together. Collaboration does not mean the absence of conflict. People may work

together and cooperate, or they may work together and come into frequent conflict.

■ Intensity of cooperative behavior in KCE: the intensity of cooperative behavior refers to the frequency with which people, whether or not on a sustained basis, engage in transactions that actually facilitate or support each others' instrumental behavior. Much of that cooperation may occur outside of explicitly collaborative contexts.

■ Intensity of conflict behavior in KCE: the intensity of conflict behavior refers to the frequency with which people, whether or not on a sustained basis, engage in transactions that actually constrain, inhibit, or block each others' instrumental behavior. Much of that conflict behavior may occur within, as well as outside, explicitly collaborative contexts.

■ Extent of withdrawal from interaction with other agents as an outcome of collaborative KCE activity: the conflict and frustration that accompany collaborative activity can sometimes result in a withdrawal from interaction with other agents in collaborative contexts. People, that is, as a result of too much collaboration-related conflict, can become disillusioned with teams, communities, and other collaborative social structures, and can simply withdraw from such collaborative activities. Such a withdrawal, in turn, can mean restriction of the KCE process to a small elite and ultimately a failure to vet knowledge claims appropriately.

■ Extent of inequality of access to previous knowledge claims: the degree to which inequality of access to previous knowledge claims exists in KCE has a pronounced effect on KCE outcomes. Those with more access are in a better position to critically evaluate knowledge claims and generally to participate in KCE processing. Those with little access are effectively disenfranchised.

■ Extent of inequality of access to sources and methods supporting KCE: inequality of access to sources and methods for KCE can be as damaging to critical evaluation of knowledge claims as inequality of access to previous knowledge claims. If all are to participate in KCE, all must have access to the sources and methods needed to perform it.

■ Ratio of messages received by an agent to messages sent by that agent related to KCE: this descriptor promises to be important in distinguishing different types of KCE subprocesses. Thus, hierarchical KCE processes will tend to be characterized by agents with either very high or very low ratios of messages sent to messages received, while more peer-oriented KCEs involving widespread participation will tend more toward one-to-one ratios.

■ Use and frequency of use of methods of interpersonal knowledge claim evaluation: knowledge claim evaluation frequently involves interpersonal methods of collaboration. It is likely that the mix of interpersonal methods, as well their frequency of use, has an impact on the efficiency and effectiveness of KCE activities. Some examples of interpersonal methods that may be useful for KCE include the Delphi Technique (Helmer 1966), Knowledge Café (Isaacs 1999), Nominal Group Technique (Delbecq and Van de Ven 1971), Joint Application Design (JAD), Joint Requirements Planning (Martin 1990; Wood and Silver 1989), focus groups, personal networking, project meetings, board meetings, and company meetings, communities of inquiry, and credit assignment processes.

■ Use and frequency of use of methods of electronic support for knowledge claim evaluation: there are various ways in which electronic methods and tools can support the interpersonal/social process methods of KCE. Here is a nonexhaustive list of some of these methods:

- Text mining
- Database querying
- Modeling (e.g., statistical and econometric, neural networks, system dynamics, fuzzy modeling, CAS simulations, etc.)
- KCE assessment modeling, using methods such as: the Analytic Hierarchy Process (AHP) (Saaty 1990, 1990a, ExpertChoice 2002) (see Appendix)
- Web-enabled searching/retrieving of knowledge claims
- Web-enabled collaboration
- Portal-enabled, server-based automated arbitration of agent-based knowledge claims (Firestone 2000a, 8)
- Credit assignment for participating in knowledge claim evaluation (Firestone 2000a, 12–13)
- Business intelligence and OLAP reporting and analysis reports (Kimball et al. 1998, Thomson 1999, Firestone 1997, 1997a)

Knowledge Claim Evaluation Outcome Descriptors

Here we cover the type of knowledge claims expressed and the characteristics of the distributed organizational knowledge claim base (the World 3 portion of the DOKB) resulting from KCE.

Type of Knowledge Claim: A Somewhat Ad Hoc Classification of Knowledge Claim Types

We have used the term knowledge claim frequently in this book and in developing this knowledge claim evaluation framework. But we have not yet presented an account of the variety of different types of expressions that this general label represents. So here is a list of knowledge claim types:

- Structured database knowledge claims
- Descriptive factual statements
- Conceptual frameworks
- Data models
- Object models
- Computer models
- Planning models
- Analytical models (mathematical or logical constructs)
- Measurement models
- Predictive models
- Impact models
- Assessment models (see Firestone 2001)
- Application software
- KCE criteria, perspectives, and frameworks
- Methods (routine step-by-step procedures for accomplishing intermediate goals)
- Methodologies (assemblages of methods)
- Metaknowledge claims (metaclaims)
- Planning knowledge claims
- Descriptive knowledge claims
- Factual knowledge claims
- Measurements of abstractions
- Knowledge claims about impact and cause and effect
- Predictive knowledge claims
- Assessment knowledge claims

Characteristics of the Knowledge Claim Base

Here we cover architectural, integration/coherence, scope, degree of relevance, level of measurement, model type, formal language type, semiformal language type, method type, methodology, and software application characteristics of the knowledge claim base. This set of characteristics illustrates the diversity represented in the knowledge claim base of any organization and may be used to develop descriptions of its knowledge claim base.

- Distributed/centralized architecture of knowledge claim base: This will affect circulation of and access to knowledge claims. If the necessary level of connectivity is present, a distributed architecture supports greater circulation and production of knowledge claims; if not, a distributed knowledge claim base may mean isolation.
- Degree of integration/coherence of knowledge claim base within or between knowledge claim types or domains: In theory, the more highly integrated the knowledge claim base, the more effective it is in providing a foundation for generating new knowledge claims. But we really know little about how this integration/coherence factor works in real organizations, and it may be the case that knowledge claim bases that are too highly integrated decrease creativity. This is an area that cries out for research and study.
- Scope of the knowledge claim base within and across information types or domains: The broader the scope, the more effective the knowledge claim base.
- Degree of relevance of knowledge claims produced to problems motivating the KLC: Clearly, knowledge claims must be relevant to the problems motivating their formulation.
- Level of measurement of attributes in the knowledge claim base within and across domains (Ellis 1966, Stevens 1959): Models whose level of measurement requirements are not being fulfilled cannot be fairly tested and evaluated against their competitors.
- Types of models used in the knowledge claim base (e.g., conceptual, analytic, data models, measurement models, impact models, predictive models, assessment models, object models, structural models). Generally, all types of models should be

represented, since all have their role in adaptation. There should not be an overconcentration in any one or a few areas.

- Types of formal languages used in the knowledge claim base (set theory, mathematics, fuzzy logic, rough sets, XML, HTML, SGML, etc.). Some problems can only be addressed by formalisms. Thus, there should be representation of formal languages in the knowledge claim base.
- Types of semiformal languages used in the knowledge claim base (e.g., Unified Modeling Language [UML], Knowledge Query Modeling Language [KQML], etc.). A similar argument holds for semiformal languages as for formal languages.
- Types of methods (features, benefits, specifications): A wide range of methods should be available in the knowledge claim base.
- Types of methodologies (features, benefits, specifications): Methodologies in the knowledge claim base should be adaptive, iterative, and incremental.
- Software applications (features, benefits, specifications, performance, interface): Software applications embed all sorts of knowledge claims including claims about what they are intended to do for users.

Other Outcome Descriptors

These fall into four categories: (1) types of meta-information (meta-claims) describing evaluated knowledge claims, (2) history of knowledge claim evaluation events, (3) types of rewards provided for participation in knowledge claim evaluation, and (4) extent of satisfaction with rewards for knowledge claim evaluation.

Types of Meta-Information (Metaclaims) Describing Evaluated Knowledge Claims

The following types of meta-information may be used to *describe* networks of knowledge claims resulting from knowledge claim evaluation. Some of these criteria are also normative and should be applied in *evaluating* KCE processes, and not just in *describing* them. They are defined more fully in the section below on fair comparison. Others, primarily useful for description, are briefly explained here.

Extent of logical consistency
Extent of empirical fit
Extent of simplicity
Extent of projectibility
Extent of commensurability
Extent of continuity
Extent of systematic coherence of knowledge claims
Extent of systematic fruitfulness
Extent of heuristic quality
Extent of completeness of the comparison set
Extent of consensus over truth, utility, and relevance of the competing knowledge claims: The extent to which consensus exists in an enterprise over the truth, utility, and relevance of competing knowledge claims is thought to be very relevant by those who believe that knowledge is distinguished from information by the degree of agreement in a community about the validity of related claims. This may be called the *democratic political criterion.*
Cognitive maps of test and evaluation meta-information. Like other information, this kind can be modeled in a cognitive map.
Extent of pragmatic priority of surviving knowledge claim components

History of Knowledge Claim Evaluation Events

This is another class of KCE outcome descriptors. It is important because it provides the opportunity to learn about the patterns of KCE in an enterprise over time, and to develop historical explanations of why KCE patterns and outcomes are what they are in a given organization.

Types of Rewards Provided for Participation in Knowledge Claim Evaluation

What do people get out of participating in knowledge claim evaluation? Recognition? Peer group approval? Influence? Reduction of risk? Financial gain? The list of rewards available for participation covers the same range as for participation in other processes. But the distribution of rewards is likely to be different as an outcome of each organization's KCE process. One of the main issues in analyzing KCE is to determine what its outcomes are in this area.

Extent of Satisfaction with Rewards for Knowledge Claim Evaluation

This outcome is an aspect of the legitimacy of the KCE process in an organization. When satisfaction is too low, the results of KCE are not likely to be accepted in the community.

Descriptors of Growth and Change in Surviving Knowledge Claim Outcomes

All of the knowledge claim outcomes listed above may be formulated as growth and change attributes. In this form, they are actually more useful for modeling causation, impact, and dynamics. That is, if we look at an attribute value at any point in time, we have no basis for the analysis and modeling of cause, impact, or dynamics. After all, what is an effect? It is always a change in an attribute or attributes from an initial state of affairs based on a change in another attribute. Here are a few examples of change attributes constructed from some of the previous attributes. Readers can construct others as necessary:

- Growth/decline of various types of validated knowledge claims
- Changes in validated knowledge claim base architecture centralization
- Growth/decline in integration/coherence of validated knowledge claim base
- Increase/decrease in scope of the validated knowledge claim base

An Approach to Evaluating Knowledge Claim Evaluation and Knowledge Claims

One of the most important activities of knowledge management is changing knowledge processing rules, including any rules that may be applied in KCE. But decisions on rule changing are based on implicit or explicit normative theory that evaluates rules and then is capable of specifying how they should be changed. This section describes an approach to such a theory. It provides both success criteria for KCE and also specifies KCE normative criteria and an outline of a normative process that is likely to bring success (to fulfill the success criteria) in knowledge claim evaluation.

Success Criteria for Knowledge Claim Evaluation

Key success criteria for the knowledge claim evaluation subprocess are discussed below.

Improvements in Cycle Time without Degradation in Quality (Efficiency)

Other things being equal, greater efficiency in knowledge claim evaluation is desirable, because it enables organizations to resolve more of their problems. But, as in other areas of endeavor, efficiency is not everything, and all things are not equal. Efficiency in the sense of decreased cycle time fails to encompass quality in the results of knowledge claim evaluation. If tested and evaluated knowledge claims may be false even though they have survived our tests, we may suspect that improvements in cycle time gained at the expense of careful testing are frequently correlated with lower rates of error elimination and lower quality of surviving knowledge claims.

Increase in Production of Surviving Knowledge Claims that are Relevant to the Problems Motivating the Knowledge Life Cycle (Effectiveness)

Since knowledge claims in KLCs are formulated in response to problems (epistemic ones), there is a strong tendency for them to be relevant to these problems. But it is also true that knowledge claims may be offered as solutions to problems and may even be tested and evaluated without refutation before it is realized that they don't offer solutions to the original problems at all. Thus, relevance is always an issue and must be a success criterion for KCE. When changing the rules in KCE, an increase in production of surviving, relevant knowledge claims is an important criterion of success.

Increase in Production of Surviving Knowledge Claims that Are Successful in Use (Effectiveness)

KCE must produce knowledge claims that work when applied in business decision making. KCE processes in some organizations, however, do not always produce knowledge that is close enough to the truth that it adequately supports business decision making (i.e., KCE may not be effective). When this happens too frequently, as judged by the organization executing its KCE process, it suggests that improvements in KCE are necessary. And such improvements are another important criterion of success for enhancing the KCE process.

Increase in Production of Surviving Knowledge Claims of Sufficient Scope to Handle Problems Motivating the Knowledge Life Cycles of the Enterprise (Effectiveness)

This success criterion goes beyond that of effectiveness expressed merely in terms of relevance and requires that changes in KCE also result in an increase in surviving knowledge claims covering the range of problems that affect the adaptation of the organization. An increase in this dimension makes the enterprise more adaptive and eventually impacts business outcomes favorably.

Realizing Knowledge Claim Evaluation Effectiveness: The Theory of Fair Comparison

The idea of "fair comparison" of competing knowledge claims is fundamental to our perspective. Not only, then, is the new KM (TNKM) differentiated from other approaches to KM by virtue of its grounding in fallibilism and falsificationism, it is further distinguished from other second-generation approaches by the manner in which it specifies how KCE should occur. Here, we make the distinction between what we shall call "biased" approaches to KCE and the TNKM approach, which is knowledge-claim-centric, nonbiased, and deeply rooted in the principle of fair comparison.

Thus, we can contrast "biased" knowledge claim evaluation with *knowledge claim evaluation through fair comparison,* and it is our claim that KCE is more effective, in the sense that it fulfills the success criteria just specified, when it is characterized by fair comparison and less effective when it is characterized by bias. *Thus, we also believe that KM-induced changes in knowledge processing rules and criteria that increase the degree of fair comparison also increase KCE effectiveness, and changes that increase the degree of bias decrease its effectiveness.*

Normatively, then, one should seek to increase KCE effectiveness and therefore increase the degree of fair comparison. We believe this can be done at the level of knowledge processing by:

- First, fulfilling background requirements (the necessary conditions) for fair comparison among the members of a set of competing knowledge claims;
- Second, implementing comparisons among the members of this *fair comparison set,* based on a number of criteria that allow us to choose among the knowledge claims of the set based on how its members perform on various tests.

Let us first examine the background requirements and then consider the criteria of comparison themselves. Keep in mind, however, that the criteria presented below provide the outlines of a theory of fair comparison, and that this theory is itself a knowledge claim in need of testing and evaluation. Furthermore, this is clearly a preliminary theory of fair comparison, so it is very unlikely that the criteria included are an adequate set either in the fair comparison requirements category or in the knowledge claim comparison category that follows from it (the theory). The adequacy of the set of criteria certainly needs to be demonstrated as research and applications in knowledge claim evaluation unfold, and the likelihood that criteria may be added to, or deleted from, the sets described below is high.

Nevertheless, when all qualifications are said and done, this preliminary theory of fair comparison represents a new departure in Knowledge Management, in that it formulates a normative standard for knowledge managers to aim at in changing knowledge processing rules. No such standard has been formulated in KM until now. Indeed, KCE has hardly been addressed in the Knowledge Management literature at all. Hopefully this situation will change, for if it does not, Knowledge Management will not succeed in enhancing knowledge production and innovation processes, and since this is the true heart of knowledge management, in the long run, if it does not, it will fail.

Fair Comparison Requirements Criteria

There are four *requirements* that must be fulfilled (i.e., they are normative) in setting up fair comparisons of knowledge claims: (1) equal specification of members of the comparison set, (2) continuity, (3) commensurability, and (4) completeness of the comparison set:

■ Ensuring an *equal degree of specification of competing knowledge claims* is necessary for fair comparison. For example, specification of systems of knowledge claims occurs in stages. Theories often begin as highly abstract knowledge claims. Then they are specified in greater detail conceptually and then empirically specified by providing them with an interpretation in terms of "observables" and metrics. To compare theories fairly, it is necessary to bring them to an equal degree of specification if they are not already there. Thus, if two or more knowledge claims are competing and one has been empirically specified with metrics and the other has not, fair comparison requires empirical specification of the second.

■ *Continuity with previous versions of the knowledge claims to be compared* is another requirement of fair comparison (i.e., the extent to which each alternative theory or model in a comparison set is faithful to its previous expressions). This criterion is a particularly subtle one. Theories evolve over time; they are changed and refined to meet challenges and criticism. It is easy to change a theory so much that its core identity is destroyed while its name remains the same. In situations like this, the original theory has been abandoned and is not part of current knowledge claim evaluation. On the other hand, a theory may change substantially in its details without changing its core identity. In such instances, the theory may be fairly compared with its competitors in knowledge claim evaluation.

If we are evaluating theory A versus theory B, then both evaluated theories must be traceable, without change of identity, to previous versions of each theory. Otherwise, the conclusion cannot be drawn that one of the theories named is preferable to the other (even though one of the theories tested may be better than the other), and the eventual consequence of such lack of continuity is destruction of the cumulative character of knowledge production.

- *Commensurability* must be created if it is not present. Commensurability refers to the extent to which alternative theories, models, or other knowledge claims may be expressed using a common conceptual framework (Popper 1970; Kuhn 1970). Knowledge claims being compared must be expressed in a common conceptual framework to achieve fair comparison. This is a requirement that grows out of the debates triggered by Kuhn's work on incommensurability in the 1960s (Kuhn 1970a; Lakatos and Musgrave 1970), by Feyerabend's (1970, 1970a) challenge to critical rationalism, and by the Duhem-Quine thesis (Duhem 1954, Quine 1953) that theories face our evaluation efforts as wholes, that all of our observations are theory-laden, and that there is no common conceptual basis on which to compare theories. The answer of Popper (1970) and other critical realists (see Niiniluoto 1999) has been to deny incommensurability as an irresolvable condition in comparisons and, at least in the case of Popper (1970) to argue that it is always possible to create commensurability even where incommensurability exists. Accepting Popper's notion that commensurability can always be constructed even when it does not initially exist, we suggest that for fair comparison to occur, commensurability must be created whenever and wherever it does not already exist.

- *Completeness of the comparison set* must be sought. This refers to the extent to which the set of alternative models evaluated (the comparison set) includes all reasonable competitive alternatives. This is not a precise criterion, but rather a regulative ideal. There is no way of knowing that a comparison set is in fact complete, just as there is no way of guaranteeing that a knowledge claim is true. New models may always be formulated and older models may easily be overlooked in searches of the literature. Still, if KCE is to be fair, its comparisons of alternatives directed at solving problems must not, intentionally or through negligence, exclude models from the comparison set on ad hoc grounds or in an effort to "stack the deck" in favor of the models or theories one prefers. Thus, a legitimate criticism of testing and evaluation involving a comparison set is that it cannot be viewed as decisive if an important competitor was excluded from the comparison set.

Direct Comparative Knowledge Claim Evaluation Criteria

(These require fulfillment of fair comparison criteria before the comparisons they produce may be considered "fair.")

These include: logical consistency, empirical fit, projectibility, systematic fruitfulness, heuristic quality, systematic coherence, simplicity, and pragmatic priority. All are briefly discussed below:

Logical consistency or coherence. This is a traditional criterion for testing and evaluation (Popper 1959), and the extent to which it is present is an important variable for distinguishing and evaluating KCE processes. It provides that logical arguments in explanations be consistent, that conclusions follow from premises, and that critics have the right to bring a consistency challenge against a network of knowledge claims, but not that one's entire theoretical network be formalized.

That is, logical consistency is of special importance to us because we can isolate conclusions whose content is inconsistent with their premises. And where we find inconsistency, we can either choose to reject (falsify) the argument's conclusion (i.e., the claim) and retain its premises, or reject (falsify) one or more of its premises. Or, in cases where we agree with the conclusion and also the premises, we can retain all of them. *The point is that we can make progress and grow our knowledge when there is inconsistency, following which we are forced to falsify at least one of our premises, or failing that, the argument's conclusion.*

But in no such case as the above can we conclude that a *proof of truth* has occurred. All we can safely say is that we believe that a conclusion deductively follows from its premises or it doesn't. As Mark Notturno puts it, "The best that a logical argument can do is *test* the truth of a statement." (Notturno 2000, 86). It "cannot force us to accept the truth of any belief," (ibid., 87) because all beliefs are fallible. "But it *can* force us, if we want to avoid contradicting ourselves, to reexamine our beliefs, and to *choose* between the truth of some beliefs and the falsity of others—because the falsity of the conclusion of a valid argument is inconsistent with the truth of its premises" (ibid.). But is this enough? Indeed it is, for as Notturno says, "so long as we regard contradictions as unacceptable, it is really quite a lot" (ibid.).

Empirical fit. The importance of this descriptor derives from the fact that it reflects the traditional empiricist requirement that deductions from models not be inconsistent with independently arrived at descriptions of the facts. If they are, logical inconsistency is incorporated into the system. This criterion is not as straightforward as it may seem, however. What if one model fits the facts better than another? Does that mean that the first model is to be favored in evaluation? Not necessarily. Sometimes, due to limitations in measurement or errors in observation, a model may be correct in its deduction of what empirical evidence should show and the measurement in question may be wrong. Alternatively, models may also be "force fitted" to data, as when too many variables are used in statistical estimation or too many nodes in a neural networking model, thus exhausting degrees of freedom of estimation. In these instances, models that fit data less closely will be the ones that will perform better on other criteria for evaluating knowledge claims.

Projectibility. This refers to extending generalized knowledge claims to new cases successfully (forecast validity). It has to do with plausibility of projections and after-the-fact measurements of predictive success (Goodman 1965), or survival of predictions in the face of reality. Organizations will vary greatly in the extent to which their knowledge claims are projectible, and this variance will be related to success in adaptation. Projectibility is one of the most important of normative criteria. The higher it is, the better.

- **Plausibility of projections.** This is a dimension of projectibility that involves judgments. And as with simplicity, these judgments may be derived from an AHP process (see the Appendix for a more thorough discussion of the AHP process).
- **After-the-fact measurements of predictive success.** This dimension of projectibility can be more "objectively" measured by keeping a track record of empirical fit comparing competing predictions.

Systematic fruitfulness. This refers to the disposition to encourage deduction of new knowledge claims implicit in knowledge claims or knowledge claim networks produced by knowledge claim formulation—in other words, the extent of our ability to facilitate deduction of new knowledge claims from previous knowledge claim networks. Some networks perform better than others in giving rise to deductions of new knowledge claims implicit in the networks.

Heuristic quality. This refers to the disposition of knowledge claims or knowledge claim networks produced by KCE to encourage formulating new conjectural knowledge claims. Some knowledge claim networks serve as heuristics for formulating new ideas. Here again, then, we're talking about the extent of knowledge claim networks to facilitate new conjectural knowledge claims; that is, some knowledge claim networks are more successful than others in supporting future knowledge claim formulation. They serve as heuristics for formulating new ideas. Organizations will differ in the extent to which the outcomes of KCE exhibit such heuristic qualities.

Systematic coherence. Networks of knowledge claims may be more or less integrated by specified linguistic relationships. And organizations may vary in the extent to which their KCE processes produce such coherence. Knowledge claim networks should be systematically coherent, both in general and in the area of relationships between abstractions and observables (measurement modeling). The effects of systematic coherence on knowledge integration and future knowledge production are not clear, though they are likely to be very significant.

■ **Coherence of measurement modeling.** The extent to which measures and descriptors are related through the propositions of a model's semantic network (Firestone 1971, Firestone and Chadwick 1975) is an aspect of systematic coherence. The connections between indicators or measures and the abstractions they are intended to measure are frequently not clearly specified in theories (Firestone 1971). Thus, the coherence of the semantic network in such theories is low and these theories' "empirical deductions" about expected indicator values don't really flow from the theories' premises.

Simplicity. This is another traditional validation criterion. Often called "Occam's razor," simplicity seems to be an intuitively clear criterion, but it is difficult to rigorously formulate, as was shown some time ago (Ackermann 1960, Goodman 1958, Rudner 1961). In any event, organizations will differ widely in the importance they place on simplicity in KCE. To apply this criterion normatively, the analytical structuring and subjective estimation techniques of the AHP process (see Appendix) may be used to compare knowledge claims on simplicity.

- **Simplicity of mathematical form of model.** The aspect of simplicity defined by the mathematical form of models is easier to assess than simplicity in linguistic expressions in general. Here, again, the AHP process (see Appendix) may be used to comparatively rate different functional forms on a ratio scale of simplicity created using the AHP Methodology (Saaty 1990, 1990a; ExpertChoice 2001).
- **Economy in number of attributes or variables entering a formal model.** Here again, the rule is the fewer the better, other things being equal. The aspect of simplicity called *economy* is relatively easy to measure since it is formulated in terms of the number of attributes used in a model.

Pragmatic Priority. Knowledge claim networks have descriptive and valuational aspects to them. They are networks with both descriptive and value interpretations (Firestone 2001, 2003, Chap. 4). And they may be compared in terms of the priority values across networks of benefits resulting from actions as specified by each knowledge claim network (or theory or model). This attribute of pragmatic priority also encompasses relevance. Thus, the greater the benefit specified in a knowledge claim network, the more relevant is the network from the pragmatic standpoint of the consequences of actions in closing gaps between goal states and actual states.

When knowledge claim networks are compared according to their pragmatic priority, we are not engaging in a comparison of epistemic values, but rather one of the estimated costs and benefits specified by each network in the comparison set. In committing to the rejection of knowledge claims as false, and relying on surviving knowledge claims in actions, the risks we take are a combination of the likelihood that our evaluation rejecting particular knowledge claim networks is in error, and the benefit/cost consequences of such errors. As a result, we might suffer the consequences predicted by the true knowledge claim network we have rejected. Thus, pragmatic priority requires that epistemic criteria be weighted by *the risk of error* in developing a comparative evaluation of knowledge claims and knowledge claim networks. This criterion does not involve wishful thinking in the sense that we will value most highly those knowledge claims that predict the greatest benefits, but rather, modest pessimism in that epistemic values are reduced based on the risk of error involved in not rejecting the surviving knowledge claim networks and in rejecting their alternatives.

Combining Comparative Evaluation Criteria in Knowledge Claim Evaluation

To make a decision rejecting some knowledge claim alternatives while failing to reject others, we need procedures for combining the evaluation criteria used to compare knowledge claims. *The key point to note about combining criteria in order to support decisions is that the procedures used can range from the very informal to the highly formal.*

Informality in combining criteria is what we normally do. That is, when we have a set of factors to be considered in choosing among a set of alternatives in KCE, we most frequently vet the alternatives with others, and may even subject them to a kind of "free-for-all" critical process, and/or weigh them using intuition and common sense, and then make our decision about which alternatives are false, which we are unsure about, and which are true (or at least most "truthlike"). The process may involve considerable critical interaction with others and often may be collaborative, since many perspectives are better than one in appreciating the importance of the various factors in a decision.

Much of the time, an informal process of vetting and weighing is also the most appropriate way of combining criteria. It is so because there may be no time for a more formal and systematic approach, or because the resources may not be available to implement one, or because what is at stake in the KCE decision may not be important enough to justify one, or because we need informality to surface criticisms, creativity, and new ideas in KCE. So, whether we should, once fair comparison requirements are fulfilled, implement a formal and systematic approach to multicriterion decision making, or an intuitive approach or something in between, depends upon available resources, time, the need for new ideas, and the cost involved—compared to what is at stake in avoiding error. If resources, time, available formal frameworks, and cost are not "right," the appropriate decision method to use in KCE may well be an informal one.

If we decide to go beyond interpersonal interchange accompanied by intuition, however, there are well established techniques one can use that have been developed over a long period of time in the field of multicriterion decision making. Multi-Attribute Utility Theory (MAUT) (Keeney and Raiffa 1976) and the Analytic Hierarchy Process (AHP) (Saaty 1990, 1990a) (see Appendix) are two contrasting approaches that focus on quantitative combination of criteria. The MAUT approach develops intervally scaled composites that may be normalized to the interval $-1.00 > 0 > +1.00$. The AHP approach develops ratio-scaled composites (that is, they have an absolute zero). Other approaches have focused on ordinal rankings (Hwang and Linn 1987, Cochrane and Zeleny 1973), and still others on fuzzy set approaches (Cox 1994, 1995) (see Appendix).

Our approach is to develop ratio-scaled composite models that map the component evaluation criteria to a ratio scale of "truthlikeness" (See Popper 1963; Niiniluoto 1987, 1999). "Truthlikeness" is similarity to the truth. The smaller the distance between a knowledge claim and the true (perhaps unstated) knowledge claim in its comparison set, the more truthlike it is. When the distance becomes zero, the knowledge claim is true. But the distance, as in the Kelvin temperature scale, can never fall to zero, because our measurement of "truthlikeness" is always subject to error. In evaluating knowledge claims, our purpose is to separate the false, least truthlike knowledge claims from the more truthlike claims that survive our tests and from those claims about which we cannot decide.

Two alternative techniques for developing composite measures of "truthlikeness" are presented in the Appendix to this chapter. The presentation requires some technical background. Readers who have the background and interest should find the Appendix interesting as a demonstration that formal approaches to measuring "truthlikeness" are available if the need and desire for a formal comparison of alternatives exists. Other readers may skip the Appendix since it is not critical to the main line of argument in this chapter.

Knowledge Claim Evaluation Software

Software does not yet provide systematic support for knowledge claim evaluation. In Chapter 11 we present the concept of the Enterprise Knowledge Portal (EKP) (Firestone 1999, 2000a, 2000b, and 2003), which provides support for KCE within the context of a broader application supporting all knowledge and knowledge management subprocesses. Here, we will describe the functionality of an application focused on KCE alone and a few structural requirements as well.

Key Use Cases in KCE Software

Based on the above analysis of knowledge claim evaluation, we believe that such an application must provide support for:

■ A high level *use case* (Jacobson et al. 1992, Jacobson et al. 1995, Jacobson, Booch, Rumbaugh 1999) for supporting humans in fairly comparing competing knowledge claims for "truthlikeness" or "survivability," including:

- Constituting comparison sets of competing knowledge claims
- Testing against fair comparison requirements criteria for comparison sets of competing knowledge claims
- Applying direct comparative validity criteria to a comparative assessment of knowledge claims
- Creating composites and making decisions ordering or rating competing knowledge claims
- Collaborating in KCE
- Partially automated testing of competing knowledge claims
- Tracking of results and history of KCE

This use case is suggested rather directly by the preceding section and provides direct support for comparing and rating knowledge claims.

■ KCE applications should also provide support for a second high level use case for creating KCE models, including support for:

- Formulating and changing KCE criteria, frameworks, and normative models
- Supporting KCE in KCE modeling

This use case supports knowledge managers in their efforts to create KCE models that would be used by the first high level use case.

■ A third high level use case, supporting automated KCE by servers and intelligent agents (IAs), should include support for:

- IAs tracking and analyzing human KCE patterns and comparing these with machine KCE patterns (from other IAs and from the servers)
- IAs learning their own KCE patterns from human and server interaction using their own learning capability
- Servers tracking and analyzing human and IA KCE patterns and taking them as inputs
- Servers learning KCE patterns from all inputs using their own learning capability
- IAs and servers applying their own KCE capability in evaluating knowledge claims coming from the IAs representing humans and tracking these for later use by humans in KCE

This high level use case provides for server and intelligent agent support for KCE. The knowledge claims emerging from automated KCE are retained for human consideration.

Structural Features of KCE Software

Structural features of KCE software include knowledge claim objects and various technical features of IAs and servers. First, Knowledge Claim Objects (KCOs) (Firestone 2003, Chaps. 10, 11, and 13) are distinguished from ordinary software business objects by the presence of *metadata (meta-information, also metaclaims) about "truthlikeness" encapsulated in the software object.* Such metadata compares the KCO to alternative, competing KCOs and may be expressed in many different forms.

The "metadata" (metaclaims) may be qualitative or quantitative, or they may be in the form of textual content where KCE has remained relatively informal. In the relatively infrequent but important special cases involving formal techniques of KCE, metadata may involve quantitative ratio-scaled ratings of a knowledge claim compared to its competitors. When the KCO is accessed by a user, data, metadata, and methods are all available, so the user can evaluate the KCO as a basis for decision against competing KCOs.

Second, a KCE application must employ an Artificial Knowledge Server (AKS) (see Firestone 2003, Chap. 10) with knowledge claim object state management and synchronization capability. Such capability provides for dynamic integration of continuous changes occurring in knowledge claim objects. The AKS must look for changes in shared objects and additions to the total pool of objects and relationships, alert all system components sharing the objects of such changes, and also make decisions about which changes should be implemented in each affected component throughout the system.

In addition, the AKS uses a persistent representation of the enterprise object model including its KCOs. The objects in the object model are reflexive—aware of their present state and any change of state. The AKS accomplishes proactive monitoring and coordinating of changes in its shared objects through their reflexivity and capacity for event-driven behavior. Since KCOs encapsulate validity metadata and the means of their manipulation, the ability to manage KCOs is the ability to manage and track the history of the KCE process in the enterprise using KCE application software.

Third, rule inference engines supply the IAs or servers in the system with the capability to respond to events as specified in the agent or server knowledge base.

Fourth, Simple Network Management Protocol (SNMP) engines provide a multithreaded capability for system wide bidirectional communications, monitoring, and control across distributed agents and servers.

Fifth, modeling capability provides the ability to model from text (including XML), semantic networks, cognitive maps, or knowledge maps communicated to or created by the agent, as well as workflows and interpersonal network.

Sixth, Complex Adaptive Systems (CAS) learning capability begins with the cognitive maps of agents or servers. Reinforcement learning through neuro-fuzzy technology modifies connection strength or removes connections. Creative learning through genetic algorithms and input from human agents or IAs adds nodes and connections that are then subject to reinforcement learning. So, IAs interact with the local environment in the KCE system and with external components to automatically formulate and evaluate local knowledge claims.

These knowledge claims are then submitted to the next higher level in the KCE system hierarchy, which tests and evaluates them against previous knowledge and claims submitted by other IAs. This process produces partially automated organizational knowledge claim evaluation and partially automated adaptation to local and global environments. We say "partially," because the KCE system is in constant interaction with human agents.

Seventh, in addition to the above general capabilities, a software capability to implement the AHP, or another tool providing the capability to build hierarchies, create ratio scales, and create composite models is also a requirement following rather directly from the use cases specified earlier.

Eighth, the use case requirement for collaboration suggests that a collaborative application providing support for communities of practice is necessary for KCE (e.g., Intraspect 2002, XeroxConnect 2002).

Ninth, the requirement for normative modeling presupposes a capability to model the KCE process as is, and this in turn requires both modeling applications such as Ventana's Vensim (2002), High Performance Systems' iThink and Stella (2002), FuzzyTech's FuzzyTech (2002), knowledge discovery in database/data mining applications, such as SAS Enterprise Miner (2002), SPSS Clementine (2002), and Statsoft's Statistica Miner (2002).

Conclusion: Significance and Questions

In this chapter, we have moved from a framework for description of knowledge claim evaluation to a normative theory, providing a high level conceptual outline of how to do KCE, to an outline of the requirements and structure of a projected KCE software application. We believe that this is significant for KM, since very few in the field are writing about knowledge claim evaluation, much less offering frameworks and techniques for implementing this critical activity in knowledge production.

Of course, for reasons of space, we have glossed over many details and potential difficulties. We can, however, indicate what they are and summarize them.

First, the approach taken to knowledge claim evaluation will be doubted by many on grounds that KCE is highly contextual in character, and that to approach it, as we have, by proposing a set of criteria and a set of rules in what is basically a normative approach simply violates the nature of the KCE process as a "form of life" requiring unique adaptations to its challenges. To those who bring objections such as this to the table, it must seem that the approach just taken is a throwback to a pre-Kuhnian philosophy of science when many believed that norms of scientific method could be formulated and prescribed for scientific practitioners. And it may further seem that this throwback is in conflict with history, sociology, and psychology of science approaches that seem to eschew prescription in favor of description.

Our response to objections of the above sort is that they accept far too readily the supposed accomplishments of subjectivist approaches to the explanation and understanding of scientific and other knowledge production activity. We think we can do better than that. Further, we do not think historical, sociological, and psychological accounts of scientific activity (not necessarily subjectivist, incidentally) preclude normative theory at all, because there is nothing inherent in them that suggests the impossibility of appropriate normative prescriptions enhancing the knowledge production process. Such studies have shown that simplistic normative prescriptions, such as full formalization of scientific theories, or value-free assessments of alternative models, face impossibility objections, but they do not show that new normative prescriptions based on better theory would necessarily share that difficulty.

Furthermore, the alternative to normative theory for enhancing knowledge production is abandonment of attempts to enhance knowledge production at all. This construal, then, restricts knowledge management to knowledge integration alone, and for reasons explained in Chapter 4, to do that is to abandon the distinction between knowledge and information and to attack the very foundations of Knowledge Management. This last argument does not imply that the anti-normative theory position in KM is necessarily incorrect, but it does indicate its inconsistency with the complex of ideas that lie at the foundation of KM as a discipline.

Second, our previous account of the component criteria for evaluating knowledge claims was overly simple in that it did not make clear that terms such as empirical fit, simplicity, systematic coherence, and others are themselves complex attributes whose measurement requires construction of more composites. Thus, the evaluation scheme developed earlier is not a two-level hierarchy with "truthlikeness" at the top and the component attributes at the bottom, but rather a multilevel analytical hierarchy, of the kind best treated with the AHP method (see Appendix), in which the second criterion level must be broken down into a third, fourth, or even fifth level of attributes before a schema for measuring "truthlikeness" is complete.

Third, the set of second-level criteria we offered in the normative model may well be incomplete, and some of its components may be incorrect. So applications of it should be free-wheeling, and modifications of it should also be undertaken freely. Moreover, the questions of the form of the composite models and the weighting used in them is left open by us, even though we provided a couple of examples of combination approaches. We believe that these aspects of the normative KCE model will vary across enterprises and that until we have much more experience in applying the model, it would be premature to suggest generalization of these aspects of it.

In short, we believe that the criteria, the form of KCE composite evaluation models, and the weights used in such models must all be open to innovation themselves, especially in an environment where we know little about the details of formal methods for evaluating KCE processes. Thus, we present the above normative framework as a working theory of KCE, as a first effort in a new direction that we need to take in Knowledge Management. We hope and believe that though this may be the first attempt at a normative model in the KM literature, it will be far from the last, and we look forward to being joined by others quickly on this important road not previously traveled in Knowledge Management.

REFERENCES

Ackermann, R.J. (1960), *Simplicity and the Acceptability of Scientific Theories*, Doctoral Dissertation, East Lansing, MI Michigan State University.

Cochrane, J. and Zeleny, M. (eds.) (1973), *Multiple Criteria Decision Making*, Columbia, SC: University of South Carolina Press.

Cox, E. (1994), *The Fuzzy Systems Handbook*, Cambridge, MA: Academic Press.

———— (1995), *Fuzzy Logic for Business and Industry*, Rockland, MA: Charles River Media.

Delbecq, A. and Van de Ven, A. (1971), "A Group Process Model for Problem Identification and Program Planning." *Journal of Applied Behavioral Science*, 7, *no. 4*.

Duhem, P. (1954), *The Aim and Structure of Physical Theory*, Princeton, NJ: Princeton University Press.

Ellis, B. (1966), *Basic Concepts of Measurement*. Cambridge, UK: Cambridge University Press.

ExpertChoice Inc. (2001) http://www.expertchoice.com.

Feyerabend, P. (1962), "Explanation, Reduction, and Empiricism", in H. Feigl, and G. Maxwell, (eds.), *Minnesota Studies in the Philosophy of Science, III*, Minneapolis, MN: University of Minnesota Press.

Feyerabend, P. (1970), "Problems of Empiricism, Part II", in R. Colodny (ed.), *The Nature and Function of Scientific Theory*, Pittsburgh, PA: University of Pittsburgh Press.

Feyerabend, P. (1970a), "Against Method: Outline of an Anarchistic Theory of Knowledge", M. Radner, and S. Winokur, (eds.), *Minnesota Studies in the Philosophy of Science, IV*, Minneapolis, MN: University of Minnesota Press.

Firestone, J.M. (1971), "Remarks on Concept Formation: Theory Building and Theory Testing," *Philosophy of Science*, **38**, 570–604.

Firestone, J.M. (1997), "A Systems Approach to Dimensional Modeling in Data Marts", *White Paper No. 1*, *Executive Information Systems, Inc.*, Wilmington, DE, March, 1997, Available at: http://www.dkms.com/White_Papers.htm.

Firestone, J.M. (1997a), "Evaluating OLAP Alternatives", *White Paper No. 4*, *Executive Information Systems, Inc.*, Wilmington, DE, March, 1997, Available at: http://www.dkms.com/White_Papers.htm.

Firestone, J.M. (1998), "Knowledge Management Metrics Development: A Technical Approach," *Executive Information Systems White Paper*, Wilmington, DE, June 25, 1998. Available at http://www.dkms.com/White_Papers.htm.

Firestone, J.M. (1999), "Enterprise Information Portals and Enterprise Knowledge Portals," *DKMS Brief*, **8**, *Executive Information Systems, Inc.*, Wilmington, DE, March 20, 1999. Available at http://www.dkms.com/White_Papers.htm.

Firestone, J.M. (2000), "Accelerated Innovation and KM Impact," *Financial Knowledge Management* (Q1, 2000), 54–60.

Firestone, J.M. (2000a), "The Enterprise Knowledge Portal Revisited," *White Paper No. 15*, *Executive Information Systems, Inc.*, Wilmington, DE, March 15, 2000. Available at: http://www.dkms.com/White_Papers.htm.

Firestone, J.M. (2000b), "Enterprise Knowledge Portals: What They Are and What They Do," *Knowledge and Innovation: Journal of the KMCI*, **1**, *no. 1*, 85–108. Available at: http://www.dkms.com/White_Papers.htm.

Firestone, J.M. (2001), "Estimating Benefits of Knowledge Management Initiatives: Concepts, Methodology, and Tools," *Knowledge and Innovation:*

Journal of the KMCI, **1**, **no.** **3**, 110–129. Available at: http://www.dkms.com/White_Papers.htm.

Firestone, J.M. (2003), *Enterprise Information Portals and Knowledge Management*, Boston, MA: KMCI Press/Butterworth–Heinemann.

Firestone, J.M. and Chadwick, R.W. (1975), "A New Procedure for Constructing Measurement Models of Ratio Scale Concepts," *International Journal of General Systems*, **2**, 35–53.

FuzzyTech (2002) at www.fuzzytech.com.

Goodman, N. (1958), "The Test of Simplicity," *Science*, **128**, 1064–1069.

Goodman, N. (1965), *Fact, Fiction, and Forecast, 2nd edition*, Indianapolis, IN: Bobbs-Merrill.

Helmer, O. (1966), *Social Technology*. New York, NY: Basic Books.

High Performance Systems (2002) at www.hps-inc.com.

Holland, J.H. (1998), *Emergence*. Reading, MA: Addison-Wesley.

Hwang, L. and Linn, M. (1987), *Group Decision Making under Multiple Criteria*, New York, NY: Springer-Verlag.

Intraspect Inc. (2002), http://www.intraspect.com.

Isaacs, David (1999), "Knowledge Café Presentation," Enterprise Intelligence Conference, December 7, 1999, Lake Buena Vista, FL.

Jacobson, I., Christerson, M., Jonsson, P., and Overgaard, G. (1992), *Object-oriented Software Engineering*. Reading, MA: Addison-Wesley.

Jacobson, I., Ericsson, M., and Jacobson, A. (1995), *The Object Advantage*. Reading, MA: Addison-Wesley.

Jacobson, I., Booch, G. and Rumbaugh, J. (1999), *The Unified Software Development Process*. Reading, MA: Addison-Wesley.

Keeney, R., and Raiffa, H. (1976), *Decisions with Multiple Objectives*. New York, NY: John Wiley & Sons.

Kimball, R., Reeves, L., Ross, M., and Thornthwaite, W. (1998), *The Data Warehouse Life Cycle Toolkit*, New York, NY: John Wiley & Sons.

Kuhn, T. (1970), "Logic of Discovery or Psychology of Research," in I. Lakatos and A. Musgrave (eds.), *Criticism and the Growth of Knowledge*, Cambridge, UK: Cambridge University Press.

Kuhn, T. (1970a), *The Structure of Scientific Revolutions 2nd edition, revised and enlarged*, Chicago, IL, International Encyclopedia of Unified Science, University of Chicago Press.

Lakatos, I., and Musgrave, A. (eds.) (1970), *Criticism and the Growth of Knowledge*, Cambridge, UK: Cambridge University Press.

Martin, J. (1990), *Information Engineering: Design and Construction, Book III*, Englewood, Cliffs, NJ: Prentice-Hall.

McElroy, M.W. (2003), *The New Knowledge Management: Complexity, Learning, and Sustainable Innovation*, Boston, MA: KMCI Press/Butterworth–Heinemann.

Niiniluoto, I. (1987), *Truthlikeness*, Dordrecht, NL: D. Reidel.

Niiniluoto, I. (1999), *Critical Scientific Realism*, Oxford, UK: Oxford University Press.

Notturno, M. (2000), *Science and the Open Society*, Budapest, Hungary: Central European University Press.

Popper, K.R. (1934), *Logik der Forschung*, Vienna, AU: Springer.

Popper, K.R. (1959), *The Logic of Scientific Discovery*, London, Hutchinson.

Popper, K.R. (1963), *Conjectures and Refutations*, London, UK: Hutchinson.

Popper, K.R. (1970), in I. Lakatos and A. Musgrave (eds.), "Normal Science and Its Dangers," *Criticism and the Growth of Knowledge*, Cambridge, UK: Cambridge University Press.

Popper, K.R. (1972), *Objective Knowledge*, London, England: Oxford University Press.

Popper, K.R. (1994), *Knowledge and the Body-Mind Problem* (edited by Mark A. Notturno), London, UK: Routledge.

Popper, K.R. and Eccles, J.C. (1977), *The Self and Its Brain*, Berlin, Germany: Springer-Verlag.

Quine, W. (1953), *From a Logical Point of View*, Cambridge, MA: Harvard University Press.

Rudner, R. (1961), "An Introduction to Simplicity," *Philosophy of Science, 28, No. 2.*

Saaty, T. (1990), *The Analytic Hierarchy Process: Planning, Priority Setting, Resource Allocation 2nd edition*, Pittsburgh, PA: RWS Publications.

Saaty, T. (1990a), *Decision Making for Leaders*, Pittsburgh, PA: RWS Publications.

SAS (2002) at www.sas.com.

SPSS (2002) at www.spss.com.

Statsoft (2002) at www.statsoft.com.

Stevens, S. (1959), "Measurement, Psychophysics and Utility," in C.W. Churchman and P. Ratoosh (eds.), *Measurement: Definition and Theories*, New York, NY: John Wiley and Sons.

Thomson, E. (1997), *OLAP Solutions*. New York, NY: John Wiley & Sons.

Vensim (2002) at www.vensim.com.

Wood, J. and Silver, D. (1989), *Joint Application Design*, New York, NY: John Wiley & Sons.

XeroxConnect (2002), at www.xeroxconnect.com.

Appendix to Chapter 5

Two Formal Approaches to Measuring "Truthlikeness"

Introduction

Sometimes the need or desire may arise to do formal comparisons among knowledge claims regarding their "truthlikeness." This could happen if one among a set of competing models will be used as a basis for important decisions—for example, competing models of the side effects of new drugs, or competing models about damage to the environment resulting from a new power plant, or competing sales forecasting models. In short, any comparison that may produce a basis for a course of action that is pregnant with consequences and not easily adjustable once taken may be a worthwhile candidate for a formal comparison if the time and resources exist to perform one. This Appendix presents two alternative formal approaches to developing ratio scales of "truthlikeness" using the framework presented in Chapter 5. The first is the Analytic Hierarchy Process approach (AHP), and the second is the "fuzzy measurement model approach." This Appendix is for readers interested in formal comparisons among

177

knowledge claims. Others may skip it. The figure numbers follow consecutively the order used in Chapter 5.

An AHP-Based Ratio Scaling Approach

Assuming the component attributes of the "truthlikeness" composite are not statistically correlated, one procedure begins with performing pairwise comparisons of the relative ability or priority of each of the criterion attributes of the composite in representing truthlikeness. For example, a knowledge worker might be asked to perform pairwise comparisons of the various criteria for comparison of knowledge claims using judgments of equal ability, weakly greater ability of one criterion over the other; essential or strong ability of one over the other; very strong or demonstrated ability of one over the other; absolute ability of one over the other; and intermediate positions between these five judgments. Thus, the rater may use one of nine ordinal judgments of degree of ability of one criterion pair-member over the other.

Sometimes judgments such as the above are elicited through use of a questionnaire. In that case, illustrated in Figure 5.2, respondents are asked to indicate their verbal judgments only by placing checks in the appropriate positions on the instrument. Sometimes, when the judgments are elicited, raters are told that they can enter numbers associated with the verbal judgments in place of these. In these instances, "equal ability" is assigned the value 1, and then each progressively stronger verbal rating including the intermediate ones receives the next integer value, until "absolute ability" receives the value 9.

Once the judgments are elicited, and sometimes as part of the judgment process, they are associated with the integer values 1 through 9 as indicated just above, and then assembled in a matrix. In the present example, our own pairwise comparison judgments for each criterion's relative ability to contribute to "truthlikeness" are presented in Figure 5.3. The integer values associated with our judgments are contained in the cells of the matrix above the 1.00 values in the diagonal. In the cells below the diagonal, the reciprocals of these values have been entered. In this way, the judgments have been interpreted and assembled in a positive reciprocal matrix and are now ready for calculations that will produce ratio scale ratings of the

Rate the relative ability to contribute to meeting your query performance requirements of the left-hand platform compared to the right-hand one, by placing a check in the appropriate position below.

	Absolute	Very Strong	Strong	Weak	Equal	Weak	Strong	Very Strong	Absolute	
L. Consistency	—	—	—	√	—	—	—	—	—	Empirical Fit
L. Consistency	—	—	—	—	—	√	—	—	—	Projectibility
L. Consistency	—	√	—	—	—	—	—	—	—	Simplicity
Empirical Fit	—	—	—	—	—	—	—	√	—	Projectibility
Empirical Fit	—	—	—	√	—	—	—	—	—	Simplicity
Projectibility	—	—	—	—	—	—	√	—	—	Simplicity

Figure 5.2

Questionnaire Instrument for Eliciting Pairwise Comparisons of Knowledge Claim Evaluation Criteria

	LC	EF	PR	S
L. Consistency (LC)	1	3	2	1/3
Empirical Fit (EF)	1/3	1	2	1/4
Projectibility (PR)	1/2	1/2	1	1/4
Simplicity (S)	3	4	4	1

Figure 5.3

Example of Pair Comparison Judgements of the Relative Ability of Criteria to Contribute to Evaluating Truthlikeness Arrayed in a Positive Reciprocal Matrix evaluative criteria relative to "truthlikeness" as well as for consistency tests of the matrix of judgments.

Saaty's (1990) preferred method of eliciting comparative judgments is justified on various grounds. The most important are: (1) the use of verbal judgments is an advantage with decision makers who often feel that quantitative pairwise comparisons are artificial, and (2) the method is by now amply justified by successful empirical work using it. This empirical work establishes that such judgments combine well enough with the AHP's mathematical methods for deriving ratio scales and consistency tests to produce useful scale numbers and tests showing high logical consistency in judgments. In addition, comparative studies evaluating the 1–9 scale against numerous others have shown that the 1–9 scale is at least as good and perhaps better than the alternatives tested.

While agreeing that Saaty's method of eliciting comparative judgments through verbal judgments and the 1–9 scale is certainly successful, it is important to note that analysis using the AHP methodology does not require the 1–9 scale. Psychometric methods provide other techniques for eliciting judgments that have been just as successful as Saaty's methods, and more important, that maybe seem more natural to raters in certain situations. Two such methods are the constant sum and proportional comparison methods.

In the constant sum method, raters are asked to split 100 points to judge the relative ability of one member of a pair compared with another. Figure 5.4 provides an instrument for eliciting pairwise comparison judgments using the constant sum method of scaling. The figure continues with the example we've been using and provides judgments, in constant sum terms, of the pairs relative to their "ability" to contribute to "truthlikeness."

Once the constant sum judgments are elicited, one arrives at the positive reciprocal matrix of ratio judgments by first dividing the left-hand rating in Figure 5.4 by the right-hand rating to get the top half of the reciprocal matrix, and then taking the reciprocals of the top half to populate the cells below the diagonal elements. Of course, the diagonal values are still 1.00, since we are comparing each element with itself.

In the proportional comparison method, illustrated in Figure 5.5, raters are asked to judge the greater or lesser ability to contribute to meeting query performance requirements of the right-hand pair

*Compare the relative ability to contribute to evaluating truthlikeness
of the left hand criterion compared to the right hand one.*

*To make your comparisons, assume that each pair of criteria has a total of 100
points of ability. Split these 100 points between the two criteria of each pair according
to your judgement of their relative degree of ability. For example, if you
are comparing Logical Consistency and Empirical Fit, you might assign 10 points
to Empirical Fit and 90 points to Logical Consistency. This would be the same as
saying that Logical Consistency has 9 times greater ability
to contribute to evaluating truthlikeness than Empirical Fit.*

Split 100 Points Between the Boxes Beside Each Pair Member

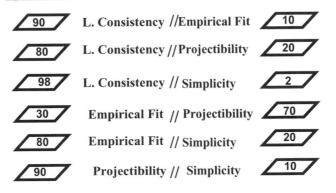

Figure 5.4

Pair Comparison Judgments Using Constant Sums

member versus the left-hand pair member in terms of the number of points given to the right-hand member compared to a baseline of 100 points assigned to the left-hand member. The instructions for the instrument indicate that the rater may evaluate the ability of the right-hand member as anything from a small fraction of that of the left-hand member to many times that of the left-hand member.

To assemble the positive reciprocal matrix from these judgments, again divide the left-hand rating (100 points) by the right-hand rating to get the top half of the matrix. Then populate the bottom half with the reciprocals of the top half and the diagonal cells with 1.00s.

The constant sum and proportional comparison methods have a long and successful history in psychometrics. More important, though, they, too, have been successful in generating ratio scales backed by consistency tests and empirical validation of the usefulness of the resulting ratio scales.

Rate the greater or lesser ability to contribute to evaluating truthlikeness
of the right-hand pair member versus the left-hand pair member.
Do this by assigning points to the right-hand pair member. Decide on the number of
points to assign the right-hand pair member by judging its ability in terms of the
baseline value of 100 points assigned to the left-hand member. If the ability of the
right-hand pair member is greater, assign it more than 100 points. If equal, assign
it 100 points. If lesser, assign it less than 100 points. If 1/5 the left-hand pair, assign
it 20 Points. If 10 times the left-hand pair assign it 1000 points, and so on. Assign
as many, or as few points as you need to make the comparison.

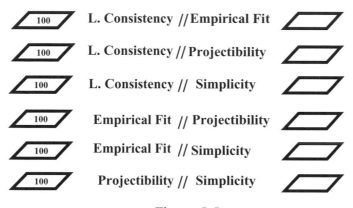

Figure 5.5

A Pair Comparison Instrument Using Proportional Comparison

The constant sum method was used in a variety of related studies performed over a five-year period (1977–1981) for both the U.S. Census Bureau and the U.S. Farmers Home Administration (FmHA). For the Census Bureau, panel studies employing the Group Value Measurement Technique (GVMT) were used to measure urban distress and rural need. Studies were done in the Detroit and Hartford metropolitan areas (under contract from the Office of the Secretary of Commerce), and in ten states (under contract from the Farmers Home Administration). Work continued at FmHA in 1981, and panel studies of rural development need were performed in three more states. Much of the urban distress work is reported in Brounstein, Firestone, Clark, Kelly, and Spoeri (1977). The work of the ten-state study is summarized in Firestone and Brounstein (1981). Four detailed technical reports on the ten-state study were also produced at FmHA.

These studies measured either suburban distress or rural development need for FmHA assistance and developed ratio scales measuring amount of distress or need, indicator importance, and in some instances, issue or subissue importance ratings. Invariably the scales derived from pair comparison ratings were validated well in multivariate analyses using empirical aggregate data. They were also shown to have very high statistical reliability across panels of raters (over .99 in certain instances), and in addition were shown to be highly consistent ratio scales using a measure called Percent Discrepancy from Perfect Consistency, which is structurally similar to the Chi-Square statistic.

The proportional comparison method was used in a forecasting study performed for the Washington, D.C., government in 1981–1982. The study used the method to compare the base year 1980 with 1985, 1990, 1995, and 2000 relative to various social indicators such as birth rate, single-family owned housing, death rate, etc. Three clusters of respondents were defined based on groupings of pair comparison responses, and some 47 ratio scales were derived from the clustered proportional pairwise comparison judgments using an approximation to Saaty's eigenvalue method (Saaty 1990) and employing the Consistency Index (CI) defined by Saaty for AHP work.

The results of the analysis indicated very high consistency of the ratio scales derived for the clusters. The mean consistency index for the 47 scales was .0006, and the standard deviation of index values was .0005. The maximum CI value (greatest inconsistency) was .0019, and the minimum CI was .0001. Saaty's criterion for acceptability of the logical consistency of a matrix of reciprocals with a derived ratio scale is CI < .10. In other words, the maximum level of logical inconsistency observed in the study was only 1/50 of the minimally acceptable value specified by Saaty, while the minimum level of observed logical inconsistency was only 1/1000 of that minimally acceptable level.

In sum, there are a number of alternatives you can use to elicit judgments for "truthlikeness" criteria using the AHP. You are safe with any of the methods discussed here and probably with other psychometric methods as well. Our recommendation is: at the beginning of an evaluation, experiment with different judgment methods. See which one the decision makers you are working with find most congenial. See which one they are most psychologically confident of and most logically consistent in using. Keep in mind that whatever method you *use should produce results that can be assembled in a positive reciprocal matrix.* This is the requirement for proceeding further to derive ratio scale values and consistency results from their ratings.

Look again at the positive reciprocal matrix of Figure 5.3. Ignore the bottom half of this matrix. Notice that the top half contains n(n-1)/2 ratio estimates, where n is the number of rows, or the number of columns, or the number of objects being compared. Thus, a 4 × 4 reciprocal matrix contains 6 ratio estimates, a 5 × 5 matrix contains 10 ratio estimates, a 6 × 6 matrix contains 15 ratio estimates, and so on. Indeed, the number of ratio estimates increases by n-1 as the order of a positive reciprocal matrix increases.

How many ratio estimates does one need to derive a ratio scale? Suppose one has a 5 × 5 matrix, including the ratios:

$$S(1)/S(2) = 1/5; S(1)/S(3) = 1/7; S(1)/S(4) = 1/3; \text{ and } S(1)/S(5) = 1/4.$$

Suppose one assigns $S(1) = 5$. Then obviously,

$$S(2) = 25; S(3) = 35; S(4) = 15; \text{ and } S(5) = 20.$$

Four ratio estimates are needed to derive 4 values of the 5-value ratio scale, with the initial value determined by assignment. The rule suggested by this example holds generally. It takes n-1 ratio estimates and an assigned anchor value to derive a ratio scale of n values.

But in the example of a 5 × 5 reciprocal matrix, there are more than n-1 (or 4) ratio estimates. In fact, according to the rule stated above there are 10 ratio estimates, six more than necessary to derive a ratio scale. So, looking at 3 more of the 10 ratio estimates, what happens if:

$$S(2)/S(3) = 1/8; S(2)/S(4) = 1/3; S(2)/S(5) = 1/6;$$
and the other judgments are as before, with $S(1) = 5$?

Then

$$S(2) = 25; S(3) = 200; S(4) = 75; \text{ and } S(5) = 150.$$

The two scales (specifically the values of S(3), S(4), and S(5)) implied by these judgments are in conflict.

So, deriving ratio scale ratings from comparative ratio judgments is not straightforward. There are alternative derivations of scale assignments depending on which set of n-1 ratio estimates one chooses to use in deriving scale values. Since there are n(n-1)/2 observed ratios available in any positive reciprocal matrix, there is generally more than enough information to allow for the logical possibility of different and conflicting ratio scales. On the other hand, the different sets of n-1 ratios may not imply different scales. It is also a logical possibility that they are consistent with each other and imply the same scale.

This situation gives rise to both a problem and an opportunity. The problem is that inconsistency can occur in the ratio estimates of the matrix. If it does, any derived ratio scale of priorities will be *arbitrary*, in the sense that it will be purely a function of our derivation procedure and will fail to represent the inconsistencies that, in fact, characterize the ratio estimates.

We can solve this problem by using AHP analytical techniques to arrive at a set of scale values, *a relative ability or priority vector* from which one can generate a new matrix of ratio *estimates having minimal inconsistency* with the original matrix of judgments. After arriving at such a scale and performing consistency tests, if it turns out that inconsistency is too high despite our efforts to minimize it, part or all of the comparative judgment task may be repeated until the scales derived from the judgments are consistent enough to satisfy us.

And this, of course, represents the opportunity. It is one of deriving a priority vector that:

- represents a logically consistent matrix;
- can be shown to represent it through a consistency test;
- therefore represents a logically coherent set of empirical judgments by decision makers comparing knowledge claim evaluation criteria or other objects being evaluated; and
- finally, is defined on a valid ratio scale that allows values to be added, subtracted, multiplied, and divided, created not from aggregate statistics or "hard data," but from human judgments provided by participants in the evaluation process.

There are two primary approaches to deriving ratio scale values of a priority vector from comparative judgments in such a way as to minimize inconsistency and test for it. The method most associated with the AHP is Saaty's Right Eigenvector Method (EM) (1990). An older method also used by Saaty and other researchers, either as an approximation to EM estimates or in its own right, is the Logarithmic Least Squares Method (LLSM), used by Torgerson (1958), Firestone (Firestone and Brounstein 1981, Brounstein et al. 1977), Saaty (1990), and Crawford (1987). The LLSM method is the easier of the two methods to implement, since it requires only a calculator that computes logarithms or a spreadsheet, but the EM is also no problem. A commercial program called ExpertChoice (2001) was developed by Professor Ernest H. Forman with Saaty's collaboration. This program makes the EM accessible in the context of providing general support for implementing the AHP. In addition, any commercial program specializing in math computations such as MATHEMATICA (2002), MATLAB (2002), etc., can easily be used to implement the EM, as can more advanced spreadsheets.

Results from both the EM and the LLSM are effective and very close when matrices are not very inconsistent (CI < .10). In cases of inconsistency, Saaty (1990, A164–A166) has proven that the EM method is preferable from a mathematical viewpoint and from the viewpoint of maintaining rank preservation, though LLSM has advantages over EM even in this context. The advantage of EM in cases of inconsistency may not be relevant, since there seems no reason to accept inconsistent results anyway, without revising comparative judgments until consistency is reached. We will not go into the details of computing EM and LLSM estimates but refer the reader to Saaty (1990) and Torgerson (1958) instead.

Once logically consistent judgments are forthcoming from the ratings task, it produces a set of relative ability ratio scaled values of weights to be applied to the criterion attributes in computing the "truthlikeness" composite. The "truthlikeness" ratio scale itself is next computed from an algorithm that multiplies the weights by the values established for each of the component criteria of "truthlikeness." The algorithm normalizes and translates each of the attributes so that their values prior to the computation of the final scores are *calibrated to one of the component criterion attributes already defined as a ratio scaled metric.* The calibration is done through simple linear regression against the criterion attribute variable and is part of the algorithm. The algorithm then proceeds to compute the composite by weighting the transformed data variables, or transformed functions of these variables (if theoretical considerations dictate using something other than a simple linear composite), and then summing the weighted transformed scores.

The result is a ratio scale since both the relative ability weights and all the component attributes in the composite have been defined on such a scale. An alternative to using regression against one of the component attributes in order to normalize all attributes to the same input ratio scale is to use a ratio-scaled criterion variable for regression that is external to the composite. The zero point for such a criterion may be established nonarbitrarily, if there are enough objects available having the ratio scaled abstract attribute to support another round of pair comparisons.

Specifically, objects can be rated comparatively in relation to the attribute being measured. Following consistency tests and computation of ratio scale values, an attribute directly scaling the objects relative to the underlying attribute is produced. At this point the procedure is completed by regressing the composite predictor of "truthlikeness" against the directly scaled attribute, or by regressing the attributes entering the composite directly against the criterion attribute. Once the composite is calibrated in this way, it can be used without the criterion variable to produce ratio scaled values.

A Fuzzy Measurement Approach to "Truthlikeness"

The second alternative technique for producing ratio scaled composites is based on fuzzy measurement modeling. The first step is to map the quantitative criterion attributes into fuzzy linguistic variables, composed of fuzzy term subsets. This mapping is called "fuzzification."

A fuzzy linguistic variable is an abstraction that maps a quantitative variable into a set of overlapping, categorical subdivisions. The overlapping categories are the values of the linguistic variable. A fuzzy term subset is one of these linguistic categories. Each fuzzy term subset is specified by a surface, called a membership function, which

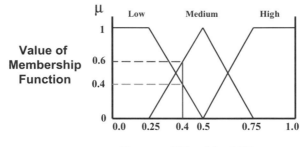

Figure 5.6

Mapping a Quantitative Variable to a Linguistic Variable with a Membership Function

maps the values of the underlying quantitative variable into the interval [0,1].

The significance of the mapping is that it measures the extent to which a value of the underlying quantity is a member of the fuzzy term subset whose surface determines the mapping. An illustration of such a mapping and its associated quantitative and linguistic variables and term subsets is in Figure 5.6.

Figure 5.6 shows a fuzzy linguistic variable with three fuzzy term subsets accompanied by three overlapping membership functions. The values of the quantitative variable are on the horizontal axis. The vertical axis provides the values of the membership functions corresponding to various points on the surfaces of these functions. The surfaces map values on the horizontal to both the term subsets and degrees of membership on the vertical axis.

In Figure 5.6, the value 0.4 units for degree of systematic coherence of knowledge claims maps to both the low and medium term sets. Its degree of membership in the low term set is 0.4. Its degree of membership in the medium term set is 0.6. Every other value on the horizontal axis is also mapped by one of the overlapping membership functions. The figure represents a measurement model for the quantitative variable systematic coherence$_1$ relative to the linguistic variable systematic coherence$_2$ and its fuzzy term subsets.

Once the mapping of quantitative to fuzzy linguistic variables and term sets is complete for all components of the composite, the output variable ("truthlikeness") is easy to estimate. Select the fuzzy term sets for the composite index, the shape of the membership functions, and the appropriate metric scale of the output quantitative variable. Degree of "truthlikeness" has a theoretical zero point, and "truth" has a theoretical (but unrealizable) value of one, so one can specify the interval between zero and one as the infinite range of values for the metric.

Next, the model can be used to formulate fuzzy rules connecting the input linguistic variables to the truthlikeness index. In the composite situation, each of these rules has the form:

If LVI(1) is A(1), and LVI(2) is A(2),
and . . . LVI(n) is A(n) then LVO is B(1)

where the LVI(1) . . . LVI(n) are linguistic variables input, A(1) . . . are fuzzy subsets (term sets), LVO is the linguistic performance output variable, and B(1) is a fuzzy output subset. The rules are linguistic expressions. An abbreviated example of such a rule is:

If degree of systematic coherence is high, and extent of empirical fit is moderate, then truthlikeness is moderate.

In a composite with ten attributes, with seven term subsets per variable, and one output variable also with seven term sets, the number of possible rules is more than 282 million, a prohibitive number to model. Fortunately, Kosko (1992, 322–326) has shown that all multiantecedent rules in a Fuzzy Associative Memory (FAM) can be composed from single antecedent rules and therefore add no new information. In the ten-attribute example, there are 490 such rules, a much more manageable number. Moreover, a system programmed with appropriate fuzzy logic algorithms will automatically generate the rules in a manner transparent to the users.

Once the rules are generated, a person needs to specify the degree of support for each rule. Degree of support is used in fuzzy inference to specify the actor's hypothesis about the validity of each rule. Degree of support can therefore be used to weight each rule in the process of inference from input to output fuzzy term subsets.

To arrive at the degree of support, the actor performs pair comparisons of the relative ability of each of the attributes of the composite to represent the abstract quantity as in the first method discussed above. The procedure produces a set of relative ability ratio scaled values of weights. These are the degrees of support to be applied in fuzzy inference. Degree of support is constant for all rules of a given linguistic variable but varies across linguistic variables. In the case of a ten-attribute composite, there would only be ten weights, each applying to 49 rules. A system incorporating an appropriate algorithm would transparently assign weights to rules for users.

When fuzzy inference is used in this type of measurement model, the scale values of the original attributes entering the composite are transformed into ratio scaled membership function values (varying between zero and one) by the membership functions specifying the term sets (see Figure 5.6). A nonzero membership function value of a member of a term set activates a fuzzy rule connecting a linguistic antecedent with a consequent *to the degree represented by the membership function value.* This degree of membership value is passed from the antecedent to the consequent in the inference process. So when inference is carried out, both a term set value (e.g., "performance is moderate") and a degree of membership value (e.g., 0.8) in the consequent term set are deduced when using a fuzzy rule.

The values generated from a single rule are one element in a fuzzy surface generated by the full set of rules as they are applied to attributes describing an object. This fuzzy surface is the full information outcome of the fuzzy inference process.

To get from this outcome to a single ratio scale composite value, the actor needs to perform "defuzzification." In defuzzification, the output surface generated by the fuzzy inference process is transformed into a single value most representative of the surface. Depending on the specific situation, different concepts of "most representative" can lead to different defuzzification calculations.

Here the centroid method of arriving at a single-valued output of the measurement process will be used. This method is essentially an average of the degree of membership values passed from the antecedent to the consequent terms during the fuzzy inference process (ibid., 315–316). Since the method operates on ratio scale values produced by the inference process, and computes a result based on the membership function values, the result is itself a ratio-scaled metric. In fact, in the truthlikeness case outcome values inferred by the fuzzy measurement model will vary over the interval from zero to one.

Other Approaches to Combining Criterion Attributes of "Truthlikeness" and KM Knowledge Production

The AHP and fuzzy measurement model to combining criteria of "truthlikeness" are only two examples of many techniques that may be used for this purpose. It is important to note that there is no shortage of techniques and that each technique provides a different interpretation of the model of "truthlikeness" proposed here, even if no change is made either in the set of criterion variables or in the requirements for fair comparison. So each technique represents an alternative model of "truthlikeness" itself subject to knowledge claim evaluation, at the level of knowledge management knowledge production distinguished in Chapter 3. It should also be clear that such a comparative evaluation of models of "truthlikeness" will itself require a model of "truthlikeness" or some other focal epistemological goal at the level of knowledge management.

References

Brounstein, S., Firestone, J., Clark, V., Kelly, P., and Spoeri, R. (1977), *Suburban Classification Project: Phase I Report*, Center for Census Use Studies, Bureau of the Census, U.S. Department of Commerce, Suitland, MD, December 29, 1977.

Cox, E. (1994), *The Fuzzy Systems Handbook*, Cambridge, MA: Academic Press.

Cox, E. (1995), *Fuzzy Logic for Business and Industry*, Rockland, MA: Charles River Media.

Crawford, G. (1987), "The Geometric Mean Procedure for Estimating the Scale of a Judgment Matrix," in Luis G. Vargas and Thomas L. Saaty (eds.) *Mathematical Modelling*.

ExpertChoice Inc. (2001) http://www.expertchoice.com.

Firestone, J.M. (2001), "Estimating Benefits of Knowledge Management Initiatives: Concepts, Methodology, and Tools," *Knowledge and Innovation: Journal of the KMCI, 1, no. 3*, 110–129. Available at: http://www.dkms.com/White_Papers.htm.

Firestone, J.M. and Brounstein, S.H. (1981), *Strategic Evaluation and Planning System (STEPS): The Needs Assessment Capability (NAC)—A*

Description of Products. Hyattsville, MD: Program Evaluation Staff, Farmers Home Administration, USDA, September, 1981.

FuzzyTech (2001) at www.fuzzytech.com.

Kosko, B. (1992), *Neural Networks and Fuzzy Systems*, Englewood Cliffs, NJ: Prentice-Hall.

Mathematica (2002) at www.wolfram.com.

Matlab (2002) at www.mathworks.com.

Niiniluoto, I. (1987), *Truthlikeness*, Dordrecht, Netherlands: D. Reidel.

Saaty, T. (1990), *The Analytic Hierarchy Process: Planning, Priority Setting, Resource Allocation 2nd Edition*, Pittsburgh, PA: RWS Publications.

Torgerson, W. (1958), *Theory and Methods of Scaling*, New York, NY: John Wiley & Sons.

Chapter 6

APPLICATIONS OF THE KNOWLEDGE LIFE CYCLE (KLC) FRAMEWORK

INTRODUCTION

By now, it should be clear to readers of this book that the knowledge life cycle, or KLC, is very much at the center of the new knowledge management. Why this is so has already been discussed in Chapters 2, 4, and 5, in particular. Now we pick up where those discussions left off and discuss several practical applications of the KLC, how it is used, and of what value it is to us as practitioners of KM. But first, let us review the basic purpose of the KLC and the general role it plays in the new KM.

In the new KM, we sometimes define KM as a management discipline that seeks to enhance Knowledge Processing (KP). Thus, we distinguish between KM the management discipline, KM the process, and knowledge processing, the range of individual and collective behaviors we're trying to enhance. This immediately presents us with a problem. How can we purport to have impact on a system, or even begin to try, until or unless we have a theory about how the system of interest to us works? In other words, how can KM lay claim to valued outcomes without first presenting us with a theory as to how knowledge processing happens in human social systems (e.g., organizations)?

This illustrates the importance of modeling in KM. When we say that a certain kind of KM investment or intervention will produce a valued outcome, we are at least implicitly invoking a model of how the target system operates and how it will—or should—respond to our efforts. Further, even if (as is often the case in first-generation KM) our goal is merely to speed up information retrieval, we must still employ models of how information retrieval generally or already occurs. Against this "as-is" benchmark, we forecast what we expect the impact of KM will be—or *should* be—upon it.

And how could it be otherwise? There's always a business case being made of some kind—hopefully—in support of investments being proposed for KM, and all such business cases invariably rest on some foundational theory of how people do their work, what aspect of their work KM will have impact on, and what the likely improvement or benefit received will be. This is modeling, if only per- formed implicitly, or "on the fly," as it were.

So if we can agree that all KM strategies rely on models of how their targets operate, what are the scope of those models, and what do they, in fact, say about how their inhabitants operate? What is it about those models that we should find compelling? Why should we accept a vendor's claim that a portal product or what have you will have a positive impact on business performance, or, for that matter, that it will have any impact at all on knowledge processing? What models are KM vendors and practitioners, in fact, using in the devel- opment of their strategies? What assumptions are they making about how knowledge is produced, shared, integrated, and adopted into practice by people in business? Do they even have an explicit model for any of this, or is their mental model a set of inchoate, unexam- ined, and probably false assumptions?

Let's further consider the implications for modeling of what we typically see in first-generation (or old) KM. Much of what we've seen there has arguably been *business-use transactional* in the sense that the purpose of KM has been seen as enhancing the delivery of information for use in episodes of business decision making and action. Investments in KM, then, are predicated on a model, a microcosmic one, that is fixated on the delivery of information in response to sudden and unpredictable needs for it in business processes, the conditions beforehand and after which, however, are of no concern to KM. For all intents and purposes, there are no such conditions. Life, for much of what passes for first-generation KM, is nothing more than unspecified experience punctuated by periodic needs for information, the effective delivery of which is KM's primary concern. Hence, our reference to its basic orientation as "business-use transactional."

Here it is worth pointing out that the well known SECI model, put forth by Nonaka and Takeuchi (1995), is also fundamentally business-use transactional in character. For a period of time in the late 1990s—and still for many people today—KM was all about making *knowledge conversions* possible. The SECI model defined four such conversions, and whole bodies of KM practice sprang forth with the express purpose of making them happen more easily.

Consider, for example, the tacit knowledge capture and conversion business (or *movement*). There, the scope of KM was pretty much confined to eliciting so-called tacit knowledge (nuggets of it) from the minds of knowers, hopefully in advance of their departure from their organizations. Once converted and codified, KM would declare victory and end, at least for those kinds of conversions (i.e., tacit to explicit ones). Three other kinds of conversions were possible in the SECI model, and KM positioned itself accordingly.

Other foundational models can be found in other corners of practice in KM, including the communities of practice arena. What are the models there? Mostly they revolve around visions of what happens in groups and the manner in which groups both create and distribute knowledge. KM to holders of those models is largely about making group formation and operation possible, the broader context of which is often lost in the process. This, too, then is transactional in scope, this time involving group transactions as opposed to individual ones. Narrowly focused communitarians, then, believe that KM should be aimed at making the formation of groups or communities possible and fruitful in their affairs. How this fits into the broader enterprise picture is not always clear because the underlying models are themselves too limited or incomplete to tell.

What many of the models in KM, explicit or otherwise, seem to suffer from is not only their limited, transactional focus, but also their apparent detachment from the bigger picture of knowledge processing. In other words, why should we be taking steps to enhance knowledge conversions or to create the conditions in which communities of practice can evolve and flourish? What do the models behind these ideas tell us about their value propositions or how they fit into the bigger picture of what people are trying to do in organizations? Unfortunately, they tend to tell us very little, precisely because of their limitations. What we hear, instead, are propositions that are themselves bounded and transactional.

The purpose of KM, many say, is to enhance knowledge sharing. Well, sharing for what purpose? And how does enhanced sharing enhance organizational performance? And where does the knowledge we hope to share more effectively come from? How do we know knowledge when we see it, and how is it different from information? In short, we need to know what the *whole* knowledge processing landscape looks like, not just some of the discrete transactions that occur within parts of it.

The Knowledge Life Cycle (KLC)

Enter second-generation (aka, the new) knowledge management. In the new KM, we begin by adopting a model of what we call *knowledge processing* in all of its dimensions, business-use transactional and otherwise. Knowledge processing, as we have said, is not the same as KM. Knowledge processing is composed of social processes that account for the production and integration of knowledge in organizations. The purpose of KM is to enhance knowledge processing. But no such enhancements are possible, much less any sort of meaningful practice of KM, in the absence of a prior understanding of how knowledge processing fundamentally happens in organizations, a model for which is badly needed. Indeed, how can we expect to have impact on a system without first having an understanding of what its shape and dynamics are? KM must be predicated on a model of knowledge processing, the absence of which in someone's work should be a warning to the wise: "Stay away, you're wasting your time."

The underlying model of knowledge processing in the new KM was largely formulated by the authors, working together with several others under the auspices of the Knowledge Management Consortium International (KMCI) over the past four years. It is known as the KMCI Knowledge Life Cycle, or KLC (see Figure 6.2). The KLC, then, is a descriptive model of how knowledge is produced and integrated in organizations. As such, it is not a normative or prescriptive model. It is a model of what *is*, not what *should be*. It is an attempt, therefore, to describe the natural patterns associated with individual and collective learning in human social systems. Its pedigree, if you will, is that it is a creature of systems theory, with a particular orientation toward Complex Adaptive Systems (CAS) theory. It also owes much to Karl Popper's ideas on problem solving (1972, 1994) and the role of problems: detecting them (while engaged in business processing), arriving at tentative solutions (knowledge claim formulation), and then performing error elimination (knowledge claim evaluation) to produce knowledge.

As both a product of CAS theory and of Popper's tetradic schema (see Chapter 2, Figures 2.6 and 2.7), the system described by the KLC is an emergent one. Not only do knowledge processing patterns form as a consequence of people interacting with one another in organizations to achieve common goals, but the order that follows is both emergent and has regularity to it. In short, knowledge processing is self-organizing and patternlike. Our model, then, begins with the belief that knowledge processing in human social systems is emergent. Moreover, because of its patternlike behaviors, we can describe it, though perhaps not predict it in detail, in fairly reliable ways. And by describing the pattern, we provide ourselves with a means of anticipating it (to at least some degree) and recognizing its appearance in organizations, as well as a basis for making KM strategies and interventions intended to enhance it. Our knowledge of the general pattern of its behavior and attributes *in advance* of our efforts makes it possible for us to anticipate to a limited degree its most likely reactions *in response* to them (i.e., in response to our interventions). This is vintage new KM—not to be found in the old KM.

At this point, astute readers may very well ask, "How can knowledge processing be emergent and yet predictable in form at the same time? Doesn't emergence preclude the possibility of prediction?" Here, as elsewhere in our explication of *the new KM*, we turn to complexity theory for guidance. Why? Because complexity science is the study of orderly behaviors in decidedly disorderly systems. Its relevance here stems from the fact that human social systems are disorderly, and yet they often display broad patterns of behavior that seem consistent and pattern-like to us. In the science of complexity, such broad patterns are referred to as "attractors," or "strange attractors" (Gleick 1987, 119–153). The term *attractor* is used here metaphorically, like something that *pulls* or "attracts" behaviors into certain patternlike formations, much like the effect a magnet has on a pile of metallic filings. The precise configurations that form from successive applications of the magnet are never exactly the same, but the broad patterns of filings that form under its influence, however, are.

There are many visual illustrations of attractors to be found in the literature, one of which we include here as Figure 6.1. Note in this illustration that no two trajectories of the pattern shown are the same, and yet all seem to follow the same general pattern. The same is true for knowledge processing in human social systems: every instantiation or expression of them is different, and yet they always follow the same broadly predictable pattern. That pattern is the KLC, of course (see Figure 6.2). The knowledge life cycle is precisely the descriptive pattern of behavior that concerns us in the new KM, the sum total of which is what we mean by "knowledge processing."

Unlike the business-use transactional focus of most old KM practices, then, the new KM is utterly holistic. It and its model look at the whole social system, and not just at discrete transactions found within it. Thus, the new KM is *macro*-KM, if you will, as well as *micro*-KM. It seeks to enhance whole knowledge processing systems, not just the piecemeal capture, codification, or movement of infor-

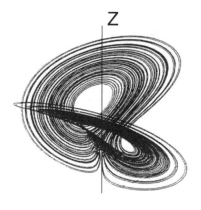

Figure 6.1
The Lorenz Attractor

mation from one mind, group, or department within an enterprise to another.

Value propositions in the new KM are, therefore, themselves not expressed in transactional terms. In the new KM, our understanding of organizational knowledge processing as expressed by the KLC makes it possible for us to work with whole-system outcomes. This allows us to formulate and move toward the achievement of actual ends, not just means. Indeed, one of the perennial shortcomings of first-generation KM is that its transactional focus never really allows us to move beyond a focus on the means to our ends and instead often commits the mistake of confusing the two. KM, according to that perspective, is judged independently of organizational outcomes. The means become the ends. Or alternatively, KM is sometimes used to describe knowledge use in business processes. Thus, the ends also may become the means.

Enhancing knowledge sharing, for example, while laudable, may or may not lead to enhanced organizational performance, higher profitability, or what have you. It is a means to an end, not the end itself. The minute we allow it to become the end, we lose sight of the bigger picture. And so value propositions or claims of that sort always leave us hanging. We never really know for sure whether or not our investments in KM are actually having beneficial impacts at the level of the whole system or at the level of the enterprise. How could we? The models that lie behind such interventions are narrowly confined to discrete transactions, as are the measurements we take of their status. The enterprise view is utterly missing.

Let us now, then, try to illustrate the value of the holistic view of knowledge processing to the practice of *the new KM* by considering its impact on several specific areas. The key issue here is *what does the KLC do for us*? What value does it offer to us in practice? To help answer these questions, we will discuss the application of the KLC to several common areas of practice in KM, including the formulation of KM strategies and some typical underlying interventions. Here are the application areas we will consider:

- Strategy formulation
- KM and knowledge audits
- Modeling, predicting, forecasting, simulating, impact analysis, and evaluation
- Metrics segmentation

- Sustainable innovation
- Methodology
- IT requirements
- Intellectual capital
- Education and training
- Open enterprise
- New value propositions for KM

KNOWLEDGE MANAGEMENT STRATEGY FORMULATION

If the purpose of KM is to enhance knowledge processing at an organizational level, how would we formulate a KM strategy in order
to do so? What would its dimensions be? Its targets of impact?
How can the KLC inform us of how best to articulate and express
KM strategy?

Let us confine our responses to these questions to the notion of
KM strategy in terms of its own externally aimed business processes.
In other words, we are not discussing strategy for the KM function
itself, or for its own internally aimed operations. Rather, we are talking about the expression of what a KM function would do in terms
of the initiatives it would undertake as it interacts with the target
knowledge processing environment of interest to it.

This last statement, then, already begins to illustrate the application and value of the KLC to the development of a KM strategy. That
is, the new KM brings a conception of knowledge processing as a
social process to the table, a vision that in a very material way gives
KM something to work with. It's not about enhancing business-use
transactions directly. It's about enhancing an end-to-end social value
network (Allee 2000) called *knowledge processing* that is described
by a model we call the KLC. The beneficial influence of the KLC on
strategy, then, is that it helps us to focus on and frame the boundaries of the environment that is the target of our strategies.

Next, consider the distinction we make between the knowledge
production side of the KLC and the knowledge integration side (see
Figure 6.2).

To put a more purposeful spin on this, we can also say that the
knowledge integration side of the KLC is "supply-side" in scope,
since its purpose is to enhance the supply of evaluated knowledge claims to its constituents (see Figure 6.3). And the knowledge

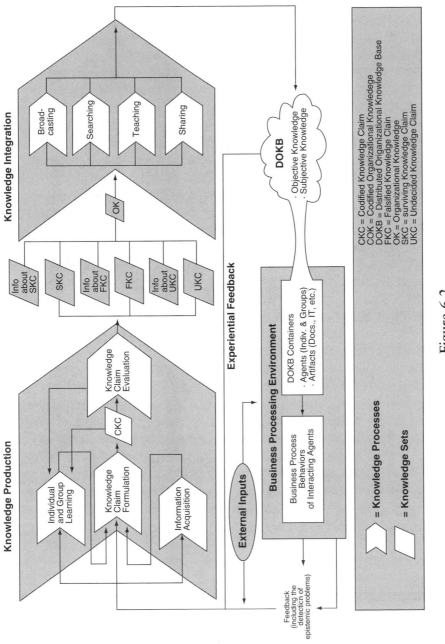

CKC = Codified Knowledge Claim
COK = Codified Organizational Knowledge
DOKB = Distributed Organizational Knowledge Base
FKC = Falsified Knowledge Claim
OK = Organizational Knowledge
SKC = surviving Knowledge Claim
UKC = Undecided Knowledge Claim

Figure 6.2
The Knowledge Life Cycle (KLC)

201

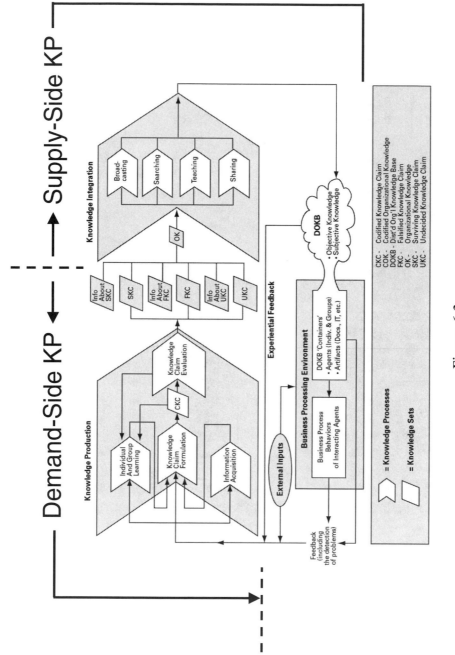

Figure 6.3
Supply- and Demand-Side Knowledge Processing

production side is, in turn, "demand-side," in the sense that its activities and subprocesses make it possible for people in organizations to satisfy their demands for new knowledge. So we have supply-side knowledge processing (KP) on the one hand, and demand-side KP on the other.

With this characterization of the KLC now firmly in mind, we can begin to formulate many different kinds of KM interventions that would be targeted at enhancing supply-side KP or, alternatively, demand-side KP. Let us say, then, that some KM interventions might be supply-side in scope while others would be demand-side in scope. So we can have *supply-side KM* and *demand-side KM*, just as we have *supply-side KP* and *demand-side KP* (McElroy 1999). The purpose of supply-side KM is to enhance supply-side KP; the purpose of demand-side KM is to enhance demand-side KP. Here again, we can attribute the beginnings of a KM strategy to the insights we receive from our understanding of the KLC, because in some organizations enhancements to demand-side knowledge processing may be more urgently needed than enhancements to supply-side knowledge processing or vice versa. Depending on what the priority is, our KM strategy is impacted accordingly.

Next in our analysis of the application of the KLC to formulating KM strategy is the recognition that the tools and methods we use to make interventions can be of two kinds: social and technological, the latter being IT-based (McElroy 2002a). Some of our interventions, therefore, could consist of the implementation of IT-based systems to enhance supply- or demand-side knowledge processing. Other interventions may have nothing to do with technology and may be comprised, instead, of the implementation of new social technologies or operating models, such as communities of practice programs, training, group decision-making processes, or what have you. This last option, in particular (i.e., social interventions), rises to our attention thanks largely to the influence of the KLC on our thinking. Social interventions make sense, we can see, because the KLC makes it clear to us that knowledge processing (our target environment), above all, *involves social processes*. We can also support it in many ways using technology, but KM is, first and foremost, a social science, not a technological one.

When we combine the supply- and demand-side KM orientations with the potential use of social versus technological tools and interventions, we get a strategic framework that shows us what the possibilities are in terms of how we might structure a very high-level plan to, in fact, make interventions (see Figure 6.4).

By formulating and expressing KM strategies in this way, we can clearly establish the relevance of our individual KM initiatives (within a particular planning period) to their individual and collective impact on knowledge processing as a whole. Were it not for our understanding and application of the KLC, this would not be possible. Today's KM strategies would be largely defined and carried out like yesterday's: very business-use transactional, and very means-oriented, with little or no capability for determining what the overall impact on knowledge processing will be at the level of the whole organization, much less its further impact on *business* outcomes.

KNOWLEDGE MANAGEMENT AND KNOWLEDGE AUDITS

In a vision of KM inspired and informed by an understanding of the KLC, what is the relevance of so-called *knowledge audits* or even, say, of *knowledge mapping*? Here we can turn to an expanded

Knowledge Processing Interventions	Demand-Side KP	Supply-Side KP	Supply/ Demand-Side KP
Social Interventions	Demand-Side Social Interventions	Supply-Side Social Interventions	S/DS Social Interventions
Technological Interventions	Demand-Side Technological Interventions	Supply-Side Technological Interventions	S/DS Technological Interventions
Socio/Techno Interventions	Demand-Side Integrated Interventions	Supply-Side Integrated Interventions	S/DS Socio/Techno Interventions

Figure 6.4
A Framework for KM Strategy

definition of KM: a management discipline aimed at enhancing the quality of knowledge processing *and its outcomes*. KM audits, then, can be aimed at both knowledge processing and related knowledge claim outputs. And it can also be aimed at itself. In other words, we can perform audits of either knowledge processing or knowledge management, the clear separation of which is revealed to us by our understanding of the KLC and the new KM in general.

Of particular interest to us here, however, are audits aimed at the processes contained in knowledge processing. Why? Well, in part because the KLC informs us of their existence and the crucial role they play in producing valuable organizational knowledge and other important outcomes. Naturally, we're also interested in building awareness of outcomes, as well (i.e., knowledge claims of various types). But the quality of our ongoing capacity to adapt has more to do with the health and well-being of our knowledge processes than with the scope and content of our knowledge *base* at any single point in time, though both are admittedly important.

So how would a KLC-inspired audit proceed? First, it is important to understand that such an audit is a very important initial and ongoing step in the formulation and administration of a KM strategy. How can we know, for example, what kinds of KM interventions should be used or prioritized in our attempts to enhance knowledge processing if we haven't first taken steps to assess the current system? What exactly, then, would we assess?

Turning to the KLC for answers, we can see that part of our assessment should be focused on knowledge production while the rest should be on knowledge integration (see Figure 6.2). Drilling down from there, we can see that in knowledge production we should be trying to assess the quality and value of individual and group learning, information acquisition, knowledge claim formulation, and knowledge claim evaluation (see Chapter 5). Similarly, on the knowledge integration side of the fence, we should be trying to determine the quality of sharing processes, broadcasting processes, searching/retrieving, and teaching. By the time we're done, we have been able to stitch together a total picture of how knowledge processing is currently performed today, who participates in it, what their influence on it is, what infrastructure they use, and what its strengths and weaknesses are. And yes, we can also add to that a profile of where knowledge currently resides, what it is, who has it, and who doesn't.

Many tools can be applied to this interpretation of how to conduct knowledge audits—knowledge processing audits, that is. Social Network Analysis (SNA) tools, for example, can be used to discover and document the strength of Communities of Practice, or groups of other kinds, who engage in group learning, knowledge claim formulation, or knowledge sharing. Similarly, other tools such as CapitalWorks' Learning Effectiveness Index™ (CapitalWorks 2002) can be applied to determining how employees in a firm acquire their work-related knowledge. Information about CapitalWorks' Learning Effectiveness Index™ and other tools and methods of theirs can be found at their Web site. Verna Allee's (2000, 2003) Value Network Analysis may be used to map out value exchanges occurring in the KLC. Tools like this make it possible to bring current individual learning processes into full relief, as well as the potential areas of future investment that KM may wish to consider.

In this respect, conducting an audit of current KLC processes and their outcomes should be seen as both an initial and ongoing task that makes strategy formulation possible on a continuing basis. Indeed, there's a gap analysis going on here. First we develop a descriptive understanding of how knowledge processing currently happens and what the disposition of its outcomes is. Then, using our modeling tools (more on that below), we analyze what the effects of potential interventions and strategies for improvement might be. We then define the hoped-for outcomes and build our strategy from there, casting it as we do in terms of policies and programs, implementations, etc., designed to close the gaps. Later on, we return to reassess the KLC; formulate new interventions; develop new strategies; and ply our trade again, as needed. A capability to perform knowledge processing audits is therefore of paramount importance to the new KM, and the basis for doing so is utterly dependent upon us having a prior understanding of the KLC.

MODELING, PREDICTING, FORECASTING, SIMULATING, IMPACT ANALYSIS, AND EVALUATION

As discussed earlier, the practice of KM is uniquely dependent upon the use of models for predicting, forecasting, and simulating the potential effects of our interventions, even if the models we use are only mental ones. How else can we be expected to credibly forecast

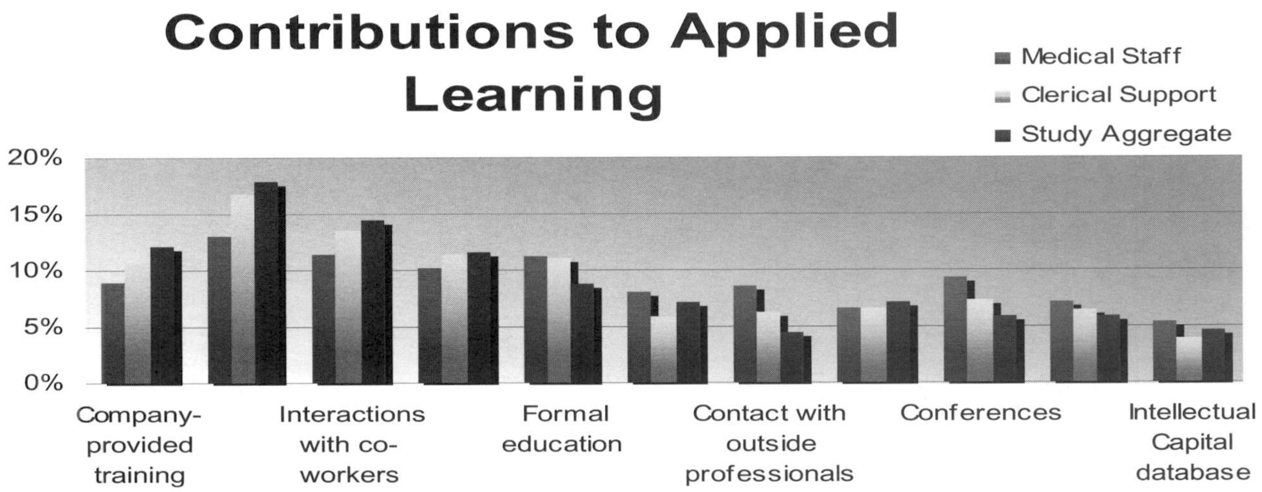

Contributions to Applied Learning

- Medical Staff
- Clerical Support
- Study Aggregate

Chart categories (left to right): Company-provided training, Interactions with co-workers, Formal education, Contact with outside professionals, Conferences, Intellectual Capital database

Y-axis: 0%, 5%, 10%, 15%, 20%

Contributions to Applied Learning

Indicators of applied learning contributions to the development of job proficiency in a regional service network of the Veterans Health Administration, U.S. Department of Veterans Affairs for Medical and Clerical Staff respondents in comparison to the **Learning Effectiveness Index**™ Study aggregate as compiled and maintained by CapitalWorks, LLC through its **Learning Value Analysis** (LVA)™ methods.

Figure 6.5
Learning Effectiveness Index™ *(sample)*

207

the likely outcomes of our efforts in systems as complex as human organizations without the aid of models? No, we must have models in the practice of KM because we must have a basis upon which we can reliably choose and carry out our strategies and interventions and then measure their impact. The KLC fulfills this requirement. How? By providing us with a representation of our target environment, thereby making it possible for us to simulate our KM interventions, observe related impacts, and evaluate their effects long before we commit ourselves to action or investments of any kind.

What, then, would a useful model for KM look like? What would its scope be? Its attributes? Questions of this sort can be answered by referring to the KLC for guidance. A useful model must, for example (if it is comprehensive in scope), reflect the dynamics of knowledge processing in all of its subprocesses and relevant dimensions. Further, it must support our needs as interventionists, so to speak, by helping us to determine what the likely impact on knowledge processing will be as a consequence of our efforts. Let us consider one such example using a model developed in 2001 by one of us (McElroy), the Macroinnovation model.

Later on below, we discuss the application of the KLC to the choice of policies and rules related to knowledge processing. Certain rules and policies can have the effect of enhancing knowledge processing, while others may, in fact, inhibit it. More on this below. For now, let us consider how the use of a model would allow us to forecast and hopefully predict the effects of different alternative interventions—policy interventions, in this case.

The tool used to develop the Macroinnovation model was a system dynamics tool called iThink, developed by the late Barry Richmond of High Performance Systems in Hanover, New Hampshire. By relying explicitly on the dynamics of knowledge processing reflected in the KLC, a model was built that made it possible to simulate the innovation behaviors of people in a fictitious organization. Here, more specifically, is the introduction to the model, which currently appears on the Macroinnovation Associates Web site (www.macroinnovation.com, 2002):

Structure and Dynamics of the Macroinnovation Simulation

The fictitious organization featured in the Macroinnovation simulation is a for-profit business consisting of 100 workers and a supervising management function. Workers account for the generation of revenue in the model, in accordance with the proportion of time they spend working versus the time spent in learning or knowledge production activities. The distribution of their time across these various activity types is, in turn, governed by knowledge-related policy choices made by management—that is, by YOU [i.e., the knowledge manager].

When you interact with the model, you assume the policy-making powers of management on matters related to knowledge production, sharing, and integration; and the effects of your choices are reported back to you in terms of what their impact has been on the rate and quality of business innovation, as well as the "bottom line."

A full description of the innovation simulator, and the simulator itself, can be found on Macroinnovation Associates' Web site. We will return to this model for more discussion in our treatment of the KLC's application to sustainable innovation shortly. For now, though, it should be seen as an illustration of the manner in which the KLC can (should) be used to inspire the creation of models that practitioners need to simulate the likely effects of their interventions.

Knowledge of the KLC can also result in the choice of many different kinds of models, not just the system dynamic ones of the sort used in the Macroinnovation model. Since organizations and their KLCs are populated with individuals, for example, each of whom has the capacity to act autonomously and to produce and integrate his or her own knowledge, agent-based models taken from the development of CAS theory can also be useful in forecasting the impact of KM interventions on, say, individual learning.

One of the more interesting kinds of models—again, inspired by an understanding of the KLC—is a model that we might call a CAS/SD, or a "Cassidy," model. A Cassidy model would make it possible to simulate the emergent behaviors of organizations at an enterprise-wide level while linking such behaviors at the same time to the individual learning and adaptive behaviors of their members "below." System dynamics models or CAS models by themselves are incapable of simulating both, even though we know that the systems we're trying to model (organizations) behave in accordance with precisely those dynamics—i.e., the emergent behavior of organizations at the top level is very much connected to the lower-level learning and adaptive behaviors of their members, albeit in nonlinear ways. The CAS models cover the lower-level learning, while the SD models cover the emergent behavioral outcomes at the top level. We know of very little work being done in this area, although Professor Jim Hines of the Massachusetts Institute of Technology claims to have built and tested models of this sort in some detail.

METRICS SEGMENTATION

Next in our discussion of KLC applications is the subject of metrics in KM, and the role that knowledge of the KLC can play in our use of them. The first consideration of importance when contemplating the use of metrics in a management discipline is to ask, "Metrics for what?" We can begin to answer this question from the perspective of the new KM by first referring to the new KM reference model (see Figure 6.6). There, as we discussed before, the KLC can be found framed on the one side by knowledge management and on the other by business processing. What are the implications for metrics?

First, the KLC is a framework for knowledge processing (KP), not KM. Knowledge management, however, has an impact on knowledge processing—indeed, that is its purpose. So right away, we can say

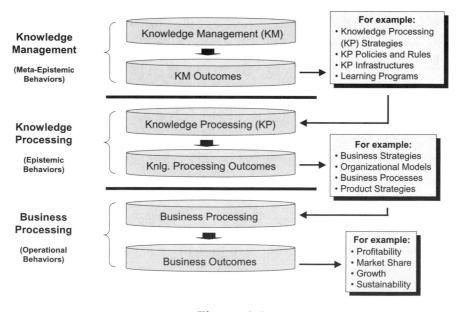

Figure 6.6
The New Knowledge Management Reference Model

that no framework of metrics in our broader treatment of KM should be regarded as complete unless it distinguishes between KM and KP and provides us with metrics for both. Moreover, since the purpose of enhancing KP is to improve business processing performance, we must also be prepared to correlate changes in knowledge processing to changes in states of affairs (outcomes) in business processing, thereby calling for the inclusion of business processing metrics in our scheme, as well.

From the argument set forth above, we can easily see that a framework for metrics in KM must have at least three levels to it (see Figure 6.7). We say "at least" because we could also, in theory, add levels of metrics above the KM level, taking into account separate activities we might undertake in order to have impact on KM itself. These might be the "meta-KM" and "meta-meta-KM" levels (Firestone 1999), etc. For simplicity's sake, however, we show only the KM level at the top of our model.

Let us now stop here and recognize that our knowledge of the KLC and the relationship that exists between knowledge processing and the KM level above and the business processing level below, is a unique consequence of the KLC itself, and the role it can play in our

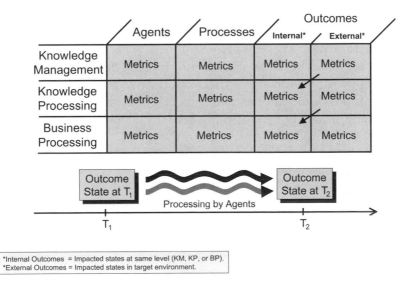

Figure 6.7
Metrics in the New Knowledge Management

thinking. Further, our specific knowledge of the KLC has a material and equally specific impact on our formulation of the approach we should take to metrics in our practice of KM—the new KM. But there's more to the story here.

To continue, we can also say that each level (or row) of the matrix shown in Figure 6.7 can be further broken down into its constituent elements, consisting of agents (people and organizational units), processes (the behaviors and patterns of tasks they display), and outcomes (the conditions brought about by agent behaviors). When we map these three dimensions into our three-level framework, we see that what results is a KM matrix for metrics that has at least nine cells inside of it. But there are actually twelve shown, aren't there? Why is that?

The outcomes dimension of the matrix has two sublayers: internal outcomes and external outcomes. What do we mean by that? Internal outcomes are outcomes local to the level. For example, some KM activities might actually be aimed at enhancing the KM function itself and not the knowledge processing level below it. Our KM metrics, then, should make it possible for us to measure the state of affairs inside the KM function itself and not just the conditions present in its target environment—knowledge processing (KP).

On the other hand, KM does, of course, engage in making investments and interventions in KP, thereby leading to changes of various sorts in the KP environment. From the perspective of KM, these kinds of changes or outcomes are *external* to itself. Note, as well, that what is external to KM can be seen as internal to KP, hence the diagonal mapping we show with arrows between the two levels. The same is true for external KP outcomes and internal business processing outcomes.

We should also point out that there are at least twelve categories of metrics required in the practice of the new KM, and that the composite view we have presented is a direct application (and result) of the KLC and its influence on our thinking. Any other approach to the specification of metrics for KM should be held to the same test: how do they distinguish between KM versus KP in their orientation, and do they, in turn, show the relationships between metrics for both, as well as between themselves and related metrics for business processing? Or do they even, for that matter, make any such distinctions at all?

Finally, in Figure 6.8 we show a more detailed illustration of the manner in which metrics for knowledge processing, in particular,

	Agents	Processes	Outcomes	
			Internal*	External*
Information Acquisition	Metrics	Metrics	Metrics	Metrics
Individual and Group Learning	Metrics	Metrics	Metrics	Metrics
Knowledge Claim Formulation	Metrics	Metrics	Metrics	Metrics
Knowledge Claim Evaluation	Metrics	Metrics	Metrics	Metrics
Broadcasting	Metrics	Metrics	Metrics	Metrics
Searching	Metrics	Metrics	Metrics	Metrics
Teaching	Metrics	Metrics	Metrics	Metrics
Sharing	Metrics	Metrics	Metrics	Metrics

*Internal Outcomes = Impacted states in same subprocess or in KLC as a whole.
*External Outcomes = Impacted states in business processing environment.

Figure 6.8
Knowledge Processing Metrics in the New Knowledge Management

should be structured. This amounts to taking the knowledge processing row shown in Figure 6.7 and exploding it into more detail. The specification of the details comes from an understanding of the KLC, the subprocesses of which constitute the dimensions of metrics for knowledge processing that should be of interest to us.

It should be clear, then, that none of what we have shown in Figures 6.6 or 6.7 would have come about were it not for the beneficial influence of the KLC on our thinking.

SUSTAINABLE INNOVATION

In our earlier discussion of the KLC's impact on "modeling, predicting, forecasting, simulating, impact analysis, and evaluation," we made reference to a KLC-based model known as the Macroinnovation model, which was developed to help illustrate the potential impact of KM interventions on knowledge processing. Reference to that model was made purely for illustrative purposes to show how the KLC can be applied in the formulation of models used by practitioners in the new KM. As it turns out, however, that particular model was developed to highlight the kinds of impacts that *policies* and related *programs* can have on knowledge processing and, therefore, on innovation. That line of thinking, too, is a direct consequence of the KLC and its impact on our thinking, as we will now show in more detail.

A very important aspect of the thinking behind the KLC is that knowledge processing is an emergent property of organizational life. Even in the utter absence of management, much less *knowledge management*, KLCs form. And they do so at multiple levels of scale (see Figure 6.9). They emerge at the levels of individuals, groups, teams, communities, departments, divisions, and certainly whole enterprises. They even emerge at higher levels, such as industries, nations, societies, coalitions, etc. To varying degrees of intensity and with different levels of effectiveness, KLCs emerge under their own steam as a natural consequence of interaction between people in social systems and their periodic detection of problems. The KLC is a problem-solving system that naturally arises as a by-product of decision processing whenever we (people) encounter epistemic problems in the course of our lives (work lives or otherwise).

What, then, might the KM implications of this insight be? How should this particular knowledge of the KLC and its nature influence choices we make about how best to practice KM?

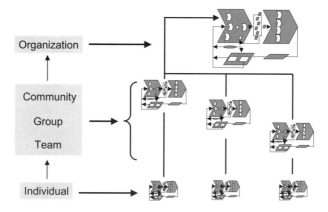

Figure 6.9
Nested Knowledge Life Cycles

When we say that the KLC is emergent, we are expressing *the new KM* view that knowledge processing in human social systems is a self-organizing phenomenon. When confronted with problems (epistemic ones), people in social systems, especially organizations, tend to self-organize around the production and integration of new knowledge. The KLC is the pattern of collective behaviors they form as they do so. Complete cycles of knowledge processing can be seen as episodes of innovation. Here, we define innovation in terms of the KLC. Let us pause and recognize for a moment, then, that the composition of the KLC provides us with valuable insight into the anatomy of innovation and also helps us understand that innovation, at its best, is a self-organizing social phenomenon.

What this tells us, first off, is that no special management is required in order for knowledge processing to occur—knowledge processing is a natural social occurrence. Strictly speaking, then, no formal or organized knowledge management is required, either. Knowledge processing has always occurred in the absence of such influences, although background or low levels of knowledge management have always been with us, as well. Why, then, should we have formal, organized knowledge management?

Despite the emergent, self-organizing nature of knowledge processing, its quality and performance is variable. Knowledge management, then, can be applied in an effort to enhance knowledge processing, or to somehow change its performance in specific ways. But this, of course, is consistent with everything we've said in this book about KM—i.e., its purpose is to enhance KP; we never said it was to create it.

Given this understanding of the nature of the KLC, it is useful, we think, to consider various styles and methods of KM practice in terms of deterministic approaches versus nondeterministic ones. Deterministic approaches work best when working with causally determined systems. Systems that are self-organizing, however, should be approached differently. We don't create or *determine* them. Nor are they caused by any set of conditions or event we can specify. They either already exist or organize themselves according to an emergent pattern. If we're happy with the general thrust of their behavior, though, we can consider *supportive* interventions as opposed to ones intended to control the system. And since we are indeed happy with the general thrust of knowledge processing in organizations (i.e., it serves a useful purpose for us), this principle has its place in the new KM. More specifically, there is a place for supportive *policy* and supportive *programs* in the new KM, a style of KM practice that is predicated on a view of knowledge processing as a self-organizing phenomenon, not a deterministic one.

In conventional management—including first-generation KM—policy is very much used in determinate ways: *"Do this because we said so,"* the voice of policy says. The theory is that desired behaviors follow from policy. In the new KM, however, the reverse is true: *policy follows from desired behaviors.* If the desired behaviors of interest to us already exist, the proper role of policy is to defer to them by supporting, strengthening, and reinforcing them.

The proper approach to the design of policy, then, when dealing with self-organizing systems is to make policy deferentially, not prescriptively. Here, policies should be less *prescriptive* than they are *permissive.* What we should have in such cases are policies that are determined by an understanding of the preexisting characteristic behaviors and dynamics in the systems of interest to us. If individual and group learning, for example, is an important element of knowledge processing—and it *is*—then we should have policies that stress its importance and which support its expression to the fullest extent. That is, our policies and programs should enhance the processing of knowledge claims by individuals and groups such that error elimination is enhanced and more robust knowledge claims survive the knowledge claim evaluation subprocess than before.

One example of this approach to KM is formally known as the Policy Synchronization Method, or PSM (McElroy and Cavaleri 2000). It gets its name from the idea of choosing policies that are synchronized with the self-organizing dynamics of knowledge processing in human social systems. By doing so, knowledge managers can enhance knowledge processing by managing the conditions in which it naturally occurs. It can do so, the PSM method reasons, by recognizing that the "conditions" of importance to us here are policies and programs. If we get the conditions right, we can enhance the emergence and performance of knowledge processing. In the wrong conditions, it withers. But none of this thinking could have occurred in the first place if the KLC hadn't been used as a source of inspiration in the development of the PSM method, as it has for every other method or practice in the new KM. How could we have conceived of the very idea of "deferential policy making" had we not, first, come to appreciate the self-organizing nature of knowledge processing, and the key subprocesses of knowledge production and integration that are the manifestation of this self-organization? That insight was handed to us by the KLC.

The connection to *programs* in this context is quite simple. Whereas policies take the form of guidelines (prescriptive, permissive, or otherwise), programs are their action-oriented implementations. They are the action consequences of policies—the fulfillments of policies, if you like. Programs are therefore downstream from policies and can be thought of as the reifications of policy. Thus, the implementation of the program side of the *policy synchronization method* could be thought of as *program synchronization*—the implementation of knowledge processing programs that seek to reinforce the self-organizing dynamics of the KLC.

Now comes the idea of *sustainable innovation*. If the KLC is a self-organizing phenomenon, it is endowed with an endogenous capacity to carry out its affairs, with or without formal KM interventions being needed to enhance it. That is, it has a certain endemic sustainability—a significant degree of autonomy and independence, if you will. Anything we might do that could conflict with or inhibit the behavior of the KLC will therefore run afoul of it, so to speak, and should not be regarded as sustainable. Here we could say that artificial knowledge processing behaviors are those that are unsustainable, to one degree or another, because of the conflicts (the friction) they encounter between themselves and the natural KLC. The KLC is, in this regard, stubborn and irrepressible.

Knowledge management strategies, tools, and methods that, in turn, fail to recognize this principle and which, instead, encourage the implementation of non-KLC-compliant knowledge processing outcomes are themselves unsustainable, because their issue will eventually come back to haunt them in the form of a surfeit of negative and unanticipated costs, both monetary and organizational.

If one's work products are unsustainable, one's work itself is not long for the world. Similarly, unsustainable knowledge processing can have its undesirable effects in the other direction: it can precipitate unwanted (and unsustainable) *business processing* behaviors and *their* outcomes. So we can see that sustainability in the conduct of human affairs has strong ties to sustainability in knowledge processing and sustainability in KM, all of which is deeply rooted in the self-organizing nature of the KLC. We believe the implications of this insight are profound, and we will return to the discussion of sustainability in Chapter 11 and in future works on the Open Enterprise.

Methodology

Perhaps the most significant contribution of the KLC to the practice of KM is in the area of methodology. Consider, for example, the broad questions of methodology and practice in knowledge management. What methodologies should we have, and what should they do for us? What is it, after all, that we're trying to accomplish? Is it to enhance knowledge sharing? Information retrieval? Collaboration? When we look at a body of KM practice, then, what do we see? What are its followers and practitioners actually doing? What is their fundamental purpose, and what methods do they use to fulfill it?

As we will discuss in Chapter 8, many KM methodologies are conceived of as instruments of strategy—their purpose is to contribute to the fulfillment of business strategy by enhancing information retrieval and knowledge sharing. As we shall argue, however, this is not the vision of the new KM. Information Management (IM) is important, but it is not the same as knowledge management, as we have shown at some length in Chapter 3. KM is not IM. Rather, in the new KM, we begin by making the all-important distinction between knowledge management and knowledge processing. From there, it's a short hop to recognizing that the purpose of KM is to enhance knowledge processing—that is, to enhance the KLC!

Does this mean that KM is completely divorced from the fulfillment of strategy? Of course not. But why confuse KM with IM? And if we do, who's left to watch the knowledge processing store, as it were? No, KM is a unique and distinct management discipline, the purpose of which is to enhance the health and well-being of the KLC. And in so doing it enhances its hosts' capacity to fulfill business strategy and to generally perform all of their business processes more competently, precisely *because of* the impact it has on knowledge processing.

But what should its methodology be?

First, let's pause for a moment to acknowledge that this conception of KM as *a management discipline aimed at enhancing the KLC* is a direct consequence of the KLC itself. Were it not for our recognition of the KLC, its role in organizations, and its characteristic pattern, there would be no such separate notion of what KM is. Thus, the KLC has informed us in a very important and fundamental way of what our understanding of KM itself should be. Now, let's consider the methodological implications more directly.

If the purpose of KM is to enhance the health and well-being of knowledge processing, then any and all KM methodologies should be held to that test. Do they support us in our goals to enhance the KLC or not? If not, then we should seriously question their relevance to our purpose. If they do, then how do they do so, and are they effective?

Here, a strong case can be made for the role of various kinds of interventions aimed at enhancing the KLC as a basis for KM methodology. Further, gap analysis techniques can also be helpful. As we consider this approach to KM, it is sometimes instructive to recall that in the new KM, it's not "knowledge management," it's "knowledge *process* management." In other words, it's KLC management; moreover, the only way that knowledge can be managed is through the impact of KM on the KLC. Changes in the KLC, in turn, then, have an impact on knowledge outcomes.

From a methodological perspective, then, we can see that we must begin the practice of KM (the *new* KM) with an attempt to understand the current complexion of knowledge processing (KP) in a firm. We must follow by modeling and analyzing the likely impact of our contemplated interventions. And last, by making the interventions themselves aimed at improving knowledge processing (i.e., KLC) performance. In other words, our interventions should be designed to help close the gaps between what we see in a current KP environment and what we think we'd *like* to see, or what we believe *ought* to be. But to arrive at interventions that will do that, our methodologies must be processes that model our interventions and their anticipated and actual effects on the KLC. Thus, the new knowledge management has produced KM Framework Methodology (KMFM) (Firestone 2001), a nonlinear adaptive methodology that is focused on producing increasingly detailed models of interventions and their impacts on the KLC.

To fully populate a KM practice with appropriate tools, techniques, and methods, then, we need to consider (a) the kinds of analytical tools needed to capture an understanding of current KLC environments, including the state of their underlying subprocesses, as well as (b) the kinds of tools, techniques, and methods required to improve them. Thus, we may use a tool like "social network analysis" to get a feel for how well group learning, knowledge claim evaluation, or knowledge sharing is taking place. Or we may use "object modeling" to formulate impact models that allow us to predict the effects of our contemplated interventions, while we turn to other tools, such as communities of practice, or IT or decision processing methods, in formulating our interventions.

In any case, this approach to methodology in the new KM would not exist were it not for the KLC itself, for without the KLC, there would be no knowledge processes to enhance, no separate conception of KM as a management discipline for doing so, and no modeling of the impact of interventions on the KLC.

INFORMATION TECHNOLOGY REQUIREMENTS

The use of IT in the new KM logically follows the thinking set forth above for methodology. If the practice of KM is to enhance knowledge processing, then all related applications and uses of IT should also serve the same purpose. This claim, however, has two sides to it. First, there is the use of IT as a tool for knowledge managers to use in their attempts to enhance knowledge processing. Thus, knowledge managers might implement IT-based solutions in their attempts to enhance knowledge processing in some way or another. Second, however, there is the potential use of IT to support the KM function itself—that is, to support its own business processes as opposed to the makeup of knowledge processing in its target environments. Let's consider these distinctions further.

First, on the knowledge processing side of the coin, there is the use of IT to enhance and support the KLC and all of its subprocesses. Here, then, we can easily envision the use of IT to support information acquisition in knowledge production, or sharing in knowledge integration. In Chapter 11, however, we go beyond the obvious uses of IT such as these and instead consider the evolution of portals that will not only make it possible for us to create, codify, share, and retrieve knowledge claims, but to manage the content of related meta-information or metaclaims, as well. Here, then, the unique importance of the KLC once again shines through.

Knowledge, as reflected in the KLC, consists of claims that have survived testing and evaluation (our efforts at error elimination) and which are therefore treated as being closer to the truth than their competitors. The record of such testing and evaluation, then, is of critical importance to the new KM. It should be possible, for example, for us not only to retrieve a so-called *best practice* from an IT-based repository of such things, but also to retrieve the evidence and arguments in its favor. Why?

Because, as we discuss in Chapter 7, so-called best practices are nothing more than *knowledge claims about practices*. As such, they, like all other knowledge claims, are fallible. How are we supposed to know the good claims from the bad ones, or the tested claims from the untested ones, or the basis of their exponents' thinking without having access to the metaclaims that lie behind them? IT can play a significant role in helping us to gain that access, an observation that is inescapably rooted in our conception of the KLC.

On the other side of the coin is the role that IT can play in support of the KM function itself. To the extent that IT has been deployed in support of knowledge processing, it presents KM with unique opportunities to measure, monitor, and observe knowledge processing activities as a by-product of related applications. The use of IT in support of communities of practice, for example, can also provide reports on related levels of activity (e.g., How many communities exist? What is their frequency of formation? Their longevity? Levels of membership in them? Degrees of activity? etc.). Similarly, usage levels and patterns related to IT systems deployed in support of information acquisition, knowledge claim formulation, knowledge sharing, broadcasting, etc., could also be generated. All of this and more can be of enormous help to KM in ways that go beyond direct support of knowledge processing.

Once again we see an application of the KLC at work here. First, it informs us of the specific role that IT can play in supporting knowledge processing, first, by virtue of its having called knowledge processing to our attention, and, second, through its articulation of the nature of the underlying subprocesses of the KLC. IT can then be targeted in very specific ways with an eye toward regulating its impact on the whole of knowledge processing. Next, since the distinction we see between KM and KP is, too, a function of the KLC's influence on our thinking, we can envision the separate use of IT to support KM itself. None of this is possible without first recognizing the KLC, and so its application to even the narrow consideration of how best to apply IT in the practice of KM is palpable.

Moreover, the specific concept of the Enterprise Knowledge Portal (EKP) is directly related to the idea of the KLC and therefore to TNKM. The first formulation of the EKP concept (Firestone 1999a), relied on a concept of knowledge processing that used categories that were a precursor of and highly similar to the KLC. Moreover, further developments of the EKP concept (Firestone 2000, 2000a, 2001a, and 2003) all rely heavily on the KLC. Specifically, the EKP is viewed as an application that must support all subprocesses within the KLC, as well as all of the management activities specified earlier in Chapter 3.

Apart from portals, the KLC is also relevant to the more general notions of Artificial Knowledge Management Systems (AKMSs) and Distributed Knowledge Management Systems (DKMSs) (Firestone 1999b, 2003). These two are also developed from the viewpoint of the KLC in Firestone (2003).

Intellectual Capital

Much has been said and written about so-called intellectual capital (IC) in the years since 1994, when Tom Stewart, a journalist for *Fortune* magazine at the time, first started writing about it (Stewart 1994). Since then, knowledge management has been firmly linked to intellectual capital in various ways. Chief among them has been to generally regard knowledge—personal and organizational—as worthy of the term "capital," deserving of all of the respect and recognition we attach to *capitals* of other kinds, thanks largely to the halo effect of the term. What exactly the term IC means, however, is still the subject of much debate, as is the question of how to measure, not to mention manage it. What is clear, though, is that the financial value of a corporation usually exceeds the so-called "book value" of its tangible assets, and so *intangibles*, as well, must have value—financial value. Has the new KM solved these problems or cracked the secret code of intangible assets? No, not entirely, but it does bring a fresh perspective to the table, one which, again, is an application of the KLC.

First, the new KM provides us with a framework for understanding knowledge and its various forms in organizations. In Chapter 1, we covered the related distinctions between World 2 (personal and subjective) knowledge and World 3 (linguistically expressed and objective) knowledge claims. These distinctions are, in turn, reflected in the KLC, both in terms of where they fit in knowledge processing and the forms that they take. Given the fundamental nature of these insights and the distinctions we can make between the different kinds of "knowledges," the new KM has some very basic and valuable contributions to make to IC, and yet the IC community has yet to fully appreciate them.

Second, there is the notion of what we call "social innovation capital," or SIC. In an earlier examination carried out by one of us (McElroy 2002) in which competing theories on IC, then and now, were reviewed, McElroy asked the question, "Where's the KLC?" If IC is all about reflecting the value of intangibles in its attempts to compute their impact on corporate valuations, then *the capacity to produce and integrate knowledge* itself should somehow figure prominently in related schemes. In other words, the only thing potentially more valuable to a firm than its prized intellectual capital should be its institutional and ongoing capacity to produce it! What form does that capacity take? Why, the KLC, of course. What he found, however, surprised us.

Consider an early (and now admittedly outdated, but still often cited) model of IC put forth at Skandia AFS by Leif Edvinsson and his team in the early 1990s (see Figure 6.10).

While outdated, the Skandia model (called "Navigator") is still emblematic of the IC community's broader failure to take *social capital*, in general, fully into account. While we see evidence of this omission in the early Skandia model and in many others since then, we have yet to see any truly rigorous attempts to incorporate social capital into the taxonomies of IC being debated in leading academic and management circles. This presents a problem for us, because the KLC is nothing if not a form of social capital. It is social in the sense that it is a particular kind of process carried out by people in social settings, and it is capital in the sense that its performance can add value (financial and otherwise) to the lives of people involved and the enterprises of which they are a part. Clearly, the quality and performance of knowledge processing has financial valuation implications in a firm.

The name we gave, then, to the particular kind of social capital represented by the KLC was "social innovation capital." In other words, the KLC is social capital of an innovation sort. Why innovation? Because we can define innovation as a social process that

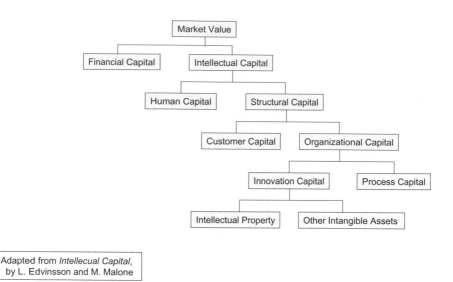

Adapted from *Intellecual Capital*,
by L. Edvinsson and M. Malone

Figure 6.10
Skandia's Navigator Model

embodies knowledge production and integration, the two major process clusters of the KLC. According to this logic, strong KLCs should add value to an organization, financial value. The capacity to innovate—sustainably so and with regularity and reliability—such as we see in companies like 3M, should be treated as deserving of value itself. We believe, therefore, that no comprehensive attempt to reflect the categorization of IC should be seen as complete until and unless it includes (a) social capital broadly, and (b) social innovation capital, in particular. We express this view, for illustrative purposes, in a modified version of the Skandia taxonomy taken from a paper on the subject published in early 2002 by McElroy (2002) (see Figure 6.11).

The influence of the KLC on the new KM's perspective on IC is dramatic and direct. Intellectual capital schemes, we have argued, should explicitly reflect the value contributions of the social capacity to produce and integrate knowledge, and not just the value of its outcomes (i.e., knowledge). Indeed, as we have said, the only thing more valuable than valuable organizational knowledge may be the organizational capacity to produce it. The KLC is perhaps the most complete, most rigorous attempt to specify the dimensions of such

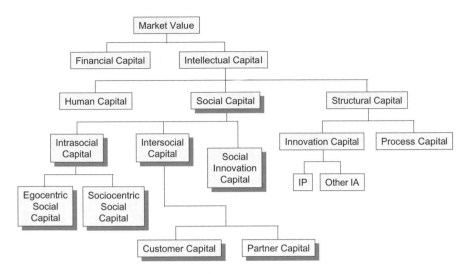

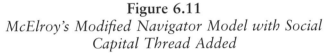

Figure 6.11
*McElroy's Modified Navigator Model with Social
Capital Thread Added*

capital, and it therefore has a significant role to play in the further development of IC management schemes. (See Chapter 10 for more discussion of the new KM's perspective on intellectual capital measurement and management schemes.)

EDUCATION AND TRAINING

There are two senses of this subject that have been impacted by the KLC and its insights. The first is how we should regard the role of education and training in organizations, and the second is the educational and training implications for KM itself. In other words, armed with our knowledge of the KLC, what sort of training should knowledge managers themselves be seeking? Let's examine these perspectives separately.

The purpose of education and training in most organizations is generally understood to be enhancing performance. People need to learn the skills required to carry out their roles and responsibilities in organizations. But is training through, say, formal corporate programs or other structured approaches really the best way to go about it? Are there other less formal and even less prescribed sources of learning that people can turn to? Well, of course there are, but it wasn't until two years ago, when a small firm called CapitalWorks LLC in Williamstown, Massachusetts, actually studied the question of where knowledge in use at work actually comes from, that the pattern was more clearly understood.

CapitalWorks, led by Jeff Kelley, conducted a survey at that time, in which hundreds of corporate workers were asked to characterize the distribution of knowledge sources relative to knowledge actually used on the job. Of the eleven categories used to classify responses, some represented formal sources while others were informal. Fully 75% of the sources cited for knowledge used on the job were informal, while only 25% were formal (see Figure 6.5).

Despite this, however, the same companies' investments in education and training were almost exclusively aimed at formal programs in exactly the opposite proportions (75% of the investments being made in learning were aimed at formal programs, with the remainder being aimed at informal ones). The disconnect between how companies were investing in learning versus the actual means and sources that employees turn to and rely on was striking.

Among the very interesting conclusions reached by Kelley and his team at CapitalWorks (CapitalWorks 2002) was that without spending any additional money at all on education and training, most companies could dramatically improve ROI from their investments in learning simply by shifting spending from formal sources to informal ones. Indeed, doing so even as overall spending is *reduced* might fetch better results!

What does any of this have to do with the KLC, you ask? As a self-organizing system, the KLC is, in a sense, an informal learning system. It is not a designed system, it is an emergent one. Further, many of its constituent subprocesses are themselves also informal. Communities of Practice, for example, are often informal, especially the most prolific ones. To wit, the very idea of the KLC itself and all that we discuss in this book and others are the products of an entirely informal group of like-minded individuals who banded together in late 1997 to form *a new KM*. The Knowledge Management Consortium International (KMCI) was/is the organizational outcome of that effort, and the KLC and many of the other ideas discussed in this book are the outcomes of *its* KLC.

So a case can be made for aiming more corporate investments toward informal learning and less on formal learning. But when we speak of "shifting spending from formal sources to informal ones" for the purpose of enhancing learning, then, exactly where should those dollars go? To enhancing the KLC, of course! In fact, bankrolling the start-up of a new KM effort in a company could come, at least in part, from dollars shifted out of training and into KM efforts to enhance the KLC. More important, Kelley's study at CapitalWorks adds fuel to the fire of the movement behind the new KM, which claims that it is the informal learning process at both the individual and collective levels that we should be seeking to support and reinforce above all else. And enhancing the KLC is the blueprint for doing so. Enhance and invest in the KLC, we argue, and higher performance in both learning and business processing will follow.

This application of the KLC, valuable as it is, also has the effect of calling into question the conventional wisdom of how people should be expected to learn in business. At the very least, we argue, managers should be attempting to strike more of a balance between investments made in formal versus informal learning programs. Kelley and his team at CapitalWorks (CapitalWorks 2002) refer to this as managing "Learning Portfolios." Is there a one-size-fits-all formula for this? Of course not. But it should be sufficient for purposes of getting started to (a) make the distinction between formal versus informal learning, (b) understand that informal learning should be prioritized from an investment point of view, and (c) that investments made on the informal side of the fence should be aimed, in particular, at strengthening the KLC and its constituent subprocesses. Even investments in *formal* learning programs should be seen and evaluated in light of their place in (and impact on) the KLC, since they, too, are reflected therein.

THE OPEN ENTERPRISE

As we discuss later on in Chapter 11, one of the most important ideas to come out of the new Knowledge Management is the concept of the Open Enterprise. Openness, in this context, is an application of the great twentieth-century philosopher Karl Popper's epistemology, whose vision of the Open Society (1945) stood in opposition to the kinds of oligarchical and coercive knowledge processing regimes associated with dictatorships and other totalitarian forms of government. But this is not surprising. Popper was a victim of such oppression, both before and during World War II, thanks to which he was forced to flee his home country of Austria and settle in New Zealand and then later on in Great Britain.

Underlying Popper's philosophy was the idea that humans can never really *know* for sure whether they have found the truth. Rather, the best we can do is to eliminate falsity (or error) wherever we find it, but to be certain that we know the truth requires a degree of omniscience that we simply do not have. This does not, however, prevent us from seeking the truth or from striving to eliminate our errors. The regulative ideal here is the truth. The activity involved is truth-seeking. And the outcome expected is enhanced closeness or proximity to the truth. We can achieve such proximity by focusing on error reduction, and sometimes we may even discover or find the truth, but even then we can never know for sure that we have done so.

Popper's (1972) focus on error reduction and his rejection of justificationist and foundationalist approaches to epistemology is known as fallibilism. Popper, along with the great American pragmatist philosopher Charles Sanders Peirce (1966), was a fallibilist. Popper (1934, 1959) was also a falsificationist—indeed, he was the founder of falsificationism, the idea that while universal knowledge claims cannot be confirmed or verified by empirical testing, they can be falsified, but also not with certainty (fallibilism).

We have taken Popper's fallibilist and falsificationist epistemology, which he previously applied in a societal context, and applied it to business. Hence, we go from Popper's vision of the open society to our own vision of the Open Enterprise. And here is where the KLC comes into play—in two important ways.

First, we have already made the very important distinction between knowledge processing (the KLC) and business processing. This is of foundational importance to the new KM. Having done so, we can see not only the distinction between them, but also the relationship they share. Knowledge *use* (in business processing) relies heavily—is *dependent* upon—knowledge processing, for without knowledge processing there would be *no knowledge to use* in business. Therefore, when we find problems with knowledge use, such as corporate behaviors we disagree with or condemn, the remedy can be found not only in making changes in business practices (which is knowledge use), but more fundamentally in knowledge processing. How, we can ask ourselves, does illicit or illegal behavior get that far in a firm? What must its knowledge processing systems be like if poor judgment can escalate from the level of ideas to the realm of practice?

Second, while our understanding of the KLC makes it possible to see both the distinctions and the connections between knowledge processing and business processing, it also gives us a place to go in terms of specific remedies. What we mean by remedies here are *solutions to problems found in knowledge processing* which, in turn, manifest themselves in unwanted business processing behaviors. More specifically, we can reasonably claim that knowledge processing regimes that are, in a sense, politically closed can be seen as being responsible for the illicit or unwanted business processing behaviors that follow. The cure for unwanted business behaviors, then, may lie more in the remediation of knowledge processing than in the reform of business processing behaviors themselves. The former leads to the latter, while the latter does not necessarily lead to the former or to sustained change of any kind.

Achieving the vision of the Open Enterprise, therefore, amounts making interventions at the level of knowledge processing in such a way that it (a) becomes more transparent to, and inclusive of, the stakeholder population it serves, and (b) revolves around the merits of knowledge claims and not their exponents. The validity of a knowledge claim should be a function of its internal merits, not the rank or status of its promoters. Thus, the Open Enterprise is *open* in the sense of participation and open in the sense that knowledge claims, or as Popper called them, conjectures, are unrestrictedly open to criticism and refutation, no matter what their source. The variables used to specify, regulate, and manage this kind of openness are precisely the attributes of the subprocesses identified in the KLC. Our knowledge and management of the KLC, then, is an indispensable element of any effort to make organizations more open, more responsible, and more adaptive. Achieving the Open Enterprise is both an important application of the KLC, as well as an illustration of how KM can be used to achieve knowledge processing outcomes, this time with enhancing organizational openness and accountability in mind.

New Value Propositions for Knowledge Management

Perhaps the most fruitful illustration of how the new KM adds value to the KM profession is made by simply calling attention to what are, in fact, its value contributions or propositions to business. At the heart of the matter is the KLC, a vision of knowledge processing that is utterly missing from the conventional practice of KM, or what we sometimes refer to as "first-generation KM." Let us first quickly review what *its* propositions are.

Most of what passes for KM tends to revolve around the idea of enhancing knowledge sharing. While it's true that the KLC featured in second-generation thinking includes sharing as well, it is by no means confined to it. First-generation thinking, however, does tend to focus almost exclusively on what we can think of as "sharing transactions." A sharing transaction would consist of one person sharing "knowledge" with another, either in person, electronically in real-time, or through use of some delayed means such as portals or IT-based repositories of other kinds. In all such cases, the business processing context is extremely narrow. It begins with someone needing information, searching for it, finding it, and acquiring it. These discrete episodes of sharing transactions are the first-generation KM equivalent of the KLC. They form the basis of most of what we see in the conventional practice of KM.

What, then, is the value proposition of first-generation KM? There are two of them. First is the ability to expedite sharing transactions. People can theoretically satisfy their demands for knowledge more quickly in the presence of a first-generation system. We call such approaches to KM "supply-side" in scope because they are designed to enhance the supply of existing knowledge from one party in an organization to another.

The second value proposition for first-generation KM is enhanced business processing performance. By shortening the cycle time of sharing transactions, less time is taken away from business processing; hence business processing behavior improves, or is at least more efficient. Thus, the ultimate value received from investments in first-generation (aka the *old*) KM is reduction in business processing cycle times.

Now comes the new KM, and with it a considerably wider view of knowledge processing (the KLC). It encompasses the first-generation view of sharing transactions but is not confined to them.

Rather, it develops a significantly wider and deeper view of knowledge processing that includes knowledge sharing but positions it as only one form of knowledge integration. Further, it rejects the first-generation tendency to simply assume that valuable knowledge exists and thereby takes up the question of how we produce it. Knowledge production processes figure prominently in the KLC for that reason.

But the new KM takes another crucial step that is entirely missing from previous formulations of KM: it defines the difference between information and knowledge and brings *that* to the table. Notice how, in the following statement heard almost universally in KM circles, the distinction between the two is glossed over and obfuscated:

> *It's all about getting the right information to the right people at the right time.*

How many times have we heard that phrase offered up as the driving vision for KM? The value proposition inside it is clear: expediting the delivery of information to people who need it in order to expedite, in turn, their business processing performance. But where is "knowledge" in this claim? We see only "information." Or are the two, from a first-generation KM perspective, equivalent? And if so, then what does "KM" bring to the table that wasn't already there in the form of IM (information management)? And where do we turn in the literature of first-generation thinking for answers to our questions? Frankly, there are none. The distinction between information and knowledge has never been satisfactorily addressed in the KM literature until, that is, the arrival of second-generation thinking, or *the new KM*.

Now this issue alone is worth the price of admission to the new KM because of the following reason: what if the information delivered "to the right person at the right time" is, in fact, false? Of what possible value could that be to the person who needs it? Or will any old information do? No, we not only need information as quickly as we can find it, we need valid information, as well. Without that, we're at best simply trading effectiveness for efficiency, because anyone can deliver false information quickly, but only valid information can make us more effective. And, at worst, by basing our decisions on false information we are assuming the risk that we will have to cope with the unexpected consequences specified in the true knowledge claims we have ignored or rejected. This last is the risk of relying on information in preference to knowledge.

This absence of focus on the relative validity of information managed and used by workers in organizations is the quiet scandal of first generation KM. How could a discipline that refers to itself using the "K" word (knowledge) be so devoid of considerations related to testing and evaluating the information it so eagerly serves up to its customers? How can it be so devoid of an emphasis on error elimination in knowledge claims?

And if the difference between information and knowledge does involve differences in the track record of competing knowledge claims in surviving testing, evaluation, and error elimination, then where do we go for knowledge about the distinction? What other branch of management theory and practice do we turn to for help not only in delivering information more quickly, but in delivering tested, evaluated, and reliable information, as well? The answer is the new KM, with its emphasis on error elimination through knowledge claim evaluation as its centerpiece.

We fully appreciate that our remarks here amount to an indictment of KM in its conventional, normal forms, but we make no apologies for declaring that the emperor has no clothes. People looking for ways of expediting the delivery of information should turn to IM, not KM. Information management has a long history of doing that, even while it, like first-generation KM, washes its hands of the validity issue and makes no representations whatsoever as to the validity of the claims contained in the objects it handles. *Garbage in, garbage out*, right?

Here, then, is what is perhaps the new KM's most significant value proposition: the ability to differentiate between "just information" and information that has survived our tests of validity over time: "knowledge." When we produce new knowledge, it exists only in the form of claims or hypotheses. Before it deserves recognition by us as something more than "just information," it must be subjected to tests, criticism (openly so), error reduction, and refutation, if appropriate. Knowledge claims (information) that survive that process thereby warrant special recognition, the name for which is "knowledge."

Notice that in the paragraph above, the process described is embodied in the formulation of the KLC shown in Figure 6.2. The KLC is, in fact, the source of this insight. But apart from the details, notice as well that the KLC has had the effect of raising the validation issue, that it has exposed the nudity of the first generation KM emperor. "What about the truth or falsity of the information we're receiving?" we can ask ourselves. What about *that*? Don't we care about the quality or relevance of the information we're receiving, or is it only about speed of retrieval? Of course we care, and the new KM provides us with a strategy for what to do about it, and the KLC is its road map.

Let us conclude this section by briefly calling attention to several other value propositions that are available to us as a consequence of the new KM and the KLC. Here they are:

- A Unified Theory of Knowledge: The KLC makes it clear to us that there are two kinds of knowledge in organizations and that both have an impact on each other, our learning, and the knowledge we individually and collectively practice. The first is subjective knowledge, knowledge in minds; the second is objective knowledge, or claims expressed in linguistic form. Both forms of knowledge play significant roles in the KLC and are explicitly shown in what the KLC identifies as the DOKB (Distributed Organizational Knowledge Base). (See Chapters 1 and 2 for more discussion on the meaning of knowledge in the new KM.)

- The Enterprise Knowledge Portal: Consistent with our discussion above, the new KM makes a sharp distinction between information and knowledge, highlighting the record of testing and evaluation behind claims as the difference that makes a difference. Thus, IT systems that purport to be "knowledge management" systems should support our need for this kind of meta information and without that should be seen by us as nothing more than information systems. Where and how to position such systems is revealed to us through close examination of the KLC. Moreover, the same systems should support the KM function itself which, as we have explained at length, is not the same as KP (knowledge processing), but is just as much in need of support. There are currently no portal products or otherwise in the market that support these applications (Firestone 2003), but the new KM and its conception of the KLC point to what KM needs from IT.

- New Perspective on the KM Function: As noted above, the idea of the KLC, and the new KM in general, makes the very important distinction between KM and KP (knowledge processing). If we are to have a meaningful and useful form of KM, then, we must approach it with the separate treatment that it deserves. KM is not knowledge sharing; it is a management discipline that seeks to enhance knowledge sharing and all of the other aspects of the KLC. The KM function itself is independent of knowledge processing, but it, too, has a KLC inside of it that produces and integrates *its* knowledge. Here we can envision a KM function that has a practice layer (people who make interventions in target KLCs); a management layer (people who manage the KM function itself); and a KLC layer (a knowledge processing environment that supports the KM function only and not the business processing environment of its target population).

■ Learning and Adaptivity: Ultimately, the most beneficial impact of enhancing the KLC is that it improves an organization's capacity to learn and adapt. This is especially true in cases where the KM strategy, in particular, strives to achieve enhanced levels of openness in knowledge processing (see Chapter 11). It should be clearly understood, then, that the KLC is the main engine room of innovation, organizational learning, agility, and adaptivity. It is where all of those things happen. Managers wishing to improve their organization's capacity to learn and adapt in the marketplace should look no further. The secret to enhanced performance in business is in the care and feeding of the KLC. Enhancing *its* performance therefore leads to improvements in business processing, since all business processing behaviors are, after all, nothing more than knowledge in use.

CONCLUSION

There are many other areas of interest to practitioners of KM where the KLC has a valuable role to play. The scope of its influence on the practice of KM is extensive, and our discussion has focused on only a few areas. Nevertheless, the breadth and significance of the applications discussed illustrate the centrality of the KLC to KM and also its utility from the point of view of practice. It also illustrates that the KLC changes everything for KM. Its implications penetrate every nook and cranny of KM as a discipline and every area of KM practice.

Again, the importance of the role that a conceptual framework or model of knowledge processing plays in the practice of KM cannot be overstated. It is absolutely critical that we begin the practice of KM with a framework or model describing in broad outline how knowledge is produced and integrated in human social systems. From there we can begin to formulate practice but always with reference to our theory. We must have grounding. All bodies of practice in KM should be held to this standard. What are their interventions? What methods do they use? How are their methods and interventions related to knowledge processing? Indeed, what is their theory *of* knowledge processing? Do they even have one? If not, how do they account for knowledge production and integration, and how does their practice relate to their theory? If not, why should we accept their value claims?

As we sometimes say, the only thing worse than all theory and no practice is all practice and no theory. In truth we need both—practice *grounded* in theory. In the new KM, the KLC is the most important focus of our theory. Many of our practices, then, are grounded in and upon it, and from the point of view offered to us by the KLC, the mission of the new knowledge management—to enhance knowledge processing—is clear!

REFERENCES

Allee, V. (2000), "Reconfiguring the Value Network," available at: http://www.vernaallee.com/reconfiguring_val_net.html.

Allee, V. (2003), *The Future of Knowledge*, Boston, MA: Butterworth–Heinemann.

CapitalWorks, LLC (2002) www.capworks.com.

Edvinsson, L. and Malone, M. (1997), *Intellectual Capital*, New York, NY: Harper.

Firestone, J.M. (1999), "The Metaprise, the AKMS, and the Enterprise Knowledge Portal," *Working Paper No. 3*, *Executive Information Systems, Inc.*, Wilmington, DE, May 5, 1999, Available at: http://www.dkms.com/White_Papers.htm.

Firestone, J.M. (1999a), "Enterprise Information Portals and Enterprise Knowledge Portals," *DKMS Brief*, **8**, *Executive Information Systems*,

Inc., Wilmington, DE, March 20, 1999. Available at
http://www.dkms.com/White_Papers.htm.

Firestone, J.M. (1999b), "The Artificial Knowledge Manager Standard: A
Strawman," Executive Information Systems KMCI Working Paper No. 1.
Wilmington, DE, Available at http://www.dkms.com/White_Papers.htm.

Firestone, J.M. (2000), "The Enterprise Knowledge Portal Revisited," *White
Paper No. 15, Executive Information Systems, Inc.*, Wilmington, DE,
March 15, 2000, Available at: http://www.dkms.com/White_Papers.htm.

Firestone, J.M. (2000a), "Enterprise Knowledge Portals: What They Are
and What They Do," *Knowledge and Innovation: Journal of the KMCI,
1, no. 1*, 85–108. Available at: http://www.dkms.com/White_Papers.htm.

Firestone, J.M. (2001), "Knowledge Management Process Methodology",
Knowledge and Innovation: Journal of the KMCI, 1, no. 2, 85–108. Available at: http://www.dkms.com/White_Papers.htm.

Firestone, J.M. (2001a), "Enterprise Knowledge Portals, Knowledge Processing and Knowledge Management," in Ramon Barquin, Alex Bennet,
and Shereen Remez (eds.) *Building Knowledge Management Environments for Electronic Government*, Vienna, VA: Management Concepts.

Firestone, J.M. (2003), *Enterprise Information Portals and Knowledge
Management*, Boston, MA: KMCI Press/Butterworth–Heinemann.

Gleick, J. (1987), *Chaos—Making a New Science*, New York, NY: Penguin
Books.

Macroinnovation Associates, LLC (2002), at:
http://www.macroinnovation.com/simulator.htm.

McElroy, M.W. (1999), "The Second Generation of KM," *Knowledge Management* (October 1999), pp. 86–88.

McElroy, M.W. (2002), "Social Innovation Capital," *Journal of Intellectual
Capital* (Vol. 3, No. 1), pp. 30–39.

McElroy, M.W. (2002a), "A Framework for Knowledge Management,"
Cutter IT Journal (March 2002, Vol. 15, No. 3), pp. 12–17.

McElroy, M.W. (2003), *The New Knowledge Management: Complexity,
Learning, and Sustainable Innovation*, Boston, MA: KMCI Press/
Butterworth–Heinemann.

McElroy, M.W. and Cavaleri, S. (2002), The Policy Synchronization
Method was developed by McElroy and Cavaleri and is the subject of a
U.S. business method patent application field in September, 2000.

Nonaka, I. and Takeuchi, H. (1995), *The Knowledge Creating Company*,
New York, NY: Oxford University Press.

Peirce, C. (1966), "Types of Reasoning," in A. Rorty (ed.), *Pragmatic Philosophy*, Garden City, NY: Anchor Books, Doubleday.

Popper, K.R. (1934), *Logik der Forschung*, Vienna, AU: Springer.

Popper, K.R. (1959), *The Logic of Scientific Discovery*, London, Hutchinson.

Popper, K.R. (1972), *Objective Knowledge*, London, England: Oxford University Press.

Popper, K.R. (1994), *Knowledge and the Body-Mind Problem* (edited by Mark A. Notturno), London, UK: Routledge.

Stewart, T. (1994), "Your Company's Most Valuable Asset: Intellectual Capital," *Fortune* (October 13, 1994) cover story.

Chapter 7

KNOWLEDGE MANAGEMENT AS BEST PRACTICES SYSTEMS—WHERE'S THE CONTEXT?

BEST PRACTICE: THE LACK-OF-CONTEXT PROBLEM

One of the many preconceived notions swirling around knowledge management for years has been that KM is all about the codification of business processes or tasks within them—that is, that KM makes it possible for knowledge workers to quickly access and apply so-called best practices on an as-needed basis. Workers with difficult decisions about what to do when faced with uncertainty are seen as spontaneously turning to KM systems for the answers—IT-based ones, of course.

More recently, this approach to KM has fallen from favor as many knowledge managers have encountered what we will refer to as *"the lack of context problem."* Their complaint? That knowledge management systems do an adequate job of delivering codified best practices but are terrible at providing insight about when to use them, much less context of any other kind that might aid in the decision about which ones to, in fact, adopt and when.

238

The devil in the details here is the precise definition of what people mean when they refer to context in, well, *this* context. Context is one of those words like culture (see Chapter 9): we all use it a lot, but it's not always clear what we mean by it (see the discussion in Chapter 4). What exactly, for example, would constitute the right kind of context in a KM system that would satisfy users and knowledge managers? Would it be more information about the circumstances in which a recommended practice should be used or not used? If so, what kind of information, in particular, would make the difference?

We agree with the concern that recommendations made in the absence of context are a problem, and that KM systems predicated on such propositions are shaky at best. The fact is that people on the front lines of business are always operating in a context of some kind, and the suitability of past practices for present day use cannot always be presumed. Indeed, this is precisely the question we ask ourselves, if only unconsciously, whenever we are faced with the option of invoking past practice for current needs. Will a decision to do so fetch the desired results? Further, what was it that made the practice desirable in the past, and what were its outcomes?

What we disagree with is (a) the tendency of many people who wrestle with this issue to put specificity aside in their definitions of context, and (b) the manner in which the questions themselves are framed. To do a proper job of resolving the lack-of-context problem, we must begin by adjusting our thinking about what a "best practice" *is* in a KM system.

KNOWLEDGE CLAIMS

Strictly speaking, best practices systems (computer-based ones) do not contain best practices at all. What they contain are *claims about* best practices. Practices are human behaviors, not claims in computer systems. So we can think of the *references* to best practices in computer systems as knowledge claims, no more. Each claim, in turn, can be thought of as an argument or an assertion, which takes the form of a linguistic, semantic network—digitally codified, of course.

Let's take management consulting, for example. In the preparation of recommendations for clients, all consultants are called upon to perform cost-benefit analyses in which the cost of implementing and maintaining business solutions are laid out in some detail. But there's more than one way to do that, some of which may be of use to a particular client while others may not. What, then, would a best practice be in situation A versus situation B? The answer, if it exists, would take the form of a claim that might read as follows:

> *Whenever faced with client situations of types 1, 2, or 3, use method A to prepare implementation and maintenance cost projections; when faced with situations 4, 5, or 6, use method B.*

The implicit claims in these two statements are as follows:

> *Method A generally works best when faced with situations 1, 2, or 3. Method B generally works best when faced with situations 4, 5, or 6.*

While not expressed in precisely these terms, the purpose behind every best practices system is quite clear: to *prescribe* behaviors of particular kinds as the best courses of action to take *in response to* situations of particular kinds: *If* you encounter A, *do* X; *if* you encounter B, *do* Y. This is generally as far as most systems go. They present the claim (in this case a rule), but not the basis behind it. Users of such systems are expected to simply accept the claim and apply it without question. Or, if discretion is allowed, the absence of evidence or arguments in support of the claim makes it all but impossible to determine its suitability.

We know from our discussion of information versus knowledge (see Chapters 1 through 5) that the difference between the two is determined by whether or not claims are accompanied by *information about claims*—i.e., by *claims about claims*, or metaclaims, if you like. Claims made in the absence of metaclaims are merely information. Think of them as unsupported assertions. Only claims that have survived our testing and evaluation made with the support of metaclaims can be seen as passing for knowledge, because they provide the argument and/or the evidence needed to help us differentiate truth from falsity. But this, of course, is exactly what most so-called best practices KM systems lack: *metaclaims*.

Metaclaims as Context

Metaclaims, to our way of thinking, comprise the most important kind of context that all knowledge processing systems should have in order to be useful. Why? Because unless we're talking about workers who function as virtual automatons, people faced with uncertainty almost always rely on their own final judgments about what to do. This is consistent with the notion of being accountable for performance and the general trend in favor of empowering individuals and encouraging them to take risks and to act in accordance with their own initiative. Work is becoming more complex and more unpredictable, not less so. Under these conditions, decision making is less centralized and more decentralized, of necessity. The act of choosing between two or more alternatives is a distributed act that goes on in the minds of countless workers—*knowledge workers*, that is. That's why we call them knowledge workers.

That said, it should be clear that what knowledge workers need are not just computer-based repositories of other peoples' ideas about what they should do, but also insights about why they (the other people) think so. If, in someone's opinion, method A should always be used in situations 1, 2, or 3, then it is incumbent upon that someone to also explain why. Why should we use method A? What is the reasoning behind that claim—its basis? And more important, what has its track record of success *and* failure been when used in the past? In other words, what we need in best practices systems (or in *any* knowledge processing system, for that matter) are metaclaims that accompany knowledge claims, and which furnish us with the record of testing and evaluation for the claims they contain. No knowledge processing system should be viewed as complete unless it contains such a metaclaim dimension (see Figure 7.1).

Once we recognize the fact that people instinctively look for and rely on metaclaims as a basis for discovering and choosing among multiple, competing knowledge claims, it's a short hop from there to appreciating that *that's* the kind of context sorely needed in knowledge processing systems and that its absence is fatal. Best practices systems that fail to provide their users with insight as to why claims are being made, what the arguments are in support of them, and what their histories of performance have been will always leave their users dissatisfied and unfulfilled. Why? Because these are the kinds of questions we ask ourselves when confronted with competing claims, and

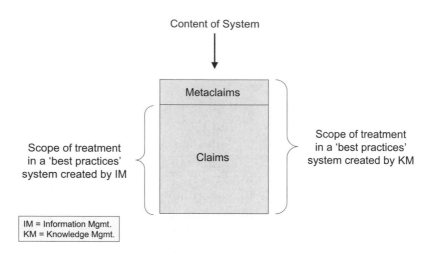

Figure 7.1
Metaclaims and Best Practices in Knowledge Management

so a system that overlooks or ignores them is bound to disappoint us and fall short of the mark. When this happens, we simply turn elsewhere for answers.

Unfortunately, most attempts to build and deploy best practices systems not only fail to address the metaclaim issue, they compound the problem by forcing people to populate their repositories with codified descriptions of practices, work products, and the like. Efforts to do so are unduly time consuming, disruptive, and are seen as having dubious value. As a result, resentment builds, and the systems themselves become distrusted, since most people come to see their content as more the result of indentured servitude than any genuine attempt to capture truly useful information or knowledge. Further, their own firsthand experience in using the system, since it consistently fails to address their basic needs for metaclaims, ultimately comes home to roost, and the reputation of KM suffers accordingly.

A BETTER WAY

Tom Davenport, who along with Larry Prusak, published one of the first well-known books dedicated to KM (*Working Knowledge*, 1998), recently published an article in *Harvard Business Review* coauthored with John Glaser, entitled "Just-in-Time Delivery Comes to Knowledge Management" (2002). In their very interesting account of KM at the Boston-based health care provider Partners HealthCare, Davenport and Glaser described a system that "bakes specialized knowledge into the jobs of highly skilled workers [i.e., physicians]—to make the knowledge so readily accessible that it can't be avoided" (ibid., 108). They do this by embedding knowledge related to the physicians' order entry process into the technology used to support it (the order entry process).

Here is Davenport's and Glaser's (ibid., 109) account of how it works:

> Let's say Dr. Goldszer [a physician at one of Partners' hospitals] has a patient, Mrs. Johnson, and she has a serious infection. He decides to treat the infection with ampicillin. As he logs on to the computer to order the drug, the system automatically checks her medical records for allergic reactions to any medications. She's never taken that particular medication, but she once had an allergic reaction to penicillin, a drug chemically similar to ampicillin. The computer brings that reaction to Goldszer's attention and asks if he wants to continue with the order. He asks the system what the allergic reaction was. It could have been something relatively minor, like a rash, or major, like going into shock. Mrs. Johnson's reaction was a rash. Goldszer decides to override the computer's recommendation and prescribe the original medication, judging that the positive benefit from the prescription outweighs the negative effects of a relatively minor and treatable rash. The system lets him do that, but requires him to give a reason for overriding its recommendation.

In sharing this account, Davenport and Glaser go so far as to suggest that integrating KM functionality into the fabric of business processes and supporting applications (IT) "could revolutionize knowledge management in the same way that just-in-time systems revolutionized inventory management—and by following much the same philosophy" (ibid., 108). It is perhaps worth pausing here to note the important distinction we make throughout this book between knowledge management and knowledge processing. Since the system developed by Partners HealthCare is designed to help physicians close their epistemic or knowledge gaps, it is a knowledge processing system, not a KM system. Knowledge management, however, can take credit for the design and implementation of the system. Deploying a knowledge processing system is an act of knowledge management; using it afterward is not.

That said, what we find most interesting about the Partners HealthCare case are two things. First is the manner in which metaclaims figure into the picture. As we have said, having access to the metaclaims that lie behind so-called best practices (or any other kind of claim) is crucial to knowledge processing. This, then, is an important step in the right direction. But recognition of the specific contribution of metaclaims as *the difference that makes a difference* in this case does not appear in the authors' analysis. This is unfortunate, for the hidden role that metaclaims play in their case study is the most important part of the story.

Second, we agree that the integration of knowledge processing functionality with business processes at Partners is important, but the lesson in it has more to do with the extent to which IT-based knowledge processing has been tightly integrated with order entry (also IT-based, in this case), and the degree to which *both* have been positioned in direct, promiscuous support of the physicians' business processes. But since our primary concern here is with the pivotal role of metaclaims in best practices systems, we will only be examining the first of these two observations in the remainder of our remarks.

The Partners HealthCare system is arguably a best practices system because of the manner in which it attempts to prescribe business processing decisions and related behaviors. From the perspective of *The New Knowledge Management*, the vignette above features a physician engaged in a business process (order entry), who is using knowledge. The physician is therefore operating in a business processing mode, which is the behavioral domain in which knowledge *use* occurs.

Periodically, however, the physician experiences "problems," that is, epistemic gaps—gaps in the knowledge required to take effective action. When this happens, the physician effectively steps out of the business processing mode and enters the knowledge processing mode. The knowledge processing mode is where knowledge *production* and *integration* occur. In other words, the physician kicks off a KLC, or knowledge life cycle (see Chapter 2), in order to produce or discover the knowledge needed. Once the knowledge is produced or obtained, the physician reverts to his business processing mode and proceeds with his order entry. Let's look at the Davenport and Glaser anecdote more closely to see where this dynamic occurs, and the crucial role that metaclaims play in the process.

Metaclaims in Action

Upon first logging onto the system, the physician develops a need to know what the patient's history of allergic reactions might be to medications. This "problem" (or epistemic gap) crops up and is detected in the business processing mode, thereby triggering a KLC at the level of the physician. The physician then steps out of the business processing mode and enters the knowledge processing mode. And since the physician has granted a knowledge production proxy to his employer, he effectively skips through the knowledge production part of the KLC and goes directly to knowledge integration. The patient's pertinent medical history is thereby broadcasted to him; he receives the answers he was looking for, and he exits the knowledge processing mode and reenters business processing.

Next, since the IT-based knowledge processing application reported that the patient did, in fact, once have an allergic reaction to a drug similar to the one the physician plans to prescribe, the computer system effectively challenges the claim that doing so would be proper. Here we have two competing knowledge claims going on, one that says ampicillin is an appropriate drug to use in this case, and another that says it might not be—or isn't. In a conventional best practices system, this might be as far as things would go. The system would advise against a certain action, or in favor of another one, leaving the user hanging, as it were, as to which alternative he should choose.

In the Partners case, however, the physician has the opportunity to challenge the computer's claim by referring to the metaclaims that lie behind it. The computer's implicit claim in this case could be interpreted as follows:

Ampicillin should be avoided in this case, since the patient has had adverse reactions to the use of similar drugs, specifically penicillin, in the past.

The physician, however, decides to challenge this claim by observing that not all adverse reactions are sufficiently undesirable to outweigh the benefits of ampicillin in cases where symptoms of the sort his patient displays are present. Here again the physician is operating in a knowledge processing mode—this time *minus* the proxy he earlier invoked with regard to his patient's records. So instead of simply accepting the computer system's claim, he subjects it to scrutiny and to his own knowledge claim evaluation (KCE) process. In other words, he is operating in the knowledge production mode of the KLC and is subjecting a knowledge claim to his own testing and evaluation process.

In this case, the physician exercises his KCE process by referring to the metaclaims associated with the claim that he should avoid prescribing ampicillin. The computer system, in turn, fetches the metaclaims consisting of the patient's previous, adverse reaction to penicillin, relying further on the metaclaim that penicillin is similar to ampicillin and that adverse reactions to one can foretell adverse reactions to the other.

Not yet satisfied, the physician digs even deeper into the metaclaims and requests more information about the symptoms previously displayed by his patient. The answer? A rash. Armed with this metaclaim, the physician then makes a KCE decision: he rejects the computer system's claim and adopts his own:

> *Ampicillin can be used in this case, despite the patient's prior adverse reactions to the use of similar drugs, because the reactions were minor, are easily treatable, and do not outweigh in consideration the anticipated positive benefits of ampicillin.*

The physician then integrates his new, tested, and evaluated knowledge claim into his own knowledge base (i.e., his portion of the organization's broader Distributed Organizational Knowledge Base, or "DOKB"), returns to the business processing mode, and applies his new claim (now "knowledge" for him).

Finally, because the computer system has a metaclaim dimension to it, the physician's reasoning behind why he rejected one claim and adopted another is of interest to its makers (i.e., the knowledge managers who produced it). Thus, in allowing the physician to override the system's claims, the knowledge processing system at Partners still "requires him to give a reason for overriding its recommendation." In other words, the system asks for the physician's metaclaims about his own claims, presumably because the system adds such claims to its content, just as it tracks the percentage of its recommendations (claims) actually accepted by physicians versus those that are not.

Davenport's and Glaser's account does not elaborate on how the Partners system handles counter-claims and counter-metaclaims. It does, however, give us a glimpse into how its own claims and metaclaims are produced—namely, they are developed by committee. Apparently, the official knowledge production and integration process at Partners (i.e., the KLC behind the knowledge-based order entry system) is staffed by panels of experts. In this way, claims are formally produced and integrated into the system, as are the metaclaims that lie behind them.

CONCLUSION

In the future, we believe that the kind of system in use at Partners will become more common. We do not, however, believe that their growth and success will be determined by the degree to which the knowledge contained in them is baked "into the jobs of highly skilled workers" (Davenport and Glaser 2002, 108). Rather, we think that the success of such systems will stem from the extent to which they make access to metaclaims possible, and by how well they reveal the relationships between metaclaims and best practices. After all, best practices systems contain nothing but claims about business processes, and all claims are predicated on metaclaims. Without having access to metaclaims, people using best practices systems are reduced to guesswork, or worse yet, uninformed decision making.

Next, we think a comment or two on this business of integrating knowledge processing functionality (they call it "KM") with business processes is warranted. That idea, and the related just-in-time metaphor that Davenport and Glaser use, is somewhat misleading. First, all knowledge processing applications are intended for use in an integrated fashion with business processes. What could the alternative possibly be? Have all knowledge processing systems historically been designed for use in a *disintegrated* fashion? Were they meant to be used apart from the business processes they were designed to support? Of course not. No, what is new and different in the case of Partners HealthCare is the extent to which IT-based knowledge processing has been tightly integrated with order entry (also IT-based), and the degree to which *both* have been positioned in direct, promiscuous support of the physicians' business processes.

Further, we think the just-in-time metaphor is also misleading. Haven't all knowledge processing systems been designed with real-time usage in mind? Or were all knowledge processing systems previously contemplated with after-the-fact use in mind? Of course they weren't. The idea has always been that as users encounter epistemic gaps, related knowledge processing systems would be available to them on an as-needed basis, in real time. Indeed, supply-side knowledge processing systems have always been about getting *the right information to the right people at the right time*.

Without a doubt, timing of delivery is important, but the real significance of the Partners HealthCare system, in our view, is the extent to which it features a metaclaims dimension. That, and not the degree of its business process integration, is the sine qua non of a best practices system. The same is true for knowledge processing systems of any other kind. If it doesn't deal with metaclaims, it's not a knowledge processing system. Indeed, *that's* the kind of context that matters most in knowledge processing, and yet few systems have it. In the "new KM," however, metaclaims are ubiquitous.

REFERENCES

Davenport, T. and Glaser, J. "Just-in-Time Delivery Comes to Knowledge Management," *Harvard Business Review* (July, 2002), pp. 107–111.

Davenport, T. and Prusak, L. (1998), *Working Knowledge*, Boston, MA: Harvard Business School Press.

Chapter 8

What Comes First: Knowledge Management or Strategy?

Introduction

Few issues in knowledge management provoke debate more fiery than the question of how KM relates to strategy and who it should report to. Is KM the servant of strategy? Or does KM somehow transcend it? Should KM be independent of strategy and not subordinate or answerable to its makers? Should strategy be seen as just another kind of knowledge claim, a product of knowledge processing? If so, and if KM is all about enhancing knowledge processing, then isn't business strategy arguably downstream from KM and not the reverse?

Further, if strategy is indeed nothing more than just another (set of) knowledge claim(s), then instead of viewing KM as a tactical tool for the fulfillment of strategy, shouldn't we instead be thinking of strategy as *an outcome of knowledge processing*, the quality of which is the chief concern of KM, and not the fulfillment of strategy? Or is KM an implementation tool for strategy? And if so, should the complexion and mission of KM change whenever business strategies change?

249

In this chapter we will examine these issues, as well as the closely related question of where KM should reside in the management hierarchy. Whether or not KM is the servant of management (and its strategy du jour) would seem to be of enormous importance to the question of who KM should report to, and where it should fit in the organizational structure.

Biased Methodologies

Clues to the presumed relationship between KM and strategy can be found in many mainstream methodologies. One of us (McElroy) encountered one such methodology while working at IBM in its KM consulting practice in 1999. In general, IBM's methodology, then and perhaps still now, unfolded in the following characteristic way:

- Step 1: Identify current business strategy.
- Step 2: Determine information resources required to successfully implement current strategy.
- Step 3: Perform IT and other organizational projects required to make information resources easily accessible and supportive of business processing.

While usually expressed in more granular or elaborated forms, this three-step pattern of activity in KM methodologies is archetypical for the field. KM methods almost always begin by taking a deferential stance toward strategy, followed quickly by a specification of the information resources needed to support it. Next comes a series of projects aimed at capturing, codifying, and/or deploying related information. Even *communities of practice* programs are typically conceived with "knowledge sharing" in mind—a social means of deploying information resources as opposed to a technological one. It's as though the unspoken, yet assumed purpose of KM is always to leverage information in support of strategy. This is the bias of most KM methods.

Let's look at another case in which the relationship between KM and strategy is codified in the form of a methodology. In a special report published by *KM Review* entitled "Crafting a Knowledge Management Strategy," authors Chuck Seeley and Bill Dietrick (1999) claim that "The realization of corporate goals must always be the aim of a Knowledge Management strategy, and it's therefore wise to ensure that investments in Knowledge Management are consistent with other corporate investments, and with the pattern of decisions made for the corporate strategy" (ibid., 4).

According to this logic, legitimate KM is only that form of KM that is consistent with current strategy. Indeed, Seeley and Dietrick hammer this point home when they say, "Those involved in crafting the Knowledge Management strategy must understand and build upon the corporate strategy to ensure that Knowledge Management is used to help realize the strategic intent of the organization" (ibid., 5). How? By "putting in place the capabilities (organizational, behavioral, technological, and informational) to unlock the organizational asset that is key to strategic realization—the knowledge and ideas of the people in the organization . . ." (ibid.).

Here we see another very clear case of KM strategy being defined in terms of deference to business strategy. It's all about KM being used to help marshal the resources required to fulfill strategy. If this sounds reminiscent of first-generation KM, there's a good reason for that—it *is* first-generation KM. To wit, Seeley and Dietrick go on to invoke one of first-generation KM's best-known slogans in their own way: "A significant challenge for organizations undertaking a Knowledge Management initiative is to distribute the right content to the right people at the right time" (Seeley and Dietrick 2000, 8)—also known as *getting the right information to the right people at the right time*, a dead giveaway for first-generation thinking.

It should be clear, then, that there are several hallmarks of first-generation (i.e., the *old*) KM, including two that we discuss in this chapter: (1) a supply-side orientation, and (2) strategy-centricity. Let us continue by examining these orientations further, as well as the assumptions that lie behind them in the context of strategy (business strategy, that is).

THE STRATEGY EXCEPTION ERROR

KM methodologies that begin by treating existing (business) strategy as a given commit what we shall call the *strategy exception error*. That is, they start out by assuming that current strategy is valid and then proceed to make investments in supporting it. Poorly conceived strategies thereby beget wasted investments in KM, a problem that advocates of strategy-centric KM methods seem unconcerned with. But why do we call this an *exception error*?

From the perspective of second-generation (i.e., the *new*) KM, strategies are nothing more than knowledge claims produced by strategy makers in organizations. As such, their content and nearness to truth is questionable. Moreover, it is not the purpose of KM to round up the information resources required to support a strategy—that role falls to any number of other organizational functions, such as IT, MIS, IS, and a host of other business-specific functions like Finance, HR, and what have you. No, the role of KM in a firm is to enhance knowledge processing and its outcomes. Unfortunately, however, most KM strategies are not expressed in these terms.

The fact that first-generation KM and its methods generally fail to make the distinction between knowledge management and knowledge processing leads to constant confusion in the industry. Consider the following statement from Seeley and Dietrick: "A Knowledge Management strategy is, therefore, a specific plan of action, laying out the activities necessary to embed Knowledge Management into the organization within a specified period of time" (ibid., 4). According to this view, then, there is no difference between KM and the targets of its interventions, much less a clear picture of what the targets are.

On the other hand, if what we are being told is that KM is supposed to enhance knowledge sharing, then it is enhanced knowledge sharing that KM interventions are meant to achieve, and not just more KM. The point here is that there is a difference between KM (the management discipline) and knowledge processing (the organizational process that KM seeks to enhance). So to say that the purpose of KM is to encourage more KM is to confuse the subject of KM interventions with their targets.

This confusion is easily resolved by simply recognizing the fact that knowledge processing occurs in all organizations—independent of KM—including in firms where there is *no* KM. KM, then, is a management discipline that we can elect to use in our attempts to enhance knowledge processing. Knowledge processing, in turn, includes things like knowledge production and integration, including knowledge sharing. In any case, knowledge management is simply not the same as knowledge processing.

In this analysis, note that from the perspective of the new KM, the purpose of KM is not to support the fulfillment of strategy nor anything of the kind. Rather, the purpose of KM is to enhance knowledge processing (i.e., the organizational capacity to solve problems, that is, close epistemic gaps through knowledge production), including the integration of associated solutions (e.g., knowledge sharing).

First-generation KM takes a different point of view. According to first-generation thinking, we should all begin by granting strategy an exception to the rule of fallibility of all knowledge claims—that is, by making the assumption that strategy knowledge is valid and that all else that follows should proceed on that assumption. There is no conception of knowledge production as of interest to KM, only knowledge sharing, nor is there any recognition of the distinction between KM and knowledge processing or knowledge processing and business processing. Strategy making and its outcomes, as well, are seen as outside the reach of KM, upstream from it, and not subject to KM's impact on knowledge processing.

The political overtones to this approach are palpable. Without saying as much, what first-generation KM practitioners are effectively saying is that some knowledge claims (and their makers) are more sacrosanct than others—untouchable, as it were. We like to think of this as *Orwellian KM*, a takeoff on George Orwell's *Animal Farm* (1946), in which some animals were described as being "more equal than others." According to first-generation thinkers, KM should follow from strategy, not the reverse, because some knowledge claims are more equal than others—KM should not focus on *strategy knowledge production*, they argue, only on *strategy fulfillment*. The proper focus of KM should, therefore, follow from strategy.

But if first-generation thinking regarding the relationship between KM and strategy is valid, then what have we been doing all these years as investments were being made in the implementation of information systems in business? Were they not intended to position information resources at the disposal of workers who presumably needed them in order to carry out strategy? Or has IT been engaged in some other enterprise all these years, somehow spending time and resources on building information systems that were *not* intended to support strategy? We doubt it. And if, in fact, there is no difference between past practices in information management (IM) and what passes for KM today, then we should stop pretending that there is and finally declare that the KM emperor has no clothes. On the other hand, if there *is* a difference between first-generation KM and past practices in IM, then let the exponents of first-generation thinking come forward and tell us what it is, because for many of us the difference has and continues to escape us.

STRATEGY AND THE NEW KNOWLEDGE MANAGEMENT

KM strategies, then, that begin by making the *strategy exception error* are arguably not KM at all. They are IM (see Chapter 3), and they have only the narrowest impact on knowledge processing, a social process vital to the survival of all organizations. Second-generation KM, by contrast, sees strategy as merely one class of knowledge claims. Strategy is an outcome of knowledge processing, but only one of many such outcomes. The chief concern of the new KM relative to strategy, then, is to see to it that the knowledge production process associated with strategy (i.e., strategy claims production) is the best it can be, with an eye toward making it possible for firms to produce the best strategies they can. KM, according to this view, precedes strategy formulation, not the reverse.

Where KM and IM part company in the integration (e.g., sharing) of strategy-related claims or information about them is in the fundamental manner in which knowledge is treated differently from *just information* (see Chapters 1 and 5). The difference that makes the difference, from a second-generation point of view, is the evidence in support of claims. Of particular importance to us is the record of testing and evaluation that accompanies knowledge claims, and the means by which we have access to *that* (the metaclaims), and not just the claims themselves. And so, while second-generation KM sees a useful role for information management and information processing, it is mostly about the support of *knowledge* processing, not *information* processing, and therein lies one of the key differences between KM and IM.

Let us now put strategy in the context of KM and KP (knowledge processing) in more direct terms. In the Seeley/Dietrick article cited above, the authors (1999) quote James Brian Quinn as defining strategy as "The pattern or plan that integrates an organization's major goals, policies, and action sequences into a cohesive whole." Fair enough. But why have a strategy in the first place? Clearly a strategy is a solution to a problem: the problem of a business or its managers not knowing what to do, or more precisely, what the general direction of the business ought to be. This is an epistemic problem, a problem of a gap in the knowledge needed to take action, not a business value problem, a gap between business goals or objectives and previous business outcomes. It triggers what Chris Argyris and Donald Schön (1974) have described as double-loop learning, and what Popper (1959, 1972, 1994) has called the method of trial and error elimination in problem solving.

We can say, then, that leaders in organizations charged with the definition of strategy must from time-to-time engage in knowledge production (i.e., strategy creation) in response to the organizational problem of not knowing how best to specify and integrate organizational "goals, policies, and action sequences into a cohesive whole" (i.e., in response to the problem of *not* having a strategy). The answers to these questions (i.e., the solutions to the epistemic problem of not having a strategy or knowing what to do) is a plan that contains claims in response. Thus, strategy is nothing more than a set of claims, usually formulated by management, about how best to configure an organization's "goals, policies, and action sequences into a cohesive whole" within and for a specified period of time. And that's all it is—a series of knowledge claims. It is no more valid than claims of any other sort in the enterprise, including business processes, organizational models, HR policies and programs, or any other domain of policy, procedure, or operations. It therefore is just as fallible as any other claim and deserves no more special status or exception from our principles of knowledge processing. Strategy, too, is fallible and is something that we produce.

In this light, we can see that the development and integration of strategy-related knowledge claims is an instantiation of knowledge processing that is performed on a periodic basis by strategy makers in organizations. In other words, it is a KLC or Knowledge Life Cycle (see Chapters 2 through 5). As such, the strategy-making process itself, and not the IM consequences of its outcomes, is the proper concern of KM, because that concern is the care and feeding of knowledge processing in all of its forms throughout the enterprise. There is no strategy exception to this rule, and there is no need for one.

In fact, if there is one set of knowledge claims that ought to be restricted from ever receiving special dispensation in a firm, it is precisely the set of claims that constitute strategy. Why? Because the cost of errors in a business strategy can be enormous. Small errors in market assessments, product direction decisions, or transaction models can potentially escalate into financial ruin or failure in the marketplace. From this perspective, anything close to granting *business* strategy a "bye" in the formulation of *KM* strategy is irresponsible at best. KM methodologies that codify and institutionalize this approach are invalid because they ignore a key area of knowledge processing in both private and public enterprises. Such approaches to KM should be severely challenged.

WHERE KNOWLEDGE MANAGEMENT BELONGS

Once it becomes clear that KM must provide oversight to the strategy-making process, rather than be subordinate to it, the next step is to consider anew the question of where KM belongs or should be fitted in the enterprise. In the article cited above, Seeley and Dietrick (2000) speak of the KM function at Seeley's former employer (Warner-Lambert) as one that reported to the "Corporate Strategic Management function." This is not surprising. A conception of KM that exists for no other reason than to distribute information to fulfill strategy would naturally be found within and subordinate to the strategy function itself. We, of course, disagree with this and have a different perspective to offer.

If strategy is, itself, an outcome of knowledge processing and if the persistent quality of knowledge processing in a firm is of paramount interest and importance to its stakeholders, then why would we continuously expose ourselves to the vicissitudes and even conflicting interests of our temporal management regimes? Do we, for example, take this approach in the management of our financial affairs? Do we defer to *personal* standards of accounting and reporting—be they high ones or low ones—that managers carry along with them as they come and go? Or do we, instead, hold all managers accountable to our own *independent* standards for financial reporting, the makeup of which *transcends* them and their designates? We of course do the latter. Why? Because it enhances our ability to perform quality control over managers. Further, it enhances the likelihood of our producing higher-quality knowledge claims (e.g., business strategies), and decreases the likelihood of bad ones surviving and escalating into bad practice. As the philosopher Karl Popper would have put it, *we must always strive to kill our bad ideas before they kill us!*

Knowledge management, therefore, should effectively report to the board of directors in a firm. Similar to a board's fiduciary role, we envision a comparable role for the new Knowledge Management, one that makes it possible for boards to provide oversight on the manner in which knowledge is being produced and integrated throughout the organization. The logic here is simple and straightforward. Risk and shareholder value are largely determined by what managers and their chains of command do in the marketplace. Organizational action, in turn, can be seen as nothing more than prevailing knowledge in use, including knowledge that derives from current strategy and related operating models. Strategy and operating models, in turn, are claims—claims about what markets to pursue, how to organize, what investments to make, and how to operationalize and do business with customers. These claims are, in turn, produced as a consequence of knowledge processing. Their quality, then, is subject to the quality of knowledge processing itself, the standards for which should not be determined solely by its users. Oversight is required here, and the board is the best place for it.

The implementation of Board oversight for knowledge processing might take the form of an ombudsman function in the firm, the name of which we could give *knowledge management*. The role of KM in this model would be to support the board's duty of maintaining rigorous standards for knowledge processing in the firm, thereby helping to serve shareholders' interests in seeing to it that *knowledge claims in use* (e.g., management strategies and operating models) are the best they can be from a production and integration point of view. Note that this model would tie nicely into the Open Enterprise (OE) vision we briefly discuss in Chapter 11, since it would provide for the enforcement and supervision of the OE by specifically placing KM under the authority of the board and not in the hands of those who would abuse it, or turn it to their own potentially conflicting immediate purposes.

CONCLUSION

This chapter raises some of the most fundamental questions concerning the role and purpose of KM in a firm and challenges the conventional (first-generation) view that KM is subordinate to strategy. In so doing, we have argued that KM is not an implementation tool for strategy and that attempts to position it as such leave us with virtually no difference between KM today and IM over the past 40 years. Indeed, we believe that there is no difference between much of what passes for KM today and what constituted IM in the past (and present, for that matter). Because of this, commonly used KM methodologies should be seen as not being about KM at all; rather, they're about IM. Or, as we have asked, are we expected to believe that all past practices in IM were somehow never about the fulfillment of strategy, were divorced from it, and that KM, having recently spotted the disconnect, has now come to the rescue? This, of course, strains credulity.

Having rejected the claim that KM is somehow different from past practices in IM, we further contend that the question of difference between the two misses the more important point: that strategy is, itself, a knowledge processing outcome. Not only does it not deserve to receive any special dispensation, as if it were infallible, but KM, as well, has nothing to do with the use of information resources in the fulfillment of strategy. That vision of KM is a first-generation idea, a kind of hangover from IM. There are plenty of preexisting management methods and IT solutions to make that happen without having to drag a new false god into the fray or trot out IM in its new more fashionable clothes. Indeed, that vision of KM doesn't hold water.

In its place we offer a vision of KM that begins by making the all-important distinction between KM and KP (knowledge processing). Described elsewhere in this book as the Knowledge Life Cycle (Chapters 2 through 6), knowledge processing is a social process that organizations rely on in order to produce and integrate their knowledge. The purpose of Knowledge Management, then, is to enhance knowledge processing. Knowledge processing outcomes, in turn, provide people with the knowledge needed to resolve epistemic problems, the behavioral outcomes from which we can observe in business processing.

Strategizing, then, is a type of knowledge making or knowledge producing activity. And strategy is a knowledge processing outcome that flows from knowledge production, the quality *itself* of which we can enhance by making KM interventions of various kinds. This is second-generation thinking in KM, and it has nothing to do with using KM to round up information resources needed to fulfill a strategy. It's all about enhancing knowledge processing, and not the implementation of some vision embodied by a strategy du jour. And if this is not the case, we ask, then who's minding the knowledge processing store?

Finally, the willful subordination of KM to strategy while committing what we refer to as the *strategy exception error* raises fundamental issues about how and where to position KM in a firm. In our view, KM should receive the same kind of attention and independence we give to the management of a firm's financial affairs, including direct accountability for oversight of knowledge processing being assigned to the board. Errors in judgment can be just as costly to a firm as errors in accounting. In fact they can cause deliberate errors in accounting that can lead to a firm's destruction. No management regime has a corner on the knowledge processing market, nor should they be allowed to behave as though they do.

On a going-forward basis, boards of directors should be held accountable for the manner in which knowledge is produced, evaluated, and integrated into practice with the shareholders' interests in mind. After all, there is nothing inherent in the concept of fiduciary responsibility that limits the idea to financial reporting. We see no reason to stop there. The integrity of knowledge processing in a firm must also be safeguarded.

Indeed, if we have learned anything from the rogues' gallery of corporate miscreants that littered the news wires and business pages since the fall of Enron, it was that the integrity of the *knowledge-making process* itself must be protected. Bad knowledge leads to bad practice, and bad knowledge is the product of bad knowledge processing. Even strategy must be accountable!

REFERENCES

Argyris, C. and Schön, D. (1974), *Theory in Practice: Increasing Professional Effectiveness*, San Francisco: Jossey-Bass.

Orwell, G. (1946), *Animal Farm*, New York, NY: Harcourt, Brace, and Company.

Popper, K.R. (1959), *The Logic of Scientific Discovery*, London, Hutchinson.

Popper, K.R. (1972), *Objective Knowledge*, London, England: Oxford University Press.

Popper, K.R. (1994), *Knowledge and the Body-Mind Problem* (edited by Mark A. Notturno), London, UK: Routledge.

Quinn, J.B. (1980), *Strategies for Change: Logical Incrementalism*, Homewood, IL: R.D. Irwin.

Seeley, C. and Dietrick, W. (1999), "Crafting a Knowledge Management Strategy, Part 1," *Knowledge Management Review*, **2**, *no. 5* (November/December, 1999).

Seeley, C. and Dietrick, W. (2000), "Crafting a Knowledge Management Strategy Part 2," *Knowledge Management Review*, **2**, *no. 6*, (January/February, 2000).

Chapter 9

KNOWLEDGE MANAGEMENT AND CULTURE

INTRODUCTION

What is culture, and what is its relationship to knowledge and knowledge management? "Cultural" barriers are often held responsible for failures to share and transfer knowledge in organizations. It is frequently said that knowledge management must undertake the difficult task of changing an organization's culture to achieve the knowledge sharing and transfer necessary to realize the full value of the organization's knowledge resources. But "culture" is one of those terms used loosely, in a multiplicity of ways, to cover a multitude of sins, so when we are told that the culture must be changed to solve a problem in KM we don't always know what that really means.

ALTERNATIVE DEFINITIONS OF CULTURE

Here are some alternative definitions of culture, summarized by John H. Bodley (2000) of the University of Washington from a longer list of 160 definitions compiled in 1952 by the great anthropologists Alfred L. Kroeber and Clyde Kluckhohn (1952):

■ **Topical:** Culture consists of everything on a list of topics, or categories, such as social organization, religion, or economy. (We don't think this definition is very relevant for KM.)

261

- **Historical:** Culture is social heritage, or tradition, that is passed on to future generations. (This may be relevant to KM in that organizations may have traditions that are difficult to change. But to use this concept in KM, we need to be very specific about which traditions in an organization impact either KM practices or activities or knowledge processing activities, and we need to realize that "traditions" generally change very slowly and most frequently as a response to behavioral change.)
- **Behavioral:** Culture is shared, learned human behavior, a way of life. (This definition is used successfully in the analysis of cultures at a societal level. To use it at the organizational level, we need to distinguish shared, learned behavior among individuals in an organization that results from *general* socialization as opposed to shared, learned behavior that results from *organizational* socialization. This may be difficult to measure. But its measurement may be important because learned behavior resulting from organizational socialization may be much easier to change than learned behavior resulting from general socialization.)
- **Normative:** Culture is ideals, values, or rules for living. (One could map organizational ideals, values, and "rules for living," but measurement is difficult. If you use behavior to measure these things, you have the problem of explaining KM, knowledge processing, and organizational behavior in terms of such behavior, rather than in terms of ideals, values, and rules for living. On the other hand, if you don't use behavioral measures, you pretty much have to do analysis of cultural products or surveys to develop measures [Firestone 1972]. In any event, ideals, values, and rules for living are emergent properties of social systems. They, like traditions, respond to changes in behavior but do not change very easily in response to organizational manipulation.)
- **Functional:** Culture is the way humans solve problems of adapting to the environment or living together. (This definition is difficult for KM, because knowledge processing tempered by knowledge management is the way humans solve such problems. So this definition does not explain or predict knowledge processing and knowledge management as much as it equates culture with these things.)

■ **Mental:** Culture is a complex of ideas, or learned habits, that inhibit impulses and distinguish people from animals. (This is the "psychologized" version of the normative definition. As stated, it is debatable because certain higher animals—e.g., primates and dolphins—also have learned habits and ideas, so this definition may not distinguish people from animals after all.

More important, this definition does not link the ideas or learned habits people have with any shared socialization. That is, ideas or learned habits resulting from individualized experiences are not distinguished from ideas or learned habits resulting from shared societal or organizational experiences. The term *culture* can only coherently be applied to the second class of ideas.

When this idea is used in KM, it is important to recognize the importance of measuring such "subjective culture" as the result of shared organizational experiences, e.g., in "boot camps," organizational ceremonies, committee meetings, performance reviews, etc. That is, when claiming that culture is a factor accounting for characteristic patterns of knowledge processing, it is necessary to show not only that attitudes, cognitive orientations, and other mental phenomena are affecting knowledge processing behavior, but also that such phenomena result from some shared experiences the organization is implementing.)

■ **Structural:** Culture consists of patterned and interrelated ideas, symbols, or behaviors. (We think this definition is too broad and doesn't distinguish between culture and other aspects of information, knowledge, or KM.)

■ **Symbolic:** Culture is based on arbitrarily assigned meanings that are shared by a society. (This is a societal concept. Is it perhaps also useful at the organizational level for KM, but this usage seems to us to be marginal.)

The upshot of this brief survey of "culture" is that when someone says that knowledge can't be shared or transferred due to cultural barriers, one really has to ask for clarification to know which sense of culture is intended. Is culture really the barrier to effective KM it is frequently made out to be? The answer may well depend on what the questioner means by "culture."

CULTURE OR SOMETHING ELSE?

Indeed, it is even possible that when people talk about cultural barriers that they are not talking about culture at all. Thus, when organizational politics is opposed to knowledge sharing and transfer, that is not culture, and while it may be difficult to change, politics is easier to change than culture. Similarly, when the organizational incentive system affecting knowledge worker behavior must be changed to facilitate knowledge sharing and transfer, that is not "culture," and it is certainly easier to change.

In fact, the claim that knowledge sharing and transfer do not occur because of culture sometimes sounds plausible because of the tacit assumption that we must somehow make knowledge workers altruistic before they will share and transfer, and that this, in turn, requires a fundamental change in "culture." But the idea that we must make knowledge workers unusually altruistic to get them to share and transfer knowledge ignores the many examples of social systems and organizations in which collaboration is based on "normal" motivations including self-interest.

We believe that the problems besetting KM are not, primarily, cultural problems in the historical, behavioral, normative, or mental senses of the term discussed earlier (the only possibilities that apply). Instead, they are problems of structural organization and change that can be managed by political means. Structural changes can align individual motivational/incentive systems, whether of individual or cultural origin, with organizational incentive systems to affect behavioral changes without cultural change. In fact, in social systems, behavioral and structural changes frequently precede and cause cultural changes.

WHAT IS CULTURE, AND HOW DOES IT FIT WITH OTHER FACTORS INFLUENCING BEHAVIOR?

As one can see from the above brief survey, there is great diversity in definitions of "culture." Is there a definition more or less consistent with previous usage that is also useful for KM? We will propose such a definition below and discuss its implications for the role of culture in KM and the relationship of culture to knowledge.

It will help in defining culture if we begin by noting that for every group and for the organization as a whole, we can distinguish analytical properties, structural properties, and global properties. These distinctions were originally introduced by Paul Lazarsfeld in the 1950s (Lazarsfeld and Menzel 1961), and later used by Terhune (1970) in a comprehensive review of the national character literature. Analytical properties are derived by aggregating them from data describing the members of a collective (a group or a system). Examples of analytical attributes include:

GNP
GNP per capita
Per capita income
Average salary
Total sales
Sales per sales representative
Number of accumulated vacation days
Number of lost work days due to injury

Structural properties are derived by performing some operation on data describing relations of each member of a collective to some or all of the others. Examples of structural properties are:

Extent of inequality of training
Extent of inequality of knowledge base distribution
Extent of inequality of knowledge access resource distribution
Extent of inequality of knowledge dissemination capability
Extent of inequality of power
Intensity of conflict behavior
Intensity of cooperative behavior
Ratio of e-messages sent to e-messages received by an agent

Last of all, global properties are based on information about the collective that is not derived from information about its members. Instead, such properties are produced by the group or system process they characterize, and, in that sense, they may be said to "emerge" from it, or from the series of interactions constituting it. Examples of emergent global attributes include:

■ Value orientations (reflected in social artifacts) (Kluckhohn and Strodtbeck 1961)
  Achievement orientation

- Self-realization orientation
- Power orientation
- Mastery over nature
- Lineality (preference for a hierarchical style in social organization)
- Extent of democratic organization of the knowledge life cycle
- Innovation propensity (the predisposition of an organization to innovate)

The classification of social system properties into analytical, structural, and global attributes is exhaustive. To define culture, let's first ask whether we should define it as an analytical, structural, or global attribute—or some combination of these?

Culture, first, is not an analytical attribute. Culture is not an arithmetical aggregation of survey results or individual man-made characteristics. It is not the percent of knowledge workers who trust their fellows, believe in systems thinking, believe in critical thinking, or are favorably disposed toward knowledge sharing. Why not? Because (a) culture influences behavior; statistical artifacts don't. And (b) the above attributes are social psychological, not cultural.

Second, culture also should not be defined as a set of structural attributes derived from relations among individual level attributes. Why not? Because "culture" refers to something comprehensive and regulative that accounts for and determines structure, and also because if we define culture as structural in character we are assuming that we can model the structural relations defining it. Do we want to assume that, or do we want to assume that culture is global in character and emergent, or some combination of the three types of attributes?

Third, the alternative of culture as a combination of attribute types may at first seem attractive, but the following considerations argue against it. (A) The character of analytical attributes as arithmetic aggregations of individual level properties is not changed by defining a construct that includes such attributes with structural and global ones. (B) Analytical attributes still are not reflective of process or system-level attributes that are regulative or comprehensive. At best they are indicators of conditions caused by structural and global level attributes and are not causal in themselves.

As for culture being a combination of structural and emergent attributes, our objection to this view lies in how we think we want to use "culture." If we want to use it as an explainer or predictor of structural patterns, it is ill-advised to confound structure with culture, that is, to confound the "form" of a social system or organization with its predispositions or "spirit." In other words, defining culture as a global attribute rather than as a combination of global and structural attributes appears most consistent with previous usage and also with our strategic need to use "culture" as a tool to account for "structure" in our models.

If culture is a global attribute of agents, we still must decide what kind of global attribute it is. The World 1-World 2-World 3 distinction of Popper's (1972, 1994), discussed in Chapter 1, is also important here. It suggests that we may distinguish three types of culture. A key characteristic of all three types is that each is man-made (or generalizing this concept, made by an intelligent agent). World 1 artifacts are material products, so *World 1 products are material culture.* World 2 culture we will call *subjective culture* (Triandis et al. 1972). And World 3 culture we will call *objective culture.*

The subjective culture of a group or organizational agent is the agent's characteristic set of emergent high-level predispositions to perceive its environment. It includes group or organizational level value orientations and high-level attitudes and the relations among them. It is a configuration of global attributes that emerges from group interactions—that is, from the organization and pattern of transactions among the agents within a group.

The objective culture of a group or organizational agent is the configuration of value orientations and high-level attitudes expressed in the agent's characteristic stock of emergent problems, models, theories, artistic creations, language, programs, stories, etc., reflected in its documents, books, art galleries, information systems, dictionaries, and other containers. It is a configuration of global attributes expressing the *content* of its information, knowledge, art, and music, apart from both the predispositions the group or its agents may have toward this content, and the material form of the artifact expressing the content. The objective culture of an organization is an aspect of the social ecology of its group agents, the cumulated effects of previous group interactions. As such, the perception of it by group agents (part of their subjective culture or psychology, depending on the type of agent) influences their behavior.

Subjective culture affects behavior within groups or organizations at two levels:

- It affects agents at the decision-making level of interaction immediately below the level of the cultural group by predisposing these agents toward behavior (see Figure 9.1).
- It affects the behavior of the group itself by predisposing it toward behavior (see Figure 9.2).

The context of objective culture in social ecology and its relationship to interaction within a group or organization is also illustrated in Figure 9.2. The focus of the illustration is the decision-making agent at the bottom left. The agent may be an individual agent or a group level agent, depending on context.

Looking at the right hand side of Figure 9.2, transaction inputs received from other agents and previous social ecology (the feedback loop on social ecology), determine the current social ecology (including objective culture) affecting an agent's decision. Next, transactions, social ecology, and previous decisions (the goal-striving outcome feedback loop) are viewed as "impacting" on the goal-directed typical agent, whose internal process then produces decisions which result in transaction outputs from agent (i) directed toward other agents j, k . . . n. These transaction outputs are inputs into the

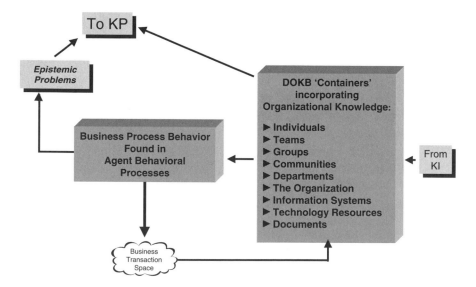

Figure 9.1
Business Process Behavior and Containers of Knowledge

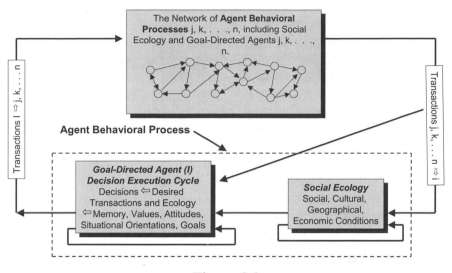

Figure 9.2
The Flow of Behavior Among Agents

decision processes of these other agents. The interaction within and among agents j, k . . . n, illustrated by the *Network of Agent Behavioral Processes* at the top, finally, produces transactions directed at agent (i) at a later time, and thereby closes the loop.

What goes on inside the goal-directed agent (i)? So long as (i) is a group level agent and its components are also groups, then the interaction process may be viewed in the same way as in Figure 9.2, *but specified at a lower level*. But if one decides to *move from a transactional to a motivational perspective* on a group level agent (i), then the conception is somewhat different.

Figure 9.3 presents a decision-making process in a prebehavior situation. Here, the prebehavior situation is filtered through the decision-making system of a group-level agent, specifically through value orientations and through attitudes existing at increasingly domain specific levels of abstraction. Subjective culture lives at the value orientation and higher-level attitude locations in this decision-making system. The interaction between the external world and the agent's predispositional reality "screens" produces a discrete situational orientation, a *"definition of the situation,"* which in turn feeds back to the predispositional (including the cultural) levels in search of choice guidance. This guidance then determines the final

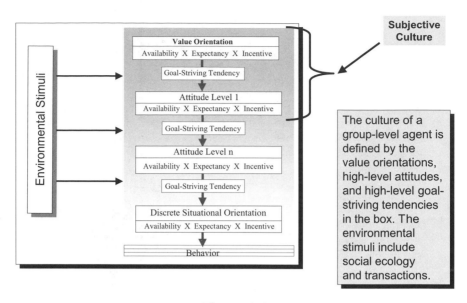

Figure 9.3
The Incentive System of a Group-Level Agent

situational orientation, which leads to behavior and to new feedbacks to the situational orientation, and to attitude and value orientation predispositions.

The predispositions in Figure 9.3 represent psychological attributes when the agent involved is an individual, but when the agent is a group, *these are the group's characteristic set of emergent predispositions to perceive its environment, including group level value orientations and high-level attitudes and the relations among them. That is, the high-level emergent predispositions in Figure 9.3 are group subjective culture.* Moreover, as in the case of the individual agent discussed in Chapter 1, the availability, expectancy, and incentive elements of high-level predispositions in combination represent *subjective cultural knowledge predispositions.*

Do Global Properties Exist?

Regarding the critics of the collective properties view, the objections are at the level of ontological assumptions. None of the critics can explain group level attributes that suggest there are such predispositions by rigorously explaining them in terms of shared mutually held individual predispositions. In fact, the doctrine of emergence suggests that such an explanation will never be possible. Therefore, the claim that group level predispositions don't exist and that "there is no *there there*" is simply a bias on the same level as the bias of some materialists who believe that "mind" really doesn't exist, and that mental phenomena will one day be explained entirely in terms of the brain.

We agree with Bateson (1972) and accept the idea of group-level consciousness. Recall the figure about the motivational system for both individuals and groups and the presence of situational orientations shown in Figure 9.3. Situational orientations with cognitive, evaluative and affective components cannot exist without thinking and, therefore, "mind." The question is: How much consciousness is there?

CULTURE AND KNOWLEDGE

Based on the above account of culture and its relationship to behavior, and on the accounts of knowledge provided in Chapter 1 and the origin of the KLC in Chapter 2, a number of conclusions about the relationship of culture to knowledge are immediately suggested:

- First, there is an organizational objective culture that is part of the social ecology of every group and individual in the organization, and which therefore is a factor in the decision making of agents at every level of corporate interaction. *Organizational objective culture is composed, in great part, of high-level generalized knowledge claims, or expressions about values, ontology, epistemology, value orientations and generalized viewpoints about the way the world works, some of them validated and surviving* (World 3 knowledge), which is shared. But not in the sense that all agree with what it says or assent to it. Indeed, it may be contradictory in many and visible ways. But it is shared in the sense that all members of the group have access to this objective culture and its World 3 content.
- Second, each group level agent, each team, each community of practice, each formal organizational group, each informal group has a *group subjective culture, largely composed of knowledge predisposition* (World 2) components of value

orientations and high-level attitudes, which affects their group decision making. So the behavior of group agents is influenced both by their internal subjective and objective cultures and also by objective organizational culture, and all three types of culture are in large part composed of knowledge.

■ Third, the most pervasive, but also the weakest subjective cultural predispositions in intensity, are the highest-level ones— those most far removed from situational stimuli. These are the most abstract value orientations and attitudinal predispositions in the hierarchy of Figure 9.3.

■ Fourth, though value orientations and high-level attitudes are both the most pervasive and the weakest influences on immediate behavior, they are also the hardest knowledge predispositions to change in a short time. This is true because they emerge and are maintained as a result of reinforcement from behavior patterns in diverse concrete situations experienced by agents in the group or organization. These most abstract patterns of any subjective culture are self-reinforcing through time. To change them, one needs to break down the structure of self-reinforcement and the integration of the many, many subsidiary patterns supporting this structure.

CONCLUSION: CULTURE AND KNOWLEDGE MANAGEMENT

As we have argued in Chapters 2 through 4, we can distinguish KM processes, knowledge processes, and business processes. And knowledge processes may be viewed in terms of the KLC framework. KLC processes produce knowledge that is used in the other business processes of the enterprise. And these, in turn, produce business outcomes. Figure 9.4 illustrates this chain of influences.

Moreover, KM processes, knowledge processes, and business processes are performed by decision-making, behaving agents. As we have seen, agents, if they are groups, have an internal culture, both subjective and objective. At the same time, the objective cultural component of social ecology also impacts agent decisions. Finally, knowledge and KM processes are affected by culture through the influence it has on behavior constituting these processes. In turn, these processes are keys to producing new knowledge and consequently changes in objective and subjective culture.

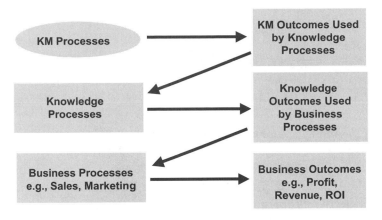

Figure 9.4

From Knowledge Management Processes to Business Outcomes

So culture is pervasive in KM, knowledge processing, and knowledge outcomes. It is part of their context, and it is also, in the long run, produced by them. But many other factors (social ecology, situational factors, transactional inputs; see Figure 9.2), also contribute to the complex interactions associated with knowledge-related processes and outcomes. Thus culture is only a small part of all there is to KM, knowledge processing, or any other business process, and therefore there remain substantial problems in measuring and analyzing its precise impact on KM or KM's impact on culture. Culture is not so much an answer to difficulties in KM as it is an issue and a problem in itself. And prescriptions that suggest that we must "change the culture" to perform effective KM and to enhance knowledge processing are not solutions to problems, but only prescriptions for movement down the wrong track toward a single factor explanation of knowledge management and knowledge processing.

REFERENCES

Bateson, G. (1972), "The Logical Categories of Learning and Communication," in G. Bateson, *Steps to an Ecology of Mind*, New York, NY: Chandler Publishing Company.

Bodley, J.H. "What is Culture," Available at: http://www.wsu.edu:8001/vcwsu/commons/topics/culture/culture-definitions/bodley-text.html.

Firestone, J. (1972), "The Development of Social Indicators from Content Analysis of Social Documents," *Policy Sciences*, *3*, 249–263.

Kluckhohn, F. and Strodtbeck, F. (1961), *Variations in Value Orientations*, New York, NY: Harper & Row.

Kroeber, A. and Kluckhohn, C. (1952), "Culture: A Critical Review of Concepts and Definitions," *Papers of the Peabody Museum of American Archaeology and Ethnology*, *47*, (*1*), (1952).

Lazarsfeld, P. and Menzel, H. (1961), "On the Relation Between Individual and Collective Properties," in Amitai Etzioni (ed.), *Complex Organizations*, New York, NY: Holt, Rinehart and Winston.

Morris, C. (1956), *Varieties of Human Value*, Chicago, IL: University of Illinois Press.

Popper, K.R. (1972), *Objective Knowledge*, London, England: Oxford University Press.

Popper, K.R. (1994), *Knowledge and the Body-Mind Problem*, Mark A. Notturno (ed.), London, UK: Routledge.

Stacey, R.D. (1996), *Complexity and Creativity in Organizations*, San Francisco, CA: Berrett-Koehler Publishers.

Terhune, K.W. (1970), "From National Character to National Behavior: A Reformulation," *Journal of Conflict Resolution*, *14*, 203–263.

Triandis, H.C. et al. (1972), *The Analysis of Subjective Culture*, New York, NY: John Wiley & Sons.

Chapter 10

A NOTE ON INTELLECTUAL CAPITAL

INTRODUCTION

Even the most casual observers of Knowledge Management, the profession, can appreciate the strong links that exist between KM and the equally active field of intellectual capital (IC). Here, we'd like to make some of those connections explicit, particularly in terms that relate to the new KM. Before we do, however, we should briefly set the stage by pointing out that the jury is still out—way out—on how best to address intellectual capital measurement and reporting. Like KM itself, the related field of IC is in a state of early, fundamental development. Competing theories abound on what intellectual capital is, how to measure it, and how to report it. The divisions among them are enormous.

It should also be useful to point out that the problems and questions posed by IC theoreticians and practitioners are almost always framed in terms of accounting. In other words, *the IC problem* is universally seen as an accounting problem, a narrow problem of computing a certain type of intangible value. What, then, is the IC problem?

275

Beginning approximately in 1980, something strange started to happen on the New York Stock Exchange: the value of stocks started to exceed the book values of its member companies by unprecedented margins (see Figure 10.1). By 1990, the value of the Dow Jones Industrial Average was actually double the book values of its 30 constituent companies; by the late 1990s, the intangibles-to-book ratio had risen to 3 : 1—all this, despite the fact that the sources of these values were utterly unaccounted for on the balance sheet. That, then, was—and still is—the IC problem.

As a result of the way in which the IC problem was articulated, the quest for solutions was launched by accountants, for accountants, and *within accounting*. There is nothing wrong with that, of course. It was a natural reaction to the problem. But we do think the manner in which a problem or question is asked, or the situational context that lies behind it should, itself, be scrutinized in the search for

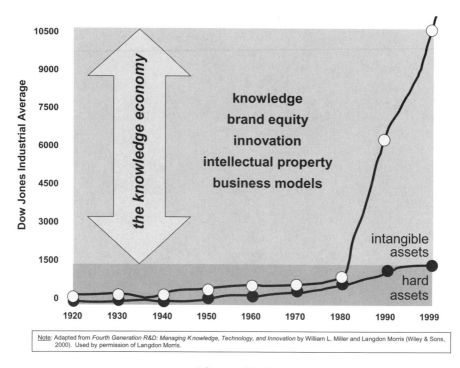

Note: Adapted from *Fourth Generation R&D: Managing Knowledge, Technology, and Innovation* by William L. Miller and Langdon Morris (Wiley & Sons, 2000). Used by permission of Langdon Morris.

Figure 10.1
Book Values versus Intangible Assets

answers to seemingly intractable problems. Why? Because the questions themselves may be wrong. Further, history shows that with intractability sometimes comes the rejection of old knowledge and the science behind it, followed by the arrival of new knowledge and new science behind *it*. The inability of old or established knowledge to answer or resolve new issues raised by new problems is a historically significant signal that the old knowledge may have all but run its course.

In his well known book on scientific revolutions, Thomas Kuhn (1970, 5) described this phenomenon in the following way:

> Sometimes a normal problem, one that ought to be solvable by known rules and procedures, resists the reiterated onslaught of the ablest members of the group within whose competence it falls.

This would seem to be a fairly accurate description of what's going on in the accounting world today. We have the economic value of companies (as reflected in their market capitalizations) exceeding the capacity of our "normal" accounting systems to, well, *account* for them. In response, we have the "ablest members" of the accounting profession working feverishly to solve the problem. And how do they see and express the problem? *How to render this slippery stuff we call intellectual capital—or "intangibles," in its broader form—measurable.* Why? So we can squeeze it into the balance sheet where they think it belongs, and thereby make the measurement system comport with what the marketplace is doing.

In sum, we think this is misguided for several reasons. Chief among them is the falsity of the claims embedded in the manner in which the questions are being asked; how the problem is being framed; and the assumptions about what a satisfactory solution would look like. What's required here, we think, is not so much a "normal" solution consistent with our existing knowledge; rather, what's needed here, we think, is a revolution of sorts—a new theory of accounting. As Kuhn puts it, what's required here is the assimilation of a new theory that involves "the reconstruction of prior theory and the reevaluation of prior fact, an intrinsically revolutionary process that is seldom completed by a single man and never overnight."

Our objections to the current manner in which solutions are being sought to the IC problem, then, are fourfold. First, there is no recognition of the economic value of social capital, in any meaningful or complete sense, by any of the prevailing IC schemes now being advanced. Second is that the solutions being sought mistakenly assume linear relationships among the components of the IC scheme. Third, there is an undue accounting-centric orientation to the formulation of the problem. And fourth, present IC schemes fail to see the market in which corporate valuations are made as a separate system that lies outside of the enterprise. We begin with the social capital issue.

SOCIAL INNOVATION CAPITAL

Earlier in this book (Chapter 6), we discussed an application of the Knowledge Life Cycle (KLC) that pertained to intellectual capital. There we made the point that most, if not all, intellectual capital valuation and reporting schemes now being bandied about fail to take *social capital* fully into account. The new KM, therefore, has an important contribution to make to the developing field of IC: the addition of social capital (and its economic value) to the balance sheet and, in particular, the addition of *social innovation capital* to the mix of things that account for corporate valuations (McElroy 2002).

Our logic here is simple. While most IC valuation and reporting schemes tend to focus only on objects or outcomes in their approach to measurement, processes, too, can add value. Further, we have argued that the capacity to continuously learn and innovate on a high-performance basis is, itself, *more* valuable to a firm than any IC outcomes it might produce, such as patents or technologies. Why? Because all knowledge is fallible and much of it is proven false or eventually expires, in that it is only relevant in light of some current situational context. That new or existing knowledge will eventually be displaced or made obsolete is highly probable. The value of most innovations is therefore ephemeral, and so learning itself must not be, but must be a continuous source of new knowledge and innovation responding to the epistemic problems that almost always arise from our existing knowledge.

The upshot of our remarks concerning the absence of social capital (and *social innovation capital*, in particular) from mainstream ideas on how to measure and report IC might first lead to the conclusion that social *capitals* should be added to the balance sheet. In fact, we should consider adding social capital in its various forms to *either side* of the balance sheet. A firm's capacity to innovate, for example (i.e., its social innovation capital), could be so poorly configured that it actually detracts from the value of a firm by dampening its capacity to learn and, therefore, adapt. A firm's social innovation capital could in some cases, therefore, be seen as not an asset at all, but as a liability. Indeed this may very well be the case in many corporations. Let's examine this closer.

Clearly, the KLC is a major source of competitive advantage in a firm, assuming it's strong and responsive, as, for example, is the KLC in an open enterprise. In such cases, we could easily see the KLC as an asset. In other cases, however, the knowledge processing environment in a firm might actually dampen or suppress learning and innovation by maintaining social conditions such as high levels of mistrust that have the effect of discouraging learning and innovation. One of us (McElroy) clearly remembers being told by a superior of his at IBM not to waste his time focusing on internal problems there— "You're not going to change anything," he said. At least for one part of IBM at the time, then, knowledge processing was narrowly controlled by senior management and was closed to the rest of us. That kind of environment arguably detracts from corporate value and should be accounted for accordingly. It's a form of negative social capital that is a liability, not an asset. And this raises the more general question of why IC models attempting to take account of intangibles do not consider intangible liabilities as well as intangible assets.

False Linearity

Among the first principles of the new KM is the view of organizations as complex adaptive systems. Outcomes are the nonlinear, emergent results of countless interactions between agents, who each have their own rule sets, are autonomous, and who at times collectively work together toward achieving common goals, but at other times work either independently or against one another and still achieve their goals. In complex adaptive systems, 1 plus 1 plus 1 is more likely to add up to 5 than 3. On other occasions it may be 6, 7, or 10, but never 3. This is anathema to conventional accounting. Balance sheets and income statements are the products of linear, or at least reductive, thinking. There is no place in them for taking account of emergent processes. Acceptable solutions when conceived from the perspective of conventional accounting, therefore, can only be ones that comport with a linear or otherwise mechanistic model of the world.

But linear and mechanical solutions are not to be had in knowledge processing. Value outcomes may be describable and explainable in retrospect, but they are not predictable in practice. Neither process, however—explanation or prediction—is dependent upon the use of linear models. Here, value is not reducible to its simple components. It is greater than the sum of its parts. By contrast, as a creature of linear and mechanical thinking, conventional accounting is entirely reductionist. The value of something can always be reduced to the value of its parts, and the values of the parts always add up to the value of the whole. Such reductionism is just plain false in the case of knowledge processing and its outcomes.

In these areas, the values of global attributes are not reducible to the sum of their parts, nor are their values specifically predictable. In order to solve the IC problem, then, those who would do so must abandon their dependence on linear and mechanical models and consider the possibility of using other tools or approaches that deal with nonlinearity and emergence. The science of complexity comes rushing to mind here. But the more general point is that global attributes of systems are generally determined by relationships among attributes that must be described by nonlinear dynamical theories and models and that often are emergent and defy explanation in terms of any model, whether linear or nonlinear in character.

The inability to predict nonlinear, dynamical outcomes has another practical implication on related accounting theories and approaches: there are no certain formulas or principles available on how best to create intellectual capital, only theories. And even the best of our theories are subject to revision or replacement in response to unexpected events that contradict them and surprise us. We do not *control* the production of IC in any simple cause-and-effect sense at all, so how can we purport to do so in ways that are as predictable and standardized as, say, the manner in which we manage fixed assets and reflect their values on a balance sheet?

Consider the following example. Three people in a department decide to collaborate with one another on the basis of their shared interest in solving a particular problem. No one asked them to do so;

they just self-organized. After many rounds of discussions and interactions, they come up with a solution that solves the problem, lowers costs, and raises revenue. The income statement reflects these effects, and a patent they later acquire shows up on the balance sheet, as well.

Meanwhile, the market notices these changes and the company's stock price increases such that its market value becomes triple its book value. Previously, its market and book values were equal. Recognizing the chain of events that led up to this new good fortune, management is then faced with two problems: (1) how to account for the new, intangible value manifested in its stock price, and (2) how to manage the firm differently in the future so that (a) it holds onto its new higher value, and (b) more of what happened happens again.

In response to the first problem, management notices that the proportion of market value now attributable to its new intellectual capital vastly exceeds the appraised value of its patent and the effects on its revenue. What's going on here, they ask? Upon reflection, they realize that part of what the market is doing is recognizing and rewarding their capacity to innovate and adapt—not just in terms of the outcomes themselves, but the newly demonstrated institutional capacity to learn. In other words, the market is placing a premium on their *social innovation capital*, and the higher price of the stock reflects it. But what are the units of measurement for social innovation capital, they ask? How do we reduce it to its constituent parts for accounting, valuation, and reporting purposes?

The truth is, they can't. Nor should they feel the need to. The driver of such questions is, itself, the problem here, not the inability to measure social innovation capital in conventional terms. What's happening is that a vestige of old knowledge (generally accepted accounting principles and their linearity) is having unwanted effects on our efforts to solve a new problem. We simply cannot measure nonlinear phenomena with linear tools, and we should stop trying to do so. Further, we need to shift our focus from the outcomes to the causal influences that produce them. Hence, our focus should be more on the social processes we call social innovation capital (and *their* quality) than on the quality and impact of their *outcomes*. This takes us to the second problem.

Should management conclude, as a result of the success they observed, that all problems from then on should be tackled by groups of three employees? Or that the process followed by the three who solved the earlier problem should be codified into a pattern and replicated throughout the firm? This, too, would be a mistake because the outcome experienced by the original three was itself an emergent outcome unaccounted for by either linear or nonlinear models. Indeed, the same three people if faced with the same problem at a different time (if even only a day later) would very likely produce a different outcome. Similarly, if the two of us sat down tomorrow or next week instead of today to write this chapter again, it would undoubtedly be different. This is the butterfly effect writ large in knowledge processing and innovation. Chances are, then, that any attempt to codify what worked well the *first* time would utterly undermine creativity *every* time thereafter.

In light of the above, we believe a credible case can be made for simply reflecting the cumulative effects of organizational activity on a company's intangible market value in one line item of the balance sheet: *organizational and market intangibles*. This would simply be the difference between market capitalization and book value. Anything that cannot be accounted for in tangible book-value form would be lumped into this new category. From there we enter the realm of management theory, insofar as we may have an interest in determining how the value of organizational and market intangibles is produced and how we can have an impact on it. If the management regime believes that making investments in strengthening social innovation capital will increase the organizational and market intangibles value of the firm, they can have at it and give it a whirl. Others can pursue their own competing theories, as well.

By reflecting the value of intangibles in a single category, the emergent *outcomes* of both the internal organizational dynamics of a firm and the separate external influence of the marketplace could be reflected in what is otherwise a linear or at least mechanistic tool for measurement and reporting. And since unlike the rest of the balance sheet's contents, emergent assets (and liabilities) are not subject to prediction or to reductionist constructions, we could relieve the accounting profession's frustration with its inability to do so and relegate the whole problem to the realm of new theory and practice. We, of course, believe that the key to growth and sustainability in the value of organizational and market intangibles lies mostly in efforts to manage the strength and composition of social innovation capital. That is where investments should be made in growing the value of a firm, and recognizing the nonlinear trajectory of related outcomes is key to their accounting.

A False Orientation

Here our remarks are only very brief because of what we have already said above. In surveying the landscape of competing ideas and theories about how best to address the IC problem, it is worth noting, we think, that the problem was born of, raised in, and will very well die of the accounting perspective. In fact, the IC problem may very well die at the hand of accounting which, when all is said in done, may wind up producing the conclusion that the problem never really was an accounting problem to begin with. Or if it was, it was the wrong accounting problem. What do we mean by this?

Why should there necessarily have to be a place in a linear/mechanistic accounting and reporting system for organizational and market "intangible" phenomena? Why must we find a way to fit the value of intangibles and their emergent character into tools that were conceived of, and designed for, linear/mechanistic analysis and reporting? Next, if the purpose of reporting is to enhance the quality of information provided to existing and would-be investors, what in the world makes us think that accountants know anything at all about organizational and market intangibles? How, then, can a solution for the measurement of emergent behaviors, processes, and outcomes possibly be hatched from within the accounting profession? In a sense what we have here is the "right problem" being addressed by the "wrong profession" using the "wrong tools." The orientation to the problem and its probable solution are, therefore, arguably false.

What we need here are social scientists, complexity theorists, and yes, knowledge managers (especially ones of *the new KM* variety) who can help take this problem out of the accounting box in which the solution is presumed to be found, and who can then recast it anew. Why? Because the first and most fundamental questions relate to the causes of intangible value in a firm. These are not accounting questions; they are social ones. They have more to do with social science, epistemology, value theory, social psychology, and economic dynamics than with bookkeeping and financial reporting. What we need is good social theory on how nonlinear value happens in human social systems, after which we can take up the related accounting issues. We, of course, believe that the KLC and other *new KM* models provide us with a large part of the answer and that investments made in strengthening KLC dynamics and KM processes should be seen as causally linked to changes in IC outcomes and related market values. But this kind of thinking is not a creature of accounting theory. Not in the least.

TWO SYSTEMS, NOT ONE

Our last criticism of the approaches taken thus far in the quest to solve the IC problem is that they all fail to recognize the fact that in looking at corporate valuations, we are dealing with two social systems (at least), not one. The first is the enterprise (any publicly traded one) and the second is the securities market(s) in which its shares are traded. Managers and employees inhabit the first system; shareholders, potential shareholders, the press, regulators, and financial analysts inhabit the second one. When we take up the question of conventional financial reporting, we are by definition speaking of value found within the former and controlled by its inhabitants, especially its managers. When we speak of intangible values, however, it is important to recognize that these are produced by the latter and controlled by *its* inhabitants, especially its stockholders, and then conferred by them onto the former. Let's explore this idea further.

Managers in businesses can in a very real sense control the book value of their companies' assets and liabilities. They can buy assets, invest in them, sell assets, depreciate them, build new buildings, sell business units, borrow money, and so on. In terms of intellectual capital, they can even buy intellectual property, sell it, license it, and reflect it in material terms on their balance sheets. In this sense, intellectual property is not "intangible" at all and should not be seen or treated as anything like social innovation capital, the composition and value of which is often nebulous at best. Ironically, the most conspicuous form of so-called intellectual capital (patents) may be precisely the one that least deserves to be included in the new category of organizational and market intangibles discussed above. Why? Because its value can be determined like any other object of asset-based accounting. Patents are, for all intents and purposes, tangible assets that can be produced, purchased, sold, licensed, and valued as such.

Managers, however, do not control the value of things above and beyond the value of their organizations' tangibles. Why not? Because such additional value is imposed on organizations following its formulation or emergence in another system (the market), which exists outside of, and separate from, the companies that operate within it. Such value is formulated, that is, by agents (especially investors) as a consequence of the dynamics at play in *their* system, the market, rather than in the system inhabited by managers and their staff (i.e., the enterprise). Enterprises then experience or inherit the effects of the emergent, nonlinear outcomes of the dynamics of their decision making as a consequence of the effect on members of the other, external system (i.e., in the form of shareholders' valuations of what the company's stock price should be as filtered through the mechanism of supply and demand). But for managers to reflect the value that such outsiders place on the firm in the same way that they measure, report, and manage *tangible* asset values would be misleading and mistaken. *That* value (intangibles) is something that managers and the enterprise, in general, receive and that they do not control.

From the perspective of the new KM, an enterprise is simply a complex adaptive system, one of many. Complex adaptive systems, in turn, have relationships with one another—ecological ones. They exchange valued things with each other, and they assign value(s) to each other, as well. The valued material (and services) that the trees in an apple orchard receive from the bees that pollinate them is in no way controlled or managed by the trees themselves. The bees, instead, confer a value to the trees while receiving value *from* them, as well. Indeed, the trees reciprocate by conferring value to the bees and their hives as a food source to them, but it would be a mistake to think that the bees are in any way *managing* the added value received by them from the trees they rely on. Both the trees and the bees have value (to themselves), part of which is directly managed while another part is not managed at all. Rather, the latter part is inherited as a by-product of their place in the ecology.

To further illustrate the point here, consider the addition to our analogy (the bees and the trees) of an orchard grower and a bee-keeper. In contemplating the purchase of the orchard (by the grower) and the beehives (by the beekeeper), each considers the tangible value of the assets of interest to them. But the grower also notices the healthy state of the local ecology and especially the presence and favorable impact of the local bees on the quality of the orchard. He adjusts his estimate of the orchard's value upward, accordingly. The beekeeper, in turn, makes a similar observation: that the size and proximity of the orchards nearby contributes to the health of the hives. He, too, adjusts his estimate of the value of his target purchase upward. Thus, we can see that the economic *intangible* value of a commercial enterprise is determined not so much by its managers, but by the separate determinations of agents in *external* systems with which the enterprise has ecological relationships. In fact in this case, there were two such external systems: (1) the market in which the buyers were situated, and (2) the orchard and the bee hives that had impacts on each others' economic valuations in the minds of the buyers.

What can we conclude from this with regard to the IC problem? First, we can say that to try and reflect the value of intangibles using conventional reporting tools is to undermine the spirit and intent behind them. Why? Because their purpose in capital markets is to report on things that managers *can* control, and not on things that they merely inherit as if they *were* controlled. Does this also mean, then, that managers should forget about trying to control the size and makeup of organizational and market intangibles? Not at all. But here again, we're still operating at a point in the development of the discipline where all we have are theories. Standardized reporting schemes, like balance sheets and income statements, call for more than that. Let the theories come forth and compete with one another on a level playing field, we say, and standards for reporting will follow. In the meantime, let's at least reflect the value of intangible outcomes in the form of the line item we have suggested: organizational and market intangibles (market capitalization minus book value). First things first.

As for how to manage in complex dynamical systems, the fact that the orchard owner cannot strictly control the attractiveness of his trees to the bees, or the value they (the bees) place on his trees, should not stop him from testing and evaluating different strategies for enhancing whatever he might think might *make* them inviting to bees. Indeed, some of his efforts may clearly enhance the growth of his trees and the extent of their flowering. But he could never manage all of the variables that contribute to assessments of value by bees any more than he could manage the many other factors that influence the behavior of bees, such as the weather or other factors outside his control. And even if he could, the nature of the system dynamics that operate between them (the variables) would seem mysterious and capricious to him. No, the best he can do is to tinker with the factors he *does* control, recognizing, however, that they are all still part of a larger emergent system that has a life and trajectory of its own.

The moral of this analogy, then, is that organizational and market intangible values are not at all controlled in the same sense that the value of tangible, book values are, nor are they even formulated from within the same system—the enterprise. Hence, we should stop pretending that they are by trying to fit them within our linear models (our reporting tools). Intangible values are determined by other actors in systems outside of the enterprise (stockholders and would-be stockholders in markets, etc.) whose independent judgments of value are extended to enterprises as projections of *their* values, not managers'. These intangible values are, therefore, conferred to enterprise systems by market-based stockholder systems and are therefore inherited by enterprises, not produced by them.

CONCLUSION

Underlying all of our comments in this chapter regarding the unsuitability of conventional accounting perspectives in the treatment of intangible values are four key points:

1. The most important source of intangible economic value in a firm is external to itself—not found at all within the firm, and therefore not directly manageable by it. The origin of such value is in the minds of current and prospective stockholders, whose valuations of a firm are determined within the dynamics of their system, not the enterprise's. Their values are then projected onto the enterprise, which in turn receives it as a kind of gift or inheritance—an inheritance, however, that is always subject to adjustment and even return.

2. Apart from being determined by agents outside of the enterprise, reflecting the value of intangibles using conventional accounting tools as though they were internally managed

suffers from another problem, as well. Balance sheets are static models. They are predicated on the assumption that it is possible to start with a market value that can then be broken down into its additive elements. Knowledge and the processes that produce and integrate it, however, are anything but additive. What we need in order to account for them both are dynamic models—nonlinear ones—not static ones. These, in turn, should come into play in conjunction with the theories of emergence they support, the composition of which will suggest reporting models and tools of their own. This is the path to solving the so-called IC problem. Ramming new realities into old frameworks simply will not work.

3. All of our warnings concerning the inability to manage emergent systems and outcomes have been precautionary but not absolute. While it's true that processes and outcomes in complex adaptive systems are emergent beyond the absolute control of managers, it is possible to have impacts on them, nevertheless—even intended impacts that give rise to corresponding (hoped for) outcomes. This, however, does not entail conventional management. Rather, management in such environments must begin with recognition of organizations as social complex adaptive systems, subject to the mostly unpredictable effects of system dynamics and emergence. Armed with this insight, it is possible to build models of organizations and their environments that are nonlinear in form and to use such models for predicting the potential outcomes of alternative management strategies, including the effects that management decisions of one kind or another might have on the externally produced value judgments assigned by markets to the enterprise. In this way, managers can have impact on the value of their organizations' organizational and market intangibles, which, so far as we're concerned, makes such values *manageable*.

4. That said, we are only prepared at this point to support the reflection of intangible values in the lump sum fashion we have proposed. It is simply too soon to suggest any other, more granular treatment of intangibles on the balance sheet. What's required, instead, is a period of trial and error, or experimentation, in which competing theories of how intangible values are produced can be tested and evaluated. As a consequence of that process, we can conceive of a point in time when the

momentum behind one or more models of how intangible values are produced matures and informs us of their management, measurement, and reporting implications. Then and only then will we have a solid basis for suggesting how best to report on the value of intangibles to stockholders. Until then, it's premature.

On the basis of the closing remarks above, we believe that the accounting profession should undertake a concerted effort to bring the additional, nonaccounting disciplines into the process of trying to discover the nature of intangible value and the role it plays in corporate valuations. These would include complexity scientists, social scientists, and knowledge managers of the second-generation (new KM) type. Until we do, and until we find ourselves testing and evaluating the use of nonlinear models, not linear ones, we should expect, as Kuhn (1970) put it, to encounter nothing but problems that seem to indefatigably resist "the reiterated onslaught of the ablest members of the group [accounting] within whose competence it [the IC problem] falls."

REFERENCES

Kuhn, T. (1970), *The Structure of Scientific Revolutions* (2nd Edition Enlarged), Chicago, IL: University of Chicago Press.

McElroy, M.W. (2002), "Social Innovation Capital," *Journal of Intellectual Capital* (Vol. 3, No. 1), pp. 30–39.

Chapter 11

CONCLUSION

VISION OF THE NEW KNOWLEDGE MANAGEMENT

The new Knowledge Management is more than just the second generation of KM—it is a new science, a social science. It is a science because its theory and practice are testable and falsifiable, yet systematic and formal, and it is a social science because of the nature of its focus on how to get human social systems to learn and adapt as best they can. The new KM can also be seen as an application of a much broader "new science": complexity science. Thus, it is a new application of Complex Adaptive Systems (CAS) theory, a vision of how living systems adapt to changes in their environment by evolving their knowledge. And because of the human social setting of its focus, the new KM also relies on organizational learning (OL) (as well as social psychological, sociological, and political) theory to round out its views. Not only do individuals learn, but the groups and organizations of which they are a part also learn. In this way, organizational learning theory, along with other social sciences that contribute to KM, help us put a human face on CAS theory, thereby accounting for the unique blend we see between OL, other social science disciplines, and CAS in the new KM.

Despite their contributions to KM, organizational learning, other social sciences, and complexity theories still need to be supplemented in one very important area: epistemology. This is (or was) a problem. After all, we can't have a discipline called "Knowledge Management"

290

that fails to adequately define its own vocabulary, or to ground itself on a theory of knowledge. For that we turned to Karl Popper (1963, 1972, and 1994; Popper and Eccles 1977). Popper's notion of the three "worlds" of existence is comprehensive and convincing. Not only does it account for knowledge held in minds (beliefs), it also provides for so-called "objective" knowledge—knowledge held in linguistic expressions, such as speech, documents, and other material recordings. In organizations, we find both "subjective" knowledge held in minds and "objective" knowledge held, or expressed, in linguistic forms.

Popper's epistemology is also highly compatible with organizational learning and complexity theory. To the former (as we have shown in Chapter 2), he adds the dynamics of knowledge claim formulation and trial-and-error as the means by which "double-loop learning" occurs; to the latter, a focus on the elimination of errors in our thinking and how error elimination can enhance our capacity to adapt. In addition, his theory of the emergent evolution of the three ontological worlds emphasizes the adaptive significance of World 2 (subjective) and World 3 (objective) knowledge in human evolution (see Chapter 1). That is, according to Popper (1972, 1994; Popper and Eccles 1977), *both types of knowledge are for adaptation, and the ability to produce both has been selected for by the environment.* This is the significance of knowledge in human evolution.

Indeed, Popper's views give managers, and other members of adaptive systems who wish to adapt, a better and more effective place to go in terms of how to approach the production of their own knowledge than do alternative theories of knowledge. That is, his views make it clear *that knowledge production by them is a legitimate and natural process that they must engage in if they and their organizations are to adapt.* Similarly, Popper's epistemology gives new meaning to the practice of KM—the new KM, that is—*by orienting organizations toward seeking out and eliminating the errors in their knowledge claims.* Institutionalizing related processes on an enterprise-wide basis is an important aspect of the mission and purpose of the new KM, because of the centrality of error elimination to adaptation.

The old KM—still widely practiced in many circles—is not entirely free of theoretical foundations itself. And it may even qualify, for some, as a science. But on both fronts, it is quite different from the new KM and considerably narrower. While mostly unspoken, we could say, for example, that the theory of first-generation KM goes something like this: *that we can assume the existence of pre-existing knowledge and that KM is about getting that "knowledge" (actually "information") to the right people at the right time.* The scope of first-generation KM's interests, therefore, is (and has been) the delivery of existing information. We say "information" and not "knowledge" because no persuasive distinction between the two has ever been made in the conventional practice of (old) KM, and the term "information" is used in the KM literature at least as often, it seems, as the term "knowledge" is.

Thus, the old KM is largely predicated on the view that valuable knowledge simply exists and that the purpose of KM, therefore, is to enhance its delivery to people who need it. But since no meaningful distinction between knowledge and information has ever been made in the practice of first-generation KM, we feel safe in concluding that the old KM has not been about "knowledge" management at all— it's been about "information" management (see Chapter 3).

Further, the assumption that knowledge (information) simply exists and that KM's role should merely be to aid in its capture and delivery is also unfounded, or at least arbitrary. While it may be convenient for some to ignore the means by which knowledge is produced—and not just *shared* or delivered—that still leaves the rest of us, who actually from time to time have a need to learn, innovate, and adapt, dissatisfied. More important still, *the essence of life, and of individuals and human organizations, is adaptation to changes in the environment. The old KM is not about such adaptation, and therefore it is basically incrementalist in orientation and not focused on the most essential of organizational functions. Compared to the new KM, then, it is unimportant, a mere diversion from the fundamental questions of organizational existence and development.*

The new KM, then, is aimed at enhancing the whole cycle of knowledge production and integration, not just the easier and more convenient tasks of rounding up documents and other artifacts for access and distribution in computer-based repositories. Its scope of attention is, therefore, considerably broader and deeper than its first-generation cousin, as are its value propositions. Moreover, the distinction it makes between knowledge and information takes it (and us) into utterly new areas of insight and opportunity. There *is* a difference between knowledge and information, and the new KM opens our eyes to it for the first time in the practice of KM.

Perhaps the most dramatic example of this new perspective is the connection we have drawn between KM and corporate malfeasance. Turning to Popper, we can interpret such behaviors as *error-ridden knowledge in practice*, employed by unscrupulous corporate executives, whose knowledge in use is not only faulty, but whose knowledge in use somehow managed to get a great deal farther along than it should have. Thus, such knowledge in use is riddled with errors, and the processes in place that produced and validated it (i.e., the knowledge processing processes) are dysfunctional, as well.

By focusing on enhancing the quality and integrity of organizational knowledge processing, the new KM can play an extremely valuable role in helping to reduce corporate malfeasance. Indeed, by calling attention to the *dimensions of errors* in our knowledge and to the importance of the processes used to produce and evaluate it, we can have a material impact on improving the quality of the business processing outcomes that follow. But since the old, first-generation KM makes no distinction between knowledge processing and business processing—much less between knowledge and information in terms of errors, validity, or anything else—no such role for KM could possibly come out of it. Its sole purpose is to enhance the delivery of information.

Deep in the heart of the new KM are two principal claims that perhaps underlie its practice more than anything else. The first, taken from Popper (1959) and from Peirce (1955), is that *there can be no certainty of truth and therefore no certain knowledge. All human knowledge is fallible.* We can, however, endeavor to get closer to the truth, and the way we can is by seeking to find and eliminate the errors in our thinking. This approach to learning is what Popper (1963) referred to as fallibilism.

The second insight follows closely on the heels of the first in the sense that *what people, in fact, seem to do as they go about the process of making decisions and learning is problem recognition, solution formulation, and error elimination through trial and error.* In this book (Chapter 2) and in other places we have described how trial and error works in the Decision Execution Cycle (DEC) (Firestone 2000, Firestone 2003), and also in knowledge claim formulation and evaluation in the KLC.

When we combine these two ideas, what we get is a fundamental dynamic found in all humans: the need to solve problems by reaching tentative solutions and then eliminating the errors in them through trial-end-error processes of testing and evaluation as a pre-cursor to decisions and action. Thus, the difference between knowledge and information is that while both consist of claims about the world, beauty, and truth, only knowledge consists of claims that have survived our tests and evaluations of whether they are in error. This doesn't make them necessarily true, but it does make them preferable to us as a basis for decisions and action, and that is why we pay so much attention to the idea of metaclaims and the role that they play in knowledge processing in the new KM.

Metaclaims are the claims about claims that we rely on (and that we also produce) as we seek to weigh the closeness to the truth of one claim against another by deciding which of the claims has survived our tests. Trying to distinguish surviving knowledge claims from false ones in the absence of metaclaims is a little bit like trying to find "middle C" on a piano keyboard whose black keys are missing. Without them, there's no way to distinguish one white key from any other.

Knowledge, then (but not truth), is entirely relative to the results of our tests and evaluations. What passes for knowledge to *us* (Firestone and McElroy) may amount to false or untested claims to you because your record of testing and evaluation may differ from ours. Moreover, some knowledge claims may be closer to the truth than others, and some may even be true, but in the end all human knowledge is fallible, and so we can never know with certainty which of our beliefs or claims are actually closest to the truth, or even coincident with it.

The best we can do is to demonstrate the absence of errors in our knowledge to the best of our ability by subjecting it to continuous criticism, testing, and evaluation. People and organizations that do this well stand a better chance of adapting and surviving in the face of change because the quality of their knowledge claims will be higher, and so their performance using them will also be superior.

The New Knowledge Management Landscape

In this book we have tried to illustrate the many ways in which The New Knowledge Management (TNKM) differs from its first-generation cousin using key issues as a vehicle for doing so. We have covered:

    The difficulties KM has had in arriving at a cogent account of knowledge;

    The problem of explaining the origin of the distinction between business processing and knowledge processing and of the origin of the KLC;

    The distinction between information management and KM and the specification of a KM framework;

    The theory of change in generations of KM;

    The nature of knowledge claim evaluation and a framework for analyzing it and performing it;

    The significance of the KLC and some of its many applications;

    The meaning of best practices and some requirements for viable best practices systems;

    The problem of KM strategy, its independence of operational management, and the question of its independent role and status in the adaptive organization;

    The problem of the role of culture in KM and the overestimation of this role in KM to date;

    The progress of the field of intellectual capital and its failure to take account of Social Innovation Capital (SIC).

There are, however, many other aspects of the landscape of The New KM (TNKM) that, for lack of space, we have left for examination in a future volume. These additional key issues on the KM landscape include:

    The SECI Model (Nonaka and Takeuchi 1995) and the need for an expanded knowledge conversion framework;

    Is KM ready for standards?

    Portal progress and KM;

    A framework for analysis and evaluation of KM software;

    TNKM metrics;

    The open enterprise and sustainable innovation;

    TNKM and the terrorism crisis;

    The role of credit assignment systems;

    Communities of practice versus communities of inquiry;

    KM methodology: linear life cycle versus adaptive "tool box" approaches;

    KM methodology: knowledge audits versus knowledge process audits;

    KM methodology: the role of the KLC in KM methodology.

We will come back to these in our discussion of the future of TNKM.

Let us now review, in summary form, a few of the most important ideas that arose from our discussion of the issues covered in the preceding chapters, while keeping in mind that our discussion neglected or only touched upon many important issues in the KM landscape.

More on Defining Knowledge

In addition to the analysis already offered in our section on the vision of TNKM, here are a number of other conclusions on the nature of knowledge in TNKM. In the old KM, the terms "knowledge" and "information" are used synonymously and without distinction, but in the new KM, as indicated in Chapter 1 and many other chapters in this book and the last section, we address the issue of making the distinction head-on. We do so by calling attention to the general ideas of knowledge claim evaluation and error elimination and to the testing and evaluation of knowledge claims. Closely associated with these ideas is the idea of claims and metaclaims, and the crucial role that metaclaims play in helping us to pick and choose from among knowledge claims based on how well they stand up to our tests—our attempts to falsify them.

In addition to knowledge in the form of claims, *knowledge also exists in the form of unexpressed beliefs and belief predispositions.* This kind of knowledge, unlike claims, is held in minds—it is mental knowledge, not artifact-based or cultural knowledge. Since one person can never directly know what another one believes, mental knowledge is personal and subjective. In order to share knowledge and make it accessible to others, it must be expressed in some way—linguistically—thereby producing "objective" knowledge in the form of a claim. But this claim is not identical to the unexpressed belief or belief predisposition. *There is an irreducible epistemic gap between what we believe and what we say.*

In the organizational setting, we find both kinds of knowledge: subjective knowledge (what we believe) and objective knowledge (what we say). Further, both kinds of knowledge can be held, or expressed, in different ways, such as tacitly, implicitly, and explicitly. Indeed, in the new KM we expand greatly beyond the SECI conversion model (see Figure 11.1) put forth by Nonaka and

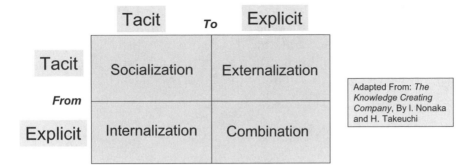

Figure 11.1
The SECI Model

Takeuchi (1995), first by asserting the existence of not just tacit and explicit knowledge, but implicit knowledge, as well; and, second, by applying all three forms to both subjective and objective knowledge. In a future work of ours, we will return to this idea and elaborate on it in more detail. Its significance, however, is that *the SECI model greatly oversimplifies knowledge conversion, and therefore KM programs based upon it neglect many important forms of knowledge conversion.* We will say a little bit more about the SECI model below.

What, then, are the KM implications of the claims and metaclaims perspective in the new KM? Most important, this perspective tells us that not only is there a difference between knowledge and information, but that artifact-based knowledge is a particular kind of information. Information is not a subset of knowledge; knowledge is a subset of information! What kind of subset?

In the case of objective knowledge, it is a linguistic subset consisting of claims that have survived our tests and evaluations attempting to falsify it and whose record of testing and evaluation is accessible to us. Thus, we can say that a knowledge processing system (be it social or technological in character) should not be regarded by us as a bona fide knowledge processing system unless it reveals and reports both knowledge claims and their metaclaims. Similarly, a KM strategy or intervention is not about KM at all unless it concerns the implementation or management of systems (social, technological or otherwise) that deal directly with the distinction between claims and metaclaims.

Here, we point out that *according to the new KM, most instantiations of KM in the past have not been about KM at all.* Perhaps this, in large part, accounts for the degree to which KM has been received with such ambivalence, reticence, and downright distrust to date. It never really *was* about *knowledge* management at all.

The Origin of the KLC

In Chapter 2, we provided a step-by-step development of the origin of the KLC in the Decision Execution Cycles (DECs) (sometimes referred to as Organizational Learning Cycles, or OLCs) that account for activity in human social systems and that, when interrelated by goals and objectives, form business processes. *We offered a theory of how DECs (see Figure 11.2), when characterized by perceived inadequate belief knowledge, can provide a context for recognition of a gap between what the decision maker knows and what he or she needs to know to make a decision. This epistemic gap is what we mean by a "problem." Problems, in turn, arouse a learning incentive system that motivates performance in a set of interrelated DECs aimed at closing the epistemic gap or solving the problem.*

This set of interrelated DECs is, in fact, the KLC pattern, where DECs are structured into information acquisition, individual and

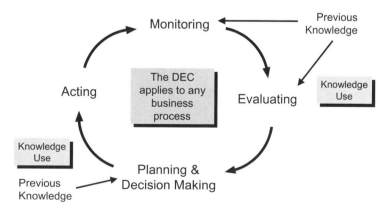

Figure 11.2
The Decision Execution Cycle (DEC)

group learning, knowledge claim formulation, knowledge claim eval-uation, broadcasting, searching/retrieving, sharing, and teaching. These are the subprocesses of the KLC (see Figure 11.3)—processes of knowledge production and integration that produce the distrib-uted organizational knowledge base, all of the mental and artifact-based knowledge that originates in the enterprise.

We have seen (in Chapter 2) *that the alternation between DECs in business processing and DECs in knowledge processing is basic to adaptation and grounded in human psychology, both at the individ-ual and group levels. It is an alternation between different types of motivation, and this alternation is the foundation of a distinction between business processing and knowledge processing and between the latter and knowledge management. This last distinction is the basis of knowledge management as a distinct process and discipline. Without it there can be no knowledge management.*

Knowledge *Process* Management and Information Management

A second key insight, now plainly obvious to many of us thanks to the new KM (see Chapters 3 and 4), is that managing "knowledge" as an outcome—even with our clarified understanding of what it is— has been a mistaken notion all along. *KM is not just about knowl-edge (claims and metaclaims) outcomes management; rather, it's about knowledge process management, as well.* Once we recognize and come to terms with the fact that knowledge is produced in orga-nizations by way of a social process, it's a short hop from there to realizing that *we can only manage the outcomes of such a process through managing the process itself.*

Here is where the new KM reveals another crucial weakness of the old KM—the premise that valuable knowledge already (or simply) exists and that the proper role of KM is merely to find it, codify it, and help make it more easily accessible to people who need it. But clearly this is not the entire story. Knowledge does not simply exist. People in organizations produce it, and they do so in regular, pat-ternlike ways.

In addition, once they produce it, they integrate their knowledge into the distributed knowledge base of the organization—also in regular, patternlike ways. To help better understand the combination

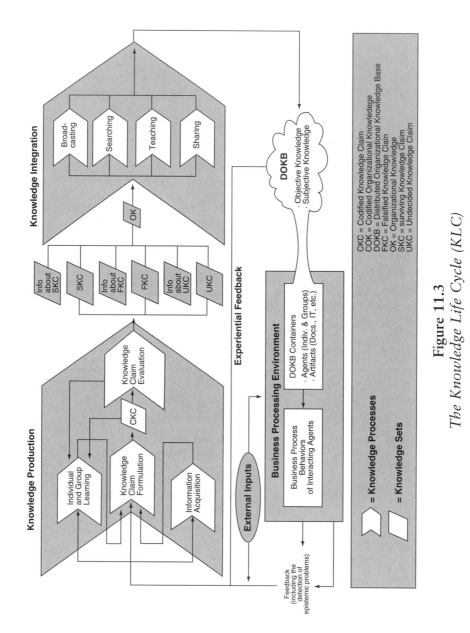

Figure 11.3
The Knowledge Life Cycle (KLC)

CKC = Codified Knowledge Claim
COK = Codified Organizational Knowledge
DOKB = Distributed Organizational Knowledge Base
FKC = Falsified Knowledge Claim
OK = Organizational Knowledge
SKC = surviving Knowledge Claim
UKC = Undecided Knowledge Claim

300

of such patternlike knowledge production and integration processes, *the new KM has given us the Knowledge Life Cycle, or KLC—a descriptive model of knowledge processing in human social systems that is unique in the field* (see Figure 11.3).

The origin of the KLC (see Chapter 2 and just above) can be traced to individual and organizational learning theories and also to theories about how living systems learn on an emergent basis as expressed in complex adaptive systems (CAS) theory. In addition, we see aspects of the KLC that are deeply rooted in psychology and cognitive science (personal knowledge), social psychology (sense making), and epistemology. When we put all of this together, we see the manner in which decision making and action are tied to sense making and the use of existing knowledge, as well as sense making and the production and integration of *new* knowledge. These are processes, not outcomes, and they can be strengthened, reinforced, and enhanced. As one of us (McElroy 1999) once remarked (to himself), "It's not knowledge management, stupid, it's knowledge *process* management."

The difference between information management (IM) and knowledge management (KM) was analyzed in Chapter 3. There we concluded that the essential difference between the two is in the area of Knowledge Claim Evaluation (KCE). KCE is a primary target for KM, but it is not logically required by the definition of IM. Moreover, the outcome of KCE is artifact-based knowledge that is distinguished from information by the tests and evaluations performed in KCE. *Thus, the management of KCE lies at the heart of the new KM because it (KCE) is the immediate source of artifact-based knowledge and its outcomes are the basis for the distinction between information and knowledge. Without management of the KCE there is only IM, not KM! With management of KCE, KM presents us with its own autonomous foundation, both as a process and as a discipline.*

In Chapter 3 we also raised the question of how KM may be specified in the form of a framework that offers a middle ground between definition and measurement and that provides a platform on which measurement may be based. We answered this question by providing a framework based on Mintzberg's (1973) classification of executive activities, the distinctions among levels of KM activity, KLC targets, social/technological, and policy/program dimensions. This framework provides the most extensive foundation for classifying KM interventions yet proposed.

Supply- and Demand-Side Knowledge Processing

Once the KLC starts to come into view, we can make a further distinction (see Chapters 4 and 5) on how its presence in organizations relates to what we do in commerce—that is, its role and impact on our business processing affairs. When we engage in business processing, we engage in knowledge use. Turning to the Decision Execution Cycle once again (see Figure 11.2), we can see that preexisting knowledge is used by us as a precursor to action whenever we monitor, evaluate, plan, and make decisions. On occasion, however, as we explained in Chapter 2, our preexisting knowledge fails us. This gives rise to epistemic gaps—gaps in what we know versus what we need to know. Cycles of knowledge processing driven by the learning incentive system then follow in order to close such gaps.

Once inside knowledge processing (the KLC), we can see that one cluster of goal-directed activity is focused on knowledge production (problem solving), while another concentrates on knowledge integration. Here we sometimes find it useful to refer to these two clusters in a shorthand manner by referring to knowledge production as "demand-side" knowledge processing and knowledge integration as "supply-side" knowledge processing. Why? *Because knowledge production is triggered by the demand for new knowledge in response to epistemic gaps; knowledge integration, in turn, is focused on the supply of knowledge only after it has been produced.* Knowledge integration is all about the propagation, diffusion, and supply of existing (old or new) knowledge across personal and organizational boundaries.

This understanding of demand- and supply-side Knowledge Processing (KP) quickly leads to a similar distinction we can make between demand- and supply-side KM (see Figure 11.4). Demand-side KM consists of KM strategies and interventions aimed at enhancing demand-side knowledge processing, or knowledge production; supply-side KM consists of KM strategies and interventions aimed at enhancing supply-side knowledge processing, or knowledge integration. *In truth, the best KM strategies are ones that cross both boundaries and which deal comprehensively with the whole life cycle, not just parts of it.* Nonetheless, we can make the demand- and supply-side distinctions, and it is often useful to do so as we consider narrower, more targeted interventions in our work.

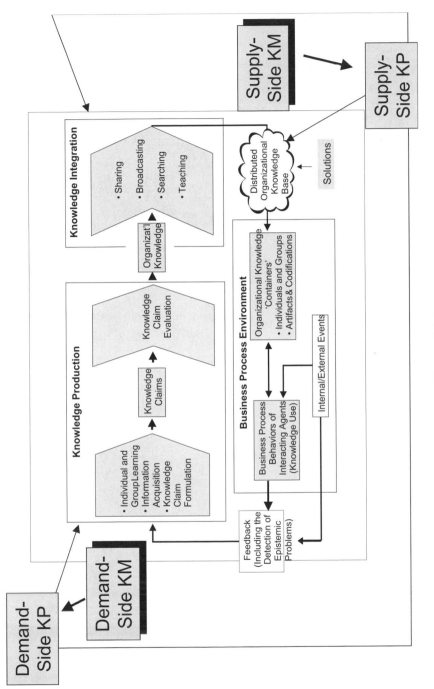

Figure 11.4
Demand- and Supply-Side Knowledge Management

303

Metaclaims and Best Practices

That the new knowledge management is so focused on the importance of knowledge claims and metaclaims is unique in the field. No other brand or style of practice in KM shares this perspective. Still, the idea seems obvious to us. Why shouldn't we think of knowledge that we express in, say, objective linguistic form as being anything other than a claim? To proclaim something as true is merely to *claim* it as such (PRO-CLAIM). And as a claim, an assertion is of course not necessarily true, for which of us can also claim to have direct contact with the truth, direct knowledge, or omniscience of a sort? *No, all knowledge claims, as well as metaclaims, are fallible.*

Adhering to fallibilism, we also agree with Popper that we can make choices between statements or claims that we believe to be true and others that we don't. *And we can do this through the use of deductive logic, which exposes inconsistency* (see Chapter 5) *and forces us to choose between premises and conclusions of arguments and therefore to falsify some of our statements and grow our knowledge.*

The practical implications for KM and for people operating in business processing modes of the idea that we can falsify our knowledge claims and to select among them from the survivors are enormous. Consider the case of "best practices," for example, as we did in Chapter 7. What is a codified "best practice" if not merely a knowledge claim? It is a claim of truth about what patterns of business processing behavior will fetch the best or most desirable results. But what are its premises? What makes its advocates think so? And why should we, as would-be users of such claims, accept them as true or as close to the truth? Where are the claims that lie behind the claims—where are the metaclaims?

The inescapable fact of such great importance to KM and to the new KM, in particular, is that *people naturally rely on metaclaims for evaluating knowledge claims as a basis for choosing to accept some knowledge claims over others (or not), even if the systems that support such decisions do not explicitly support metaclaim production, integration, or use.* In other words, the processes we use to evaluate knowledge claims, such as "best practices" claims, are always broader in scope than the systems we have historically relied on to support us have been.

A conventional IT-based best practices system will always report claims, but rarely will it provide us with the evaluative metaclaims that lie behind them. Nonetheless, we still subject such knowledge claims to our own search for the metaclaims behind them, and then we always subject all of that (the claims and their metaclaims) to our tests of consistency, simplicity, projectibility, and other evaluation criteria or perspectives. Rarely do individuals simply accept a claimed best practice and put it into use without at least asking themselves, *does this make sense?*

Metaclaims that evaluate knowledge claims, like the black keys on a piano, are the context that matters most in knowledge processing, for how can we safely conclude that "middle C" is where we think it is without them? *I know where it is because of where it sits relative to the black keys behind it, and it always sits thus so.* In knowledge management, this changes everything. *There is no KM in the absence of metaclaims that evaluate, only IM (Information Management). Nor is there any knowledge processing in the absence of metaclaims.* The truth is that people in organizations—indeed, all of us—rely heavily on the content of metaclaims from one minute to the next as we constantly try to sort between claims that we ought to accept and the ones we shouldn't. *Knowledge management systems, then, conceived with the idea of enhancing knowledge processing, must make and support the distinction between claims and metaclaims in order to be useful and complete, and this means that management of the knowledge claim evaluation subprocess is a central fulcrum of KM* (see Figure 11.5).

Knowledge Claim Evaluation

In Chapter 5, we presented a framework for description of knowledge claim evaluation, then a normative theory, called *the theory of fair comparison,* providing a high level conceptual outline of how to do KCE, and last an outline of the requirements and structure of a projected KCE software application. *We believe that this analysis is significant for KM, since very few in the field are writing about knowledge claim evaluation,* much less offering descriptive frameworks, normative models, and techniques for implementing this critical activity in knowledge production.

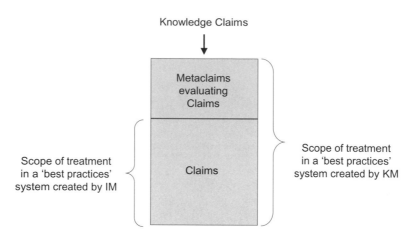

Figure 11.5
Claims versus Metaclaims

The idea of "fair comparison" of competing knowledge claims is fundamental to our perspective. We contrast "biased" knowledge claim evaluation with knowledge claim evaluation through fair comparison and assume further that KCE is more effective, in the sense that it fulfills certain success criteria, when it is characterized by fair comparison and less effective when it is characterized by bias. *Thus, we believe that KM-induced changes in knowledge processing rules and criteria that increase the degree of fair comparison also increase KCE effectiveness, and changes that increase the degree of bias decrease its effectiveness.*

Normatively, of course, one should seek to increase KCE effectiveness and therefore increase the degree of fair comparison. We believe this can be done at the level of knowledge processing by:

- First, fulfilling background requirements (the necessary conditions) for fair comparison among the members of a set of competing knowledge claims; and
- Second, implementing comparisons among the members of this *fair comparison set,* based on a number of criteria that allow us to choose among the knowledge claims of the set based on how its members perform on various tests.

The theory of fair comparison specifies *equal specification of members of the comparison set, continuity, commensurabiliy,* and *completeness of the comparison set* as four necessary conditions of fair comparison. It also names *logical consistency, empirical fit, projectibility, systematic fruitfulness, heuristic quality, systematic coherence, simplicity,* and *pragmatic priority* as criteria for evaluation of competing alternatives once a fair comparison set is constituted. In Chapter 5, we discussed what we mean by each of the above criteria, and also pointed out that in KCE our procedures for combining criteria can range from the very informal to the highly formal.

Informality in combining criteria is what we normally do. That is, when we have a set of factors to be considered in choosing among a set of alternatives in KCE, we most frequently vet the alternatives with others, and may even subject them to a kind of free-for-all critical process and/or weigh them using intuition and common sense, and then make our decision about which alternatives are false, which ones we are unsure about, and which are true (or at least most "truth-like"). The process may involve considerable critical interaction with others and often may be collaborative, since many perspectives are better than one in appreciating the importance of the various factors in a decision.

Much of the time an informal process of vetting and weighing is also the most appropriate way of combining criteria. It is so because there may be no time for a more formal and systematic approach. Or because the resources may not be available to implement one. Or because what is at stake in the KCE decision may not be important enough to justify one. Or because we need informality to surface criticisms, creativity, and new ideas in KCE. So whether we should, once fair comparison requirements are fulfilled, implement a formal and systematic approach to multicriterion decision making, or an intuitive approach or something in between, depends upon available resources, time, the need for new ideas, and the cost involved, compared to what is at stake in avoiding error. If resources, time, available formal frameworks, and cost are not "right," the appropriate decision method to use in KCE may well be an informal one.

Knowledge claim networks, including metaclaims, have descriptive and valuational aspects to them. They are networks with both descriptive and value interpretations (Firestone 2001, 2003, Chap. 4).

And they may be compared in terms of the priority values across networks of benefits resulting from actions as specified by each knowledge claim network (or theory or model). The criterion attribute of *pragmatic priority* listed above also encompasses relevance. Thus, the greater the benefit specified in a knowledge claim network, the more relevant is the network from the pragmatic standpoint of the consequences of actions in closing gaps between goal states and actual states.

When, during KCE, knowledge claim networks are compared according to their pragmatic priority, we are not engaged in a comparison of epistemic values, but rather one of the estimated costs and benefits specified by each network in the comparison set. In committing to the rejection of knowledge claims as false, and relying on surviving knowledge claims in actions, the risks we take are a combination of (a) the likelihood that our evaluation rejecting particular knowledge claim networks is in error, and (b) our assessments of the benefit/cost consequences of such errors—and that, as a result, we might suffer the consequences predicted by the true knowledge claim network we have rejected. *Thus, pragmatic priority requires that epistemic criteria be weighted by the risk of error in developing a comparative evaluation of knowledge claims and knowledge claim networks.* This criterion does not involve wishful thinking, in the sense that we will value most highly those knowledge claims that predict the greatest benefits, but rather modest pessimism in that epistemic values are reduced based on the risk of error involved in not rejecting the surviving knowledge claim networks, and in rejecting their alternatives.

We expect that *the set of direct comparative evaluation criteria we offered in the normative model may well be incomplete and that some of the model's components may be incorrect. So applications of the model should be freewheeling and adaptive, and modifications of it should be undertaken freely.* Moreover, the issues of the form of the composite models and the weighting used in them are left open by us, even though we provide a couple of examples of combination approaches in Chapter 5. We believe that these aspects of the normative KCE model will vary across enterprises and that until we have much more experience in applying the model it would be premature to suggest generalization of these aspects of it.

In short, we believe that *the criteria, the form of KCE composite evaluation models, and the weights used in such models must all be open to innovation themselves*, especially in an environment where we know little about the details of formal methods for evaluating KCE processes. Thus, *we present the normative framework of Chapter 5 as a working theory of KCE, as a first effort in a direction that we need to take in knowledge management.* We hope and believe that though this may be the first attempt at a normative model in the KM literature, it will be far from the last, and we look forward to having others join us quickly on this important road not previously traveled in knowledge management.

The Centrality of the Knowledge Life Cycle

What is perhaps most surprising about the old, first-generation KM is its failure to specify the nature or behavior of its target in any sort of systematic or rigorous way. Worse yet may be its failure to acknowledge that a target of its interventions exists. What do we mean by this?

In the new KM, when we make a KM strategy or engage in an intervention of some kind, we are always seeking to enhance the performance of knowledge processing in human social systems. The target of our interventions, that is, is a social process that we are trying to improve. Moreover, the social process of interest to us has a particular shape and content. It has internal elements, subprocesses that we understand in advance of our efforts and which we can target more narrowly if we choose (see Figure 11.6). This social process that we speak of is, of course, the Knowledge Life Cycle, or KLC.

In the new KM, the KLC is of central importance. It is as important to us as practitioners of KM as knowledge of the patient is to a physician. And just as patients and their illnesses figure prominently in the practice of medicine, so do the KLC and its illnesses figure prominently in the practice of the new KM. It is our job, that is, to ensure the health of the KLC and to enhance its performance whenever we can. And just as a patient in a hospital has a mind and a body for physicians to work with, so does the KLC have substance and regularity to its form. We can see it, touch it, measure it, anticipate its behaviors, alter its behaviors, change the conditions in which it operates, tinker with its internals, and experience its outcomes. In a very real sense, the KLC is a living system, and it falls to the new KM to ensure its well-being.

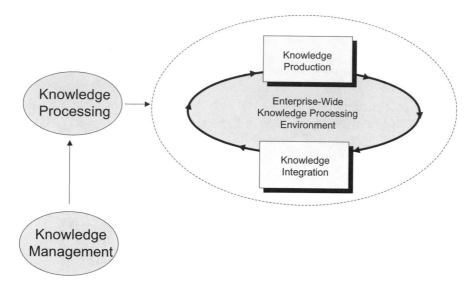

Figure 11.6
Knowledge Management versus Knowledge Processing

What, then, could the equivalent of the "patient" possibly be in the practice of first-generation KM? For all of the obsessive talk of enhancing knowledge sharing that occurs on that side of the fence, we can only guess that it must be the act of offering someone else one's knowledge. Or is it the act of accepting or retrieving such knowledge once offered? In any case, in first-generation KM, there is no distinction between knowledge management and knowledge processing. There is no social process that comprises knowledge processing. There is no model or framework of knowledge processing that can serve as a target of KM interventions or strategies of any kind. There seems only to be life in organizations that is periodically punctuated by sudden needs for information (not knowledge, mind you), backed up by constant browbeating (or stories, or shallow incentives) from management to get people to share it.

Indeed, in the old KM, the raison d'etre for KM strategies and interventions seems singularly aimed at knowledge sharing and use events that, from the perspective of the new KM, are isolated transactions in a much bigger knowledge processing system. And while the new KM sees knowledge processing as the heart of the adaptive engine that makes organizations tick and helps them to survive, the old KM seems inexorably fixated on only their transactional needs. Ensuring that individual acts of sharing and information retrieval occur as best they can is the sole priority of the old KM. Never mind that the firm may be sinking fast, or that managers are looting the treasury, or that the broader adaptive performance of the company is trending downward. There is no higher purpose in the old KM, no KLC, no knowledge processing system, no complex adaptive system, no decision execution cycle—none of that. There are only people who have information and others who need it.

If in the new KM, we can say that the Knowledge Life Cycle lies at the heart of its practice, in the old KM it must be the Information Delivery Cycle (IDC). The IDC has two parts to it: (1) information sharing and (2) information retrieval. And if this is true, then what is the difference between information management and knowledge management in the old KM when all is said and done? The answer is unclear. But in the new KM, the makeup and purpose of the patient *is* clear. *The organization is a complex adaptive system, and the knowledge life cycle is its adaptive engine.* It has a "physiology" with recognizable regularity to it that we can clearly observe, understand, and have impact on. Our purpose, then, is equally clear—to enhance the health and performance of the KLC!

In Chapter 6 we illustrated the centrality of the KLC by illustrating various areas of its application. There we discussed how the KLC is applied to KM strategy, KM and knowledge audits, modeling, predicting, forecasting, simulating, impact analysis and evaluation, metrics segmentation, sustainable innovation, methodology, IT requirements, intellectual capital, education and training, the open enterprise, and new value propositions for KM.

There are many other areas of interest to practitioners of KM where the KLC has a valuable role to play. *The scope of its influence on the practice of KM is extensive, and our discussion in Chapter 6 focused on only a few of them. Nevertheless, the breadth and significance of the applications discussed illustrate the centrality of the KLC to KM and also its utility from the point of view of practice. It also illustrates that the KLC changes everything for KM. Its implications penetrate every nook and cranny of KM as a discipline and every area of KM practice.*

Again, the importance of the role that a conceptual framework or model of knowledge processing plays in the practice of KM cannot be overstated. It is absolutely critical that we begin the practice of

KM with a framework or model describing in broad outline how knowledge is produced and integrated in human social systems. From there we can begin to formulate practice, but always with reference to our theory. We must have grounding. All bodies of practice in KM should be held to this standard. What are their interventions? What methods do they use? How are their methods and interventions related to knowledge processing? Indeed, what is their theory *of* knowledge processing? Do they even have one? If not, how do they account for knowledge production and integration, and how does their practice relate to their theory? If not, why should we accept their value claims?

As we sometimes say, the only thing worse than all theory and no practice is all practice and no theory. *In truth we need both—practice grounded in theory.* In the new KM, the KLC is the most important focus of our theory. Many of our practices, then, are grounded in and upon it, and from the point of view offered to us by the KLC, the mission of the new knowledge management—to enhance knowledge processing—is clear!

KM and Strategy

Another of the most common mistakes made in the practice of the old KM is what we call the "strategy exception error." The strategy exception error mostly shows up in the composition of first-generation KM methodologies. *The error is committed by turning to existing business strategy as the starting point for KM strategy.* The logic behind the error is that (1) the purpose of KM is to help fulfill strategy (business strategy), and (2) that all KM interventions must therefore be planned by first making reference to the content of current business strategy. The error continues, then, by making yet another one—that there is no difference between information and knowledge (no claims and metaclaims) and that the proper role of KM is to improve information delivery in the service of strategy.

KM methodologies that commit this error usually go on to specify steps that run something like this:

- Step 1: Identify current business strategy.
- Step 2: Determine information resources required to successfully carry out current strategy.

■ Step 3: Perform IT and other organizational projects required
to make information resources easily accessible and supportive
of business processing.

The result, of course, is a transactional one. In other words, at best,
KM strategies carried out according to this methodology wind up
improving fleeting acts of information sharing and retrieval, but not
necessarily anything else. Here again, this has the effect of reducing
KM to nothing more than information management trotted out in
today's more fashionable clothes, even as it breeds ill will in the business community for what appears to be a grand deception, or at least
an irresponsible form of self-delusion. We're here, of course, to point
out that the old KM emperor, in fact, has no clothes.

What, then, is the relationship of strategy to KM? Quite simply,
strategy is an outcome of knowledge processing. So in order to
answer the question, one must first be equipped with an understanding of the difference between business processing, knowledge
processing, and knowledge management (see Figure 11.7). Business

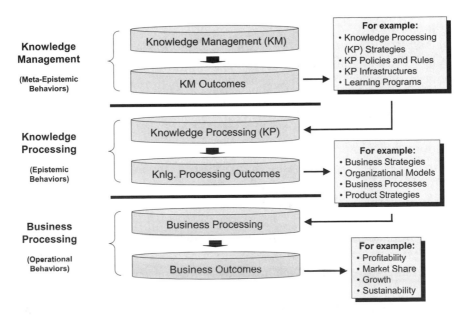

Figure 11.7
The New Knowledge Management Reference Model

processing is the domain of business strategy and related behaviors. *Knowledge processing, however, is where business strategies are hatched. They (strategies) are the manifest resolutions of epistemic gaps between what managers in organizations need to know about strategy and what they, in fact, do know. Thus, a business strategy is a network of knowledge claims produced as a consequence of knowledge processing.*

Knowledge management, in turn, is not subject to strategy, nor is it supposed to help fulfill it. That role falls to information management and to operational business processes, not KM. KM's role transcends strategy. KM's role is to enhance the quality and performance of knowledge processing behaviors, not business processing ones. Indeed, the quality of a business strategy depends heavily on the quality of knowledge processing, its source, and thus indirectly, as well, on the quality of KM. *But strategies, like all knowledge claims, are fallible; they come and go.* KM, though, like good financial management practices, is permanent and transcends strategy. It's above and apart from strategy, not within or below it.

This perspective on the proper role and positioning of KM in a firm raises another important issue for which the new KM has an emphatic answer. *The question is where KM belongs in the functional configuration of a company. The answer, we believe, is that it should be reporting directly to the board of directors and to no one else.* Why? Because maintaining the independence and integrity of knowledge processing in a firm is a fiduciary matter, just as the quality of financial management is. Oversight for both, therefore, is best placed at the level of the board.

Anyone who has any doubt about this need not think for long about what's happened in the United States over the past year or so. When we look at the crises that occurred at such firms as Enron, Worldcom, ImClone, Tyco, and others, what we see are bad strategies, or parts of them, in use. What we can ask ourselves, then, is *what must the knowledge processing systems be like in such firms that knowledge claims of such poor quality manage to survive their internal tests and evaluations?* Who was watching the knowledge processing store there? Was anybody watching it?

Perhaps it can be said that one consequence of the information or knowledge age that few of us fully appreciate is that with the ascendance of knowledge as the new prized asset in corporations has come the need to exercise oversight on its production. *The time has come for boards in businesses (especially publicly traded ones) around the world to formally embrace oversight for knowledge processing as a fiduciary duty, and to recognize the fact that the knowledge we practice in organizations is the knowledge we produce.* Boards must rise to this challenge, and the new KM can help show them the way.

KM and Culture

What is culture, and what is its relationship to knowledge and knowledge management? "Cultural" barriers are often held responsible for failures to share and transfer knowledge in organizations. It is frequently said that knowledge management must undertake the difficult task of changing an organization's culture to achieve the knowledge sharing and transfer necessary to realize the full value of the organization's knowledge resources. In Chapter 9, we showed that this viewpoint is incorrect, and that the widespread belief in it is probably due to the use of the term to describe many different factors that are social, political, or psychological, rather than cultural in character. Our analysis produced the following definitions of culture.

The subjective culture of a group or organizational agent is the agent's characteristic set of emergent high-level predispositions to perceive its environment. It includes group or organizational level value orientations and high-level attitudes and the relations among them. It is a configuration of global attributes that emerges from group interactions—that is, from the organization and pattern of transactions among the agents within a group.

The objective culture of a group or organizational agent is the configuration of value orientations and high-level attitudes expressed in the agent's characteristic stock of emergent problems, models, theories, artistic creations, language, programs, stories, etc., reflected in its documents, books, art galleries, information systems, dictionaries, and other containers. It is a configuration of global attributes expressing the *content* of its information, knowledge, art, and music, apart from both the predispositions the group or its agents may have toward this content, and the material form of the artifact expressing the content. The objective culture of an organization is an aspect of the social ecology of its group agents, consisting of the cumulated effects of previous group interactions. As such, the perception of it by individual and group agents (part of their subjective culture or psychology, depending on the type of agent) influences their behavior.

As we argued in Chapters 2 through 4 and just above, we can distinguish KM processes, knowledge processes, and business processes. And knowledge processes may be viewed in terms of the KLC framework. KLC processes produce knowledge that is used in the other business processes of the enterprise. And these, in turn, produce business outcomes. Figure 11.8 illustrates this chain of influences.

Moreover, KM processes, knowledge processes, and business processes are performed by decision-making, behaving agents. As we have seen, agents, if they are groups, have an internal culture, both subjective and objective. At the same time, the objective cultural component of social ecology also impacts agent decisions. Finally, knowledge and KM processes are affected by culture through the influence it has on behavior constituting these processes. In turn, these processes are keys to producing new knowledge and consequently changes in objective and subjective culture. The interplay between KM processes and culture is bidirectional.

So culture is pervasive in KM, knowledge processing, and knowledge outcomes. It is part of their context, and it is also, in the long run, produced by them. But many other factors (social ecology, sit-

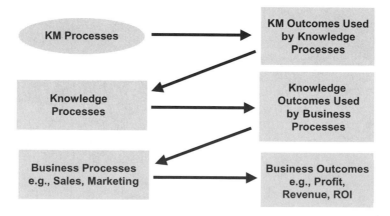

Figure 11.8
From Knowledge Management Processes to Business Outcomes

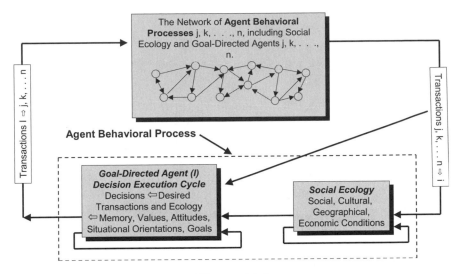

Figure 11.9
The Flow of Behavior Among Agents and the Role of Culture

uational factors, transactional inputs; see Figure 11.9) also contribute to the complex interactions associated with knowledge-related processes and outcomes. Thus, culture is only a small part of what there is to KM, or any other business process, and therefore there remain substantial problems in measuring and analyzing its precise impact on KM, or KM's impact on culture. *Culture is not so much an answer to difficulties in KM as it is an issue and a problem in itself.* And prescriptions that suggest that we must "change the culture" to perform effective KM and to enhance knowledge processing are not solutions to problems, but only prescriptions for movement down the wrong track toward a single-factor explanation of knowledge management and knowledge processing.

The Open Enterprise

This is perhaps the most exciting idea to come out of the new KM. In a phrase, *the Open Enterprise (OE) is a normative model for knowledge processing and knowledge management designed to achieve sustainable innovation and transparency in management. It is the antidote to Enron-like styles of management even as it also enhances innovation and the organizational capacity to adapt.* Unlike the KLC, which is a descriptive model, the open enterprise is a prescriptive one. The OE is largely specified in terms of the KLC's subprocess dimensions, with a particular emphasis on problem detection in business processing, knowledge claim formulation, and knowledge claim evaluation.

What makes the OE so exciting to us is that it is the first comprehensive, normative vision of knowledge processing to appear on the KM landscape. As such, it can equip knowledge managers with a specific target environment, a to-be picture of what to shoot for in the area of KM strategy and practice. *It therefore provides us with a description of how knowledge processing ought to be in a firm, in terms specific enough that we can translate them into KM strategy and action.* And unlike the narrow, transactional bandwidth of the old KM, according to which the to-be environment is confined to individual acts of information sharing and retrieval, the OE is system- and process-wide in scope. It offers a vision of what high-performance knowledge processing should (or can) look like in all of its dimensions and at all levels—enterprise-wide.

The Open Enterprise has several important value propositions not found elsewhere on the KM landscape. First, it enhances an organization's capacity to detect epistemic problems by effectively engaging the whole firm in the process, not just the designated elites in management who can't possibly have the full range of view required to detect problems on a distributed basis. Second, it implements its policy of broad inclusiveness by enfranchising all of the organization's members in the knowledge production side of the KLC, especially in terms of knowledge claim formulation and evaluation. Thus, the full human resource complement in a firm, as opposed to only a fraction of it, becomes engaged in knowledge processing.

Also different in the OE are the rules that relate to knowledge processing. No longer is information or knowledge held close by management hierarchies. Instead, knowledge processing itself is more distributed as is the previous knowledge that informs it. In the OE, the separation of business processing and its management from knowledge processing and its management are made explicit. The monopoly on knowledge processing control once held by business processing managers is repealed. Knowledge processing becomes open to all stakeholders in a firm, not just its managers. This, however, does not mean that management is "undermined." To the contrary, the power to control and direct resources remains with management on the business processing side of the equation.

Considering the issue of terrorism, to be discussed in more detail below, we believe that the specific contribution the new KM can make to the quest for security in the United States and elsewhere is to show how knowledge processing can be improved by bringing powerful new normative (i.e., prescriptive) models, such as the OE, to the table. Only when knowledge processing systems are fully open in terms of the kinds of structural and operational attribute values present in the OE pattern will intelligence be capable of operating fully at its peak. Had the U.S. intelligence system been operating in accordance with our vision of the OE, it may well have been able to "connect the dots" long before the attacks of 9/11/01 took place. We hope to substantiate this claim in more detail as the full scope of the OE is developed in the months ahead.

Intellectual Capital

Underlying all of our comments in Chapter 10 regarding the unsuitability of conventional accounting perspectives in the treatment of intangible values are four key points:

1. The most important source of intangible economic value in a firm is external to itself—not found at all within the firm, and therefore not directly manageable by it. The origin of such value is in the minds of current and prospective stockholders, whose valuations of a firm are determined within the dynamics of their system, not the enterprise's. Their values are then projected onto the enterprise, which in turn receives it as a kind of gift or inheritance—an inheritance, however, that is always subject to adjustment, and even return.

2. Apart from being determined by agents outside of the enterprise, reflecting the value of intangibles using conventional accounting tools as though they were internally managed suffers from another problem, as well. Balance sheets are static models. They are predicated on the assumption that it is

possible to start with a market value that can then be broken down into its additive elements. *Knowledge and the processes that produce and integrate it, however, are anything but additive. What we need in order to account for them all are dynamic models—nonlinear ones—not static ones.* These, in turn, should come into play in conjunction with the theories of emergence they support, the composition of which will suggest reporting models and tools of their own. This is the path to solving the so-called IC problem. Ramming new realities into old frameworks simply will not work.

3. All of our warnings concerning the inability to manage emergent systems and outcomes have been precautionary, but not absolute. *While it's true that processes and outcomes in complex adaptive systems are emergent beyond the absolute control of managers, it is possible to have impacts on them, nevertheless—even intended impacts that give rise to corresponding (hoped for) outcomes.* This, however, does not entail conventional management. Rather, management in such environments must begin with recognition of organizations as social complex adaptive systems, subject to the mostly unpredictable effects of system dynamics and emergence. Armed with this insight, it is possible to build models of organizations and their environments that are nonlinear in form and to use such models for predicting the potential outcomes of alternative management strategies, including the effects that management decisions of one kind or another might have on the externally produced value judgments assigned by markets to the enterprise. In this way, managers can have impact on the value of their organizations' organizational and market intangibles, which, so far as we're concerned, makes such values *manageable*.

4. That said, we are only prepared at this point to support the reflection of intangible values in the lump-sum fashion we have proposed. It is simply too soon to suggest any other, more granular treatment of intangibles on the balance sheet. *What's required, instead, is a period of trial and error, or experimentation, in which competing theories of how intangible values are produced can be tested and evaluated.* As a consequence of that process, we can conceive of a point in time when the momentum behind one or more models of how intangible values are produced matures, and informs us of their manage-

ment, measurement, and reporting implications. Then and only then will we have a solid basis for suggesting how best to report on the value of intangibles to stockholders. Until then, it's premature to attempt such a report.

On the basis of these remarks, we believe that the accounting profession should undertake a concerted effort to bring additional, nonaccounting disciplines into the process of trying to discover the nature of intangible value and the role that it plays in corporate valuations. These would include complexity scientists, social scientists, and knowledge managers of the second-generation (new KM) type. Until we do, and until we find ourselves testing and evaluating the use of nonlinear models, not linear ones, we should expect, as Kuhn (1970) put it, to encounter nothing but problems that seem to indefatigably resist "the reiterated onslaught of the ablest members of the group [accounting] within whose competence it [the IC problem] falls."

Information Technology and the New KM

No summary of the landscape of KM (new, old, or otherwise) would be complete without making some remarks about the IT implications of related practice. In the case of the new KM, the story, we're afraid (see Firestone 2003, Chaps. 10–19), is a short one. *At present, there are no software applications that we know of that explicitly address the claim/metaclaim distinction so central to the new KM, or provide explicit support for knowledge claim evaluation.*

In particular, the Enterprise Knowledge Portal (EKP) (Firestone 1999, 2000a, 2003, Chap. 13) is an application that comprehensively supports knowledge processing and knowledge management. *Despite claims to the contrary, such an application does not yet exist. But the last two years have brought progress toward achieving this essential objective of TNKM.* Firestone's (2003) review of various KLC and KM categories of TNKM framework provides a view of the gap between the current state of portal progress and what is needed for an EIP that would support knowledge processing and knowledge management—that is, for an EKP.

Specifically, current EIPs provide support for those subprocesses in knowledge processing and knowledge management that are common to KM and information processing and information management. However, they don't support individual and group learning, knowledge claim formulation, knowledge claim evaluation, knowledge outcomes, the DOKB, KM knowledge processing, resource allocation, or negotiation well.

The most glaring departure from TNKM requirements is in the area of knowledge claim evaluation. Here, current portal products provide almost no support and the idea of providing it is apparently not even on the radar screen of any vendor. Perhaps that will change. But we are still probably years away from having a real knowledge portal. In Firestone (2003, Chaps. 13, 17, and 19), we outlined "how to get there from here."

Slow progress is perhaps due to the relative obscurity of ideas about the KLC, KCE, and metaclaims in conventional KM circles. We hope, of course, that this book and other writings of ours will help to change this and that progress will be made in recognizing the centrality of the KLC and KCE and the role that claims and metaclaims play in our knowledge processing affairs.

That all said, the landscape here is not entirely barren. Using the KLC as a backdrop, we can easily see existing technologies and applications that support aspects of knowledge processing. E-learning systems, for example, clearly support individual learning on the knowledge production side of things—though not yet very well in a work-oriented problem-solving context—as well as training on the knowledge integration side. Similarly, communities of inquiry that support at least the human interaction, if not the recording and tracking side of error elimination in knowledge processing, can be supported by a wide range of tools aimed at collaboration and group learning. And certainly the information acquisition subprocess is extensively supported by a whole host of applications, some of which have been around for some years.

Of particular interest to us, however, are the new technologies that support the analysis and management of knowledge claims in artifacts. Tools that rely on semantic network analysis, neural network analysis, fuzzy logic, and other technologies aimed at teasing out claims and the metaclaims behind them in e-mail messages, documents, and other electronic files are particularly promising here. But the best in new KM technologies is yet to come, as we discuss in the next section on the future of the new KM.

THE FUTURE OF THE NEW KM

In Popperian epistemology, the development of new knowledge always raises new problems, and therefore a need for more new knowledge. The new KM is no exception. As a new science, much of its content and methodology is still not fully defined, and many of the new questions it raises have not yet been answered. In some cases, these are entirely new questions; in others they are old questions answered by the old KM, for which the new KM has new answers to offer. What we offer here, then, are some brief discussions of new KM perspectives on some new and old problems in KM. In forthcoming works of ours, we plan to address each of these issues in more detail. For now, simply naming and describing the problems to be worked on will do.

SECI Model

Among the many important implications of the new knowledge management is that the once, and perhaps still, popular SECI model put forth by Ikujiro Nonaka in his 1995 book with Hirotaka Takeuchi, *The Knowledge-Creating Company*, may be, as we indicated earlier, materially incomplete and seriously flawed. While the reformulation of Nonaka's model by us is not yet fully completed, we can say that the original SECI model (Socialization/Externalization/Combination/Internalization) suffers from two important oversights.

First, the SECI model has many flaws at the level of psychological and cognitive theory. Thus, it neglects to include consideration of implicit knowledge and in the process provides us with an ambiguous rendition of tacit knowledge. As Michael Polanyi, an early source of theory for the nature and meaning of tacit knowledge, pointed out, some tacit knowledge consists of that which one can know but never tell— ". . . *we can know more than we can tell.*" (Polanyi 1966, 4). Tacit knowledge is, therefore, inexpressible. There is no conversion from it to explicit form, thus Nonaka's notion of externalization (acts of converting tacit knowledge to explicit knowledge) is misleading. Implicit knowledge, however, can be converted to explicit form. But Nonaka and Takeuchi made no provisions for implicit forms of knowledge, even though Polanyi mentions it in his work (Polanyi 1958, 286–288).

Further, the SECI model also fails to distinguish between knowledge predispositions and situational orientations. The distinction between tacit and explicit knowledge may either be interpreted as applying to predispositions or to orientations. But if it's applied to predispositions, it has no meaning because there are no predispositions that are explicit. On the other hand, if tacit knowledge is applied to orientations, then it is clear that much of the "tacit knowledge" that people have referenced in examples, such as the ability to ride a bicycle, doesn't fit such a notion of tacit knowledge, because such abilities are predispositional in character.

Second, with the arrival of the new KM comes the distinction between subjective knowledge in minds and objective knowledge in artifacts. This, too, materially expands the range of possible forms from which knowledge can be converted. Instead of just tacit, implicit, and explicit forms of knowledge, we now have all three for *both* subjective and objective knowledge to consider. Thus, we have up to six categories of knowledge to deal with in the new KM knowledge conversion model, not just two as in the case of Nonaka's SECI model. In truth, however, there are only five such categories since we have already rejected the notion of tacit objective knowledge, or tacit knowledge held in anything other than minds.

All of this leaves us with a dramatically expanded matrix, which takes us from a two-by-two matrix with four cells to a five-by-five matrix with twenty-five cells. The implications of this insight are enormous. *Among other things, it means that all of the KM practices and practitioners out there that have been basing their knowledge conversion efforts on the SECI model may have been engaging in fantasy for the past several years. There is no conversion of tacit knowledge to explicit knowledge; there never has been and never will be.* At best, they've been dealing with implicit knowledge, not tacit knowledge, but the SECI model never allowed for that. Here we see a dramatic example of how theory matters greatly to practice. Faulty theory can lead to faulty practice, which can, in turn, lead to colossal wastes of time.

In sum, then, the landscape of ideas contained in the new KM raises several important questions about the falsity and usefulness of the Nonaka SECI model, thanks to the new KM's identification of implicit knowledge, objective knowledge, and subjective knowledge as forms of knowledge that the SECI model simply overlooks. In a future work of ours, we plan to unveil a fully reformulated knowledge conversion model that corrects these errors—which, of course, will be nothing more than a new knowledge claim complete with its own set of new questions and epistemic problems.

The EKP

A vital task for the new KM is development of the Enterprise Knowledge Portal (EKP), because it is that application that provides comprehensive support for both the KLC and for KM. In addition, the EKP is vital for the open enterprise as well. In Firestone (2003, Chap. 13), one of us outlined the steps that should be taken to advance from present EIP platforms to the EKP. *The Enterprise Knowledge Portal is an application on the verge of development. The technology it requires is in existence now. The cost of its development is low as software applications go, since its implementation is largely a matter of systems integration, with the exception of its Intelligent Agent (IA) component that exceeds current IA capabilities. On the other hand, the benefits associated with the EKP are great. They are nothing less than realization of the promise of the Enterprise Information Portal (EIP) to achieve increased ROI, competitive advantage, increased effectiveness, and accelerated innovation.*

EIPs are risky because (neglecting data quality applications which involve relatively superficial quality issues) they fail to evaluate the information they produce and deliver for quality and validity. Nothing, including EKPs, can ensure certainty about information, models, or knowledge claims. But EKP applications incorporate a systematic approach to knowledge claim testing and evaluation that eliminates errors and produces quality assured information. In the category of portal technology they, not EIPs, are the best we can do. They, not EIPs, are the future of portal technology.

Framework for Analysis of KM Software

The EKP concept provides the basis for a comprehensive framework for evaluating knowledge processing and KM software. Currently there is no such framework. Vendors offer claims about the support they provide for KM, but there is no benchmarking framework against which to evaluate such claims. A future task for the new KM development is to use the EKP concept to produce such a framework.

Role of Credit Assignment Systems in KM Software

The New KM (TNKM) suggests that the primary motivation for using KM software will be the desire to solve problems. However, a long-recognized problem in the old KM has been that of "incenting" people to participate in knowledge sharing initiatives and specifically in software designed to support knowledge sharing. Thus, a natural question is whether the same problem will exist in TNKM. That is, what kinds of incentives will be needed to encourage knowledge worker participation in TNKM software applications? Will credit assignment systems be necessary? Or will it be sufficient to simply involve people in KLCs by giving them free rein to solve their own problems?

TNKM Metrics

In Chapter 6, we discussed the application of the KLC model to metrics development and showed how it could be used as a guide to metrics segmentation. Of course, the KM approach developed in Chapter 3 can also be used to supplement the KLC. Preliminary work has been done in this area by Firestone (2000) and Firestone and McElroy (2002). However, previous work has only initiated the process of KM metrics development. This will be a primary and ongoing activity of TNKM.

TNKM and Terrorism

After the 9/11/01 attacks, much of the criticism levied against U.S. intelligence agencies revolved around their failure to "connect the dots." Critics argued that internal warnings and red flags should have been noticed and that sufficient evidence existed prior to the attacks to suggest that danger was imminent.

From our perspective, the failure of U.S. intelligence agencies to potentially anticipate the 9/11 attacks was a failure of knowledge processing. Using the KLC as an analytical tool, we could say that there was a breakdown in knowledge claim formulation on a grand scale, but also that on a micro scale certain knowledge claims made by specific agents in the system were too quickly discarded or overlooked. In that case, it was knowledge claim evaluation that failed us, because authoritarian and bureaucratic rather than epistemic and appropriate value criteria were used to falsify promising knowledge claims in favor of others that proved false in the end.

Intelligence is an industry that is in the knowledge processing business. It exists for no other reason than to close epistemic gaps—gaps in the knowledge we need about threats to our security versus the knowledge we have. *One could argue, therefore, that there is no more important, more urgent need for the new KM than in the intelligence business, for the KLC provides it, and us, with a roadmap of how knowledge processing happens, and therefore a framework for aiming strategies, tools, and interventions at its improvement.*

Further, it may also be the case that the most urgent software application for an interagency intelligence system is an EKP. Indeed, if the open enterprise can be described as an enterprise-wide knowledge processing system with maximum inclusiveness, then the EKP can be seen as its indispensable IT infrastructure. From the perspective of the EKP, every stakeholder in a firm is a full participant in knowledge processing. If a memorandum written by some far-flung agent in Phoenix, Arizona, suggests that terrorists are going to fly fully loaded passenger jets into the World Trade Center towers in New York City, the EKP picks up on that, connects the dots, and broadcasts its knowledge claims—without fail and without additional human intervention—to appropriate stakeholders in the system. Why? Because the OE is a knowledge-claim-centric construct, not a management-centric one. A credible claim is a credible claim, regardless of who develops it or what their rank or status is in the firm. The knowledge processing ethic of the OE is blind to such things, and the EKP does nothing but doggedly hunt for dots and explore ways of connecting and evaluating them.

The Open Enterprise, Again

The Open Enterprise (OE) is a vital part of the future of TNKM. In future work of ours, we will be developing the model of the OE comprehensively and in much more detail than was possible in this book. Out of this work will come new and potentially powerful applications of the OE for enhancing national security and reducing terrorism, as the approach the OE prescribes will make it possible for intelligence agencies to dramatically enhance their capacity to detect and solve epistemic problems.

The OE ethic of inclusiveness and aggressive knowledge claim formulation will have equally dramatic effects in less urgent settings such as businesses. This, of course, will be its most common application. In businesses, the OE will, by definition, lead to greater transparency and inclusiveness, since its most important precept is that knowledge processing must be a politically open process. While there will always be a place for secrecy, privacy, and confidentiality in the OE, a great deal of what today passes for closely held knowledge in organizations will be more widely shared in the OE.

The effects? Greater transparency will lead to fewer cases of management malfeasance as inherently bad ideas get swept aside long before they escalate into practice. In addition, the advent of such tools as free employee presses in which employees can openly review and critique management decisions, related strategies, and assumptions will make it easier for stockholders to witness and understand management's actions and intent, as well as the risks associated with both. And finally, the rate and quality of innovation will improve, as more of the firm's employees and other stakeholders become directly involved in problem detection and knowledge production.

Of additional importance to the OE will be normative models for OE-related KM tools and methods. In other words, if the OE is an attractive end-state model, the next question, and one we will devote much attention to in our future work, is *how do we get there from here?* Much work in the new KM has already occurred here, in that a technique known as the *Policy Synchronization Method* (PSM) has been developed and continues to be refined (McElroy and Cavaleri 2000). PSM is a KM method predicated on the view of knowledge processing as a self-organizing complex adaptive system. It therefore concentrates its focus not so much on the system itself, but on its background conditions instead. *Getting a knowledge processing system to function at its peak capacity, according to the PSM method, is best accomplished by managing its background conditions so that they are synchronized with the problem-solving predispositions of people and groups inside of it (the system). Once such conditions are properly set, sustainable innovation and high-performance knowledge processing flourish.*

The importance and significance of the open enterprise cannot be overstated here. The potential contribution that the OE can make to business and society in general is enormous. Anything that can improve our collective capacity to detect problems, eliminate errors in our knowledge, and choose actions that enhance the sustainability of our course is desperately needed at this time. This is the promise of the OE. It is a normative model for knowledge processing in human social systems designed to enhance our capacity to learn, avoid errors, and adapt.

Communities of Inquiry (CoI)

The old KM is much concerned with Communities of Practice (CoPs) because of their usefulness for knowledge sharing. Practitioners in the CoP area often believe that they are useful for knowledge production too. But TNKM perspectives raise the concern that knowledge production in CoPs is likely to be characterized by the use of consensus as a validation criterion for knowledge claims. This communitarian form of knowledge production is inconsistent with fallibilism and an orientation toward error elimination. Therefore, TNKM must develop an alternative model to the CoP construct specifying the attributes and characteristics of communities dedicated to the discovery and elimination of errors in knowledge that differ from CoPs in behavior and intent. We call such communities Communities of Inquiry (CoI). Thus, CoIs are the counterpart to the OE at the group or community level.

Knowledge Management Methodology

KM project methodology (Firestone 2001a) is another important aspect of TNKM we have not been able to cover in this work. Clearly, however, it must be a continuing concern of TNKM. In a future work on TNKM, we will take up three TNKM methodology issues. First, should TNKM methodology be a life cycle methodology or should it be an adaptive, iterative, incremental methodology? Second, what implications does TNKM have for the form of that most common of KM initiatives: the knowledge audit? And third, what is the role of the KLC in KM methodology?

Value Theory in Knowledge Management

In Chapters 5 and 10 in passing, we introduced the idea that valuational knowledge claims enter the Knowledge Claim Evaluation (KCE) process. That raises the more general question of the place of valuational models in TNKM. We can approach this question through the KLC. If we do, it is immediately apparent that problem recognition, as well as every subprocess of the KLC, involves making value judgments. However, the subprocess where the value judgments we make seem most controversial is the KCE process. And the reason for that is the legacy of "value free," "objective" inquiry—an idea that was dominant in scientific philosophy for a good part of the last century, but which is far from dominant now.

In TNKM, our notion of objective inquiry views value theory as playing a vital role in the KCE process. Let's review that role and see what it implies. In developing our normative model for KCE we included a category of criteria called *pragmatic priority*. All the other criteria discussed fall into the category of traditional epistemic criteria for comparatively evaluating *factual* knowledge claims. But pragmatic priority involves taking account of the valuational consequences of rejecting knowledge claims as false and relying on surviving knowledge claims as a basis for action.

The risks we take are a combination of the likelihood that our evaluation rejecting particular knowledge claim networks is in error, and the benefit/cost consequences of such errors. If we are in error in our falsifications, we must suffer the valuational (cost and benefit) consequences predicted by the true knowledge claim network we have rejected. *To take account of these risks in estimating pragmatic priority, we must formulate valuational knowledge claims that provide a value interpretation of our descriptive knowledge claim network. So, to estimate pragmatic priority we have no choice but to formulate a value theory and to use it in making our estimates and in comparatively evaluating factual knowledge claims.*

Now, taking this one step further, the value theory we use to estimate pragmatic priority is only one of a set of alternative value interpretations that might be applied in the specific KCE context in question. And just as we have constructed a fair comparison set of factual knowledge claims that our KCE process must test and evaluate, we also must construct a fair comparison set of alternative value interpretations for testing and evaluation and seek to eliminate error in that comparison set.

So the implication of the role of valuational knowledge claims in KCE that we have just outlined is that objective inquiry requires not only the formulation of valuational knowledge claims, but their testing and evaluation as well. *Valuational knowledge claims are just as important as factual knowledge claims in our knowledge claim networks, and they are just as approachable as factual claims through applying Popper's method of conjecture and refutation focused on error elimination.*

In the case of factual knowledge claims, the goal that regulates inquiry is the truth. In the area of value inquiry, the goal is "the legitimate." But in both cases, the Popperian tetradic schema for problem solving can still be applied to grow our knowledge. Because in each area, inquiry starts with a problem, continues with tentative solutions, proceeds to error elimination, and then gives rise to a new problem. And the orientation of TNKM and the open enterprise are both just as relevant to the production and integration of value knowledge as they are to the production and integration of factual knowledge.

In the last several paragraphs we have expanded on our account in Chapter 5 and presented a broader perspective on the role of value theory in KCE. That role has implications for the future of TNKM. First, part of our program must be to refine the normative model presented in Chapter 5 and evolve it toward a KCE methodology. Second, we must clarify in future work how value interpretations and value theories are formulated. One of us (Firestone 2001) has performed previous work on value interpretations. Third, we must develop a parallel normative model for evaluating the legitimacy of valuational knowledge claims, i.e., the value interpretations that transform factual theories into valuational theories. And fourth, we must, in TNKM, begin to formulate value interpretations along with our theories about fact.

The New Knowledge Management and Knowledge Management Standards

We close this chapter and the book itself with some final words about standards for KM. We offer our remarks by first acknowledging that there are currently many efforts around the world now under way to develop standards for KM, though generally these are not coordinated. We believe that all such standard formulation efforts are premature at best and seriously misguided at worst. They have the potential of doing great damage to the continued growth and evolution of the field. How? By locking KM and knowledge processing in the industry into patterns of behavior that may, in fact, be harmful to sustainable innovation, organizational intelligence, and organizational adaptation.

Jan Hoffmeister, one of our colleagues on the board of the Knowledge Management Consortium International, points out that in the development of any new field, there are three basic stages of development. The first stage is the stage of relative chaos. Hoffmeister, who serves as Skandia's Global Director of Intellectual Capital Reporting, has seen this firsthand in his own immediate field, intellectual capital (reporting), for which there presently are no standards. This is the stage, then, in which many competing and discordant ideas are bandied about, even in the absence of commonly held views on what the questions are, or the guiding principles that help determine the answers.

The second stage is the stage in which commonly held principles start to form. In knowledge management, for example, we could say that if the frameworks put forth in the new KM, such as the KLC and the unified theory of knowledge that it embraces, rise to the level of commonly held knowledge, the second stage of KM will have at least begun. *And once it has, and after it has established itself on a more stable footing, it will be time to proceed to the third stage and to consider the development and adoption of standards for KM. But not before!*

We are nowhere near the third stage of development in KM, nor are we barely beyond the first. That scene has yet to be played out. At best, we are in the early period of the second stage, but even that is mere speculation. To undertake the development of standards for KM at this juncture in time borders on the irresponsible. Let's consider some of the errors reflected in many of today's KM standards efforts to help illustrate why current efforts at forming KM standards are highly premature.

First, how can we possibly have standards for KM when most such efforts fail even to make the most rudimentary distinction between knowledge management and knowledge processing? Worse yet is the constant confusion that continues to exist about the two, the result being that some of what we see in related standards efforts are arguably KM-related while others are clearly knowledge processing related. This, of course, is necessarily accompanied by expressions of *what KM is* that are foggy at best. Is it to enhance knowledge processing? Is it to enhance knowledge sharing? Is it to help harvest the economic value of "intellectual assets"?

A quick survey of the many KM standards efforts now under way will reveal that apparently it's all of the above. Which, of course, means that it's none of them, for how can we have standards for the same thing in different places around the world that in very material ways contradict one another? The answer is we can't, or at least we shouldn't. If ever there was a case of standards-making efforts being launched prematurely, this is it. We're now actually codifying our prematurity in the form of conflicting sets of standards.

Second, it is embarrassing to watch the deeply ironic manner in which standards in KM are being pursued in venues that, themselves, are engaging in KM without the slightest bit of self-consciousness about what it is they are doing. The American National Standards Institute (ANSI), the British Standards Institute (BSI), and the International Standards Organization (ISO) are three that come immediately to mind, although KM standards development efforts are now also under way under the auspices of several other standards-making organizations around the world. But what is a standards-making organization if not a formal knowledge management system, itself? And what, for that matter, is a standard if not a set of codified knowledge claims? And what is a KM standard if not a set of knowledge claims about knowledge management or knowledge processing?

Indeed, the processes that organizations like ANSI, BSI, ISO, and others prescribe and enforce are normative knowledge processing systems, the purposes of which are to produce validated knowledge claims (i.e., standards). The irony here is palpable! Let us put it in explicit terms. If a group of people is interested in developing standards for how organizations and their managers should go about managing knowledge processing, why not just adopt the processes already in use by the standards-making organizations themselves, which they (the would-be KM standards developers) apparently already find acceptable? Why not just take the ANSI process, or the ISO process or what have you, embrace it as the KM standard, declare victory, and move on?

It would be even more ironic if any of the now underway KM standards efforts were to actually produce outcomes that conflicted with those enforced by the standards-making bodies under whose auspices their work occurred. The hypocrisy here would be overwhelming. How can a group accept the validity of one set of rules for knowledge processing and yet ratify another, even as it relies on the legitimacy of the first set (which it then implicitly rejects) as the basis for producing the latter? No, intellectual honesty would seem to demand that any KM-standards related group that subordinates itself to the standards-making procedures of an ANSI, BSI, ISO, or what have you should immediately be seen as having embraced, and thereby endorsed, the knowledge management model of their overseers and the knowledge processing systems they prescribe. Why, then, continue with the development of yet another, new set of KM (or knowledge processing) standards as if the ones practiced and enforced by the overseers didn't already exist?

Third, in light of this criticism of KM standardization efforts, what can we say about the future of such efforts? (1) We can safely assume, we think, that the maturity of standards that conflict with one another in KM will have precisely the opposite effect of what their makers hope for. The only thing worse than conflicting theories and practices in KM is standards that codify them rigidly into place.

(2) It is our hope that the overseers now reigning supreme in the development of KM standards efforts will themselves be seen as enforcers of an approach to KM *and knowledge processing* that is unduly determinative of outcomes and biased in its effects. Why? Because even a cursory inspection of the standards-making processes enforced by ANSI, BSI, ISO, and the rest will reveal the fact that they are (a) KM organizations themselves whose methods we are expected to adopt, and (b) whose enforced knowledge processing system is fundamentally communitarian and therefore deeply flawed.

Communitarian systems employ consensus as the basis of knowledge claim evaluation in their knowledge processing schemes. According to that logic, a standard could (and will) be adopted simply by virtue of its popularity or the degree to which a consensus builds behind it. Once this consensus is reached, communitarian systems are not open to continuous testing and evaluation of the knowledge claims backed by the consensus, for the simple reason that the criterion of truth in such systems is the consensus that has already been reached. Never mind the veracity of the claims themselves or their closeness to the truth. Communitarian systems seek harmony and agreement amongst their stakeholders, regardless of the quality or integrity of the knowledge they produce.

Let us conclude our remarks on this subject, and the book itself, then, by pledging to do whatever *we* can to continue to call attention to the prematurity and hypocrisy of KM standards-making efforts under current industry and institutional circumstances. This, too, is liable to change under the influence of the new KM in the days ahead.

REFERENCES

Firestone, J.M. (1999), "Enterprise Information Portals and Enterprise Knowledge Portals," *DKMS Brief*, 8, *Executive Information Systems, Inc.*, Wilmington, DE, March 20, 1999. Available at http://www.dkms.com/White_Papers.htm.

Firestone, J.M. (2000), "Knowledge Management: A Framework for Analysis and Measurement," *White Paper No. 17, Executive Information Systems, Inc.*, Wilmington, DE, October 1, 2000, Available at: http://www.dkms.com/White_Papers.htm.

Firestone, J.M. (2000a), "Enterprise Knowledge Portals: What They Are and What They Do," *Knowledge and Innovation: Journal of the KMCI*, *1, no. 1*, 85–108. Available at: http://www.dkms.com/White_Papers.htm.

Firestone, J.M. (2001), "Estimating Benefits of Knowledge Management Initiatives: Concepts, Methodology, and Tools," *Knowledge and Innovation: Journal of the KMCI*, *1, no. 3*, 110–129. Available at: http://www.dkms.com/White_Papers.htm.

Firestone, J.M. (2001a), "Knowledge Management Process Methodology", *Knowledge and Innovation: Journal of the KMCI*, *1, no. 2*, 85–108. Available at: http://www.dkms.com/White_Papers.htm.

Firestone, J.M. (2003), *Enterprise Information Portals and Knowledge Management*, Boston, MA: KMCI Press/Butterworth–Heinemann.

Firestone, J.M. and McElroy, M.W. (2002), *Certified Knowledge and Innovation Manager (CKIM) Level I Course Notes*, Hartland Four Corners, VT: KMCI.

Kuhn, T. (1970), *The Structure of Scientific Revolutions (2nd Edition Enlarged)*, Chicago, IL: University of Chicago Press.

McElroy, M. (1999), "The Second Generation of KM," *Knowledge Management Magazine* (**October, 1999**), 86–88.

McElroy, M. and Cavaleri, S. (2000), "The Policy Synchronization Method" is the subject of a U.S. patent application filed in September 2000 by McElroy and Cavaleri. It currently holds patent-pending status.

Mintzberg, H. (1973), "A New Look at the Chief Executive's Job," *Organizational Dynamics*, AMACOM, **Winter, 1973**.

Nonaka, I. and Takeuchi, H. (1995), *The Knowledge Creating Company*, New York, NY: Oxford University Press.

Peirce, C. (1955), "The Scientific Attitude and Fallibilism," in J. Buchler (ed.) *Philosophical Writings of Peirce*, New York, NY: Dover Publications, 1955.

Polanyi, M. (1958), *Personal Knowledge*, Chicago, IL: University of Chicago Press, 1958.

Polanyi, M. (1966), *The Tacit Dimension*, London, UK: Routledge and Kegan Paul.

Popper, K.R. (1959), *The Logic of Scientific Discovery*, London, Hutchinson.

Popper, K.R. (1963), *Conjectures and Refutations*, London, UK: Hutchinson.

Popper, K.R. (1972), *Objective Knowledge*, London, England: Oxford University Press.

Popper, K.R. (1994), *Knowledge and the Body-Mind Problem* (edited by Mark A. Notturno), London, UK: Routledge.

Popper, K.R. and Eccles, J.C. (1977), *The Self and Its Brain*, Berlin, Germany: Springer-Verlag.

Rudner, R. (1953), "The Scientist Qua Scientist Makes Value Judgments," *Philosophy of Science*, **20**, 1–6.

GLOSSARY OF ACRONYMS

AHP	Analytic Hierarchy Process
AKMS	Artificial Knowledge Management System
AKPS	Artificial Knowledge Processing System
AKS	Artificial Knowledge Server
ANSI	American National Standards Institute
BP	Business Processing
BPE	Business Processing Environment
BPR	Business Process Re-engineering
BSI	British Standards Institute
CAS	Complex Adaptive Systems
CEO	Chief Executive Officer
CFO	Chief Financial Officer
CIO	Chief Information Officer
CKO	Chief Knowledge Officer
CoI	Community of Inquiry
CoP	Community of Practice
DEC	Decision Execution Cycle
DKMS	Distributed Knowledge Management System
DLL	Double-Loop Learning
DOKB	Distributed Organizational Knowledge Base
DSS	Decision Support Systems
EIP	Enterprise Information Portal
EKM	Enterprise Knowledge Management
EKP	Enterprise Knowledge Portal
FGKM	First-Generation Knowledge Management
HR	Human Resources
HRD	Human Resources Development
HTML	Hyper-Text Markup Language
IA	Intelligent Agent

IC	Intellectual Capital
IDC	Information Delivery Cycle
IM	Information Management
ISO	International Standards Organization
IT	Information Technology
KBMS	Knowledge Base Management System
KCE	Knowledge Claim Evaluation
KCF	Knowledge Claim Formulation
KLC	Knowledge Life Cycle
KM	Knowledge Management
KMCI	Knowledge Management Consortium International
KMFM	Knowledge Management Framework Methodology
KP	Knowledge Processing
KP	Knowledge Processing
NKMS	Natural Knowledge Management System
NKPS	Natural Knowledge Processing System
OD	Organizational Development
OE	Open Enterprise
OLC	Organizational Life Cycle
PCAS	Promethean Complex Adaptive System
PLC	Problem Life Cycle
PSM	Policy Synchronization Method
ROI	Return on Investment
SECI	Socialization/Externalization/Combination/Internalization per Nonaka and Takeuchi
SGKM	Second-Generation Knowledge Management
SIC	Social Innovation Capital
SLL	Single-Loop Learning
TNKM	The New Knowledge Management™
XML	Extensible Markup Language

INDEX

A

Agent interaction, transactional systems model of, 41–48
  coping behavior classes, 44
  interpreting environment stimuli, 43–44
  motivational behavior aspects, 43–47
  motivational hierarchy, 41–43
  sense making, 47–48
Ages of knowledge management, 88–89, 94–97; *see also* Generations of knowledge management
  difficulties with, 95–97
  Snowden on, 94–95, 96
  third age and sense making and complex adaptive systems, 113–115
  third age forecast by Snowden, 104–134
Allocating resources, 80
Analytic hierarchy process (AHP), 171, 172, 177, 191
  consistency index (CI) and, 183
  logarithmic least square method (LLSM) and, 186
  ratio scaling approach based on, 178–187
  right eigenvector method (EM) and, 186
Artificial knowledge management systems (AKMs), 222

Artificial knowledge server (AKS), 169–170

B

Behavior flow among agents, 107
Best practices systems, 238–248
  conclusions, 247–248
  fallibility of, 221
  first stage of knowledge management and, 90, 99
  information-based, 305
  knowledge claims, 239–240
  knowledge management as, xxiv, 238–248
  lack of context problem, 238–239
  metaclaims as context, 241–242, 304–305, 306
  metaclaims in action, 245–247
Building relationships with individuals and organizations external to enterprise, 78
Business process
  decision executive cycle and, 49, 51
  definition, 48
  environment, 49, 50
  hierarchy and activity, 49
  knowledge process level and, 74
Business process reengineering (BPR), 94

C

CapitalWorks Learning
  Effectiveness Index, 206, 207
CAS. *See* Complex adaptive
  systems
Cassidy model, 209
Codified knowledge claims (CKCs),
  54, 56
Communities of inquiry (CoI), 329
Communities of practice, 91, 226,
  250, 329
Complex adaptive systems, xx, 61,
  62, 106, 113–115, 290
  application of, 131
  Cynefin model and, 121–122,
    128, 129–130
  ecological relationships, 285
  false linearity and, 279
  generational view of knowledge
    management and, 98
  knowledge claim evaluation and,
    148, 170, 209
  knowledge life cycle and, 197,
    301
  Level Zero knowledge and, 72
  natural, 121
  Promethean, 121, 122, 125,
    126–127, 133
  sense making and, 113–114
  viewing, 90
Content management, 92, 94, 100
  third age of knowledge
    management and, 105–110
Crisis handling, 80
Culture, 261–274, 315–317
  analytic attributes, 265
  barrier question, xxv, 264
  conclusion, 272–273
  definitions, alternative, 261–264,
    315
  fitting with other factors
    influencing behavior,
    264–271

global attributes, 265–266
global properties question,
  270–271
introduction, 261
knowledge and, 271–272
objective, 267, 268, 271, 272,
  315–316
structural properties, 265
subjective, 267–268, 270,
  271–272, 315, 316
Cynefin model, xxiii
  abstraction definition for,
    117–118
  changes needed for, 132–134
  commentary about, 116,
    117–118, 119, 120, 121,
    122–124, 125–126,
    127–128, 129–130,
    131–132
  conclusions about, 132–134
  diagram of, 116
  information about, 115–116,
    118, 119, 120, 121, 122,
    124, 125, 126, 127, 128,
    130–131
  problems of, 115–132
  purpose of, 118

D

Data versus information versus
  knowledge versus wisdom,
  17–20
Davenport's definition of
  knowledge management, Tom,
  68–69
DEC. *See* Decision Execution Cycle
Decision Execution Cycle, xxii,
  33–37, 39
  acting and, 34
  of agent, 107, 108
  business processes and, 49, 51
  diagram of, 35, 108, 298
  evaluating and, 35

knowledge claim evaluations
and, 143, 145, 146
knowledge integration process
and, 53
knowledge life cycle and, 56,
57, 298, 299
knowledge produced by, 40
monitoring and, 35
motivation of, 34
phases of, 34, 35, 36
planning and, 34
pre-existing knowledge and, 302
problem life cycle and, 45–47
problem solving adaptive
responses arising out of,
41–48
purpose, 34, 35
rules and, 79
sense making and, 119
trial and error in, 293
Decision-making activities, 77,
79–80, 84
Decision Support Systems (DSS),
95, 102
Demand-side knowledge, xix–xx,
89, 97
age of, 99
concerns, xx
focus of, 97
generational view of knowledge
management and, 98
processing, 202, 203, 302–303
Distributed knowledge management
systems (DKMs), 222
Distributed organizational
knowledge base, 35–37, 45,
49, 61, 246
knowledge integration process
and, 53
knowledge life cycle and, 49,
51, 233
problem life cycles and, 40,
45–47, 51

role of, 36
World 2 and World 3
knowledge and, 53, 152
DLL. *See* Double-loop learning
DOKB. *See* Distributed
organizational knowledge base
Double-loop learning, xxii, 37–38,
39, 40, 45, 49
combining with tetradic schema,
39–41
knowledge gap and, 255
means for, 29
Duhem-Quine thesis, 161

E
Education and training, 225–227
EIP. *See* Enterprise information
portal
EKM model. *See* Enterprise
knowledge management
model
EKP. *See* Enterprise knowledge
portal
Emergent behavior, 61
Enterprise information portals,
105, 321–322, 325
Enterprise knowledge management
model
Level One knowledge in, 72, 73
Level Two knowledge in, 73
Enterprise Knowledge Portal,
167–168, 222, 233, 321, 325,
327
Experimental learning cycle, 33
Explicit knowledge
Polanyi on, 95
tacit knowledge and, 20–21, 22
World 3 knowledge and, 22, 23

F
Fallibilism, 228, 304
Falsified knowledge claims (FKCs),
51, 144, 145

Figurehead or ceremonial
    representation knowledge
    management activity, 77
Future of new knowledge
    management, 323–335
Fuzzification, 187–190
Fuzzy Associative Memory (FAM),
    189

G

Generations of knowledge
    management, xxii–xxiii,
    88–141
  change in knowledge
    management, three views of,
    88–90
  conclusion, 134–136
  first generation shortcoming, 199
  knowledge claim evaluation and,
    144
  knowledge life cycle and, 230,
    231
  Snowden's forecast of third age
    of knowledge management,
    104–134
  start of first generation, 99
  strategy and, 253, 254
  theory of first generation, 292
  two generations, 97–104

H

Hierarchical versus organic
    knowledge management,
    62–63
Human organizations, data versus
    information versus knowledge
    versus wisdom in, 17–20
  World 2, 19–20
  World 3, 17–19

I

IC. See Intellectual capital
IM. See Information management

Implicit knowledge, 21–23
Incentive system of agent, 107,
    108, 109
Individual and group (I&G)
    learning, 54
Information delivery cycle (IDC),
    311
Information management
  knowledge management and,
    xxii, 60–87
  differences, 69–70, 84–85
  interpersonal behaviors, 84
  knowledge management versus,
    69–70, 84–85, 218, 301
  knowledge process management
    and, 299, 301
  knowledge processes versus, 70
  validity, 231–233
Information processing and
    knowledge, 76, 78–79
Information production, 70
Information technology
  to enhance supply- or demand-
    side knowledge processing,
    203
  as initial stage of knowledge
    management driver, 90, 91,
    93, 95
  new knowledge management
    and, the, 321–322
  requirements for knowledge life
    cycles, 220–222
Information versus data versus
    wisdom, 17–20
Information versus knowledge, 14,
    55, 143, 146, 240
Innovation management (IM), 98,
    99
Intellectual capital, 90, 222–225,
    275–289, 319–321
  accounting and, 275–278,
    283–284, 287–289, 321
  appearance of term, first, 90

conclusion, 287–289
false linearity, 279–283
false orientation, 283–284
frameworks foundation, xxv
introduction, 275–278
knowledge life cycle and,
    222–225, 278
problem, 275–278
social innovation capital,
    278–279
as two social systems, 284–287
Intelligent agents (IAs), 168–169,
    170
Interpersonal knowledge
    management behavior, 76,
    77–78
Introduction, xviii–xxvii
IT. *See* Information technology

J
Justification of knowledge, 55, 146

K
KCE. *See* Knowledge claim
    evaluation
KLC. *See* Knowledge Life Cycle
KM. *See* Knowledge management
KMP. *See* Knowledge management
    process
Knapp's definition of knowledge
    management, Ellen, 65
Knowledge
    culture and, 271–272
    data versus information versus
        wisdom versus, 17–20
    defining, 296–298
    definitions, 3–11, 111; *see also*
        Knowledge conundrum
    information processing and,
        78–79
    information versus, 14, 55, 143,
        146, 240
    methodology, 329

paradox in definition of,
    112–113
process or outcome question,
    110–113
types of, 5–6, 28
typology table, 26–27
World 2 definitions of, 11–13
World 3 definitions of, 13–17
Knowledge audits, 204, 205–206
Knowledge claim evaluation, 38,
    45, 142–176, 296, 305–309
    artificial knowledge server and,
        169–170
    base characteristics, 153–154
    commensurability, 161
    comparative evaluation criteria
        combined with, 166–167
    complex adaptive systems and,
        148
    component criteria, 172–173
    contexts, 148
    decision executive cycle and,
        143, 145, 146
    direct comparative criteria,
        162–166
    distributed/centralized
        architecture of, 153
    effectiveness, 158–167, 306
    electronic support for, 151
    empirical fit, 163
    evaluation approach, 156–157
    events history, 155
    fair comparison requirements
        criteria, 160–162
    fair comparison theory
        realization, 158–167, 331
    framework for describing,
        146–156
    groups participating in, 56
    heuristic quality, 164
    improvements in cycle time, 157
    information management versus
        knowledge management, 301

integration degree, 153
interpersonal methods for, 151
introduction, 142–143
knowledge life cycle and, 143, 147, 205
knowledge produced by, 144–146
knowledge production and, 70
languages used, 154
logical consistency or coherence, 162–163
metaclaims described, 154–155
outcome classifications of, 144, 145
outcome descriptors, 152–156
pragmatic priority, 165–166
process descriptors, 149–151
production increase, 157–158
projectibility, 163
relevance, 153
reward types, 155–156
role of, xxiii
significance and questions, 171–173
simplicity, 164–165
software, 154, 167–171
specific, 147–156
success criteria for, 157–158
support, lack of, 322
systematic coherence, 164
systematic fruitfulness, 163–164
task cluster, 54
testing, 148
types classifications, 152
as validation, 85
World 2 knowledge and, 143, 145, 146, 147
World 3 knowledge and, 143, 144, 145, 146, 147
Knowledge claim formulation, 38, 45, 53, 70, 197, 205

Knowledge claim objects (KCOs), 169, 170
Knowledge conundrum, xxi–xxii, 1–31
    conclusion, 28–29
    definition discussion, 2–3
    importance of defining, 2–3
    introduction, 1–2
    solution proposal, 26–27
    tacit and explicit knowledge, 20–21
Knowledge conversion, 96
    knowledge models and, 195–196
    SECI model and, 103
Knowledge ecology. See Organic knowledge management
Knowledge integration, xix, 79
    definition, 53
    included in, 70
    knowledge life cycle and, 205
    organizational knowledge and, 56
    process, 53
    result of, 53
Knowledge Life Cycle
    applications, xxiii–xxiv, 193–237
    Cassidy model, 209
    centrality of, 309–312
    changes in knowledge management and, 135
    character, xxii
    complex adaptive systems and, 197, 209
    conclusion, 57
    Cynefin model and, 131
    decision execution cycles versus, 57
    description of, 196–200
    diagrams of, 52, 101, 203, 300
    education and training and, 225–227

elements of, 18–19
execution of processes, 56
as expression of change in
   instrumental motivation,
   48–57
framework applications,
   193–237
framework of, 100, 101
individual and group learning
   and, 54
information technology
   requirements, 220–222
intellectual capital and,
   222–225, 278
introduction, 32–33, 193–196
knowledge audits and, 204,
   205–206
knowledge claim evaluation and,
   143, 147
knowledge management strategy
   formulation and, 200–204
learning and adaptivity, 239
Macroinnovation model based
   on, 208–209, 213
methodology, 218–220
metrics segmentation, 210–213
models, 206, 208–210
nested, 214
nesting, 54
open enterprise and, 227–229
organizational learning cycle
   versus, 32–33
origin, xxii, 32–59, 298–299,
   300, 301
social innovation capital and,
   278, 279
sustainable innovation and,
   213–218
unified theory of knowledge
   and, 233
as value propositions for
   knowledge management,
   230–234

World 2 and World 3
   knowledge and, 20
Knowledge management. See also
   The New Knowledge
   Management
activities classification, 83–84
ages of, 88–89, 94–97, 104–134
approach to, 60–61
as best practices systems, xxiv
change in, three views of, 88–90
complex adaptive systems and,
   62
culture and, 315–317
definition and specification of,
   70–84
definitions, 63–69; see also
   Knowledge conundrum
diagram, 57
dimensions of, 71
generations of, xxii–xxiii,
   88–141
hierarchical versus organic,
   62–63
information management and,
   60–87
information management versus,
   69–70, 84–85, 218, 301
initiatives examples, 82
knowledge processing versus,
   97–98, 196, 243–244, 252,
   310
levels of, 71–76
methodology, 329–330
modeling importance, 193–195
objective of, 62
policies versus programs
   initiatives, 83
process or outcome question,
   110–113
processes breadth, 76–80
processes to business outcomes
   diagram, 273
producing and integrating, 56

purpose of, 219
specification gap, 85
stages of, three, 88, 90–94
standards and, 332–335
strategy formulation, 200–204, 312–315
strategy versus, xxiv
targets of, 80–81, 82
task cluster types, 76–77
tools and their unimportance in measuring, 101–102
value theory in, 330–332
where it belongs, 256–257
Knowledge management process, 70–71, 299, 301, 316
Knowledge mapping. *See* Knowledge audits
Knowledge processes, 49, 50
information processes and, 70
knowledge production as, 78–79
level, 72, 74
outcome versus, 110–113
Knowledge processing, 56
adapting model of, 196
fair comparison and, 159
information technology and, 221
knowledge life cycles and, 198, 200
knowledge life cycles and organizational learning cycles and, 57
knowledge management versus, 97–98, 196, 243–244, 252, 310
metrics segmentation and, 212–213
nature of, xxii
rules, changing, 79–80
self-organizing nature of, 215
Knowledge production
from agents viewpoint, 55–56
included in, 70

information production versus, 54, 146
knowledge claim evaluation role in, xxiii, 142–176
knowledge life cycle and, 53–54
as knowledge management and knowledge process, 78–79
learning and, 39–41
levels, 71
second generation of knowledge management and, 97
Knowledge validation, 55–56
Knowledge wars, xxi–xxii
Knowledge workers, 241
KP. *See* Knowledge processing

L
Leadership, 77–78
Levels of knowledge management, 71–76
Level One, 72, 73, 75, 79
Level Three, 75
Level Two, 73, 75, 79
Level Zero, 72, 73, 75, 79
other names for, 74
relationship diagram, 73, 74
Lorenz attractor, 198

M
Macro-knowledge management, 198
Macroinnovation model, 208–209, 213
Malhotra's definition of knowledge management, 63–64
Management
key issues, xix
Metaclaims, 8, 296
in action, 245–247
best practices and, 241–247, 304–305
claims versus, 240, 306
as context, 241–242

definition, 294
knowledge claim evaluation
software and, 169, 170
knowledge claim evaluations
and, 144, 154–155
role of, 322
Metaknowledge management, 74,
75, 211
Metaknowledge process level, 74,
75
Meta-meta-knowledge
management, 75, 211
Methodologies, biased, 250–251
Metrics segmentation, 210–213
Micro-knowledge management,
198
Murray's definition of knowledge
management, Philip C., 67–68

N
Natural complex adaptive systems
(NCASs), 121
Natural knowledge processing
system, 61
complex adaptive systems and,
62–63
Negotiating agreements, 80
NKPS. *See* Natural knowledge
processing system

O
Objective knowledge, 16
OE. *See* Open enterprise
OLC. *See* Organizational Learning
Cycle
Open enterprise, 227–229,
317–319
board oversight of knowledge
management and, 257
future of The New Knowledge
Management and, 328–329
knowledge processing and,
318–319

as knowledge-claim-centric
construct, 327
model of knowledge production,
126
terrorism and, 319
value propositions, 318
Organic knowledge
hierarchical knowledge
management versus, 62–63
motto of, 62
Organizational development (OD),
98
Organizational knowledge (OK),
51, 53, 54
knowledge integration and, 56
predispositions, 114
Organizational learning (OL), 98,
99, 114, 290
Organizational Learning Cycle,
xxii, 33–37
knowledge life cycle versus,
32–33, 298

P
PLC. *See* Problem Life Cycle
Policy synchronization method
(PSM), 216, 328–329
Popper's tetradic schema, 38–39,
45
combining with double-loop
learning, 39–41
knowledge learning cycle and,
197
Problem Life Cycle, 40, 49, 56
decision execution cycle and, 40,
45–47, 51
as knowledge life cycle, 51
knowledge produced by, 40–41
as motivation of intelligent
agents, 45
Promethean complex adaptive
systems (PCASs), 121, 122,
125, 126–127, 133

S

Scientific management and knowledge management, 105
SECI model. *See* Socialization/Externalization/Combination/Internalization model
Sense making, xxii, 113–115
  complex adaptive systems and, 113–114
  Cynefin model and, 118–120, 123–125
  decision executive cycle and, 119
  in transactional system, 47–48
Simple Network Management Protocol (SNMP), 170
Single-loop learning, 36, 37, 39, 45
  knowledge integration process and, 53
Social acts, 14
Social and technological, and policy and program interventions, 81, 82–83
Social innovation capital (SIC), 223, 224, 225, 278–279, 281
Social Network Analysis (SNA), 206
Socialization/Externalization/Combination/Internalization model, 89, 195, 296–297
  falibility of, 103–104, 110, 323–324
  future and, 323–325
  stage 2 of knowledge management and, 91, 94–95, 102–103
Software
  analysis framework, 325–326
  for knowledge claim evaluation, 154, 167–171
Stages of knowledge management, three, 88, 90–94

Standards, 332–335
Strategy
  biased methodologies, 250–251
  definition, 254, 255
  exception, 251–254, 259
  introduction, 249–250
  knowledge management versus, xxiv, 249–260, 312–315
  The New Knowledge Management and, 254–256
  where knowledge management belongs with, 256–257
Strategy-centricity, 251, 252
Supply-side knowledge, xix, xx, 89, 97, 230
  age of, 99
  concerns, xx
  focus of, 97
  generational view of knowledge management and, 98, 99, 102, 104
  processing, 200, 202, 203, 302–303
Supply-side orientation, 251
Surviving knowledge claims (SKCs), 51, 53, 144, 145
Sustainable innovation, xx, 213–218
Sveiby's definition of knowledge management, 64–65

T

Tacit knowledge
  capturing, 195
  explicit knowledge versus, 20–21
  Polanyi on, 12, 20–21, 22, 95
Targets of knowledge management, 80–81, 82
Task, task pattern, task cluster, 48, 54, 56, 70, 79
Task clusters of knowledge management, 76–80

Tetradic schema. *See* Popper's tetradic schema

The New Knowledge Management. *See also* Knowledge management
characteristic, defining, 89
definition, xix, 193
future of, 323–335
information technology and, 321–322
introduction to, xix–xxvii
issues, xxi–xxv, 295
landscape, 294–335
metrics, 326
open enterprise and, 328–329
as a paradigm, xx
reference model diagram, 210, 313
software usage reason, 326
standards, 332–335
strategy and, 254–256
terrorism and, 326–327
theory and practice in, xxiii–xxiv
viewing, 88–90
vision of, 290–294

TNKM. *See* The New Knowledge Management

Training and education, 225–227

Transactional systems model of agent interaction, 41–48
coping behavior classes, 44
interpreting environment stimuli, 43–44
motivational behavior aspects, 43–47
motivational hierarchy, 41–43
sense making, 47–48

"Truthlikeness"
analytic hierarchy process-based ratio scaling approach to, 178–187, 191
approaches to measuring, two formal, 177–192
definition, 167
developing composite measures of, 167
introduction, 177–178
knowledge claim evaluation software and, 169
knowledge management knowledge production combining criterion of, 191
measurement approach to, fuzzy, 187–190, 191

U

Undecided knowledge claims (UKCs), 51, 144, 145
University of Kentucky's definition of knowledge management, 65–66

V

Validation of knowledge, 55–56
Value Network Analysis, 206
Value theory in knowledge management, 330–332

W

Wiig's definition of knowledge management, Karl, 66–67
Wenig's definition of knowledge management, R. Gregory, 67
Wisdom versus data versus information versus knowledge, 17–20
World 1 knowledge, 23
culture and, 267
definition, 5
evolution and, 10–11
genetically encoded knowledge and, 20
World 2 versus, 6

World 2 knowledge
  beliefs, 7
  culture and, 267, 271
  data, information, and
      knowledge, 19–20
  definitions, 6, 11–13
  distributed organizational
      knowledge base and, 53
  explicit knowledge and, 22, 23
  in goal-directed agent, 24, 25
  knowledge claim evaluation and,
      143, 145, 146, 147
  motivational hierarchies and,
      individual level, 23–28
  objects, 7, 51
  as subjective, 55, 146, 222,
      291
  system of agent, 43
  World 1 versus, 6

World 3 versus, 8–10, 12,
      16–17, 22, 23
World 3 knowledge
  claims, 7–8, 51
  as cultural factor, 24, 267, 271
  data, information, knowledge,
      and wisdom, 17–19
  definitions, 6, 8, 13–17
  distributed organizational
      knowledge base and, 53,
      152
  implicit knowledge and, 22, 23
  included in, 6–7
  knowledge claim evaluation and,
      143, 144, 145, 146, 147
  as objective, 55, 146, 222–223,
      291
  World 2 versus, 8–10, 12,
      16–17, 22, 23

About the Authors

Joseph M. Firestone, Ph.D., is vice president and Chief Knowledge Officer (CKO) of Executive Information Systems (EIS) Inc. Joe has varied experience in consulting, management, information technology, decision support, and social systems analysis. Currently, he focuses on product, methodology, architecture, and solutions development in enterprise information and knowledge portals, where he performs knowledge and knowledge management audits, training, and facilitative systems planning, requirements capture, analysis, and design. Joe was the first to define and specify the Enterprise Knowledge Portal (EKP) Concept, and he is the leading writer, designer, commentator, and trainer in this area. He is widely published in the areas of decision support (especially enterprise information and knowledge portals, data warehouses/data marts, and data mining), and knowledge management, and he has completed a full-length industry report entitled "Approaching Enterprise Information Portals." He is also the author *of Enterprise Information Portals and Knowledge Management.*

Joe is a founding member of the Knowledge Management Consortium International (KMCI), its corporate secretary, and executive vice president of education, research, and membership, the CEO in these areas directly responsible to KMCI's board. He is also the director of the KMCI Knowledge and Innovation Manager Certification (CKIM) Program (see http://www.kmci.org/Institute/certification/ckim_details.htm), and director of the KMCI Research Center. Joe is also a frequent speaker at national conferences on KM and portals and a trainer in the areas of enterprise information portals, enterprise knowledge portals, and knowledge management (KM). He is also developer of the Web site www.dkms.com, one of the most widely visited Web sites in the portal and KM fields.

Joseph M. Firestone, Ph.D.
Chief Knowledge Officer
Executive Information Systems Inc. (EIS)
Executive Vice President, Education, Research, and Membership
Knowledge Management Consortium International (KMCI)
(703) 461-8823
eisai@comcast.net

Mark W. McElroy is a thought leader, consultant, and award-winning author in the fields of knowledge management, organizational learning, intellectual capital, and innovation. He is a twenty-five year veteran of management consulting, including time spent at Price Waterhouse and KPMG Peat Marwick. While at KPMG, he served as U.S. national partner-in-charge of the enterprise networks practice. He was also a principal in IBM's knowledge management practice in Cambridge, Massachusetts.

At present, Mark is president and CEO of Macroinnovation Associates LLC, a management consultancy based in Windsor, Vermont. He is the principal developer of the "Policy Synchronization Method" (PSM), a patent-pending technique for enhancing transparency, openness, and innovation in business. The PSM method is based on a unique blend of organizational learning and complexity theory and is offered to end-user organizations around the world through free and perpetual licenses.

Mark is also president of the Knowledge Management Consortium International (KMCI), the largest professional association of KM practitioners in the world. He serves on the board there, as well, and has been affiliated with KMCI since 1998. He is also the author of *The New Knowledge Management—Complexity, Learning, and Sustainable Innovation*.

Mark W. McElroy
President and CEO
Macroinnovation Associates LLC
10 Ogden's Mill Road
Windsor, VT 05089
(802) 436-2250
www.macroinnovation.com
mmcelroy@vermontel.net